DI061472

ROBERT MANNING
STROZIER LIBRARY.

AUG 8 1994

Tallahassee, Florida

Managing Commodity Price Risk in Developing Countries

Stijn Claessens and Ronald C. Duncan,
Editors

Published for the World Bank
The Johns Hopkins University Press
Baltimore and London

© 1993 The International Bank
for Reconstruction and Development / The World Bank
1818 H Street, N.W., Washington, D.C. 20433, U.S.A.

The Johns Hopkins University Press
Baltimore, Maryland 21211-2190, U.S.A.

All rights reserved
Manufactured in the United States of America
First printing December 1993

The findings, interpretations, and conclusions expressed in this publication are
those of the authors and do not necessarily represent the views and policies of the
World Bank or its Board of Executive Directors or the countries they represent.

The material in this publication is copyrighted. Requests for permission to
reproduce portions of it should be sent to Director, Publications Department, at
the address shown in the copyright notice above. The World Bank encourages
dissemination of its work and will normally give permission promptly and, when
the reproduction is for noncommercial purposes, without asking a fee.
Permission to photocopy portions for classroom use is not required, though
notification of such use having been made will be appreciated.

The complete backlist of publications from the World Bank is shown in the
annual *Index of Publications,* which contains an alphabetical title list and
indexes of subjects, authors, and countries and regions. The latest edition is
available free of charge from Publication Sales Unit, The World Bank, 1818 H
Street, N.W., Washington, D.C. 20433, U.S.A., or from Publications, The
World Bank, 66 avenue d'Iéna, 75116 Paris, France.

Library of Congress Cataloging-in-Publication Data

Managing commodity price risk in developing countries / Stijn
    Claessens and Ronald C. Duncan, editors.
        p.   cm.
    Includes bibliographical references and index.
    ISBN 0-8018-4662-5
    1. Commodity futures—Developing countries.   2. Prices—Developing
countries.   3. Hedging (Finance)   4. Risk management—Developing
countries.   5. Financial instruments—Developing countries.
I. Claessens, Stijn.   II. Duncan, Ronald C.   III. World Bank.
HG6051.D44M36   1993
332.63'28—dc20   93-23482
                                                                      CIP

Contents

Foreword

Large fluctuations in the prices of commodities are one of the main reasons for the difficulties that many developing countries experience in economic management. For many developing countries, commodities represent more than half of their export earnings, and, on average, petroleum and petroleum products account for about 10 percent of total imports. Hedging the exposure to commodity price risk is therefore important. Developing countries also face other substantial external risks arising from financial liabilities and assets: exchange rate and interest rate risks. Better management of all these risks would result in substantial gains in welfare.

Hedging of external price risk for short horizons by using financial instruments such as futures has been possible for a long time. One of the most promising developments for developing countries over the past few years has been the emergence of financial instruments that allow commodity price risks to be hedged over longer periods and finance to be raised on a commodity price–linked basis. Although these new instruments appear to offer much promise, they have been little used by developing countries. Indeed, comprehensive use of short-horizon hedging instruments for commodity risk management is rare.

It is hoped that an increasing number of developing countries can be encouraged and assisted to use the full range of financial instruments, including longer-term instruments, to manage commodity risk. This book, which is a by-product of a research and technical assistance program in the International Trade Division of the World Bank, is intended to help this process along by providing detailed information about financial instruments for managing external commodity price risks, creating awareness of the institutional constraints that must be removed to allow full access to these instruments, and illustrating the kinds of technical assistance and education needed to enable good use of the instruments.

D. C. Rao
Director
International Economics Department

Preface

Since 1987 the International Trade Division of the World Bank has researched the possibilities for use of commodity price–linked financial instruments by developing countries.[1] This research has confirmed that these instruments are of potential use to developing countries in hedging commodity price risks and raising finance, but that the actual use of these instruments is very limited. In 1990 the division began to assist developing countries in using these instruments to manage their exposure to commodity prices.[2]

The technical assistance program began with the idea that work would be concentrated initially in only a few countries in order to develop successful models for others to follow. It was understood that this work was as much one of research into problems to be resolved and issues to be discussed as it was one of actual assistance to particular countries. Most of the work has been done in Colombia and Costa Rica, and in both countries commodity price risk management using financial instruments is now being undertaken. The technical assistance program is being extended to other countries as well, following the format developed in Colombia and Costa Rica. An initial "needs assessment" survey pinpoints the commodity price exposures and the entities that should manage those risks. The survey is followed by workshops to train people in both the private and the public sectors in the design and use of financial risk management instruments as part of a hedging or financial strategy.

Most of the chapters in this book are based on the financial technical assistance undertaken by the International Trade Division in these pilot countries. The case studies presented in the book are drawn either from the needs assessment surveys or from analysis and are intended to demonstrate the purpose, benefits, and costs of particular instruments or hedging strategies. Many of these case studies have been used as teaching aids in training workshops.

In addition to presenting case studies, the book discusses the different kinds of financial instruments, the markets that are available for these instruments, and the current regulatory framework for commodity-linked instruments. The book also documents the experiences of more traditional domestic price stabilization schemes that have been used in developing countries to complement or substitute for market-based financial risk management instruments.

The case studies demonstrate that developing countries can benefit significantly from using financial instruments to manage the risks of commodity price changes. The fact that very few developing countries or entities in these countries have used these instruments, in particular the newer instruments, is attributed to a lack of awareness of the risks that are faced; to a lack of knowledge of the potential use of market instruments; to domestic regulatory, institutional, and legal constraints; and to considerations in the marketplace regarding the countries' creditworthiness. The obvious conclusions are that technical assistance, training and education, and credit enhancement by third parties are necessary to allow developing countries to benefit fully from the use of these instruments.

The first five chapters of this book present general concepts on commodity price risk management. The rest of the book consists of case studies.

Chapter 1 indicates the importance of improved commodity risk management in developing countries and identifies the role financial instruments can play in managing commodity price risk, providing access to external finance, and lowering credit risk. On the basis of the case studies, the chapter draws some general recommendations about what is necessary to improve commodity price risk management in developing countries.

Chapter 2 describes how domestic schemes to stabilize commodity prices work and the experience that developing countries have had with such schemes. The chapter allows one to understand how financial instruments for managing commodity risk relate to the more traditional stabilization schemes, and it demonstrates that the two can be seen either as complements or as substitutes. Chapter 3 presents applications of financial risk management instruments within the context of traditional domestic price stabilization schemes, further demonstrating the complementarity of the two.

Chapter 4 discusses the financial instruments that are available for external risk management, focusing on instruments that manage commodity risk. Chapter 5 discusses some of the practical and regulatory constraints to using commodity risk management instruments. The focus is on longer-term hedging instruments, such as commodity bonds, and instruments that combine traditional forms of finance with commodity-linked payoffs (so-called hybrid instruments).

The second part of the book contains, first, the chapters that report (simulated) case studies for Costa Rica, Papua New Guinea, Colombia, and Sub-Saharan Africa (chapters 8 through 13). These chapters analyze the use of financial risk management instruments either at the level of the different entities (private or public) that are exposed to commodity price risk or at the country level. Chapters 14 and 15 analyze, in turn, the newly established futures exchange in Hungary and the possibilities for tariff-based commodity price stabilization schemes in Venezuela. The final chapter looks at the integration of spot commodity markets and the role that futures can play as a tool for hedging and price discovery. The focus in that chapter is on the international rice market.

Notes

1. The early, mainly theoretical work on the potential role of the new, longer-term instruments was published in Priovolos and Duncan (1991).

2. This technical assistance is provided within the Bank's broader program of financial technical assistance to developing countries. Within this broader program, assistance is provided by the International Trade Division, the Debt and International Finance Division, the Financial Technical Assistance program in the Treasury Vice Presidency, and the Co-financing and Financial Advisory Services Vice Presidency.

Acknowledgments

We are grateful for the financial support of the World Bank, in particular the support from its Research Committee and the regional vice presidents' offices. We are also grateful for financial support from the government of Switzerland's Federal Office for Foreign Economic Affairs for continuation of the risk management program in Costa Rica and other countries. Our gratitude is extended to people in government and in the private sector in the various countries that have participated in the technical assistance program.

We would like to thank the two referees of the Editorial Committee of the World Bank who provided constructive suggestions. We acknowledge with many thanks the encouragement and support of Stanley Fischer, chief economist at the World Bank when this work was initiated, and Lawrence Summers, former chief economist, who has given his continued support.

We also owe a debt to our colleagues in the International Economics Department for their advice and their comments on drafts of the various papers. We have benefited from the comments and suggestions of a number of others in the World Bank Group as well, including Ishac Diwan, Tom Glaessner, Peter Hazell, Ishrat Husain, D. C. Rao, Lester Seigel, and John Underwood, as well as those outside the World Bank Group, including Mike Dooley (University of California, Santa Cruz), Bob Myers (Michigan State University), John O'Connell (Refco, Inc.), Krishna Ramaswamy (Wharton School), and Charles Smithson (Chase Manhattan Bank).

The finalization of this book has been a challenging task, but we were fortunate to have had much support. Many thanks go in particular to Alfred Imhoff and Michael Treadway of the World Bank's Editorial and Production Unit for putting the book into its final shape and to Esther Riley for excellent copyediting; to Julie Carroll, Joan Hawkins, and Sarah Lipscomb for secretarial assistance; and to Nacer Megherbi for graphics production assistance.

Contributors

Ronald Anderson is professor of finance in the Département des Sciences Economiques, Université Catholique de Louvain, Belgium.

Stijn Claessens, formerly in the Debt and International Finance Division at the World Bank, is senior financial economist in the Bank's Europe, Central Asia, Middle East, and North Africa Technical Department.

Jonathan R. Coleman, formerly a consultant to the World Bank, is a senior economist at Sparks Companies, Inc.

Ronald C. Duncan, at the time of writing chief of the International Trade Division at the World Bank, is professor of economics at the Australian National University.

Christopher L. Gilbert is professor in the Department of Economics, Queen Mary and Westfield College, London, England.

Jeannette Herrmann, formerly with the Chicago Board of Trade, is now a consulting economist with offices in Boston and Chicago.

Donald F. Larson is an economist in the International Trade Division at the World Bank.

Toshiya Masuoka is an investment officer in the Infrastructure Department of the International Finance Corporation.

Robert J. Myers is associate professor in the Department of Agricultural Economics, Michigan State University, East Lansing.

Michael Occhiolini has been a consultant to the World Bank and is now an associate at the law firm of Wilson, Sonsini, Goodrich, and Rosati, P.C.

Andrew Powell is lecturer in economics at the University of Warwick, Coventry, England.

Ying Qian is a research analyst in the International Trade Division at the World Bank.

Stanley R. Thompson, formerly in the Department of Agricultural Economics at Michigan State University, East Lansing, is professor and chair of the Department of Agricultural Economics and Rural Sociology at Ohio State University, Columbus.

Panos Varangis is an economist in the International Trade Division at the World Bank.

P A R T I

Overview and Background

1

Overview

Stijn Claessens and Ronald C. Duncan

The Importance of Managing Commodity Price Risk

The significance of instruments to manage commodity risk can be appreciated when one examines the importance of primary commodity earnings and expenses for developing countries; the volatility and uncertainty in commodity prices and other external prices; and the effect of commodity price uncertainty on planning at the micro and macro levels.

The Importance of Commodity Earnings and Expenses

Because of their export revenue profile, many developing countries are highly exposed to fluctuations in world commodity prices. Not only export revenues in these countries are vulnerable but also government revenues, import expenditures, and the incomes and profits of state and private enterprises. Commodity price swings are also reflected in the unsatisfactory performance of domestic price stabilization schemes and commodity marketing boards.

The exposure of developing countries to commodity price risk is illustrated in table 1-1, which shows the number of developing countries in which primary commodities (those represented in the World Bank primary commodity price index) as a share of total exports exceeds certain percentages. Table 1-1 shows that, for forty-four countries, nonfuel primary commodities account for more than 50 percent of total exports; if fuel is included, the number of countries for which primary commodities account for more than 50 percent of total exports rises to sixty-seven. For several developing countries (for example, Burundi and Burkina Faso) the exports of a single commodity (coffee) account for more than 90 percent of total export earnings. Overall, primary commodities

3

Table 1-1. *Export Concentration in Eighty-nine Countries, 1984–88*

Primary commodities as share of exports	Number of countries with primary commodity export share larger than indicated percentage[a]	
	Primary commodities, excluding fuels	Primary commodities, including fuels
>90%	12	24
>80%	24	47
>70%	32	55
>60%	39	63
>50%	44	67
>40%	53	74

a. Figures are averages for 1984–88.
Source: World Bank data.

account for 68 percent of the total export earnings of low-income developing countries and 44 percent of the total export earnings of high-income countries.

Some developing countries have been able to diversify away from primary commodity exports. For instance, Southeast Asian countries have reduced the share of primary commodity exports in their total exports from an average of 74 percent in 1965–69 to 43 percent in 1984–88. However, dependence on primary commodity exports has remained high in several countries, especially in Sub-Saharan Africa, where the decline in the share has been small—from 87 percent in 1965–69 to 70 percent in 1984–88 (see chapter 13). For some countries, the dependence has actually increased. For instance, in the case of Madagascar, the average share of the top commodity export, coffee, has increased from 30.6 percent in the period 1974–76 to 40.7 percent in 1984–86.

As mentioned above, the exposure of countries to commodity price risk is not limited to their export earnings; it also affects government revenues, the incomes of state enterprises, and, in the end, the incomes of primary producers. Often government revenues are extremely sensitive to movements in international commodity prices, because tax revenues depend in a progressive manner on earnings from a few commodities. This is the case when commodity exporters have to pay an additional profit or export tax when commodity prices exceed a certain level. State enterprises that concentrate on international commodity exports are, of course, affected through their net income. Government-authorized marketing boards are also affected by price swings, especially when the marketing boards guarantee a price to producers. Even when domestic stabilization schemes, export taxes, and market intermediation activities cause domestic commodity prices to diverge from international prices,

Table 1-2. *Import Concentration in Eighty-nine Countries, 1984–88*

	Number of countries with primary commodity import share larger than indicated percentage[a]	
Primary commodities as share of imports	Primary commodities, excluding fuels	Primary commodities, including fuels
>30%	8	54
>25%	16	64
>20%	34	80
>15%	59	85
>10%	76	88
> 5%	87	89

a. Figures are averages for 1984–88.
Source: World Bank data.

uncertainty about international prices still often results in substantial uncertainty in local-currency prices for final producers.

Uncertainty in international commodity prices also affects the import expenses of developing countries (see table 1-2). Many developing countries import basic consumer goods, including foodstuffs, and thus changes in international prices greatly affect consumer welfare and even political stability. Chapter 15 describes Venezuela's reliance on imports of foodstuffs. To cope with import price variability, many developing countries have tried to stabilize the domestic price of imported commodities by using schemes similar to those used for exported commodities or have reduced price variability by imposing trade restrictions. The increase in crude oil prices in late 1990 highlighted again the effect of oil price fluctuations on the import expenses of developing countries.

The Effect of Commodity Price Uncertainty

The impact of volatility in commodity prices is not limited to its contemporaneous effect on cash flows. It also affects production and investment decisions, although, theoretically, these effects are not clear. On the one hand, uncertainty about future prices should reduce investment, because the possibility increases that, ex post, resources will be misallocated as (relative) prices are realized.[1] Because investors can suffer from being locked into what turns out to be an unprofitable project, they will tend to reduce investment in the face of large price uncertainty. On the other hand, convexity of the profit function with respect to commodity prices implies that an increase in price uncertainty increases the expected profits in the commodity sector and consequently should lead to higher investment. Still, existing empirical work suggests a strong and negative relationship between price uncertainty and investment (see, for instance, Caballero and Corbo 1989).

Commodity price swings also have major macroeconomic effects on the other sectors of an economy. For many economies, the sharp increases in commodity prices in the late 1970s (in particular, for cocoa, coffee, tea, and crude oil) were mixed blessings. Many economies suffered in this way from what became known as the Dutch disease (see Cuddington 1989). The Dutch disease—named for the experience of the Netherlands after the discovery of large quantities of natural gas—begins with an appreciation of the real exchange rate as a result of a commodity boom. This appreciation reduces the competitiveness of other export sectors in the economy and favors import substitution. A subsequent fall in commodity prices, as happened for many (primary) commodity prices in the 1980s, requires the economy to adjust—through a round of sharp macroeconomic adjustments, including a depreciated real exchange rate. In the meantime, however, valuable productive capacity is lost in the economy as other (export) sectors fail to develop.

Developing countries operate under stress when fluctuating prices for primary commodities generate severe terms-of-trade shocks. Observation of the day-to-day performance of developing countries that are experiencing these conditions suggests strongly that these episodic events are inimical to the development process. Sharp upturns in commodity prices seem to have been as disruptive of long-term development programs as sharp declines. Both kinds of shocks have consequences that require the diversion of scarce management skills from tasks essential to generating growth and development to short-term crisis management, wherein the battles to maintain policies favorable to development are frequently lost.

The Volatility of Commodity Prices

The prices of primary commodities have long been volatile.[2] As chapter 2 reports, volatility in agricultural food commodities originates mainly in supply disturbances, whereas for industrial raw materials, both agricultural and metallic, the origin is largely demand disturbances. In conjunction with low short-run demand and supply elasticities, these disturbances give rise to sharp price variations. Stockholding leads to some price smoothing, but when stocks are low, prices can jump sharply as a result of demand and supply disturbances. Price cycles for minerals and tree crops are aggravated by long gestation periods for investments. Often the result is lower prices and excess supply as investments made in periods of high prices come on stream, the reverse being true for the investment response to low prices.

In general, the pattern for commodity prices is one of high instability, with occasional high, short-lived peaks. Observing the behavior of commodity prices over the 1900–87 period, Deaton and Laroque (1992) noted that commodity prices have high autocorrelation coefficients of the first and second order, that a current shock does not persist into the distant future, and that positive shocks are more frequent than negative ones. The existence of storage, which cannot be negative, appears to explain this asymmetric pattern.

The high uncertainty in commodity prices is likely to continue, because technological and policy shocks and demand and supply disturbances will continue. Moreover, it has to be recognized that forecasting of commodity prices is very difficult, given the large stochastic component of commodity price series and the fact that the stochastic process of commodity prices is not always well understood. A recent analysis of price forecasts by the International Trade Division of the World Bank found that the standard deviation of the actual price from the forecast price (for only a one-year horizon) was considerable—about 25 percent.[3] The high volatility of commodity prices, combined with their sharp recent downward trend in real terms (when compared with the prices of manufactured goods imported by developing countries), presents special difficulties for developing countries. Financial risk management will not prevent or reverse this deterioration in developing countries' terms of trade, but it can mitigate short-term volatility. To offset the unfavorable trend in real commodity prices and achieve real income gains, developing countries will need to improve the productivity of their existing activities and continue the process of export diversification.

Other External Risks

Although this book concentrates on managing commodity price exposures, developing countries are exposed not only to risks arising from trade (commodity risk), but in many cases also to risks arising from financial liabilities and assets (exchange rate and interest rate risks). Good economic management dictates that commodity price risk management and commodity price–linked finance be placed in the broader context of the management of all external risks, for several reasons. First, there may exist relationships between the different external risks that make integrated management preferable. For example, some of the risks may offset each other. Also, many financial instruments have significant overlaps. For instance, there are commodity price–linked financial instruments that have some risk management as well as new finance features. Finally, a country needs to have an overall strategy for external liability management which, among other things, addresses issues such as the desirable forms of external finance for projects, the institutional structure for liability management, the overlap between instruments, and the allocation of management and control for external risk management.[4]

Experiences in Managing Commodity Price Risks

In principle, the adverse impact of commodity price swings on private and public consumption can be overcome through various mechanisms. Access by domestic consumers and producers to domestic credit and deposit markets, to storage facilities, or to forms of insurance can result in a smoothing of the impact of temporary commodity price movements on consumption and income. In many industrial countries, these instruments have allowed commodity producers and consumers to cushion the impact of commodity price swings. In most developing countries, however, these instruments have not been available, or available only on unfavorable terms or in informal markets, and consumers and producers have been able to smooth the impact of temporary price shocks only to a limited extent.

In order for an economy as a whole to smooth consumption, it has to borrow or lend in international capital markets. But access by developing countries to international capital markets in order to smooth the impact of price swings has been constrained. And when countries have had access to international credit markets, these markets have often been procyclical instead of countercyclical, providing easier access in times of high commodity prices and less access in times of lower commodity prices (see Cuddington 1989).

Because access to international capital markets is constrained, and because determining whether price swings are temporary or permanent is difficult, a large number of developing and industrial countries and international institutions have individually or collectively taken measures to stabilize commodity prices and to reduce the impact of commodity price fluctuations on developing countries' economies. These measures can be classified into two types: measures to stabilize international prices, and measures to reduce the effects of international price movements on the domestic economy. Chapter 2, by Gilbert, discusses these measures in detail. We will review them briefly here, because commodity risk management and finance instruments can substitute for these measures or complement them.

International Price Stabilization

International commodity agreements have ranged from formal arrangements between producers and consumers (such as for coffee, cocoa, and tin) to informal producer cartels (such as for bananas). The aim of these agreements has generally been to stabilize world prices, often at as high a level as possible. This function has been performed through the use of a variety of instruments, including buffer stocks, buffer funds, export quotas, import quotas, and quotas on production or consumption or both. For the most part these agreements have failed to be reliable mechanisms for managing price risk.

The widespread failure of the schemes to achieve their goal stems from problems of two kinds. First, it is difficult if not impossible to determine the long-run price trend. In order for such schemes to be viable, the levels at which prices (or quantities, in the case of quotas) are to be stabilized need to be set, and occasionally adjusted, to ensure long-run balance between demand and supply. This task has proved difficult, and most schemes have failed because they were unable or unwilling to adjust to changing market conditions. Second, coordination of the different interests of members of the agreement, and sometimes of parties extraneous to the agreement, has been difficult. Lack of enforcement mechanisms, evasion of rules, smuggling, and free-riding are problems common to most agreements. Both kinds of problems have contributed to the demise of these agreements in recent years and their virtual elimination from the international policy agenda.[5]

Domestic Price Stabilization

Schemes that aim to minimize the impact of (negative as well as positive) commodity price changes on the domestic economy can be put into two groups: (a) self-insurance schemes and (b) third-party and other insurance schemes. The first group includes instruments and actions such as macroeconomic policies, domestic commodity price stabilization schemes, reserve management schemes, infrastructure programs such as irrigation schemes and roads, and production and export diversification. The second group includes the financial market instruments described in chapter 4, which are the primary focus of this book, and other financial schemes, including compensatory financing schemes such as the European Community's Stabilisation of Export Earnings (STABEX) and System for Safeguarding and Developing Mineral Production (SYSMIN) and the International Monetary Fund's Compensatory and Contingency Financing Facility (CCFF).

Chapter 2 provides a good summary of experiences with self-insurance schemes. The most important self-insurance mechanism has been the adjustment of macroeconomic policies in response to a commodity price change—that is, fiscal adjustments, real exchange rate corrections, monetary measures, and currency and capital controls. These forms of self-insurance are likely to continue to play an important role in many developing countries (an example being the adjustments made in response to the late-1990 oil price shock). As Gilbert argues in chapter 2, however, use of macroeconomic policies in response to an exogenous price movement may be inappropriate and result in serious disruption to the whole economy and significant misallocation of resources. This is likely to be the case when the initial commodity price shock affects only part of the economy. The major macroeconomic disruptions in many developing countries as a result of commodity booms in the late 1970s and early 1980s ("Dutch" or "Nigerian" disease) can be seen, in retrospect, to be linked to the inappropriate use of macroeconomic instruments. Use of macroeconomic policies, therefore, is not usually the most efficient self-insurance mechanism for handling commodity price fluctuations.

More formally structured self-insurance mechanisms are domestic stabilization schemes. Newbery and Stiglitz (1981) provide much of the economic analysis of domestic price stabilization schemes. Chapter 2 describes the recent experiences of these schemes in detail. The type of scheme depends on whether the commodity in question is an export or import (competing) good or whether it is nontraded. Gilbert identifies schemes such as export marketing boards (for export goods), variable tariff schemes (for import goods), and food marketing boards (for nontraded goods). The choice of scheme has also depended on whether the commodity in question is storable or not and whether an individual country's share in the world market is sufficiently large to influence the world price. Schemes have been implemented using a variety of mechanisms, such as buffer stocks, buffer funds, variable rate tariffs, subsidies, price bands, support prices, quantity controls, and direct intervention. Coleman and Larson (chapter 15) analyze the properties of some of these mechanisms in the context of Venezuela's imports of foodstuffs. They focus on the possible effects of a number of tariff-based schemes on domestic prices and domestic production and conclude that a price band scheme may be the most appropriate for Venezuela.

In chapter 2 Gilbert observes that when the schemes distribute the effects of commodity price changes over other parts of the economy—via the government budget—the schemes are effectively the equivalent of macroeconomic policies, except that the schemes may lead to relative price distortions.[6] Gilbert documents how this has been the case in a few African countries. It is only when policies to manage the foreign exchange reserve are used as part of the scheme—and sterilization occurs—that spillover effects of the scheme onto other parts of the economy can be prevented.[7]

Gilbert shows that for all stabilization schemes there will be a tradeoff between the welfare benefits of price stabilization and the efficiency of investments and resource allocation. Stabilization efforts can lead to domestic prices that do not reflect (worldwide) long-run conditions of supply and demand, and the result over the long run may be a loss in efficiency.[8] Furthermore, taxes and subsidies that are used to implement the stabilization scheme can distort investment and consumption decisions.[9]

Requirements for Successful Price Stabilization Schemes

Key factors, identified by Gilbert in chapter 2 and stressed by the authors of other chapters, determine the success of a domestic stabilization scheme: (a) the ability to determine the long-run price trend, (b) the insulation of the scheme from the general government budget, (c) the sterilization of the scheme from the national economy, and (d) the pursuit of compatible goals. Stabilization schemes almost always involve the determination of a long-run price trend, because the schemes are usually defined with respect to a band around a central price or with respect to deviations from a central price. The central price must be related to the long-run trend in the international price in order to minimize efficiency losses and to ensure that the scheme is viable in the long run. (Efficiency losses would result from production misallocation related to the delinking of the domestic price and the international price.) Insulation from the general government budget should have two aspects: first, the scheme should not be used as a taxing vehicle, and second, the deficits and surpluses of the scheme should not enter the government budget. Sterilization of commodity price fluctuations is achieved by diversifying outside the economy.

The experiences recounted by Gilbert demonstrate that these schemes often failed because of a lack of clear objectives or a mixture of incompatible goals. Often schemes had objectives related to income distribution, income stabilization, control of supply or demand, or the raising of tax revenues—in addition to the goal of price stabilization. Commodity price stabilization schemes are not the most effective means of meeting these other objectives. One conclusion that should be drawn is that the starting point for any scheme for managing commodity risk should be a clear identification of objectives.

The Market for Financial Instruments to Manage Risk

The financial environment of the 1980s has been marked by the emergence of a host of new financial instruments and financing techniques. These include adjustable-rate preferred equity, foreign currency–

denominated bonds, interest and currency swaps, and the increased use of futures, forwards, and options. Chapter 4, by Masuoka, reports on these developments. The markets for financial instruments to manage currency and interest rate fluctuations developed earliest and have reached a mature stage. In general, the increased demand for such instruments arose from the large increase in uncertainty about interest rates and foreign currency prices, beginning in the 1970s. More recently there have been developments in the market for financial instruments to manage commodity risk. These developments have arisen from perceptions of increased uncertainty about commodity prices and from the breakdown of existing measures for risk management—such as international commodity agreements and forward contracts. Masuoka shows that the market for instruments to manage commodity risk largely imitates the markets for instruments to manage exchange rate and interest rate risk. The principal features of these instruments take either one of two forms: (a) contracts indexed on a commodity price with respect to principal or interest payments or both and (b) contracts that give the holder the right—but not the obligation—to buy or sell a commodity at a particular price and, conversely, give the seller the obligation to perform if the buyer exercises its right (option-type contracts). The first group of instruments includes futures, forwards, swaps, long-term contracts, and commodity-indexed bonds. The second group includes call and put options, warrants, and swaptions. Both features are often combined in one instrument.[10]

As Masuoka reports, the market for short-term instruments to manage commodity risk—that is, for futures and options traded at exchanges— has grown over the years. For example, the volume of outstanding contracts for commodity futures increased by 19 percent between 1989 and 1990. In chapter 5 Occhiolini documents the steps that are necessary for a developing country to gain access to futures exchanges and the various regulations and requirements under which a developing country operates.[11] He concludes that there are few requirements for using exchange instruments that are specific to a developing country.[12]

The relative ease of access to trading in futures and options does not necessarily imply that futures and options will be the preferred instruments to manage risk: their demands in terms of human resources required for accounting, institutional organization, legal practice, management, and control are quite high. This is especially so because trading in futures and options requires almost continuous cash flows (because of the marked-to-market features) and frequent participation in the markets. The case studies for Costa Rica, Venezuela, Papua New Guinea, and Colombia confirm this conclusion and report on the many necessary steps for establishing an effective risk management program using short-term instruments.

The most promising recent development in the markets for instruments to manage commodity risk has been in transactions between financial intermediaries—the so-called over-the-counter market—and in the capital market.[13]

The Over-the-Counter Market

In recent years, many financial intermediaries have made commodity risk management instruments available that are "tailor-made" to a particular client's needs. The increased involvement of financial intermediaries has been accompanied by significant product innovation, especially in the area of longer-dated instruments, that is, instruments with a maturity of between one year and ten to fifteen years. One of these innovations has been the commodity swap, a financial transaction that works this way: One of two parties agrees that at fixed points in time over a certain period it will pay the monetary equivalent, at the then-current price, of a fixed amount of a physical commodity. In exchange, the other party agrees to pay a fixed monetary amount at the same points in time. There are no exchanges of physical commodities in a commodity swap; all transactions take place through the exchange of monetary amounts. A commodity swap thus allows one of the parties to lock in a price over a long period of time. A producer could use a commodity swap to lock in part or all of its revenues; a consumer could use it to fix its expenses in relation to a commodity. A parallel development in financial intermediation has been the commodity price–linked loan, in which the repayment of interest or principal or both has been linked to the price of a certain commodity or an index of commodity prices.[14]

The financial intermediary offering the long-term instruments for managing commodity risk will—in the absence of a directly available matching counter swap—manage the price risk on the swap by using the short-dated futures and options markets. By dynamic hedging through the use of short-dated instruments, the intermediary can duplicate a long-dated hedge. The simplest form of a dynamic hedge is a "rollover" (that is, a renewal of a short-dated hedge at maturity). In practice, the protection offered by a rollover will be considerably less than that of a long-dated instrument because of basis risk arising from changes in the relation between spot and futures prices.[15]

The Capital Market

An important development in the capital market has been the increase in the number of commodity price–linked bonds that have been issued (see also Priovolos and Duncan 1991). In these bonds, the coupon or the principal repayment or both are expressed as a fixed amount of a particular commodity, but the payments are settled monetarily.[16] Effectively, these commodity price–linked loans and bonds combine financing and hedging in a single instrument. They therefore assist in reallocating risks, while at the same time creating and facilitating access to credit. As Masuoka argues, one of the main advantages of combining financing and hedging in a single financial obligation is that it can reduce default risks.

The Development of the Market

The use of long-term contracts with fixed prices—the traditional means of sharing commodity price risks between consumers and producers—was largely abandoned with the large movements in commodity prices during the late 1970s and 1980s, when many long-term fixed price contracts were broken.[17] Since then, most sales contracts have been on a variable price basis, and commodity price exposures have thus increased. The breaking of contracts showed that one of the main problems with fixed price contracts is credit risk. The breaking of forward contracts and the realization of credit risk, together with the collapse of international commodity agreements, led banks to develop longer-term instruments for managing commodity risk, instruments that allowed the banks to put to good use their capacity for credit analysis.

So far, the development of the market for longer-term management of commodity risk has been slower than the earlier development of markets for the management of currency and interest rate risk.[18] The reasons for the slower development may shed some light on the potential of the market for longer-term management of commodity risk for developing countries. The chapters by Masuoka and Occhiolini identify a number of factors.

First, the legal and regulatory framework under which banks and financial intermediaries operate has at times been a barrier to the introduction of longer-term instruments. Many countries have traditionally regulated and controlled some aspects of the market for physical commodities and short-term risk management (futures and options exchanges). Part of this regulation "spilled over" when longer-term financial tools for risk management were developed, but this process created certain anomalies. In chapter 5 Occhiolini discusses some of the current problems and anomalies, concentrating on the United States, where the regulatory framework is the most complicated. He describes the kind of commodity swaps and commodity price–linked capital market instruments (so-called hybrids) that are currently allowed.[19] The liberalization of the financial market in many industrial countries will likely allow these markets to develop more freely,[20] but important economic and financial linkages between the physical (or spot) and short-term financial markets and the longer-term financial markets may continue to dictate a need to regulate the longer-term market.

Second, the large number of commodities, the relative lack of standardization of commodity prices, and the links with the underlying markets for physical commodities have made it more difficult to establish procedures for pricing, documentation, settlement, and so on than in the case of exchange rate and interest rate instruments. A related issue concerns the market influence of large suppliers (or consumers) of a commodity. Furthermore, the peculiar characteristics of commodity markets, many of which have seasonal or perishable products, make pricing complicated.[21]

Third, it is only recently that firms in industrial countries have expressed an increased demand for instruments to manage commodity risk. This demand has come about with the firms' realization that they need to focus on their core business and eliminate as much as possible the influence of external price movements on their operating cash flows.

Some of these constraints have been—and will continue to be—overcome through financial deregulation and innovation. It is expected that the markets for long-dated instruments will expand significantly, especially for commodities with characteristics that allow easy standardization, for example, gold, copper, silver, steel, timber, crude oil, and petroleum products and derivatives. Long-term instruments for risk management exist for other commodities of particular importance to developing countries, for example, coffee, cocoa, and cotton, but the development of markets for these instruments will depend on overcoming some hurdles. So far, very few transactions have been completed for these commodities.

The Costs of Financial Instruments

It is important to recognize that it cannot be expected that managing commodity risk will lead consistently to higher export prices or, conversely, lower import prices. Risk management effects a tradeoff between the assurance of predictable future cost against future factor price movements that could produce either large windfalls or equally large losses, or a protection against downside risk in exchange for some current or future costs. Whether the hedge has avoided losses or gains to the economy depends on the (ex post) trend in international factor prices, which cannot be anticipated.

The chapters by Masuoka and Herrmann—and several other chapters in this book—also analyze the costs of using financial tools for risk management. Near-term instruments, covering periods of up to one to two years, are efficient for short-term risk management because the liquidity of these instruments is generally high.

The longer-term instruments are becoming less costly as the markets develop. The costs of participating in the futures and options markets can be decomposed into two components, one easily measurable and the other more elusive. These are, respectively, transaction costs and risk premiums. Transaction costs consist of brokerage fees, bid-ask spreads, possible liquidity costs (for example, a reduced bid price for selling a large volume), and the costs of providing a margin. Typically, these costs will amount to no more than a fraction of 1 percent of the contract value—about one-eighth to one-half of 1 percent for commodities with developed futures and options markets—although in brief periods of exceptionally high price volatility they may be significantly higher.[22]

Risk premiums represent the return that hedgers have to pay to other agents to bear the risk of price movements over the life of a contract. They should be defined as the expected difference in cash flow as a result of the use of the risk management instrument compared with an unhedged ("open") position. A priori one would expect risk premiums to be positive. It is this expected difference that should be evaluated against benefits achieved in risk reduction.

In practice, estimates of the expected difference are extremely difficult to make. Masuoka and Herrmann report on some empirical studies that have shown that, even though the expected difference tends to vary significantly over time and cannot be modeled accurately, it is relatively low. Furthermore, the difference between futures prices and future spot prices can be split into a forecasting bias and a risk premium. The division of the forecasting bias between the expectational error and the risk premium is the subject of intense academic debate, and it is extremely difficult to disentangle the two effects. On balance, empirical studies tend to suggest that the risk premiums are low and vary by commodity and that forecasting biases are low as well. The implication is that the costs of using risk management instruments are likely to be low in relation to the risk reduction benefits, especially in developing countries. The instruments are therefore attractive.

Using Financial Instruments: General Considerations

The starting point for any scheme to manage commodity risk, including any that uses financial instruments, should be a clear identification of objectives. Objectives need to be realistic and should interfere as little as possible with the efficient allocation of resources within the country. All the case studies reiterate this need for realistic and efficient objectives.

The objectives of commodity risk management will differ from case to case. In general, realistic objectives can include improving the predictability of the following: the country's future export revenues or import expenses; the government's budget; state and private enterprises' revenues and expenses related to the production or export of commodities; and the prices of goods for producers, consumers, and investors.

How financial instruments fit into the broader range of stabilization mechanisms leads to the question of whether they are complements of or substitutes for other schemes. Analytically, one can conclude that financial instruments can have several advantages over traditional schemes and therefore should be substitutes. First, financial instruments are more efficient. Schemes to stabilize commodities tie up physical (stocks) or monetary resources that could be used more productively elsewhere; tools to manage financial risk do not. Second, for some commodities, financial instruments (especially commodity swaps) can provide stabilization of prices over longer horizons; none of the traditional stabilization schemes has been able to do this in a reliable manner. The expectation of price stability in the longer term can aid both consumers and producers in the investment or planning process. Third, because financial instruments rely on markets to determine their terms, the instruments provide information on world market expectations of future prices. This so-called price discovery element, which is stressed by Herrmann (chapter 16) for the international rice market, reduces the need for long-term forecasts of prices, an advantage when the stochastic process of a commodity price is not well understood.[23] Fourth, because financial instruments are market-based, they are less likely to introduce distortions in investment and consumption decisions and less likely to lead to the conflicts between objectives that have plagued other schemes. Most importantly, they can complement efforts by developing countries to reduce and reform the role of the state and aid in the liberalization process.[24] Fifth, financial risk management instruments always involve external diversification of risk, which, as argued above, is one of the conditions for successful price stabilization. Of these advantages, the market-based character appears from the case studies to be the most important.

On a practical level, the case studies indicate that financial instruments for risk management can be used as complements to other stabilization schemes, especially in cases where well-designed and well-functioning stabilization schemes already exist.[25] The chapters by Claessens and Coleman on Papua New Guinea, by Coleman and Larson on Venezuela, and by Powell on Colombia show that financial instruments can be used effectively within the context of existing stabilization schemes. Furthermore, the existing schemes, if well run and not permanently subsidized, can serve a useful function when markets for commodity-linked instruments are not complete. But, in general, moving toward market-based schemes is recommended.

The case studies confirm that financial instruments do not, however, overcome the need to correct deficiencies and failures in other (intertemporal) markets in the developing country. Where failures in other markets give rise to some form of commodity risk management by the government, the long-run objective should be to make institutional changes in the domestic market. These reforms should be an integral part of an effort to minimize economic losses arising from price uncertainty. An example is given by Anderson and Powell for Hungary, where the introduction of instruments to manage commodity risk required substantial institutional changes in the market structure for grains, including changes related to warehousing, transportation, and insurance.[26]

Implementation: Some Guiding Principles

Commodity risk management and finance operations should fit into a country's overall strategy for managing external risk and liability, including management of the exchange rate and interest rates. Having an overall strategy is important from a management and control point of view, given the similarities, overlaps, and interactions between the different financial instruments. Its importance is exemplified in chapter 12, on Colombia, and in chapters 10 and 11, on Papua New Guinea. In chapter 10 Powell argues that an overall strategy for risk management for Colombia is required because movements in cross-currency exchange rates offset movements in coffee prices. Because Colombia is heavily dependent on coffee export earnings and because its debt is largely nondollar debt, management of commodities and of the exchange rate needs to be modified, less hedging being required for both.[27] Furthermore, because some financial instruments can serve a financing as well as a hedging function, risk management and financing need to be integrated. This was the case in Algeria, mentioned by Masuoka, where financing linked to the price of oil was raised.

An important relationship is the one between prices and quantities, for it affects revenues and expenses. Depending on the world market structure for the commodity (for example, the elasticity of supply and demand) and the market share of the country, price changes can be offset to some degree through changes in the quantities exported or imported.[28] In the case studies for Colombia, Papua New Guinea, and Sub-Saharan Africa, the commodity risk management that was proposed accounted for this relationship.

The case studies showed that, as with other forms of external finance, the creditworthiness of the country is an important constraint. This is true not only for commodity price–linked financing but also for hedging instruments, because the use of a hedging instrument involves the assumption of credit (default) risk by the institution providing the instrument. Creditworthiness applies to commodity risk management not only in the public sector but also in the private sector because of concerns about possible capital controls, currency inconvertibility, and so on. Credit risk is less of a constraint for many of the short-term instruments because these often require margin accounts and sometimes collateral, which largely overcome the credit problem. As seen from the case studies, credit risk is a more serious problem for longer-dated instruments.[29]

In principle, the use of risk management instruments will mitigate the risk of an interruption in payments by reducing the price risk. Therefore the credit risk on commodity price–linked or hedged financing should be less than on a conventional loan. However, indexing the obligation to the ability of the debtor to repay cannot completely eliminate credit risk, and other measures (as in the case of private firms in developing countries, instruments with collateral, and instruments that create special claims on future exports) may be necessary.[30] An example of how credit risk can be managed is the financing arranged for Mexicana de Cobre, as discussed by Masuoka. This financing benefited from a reduction in credit risk through a commodity (copper) swap as well as through use of an escrow account.

The case studies also indicated that risk management requires a great deal of organization and coordination. Parties need to beware of the objectives of the program. A committee to provide oversight and control may be necessary. Lines of communication and procedures need to be established between governmental agencies to enable, for example, access to foreign exchange on short notice for margin accounts. Domestic pricing procedures may need to be modified. And so on. The chapter by Claessens and Varangis on the oil sector indicates some of the steps involved in implementation.

Moving from External to Internal Risk Management

The case studies showed that the impact of international price changes is often allocated in a complex way across different parties in the economy. Some of the impact is absorbed by the firms that export or import the commodity, some by the final producers or users, some by intermediaries, and some by the government in the form of changes in taxes and transfer payments. It is basically the country's institutional structure that determines the allocation of its exposures.

Commodity export revenues, for example, are affected by taxes, tariffs, and subsidies, as documented by Powell with regard to the coffee sector in Colombia. There, portions of the ad valorem taxes levied on exports go to the government, to the National Coffee Federation, and to departmental committees. The National Coffee Federation receives subsidies or pays taxes, depending on the level of the international coffee price in relation to the price paid to farmers.

The appropriate use of commodity risk management may therefore differ significantly from what may be expected on the basis of an "on-the-border" risk profile. Thought should be given to which party can most efficiently execute the risk management, considering the possible effects on other parties. An example, on the coffee sector in Costa Rica, is given by Myers in chapter 6 and illustrated further by Claessens and Varangis in chapter 7. Coffee producers receive an advance on their crops when the coffee beans are brought to a mill, but do not receive final payment on this crop until the mill has sold all of the current harvest. This means that producers face a price risk while the crop is being sold by the mill. The advance the producer receives provides some insurance against large price falls during this period. The mill has also taken on some part of the risk of price movement, because if prices fall sharply, the revenue obtained from selling the coffee abroad may not be sufficient to cover the advance provided to the farmer. The government is also exposed, because its tax revenues depend on the profits of farmers and millers and thus also vary with coffee prices. Claessens and Varangis indicate the institutional changes that are required to induce and allow millers and exporters to hedge on behalf of the producers.

In some cases, use of new financial instruments needs to be designed around existing risk-sharing mechanisms and take into account methods already used domestically or abroad to manage commodity price risks. Many countries have informal risk-sharing mechanisms, such as sharecropping and intrafamily credit. In such cases, the exposures to commodity price changes and hedging needs will be different. An efficient program to manage external commodity price risks, then, cannot be implemented independently of a reform of the domestic market structure; in general, liberalized domestic prices are a sine qua non for an efficient program.

Choosing the Appropriate Strategy

The case studies demonstrate that management of commodity price risk may need to be different for each country and that different commodities need different approaches. The studies also indicate, however, that there are common elements in the risk management strategies for countries with similar risk exposures, for example, exporters of precious metals, crude oil, or agricultural commodities; countries with large numbers of state enterprises; and countries with large mineral extraction industries. This section discusses some of the common elements. It makes a distinction between risk management of a firm engaged in an enclave type of commodity production or consumption (for example, mineral extraction, crude oil production, or production based on imported goods) where there is little in the way of linkages between the firm and the rest of the economy, and risk management where there are many smallholder producers and many consumers.[31]

Risk Management for Firms

In firm-specific risk management, such as for large exporting or importing state or private enterprises that extract minerals or petroleum or that import commodities for their own production process, there is little or no need to integrate the management of external commodity price risk with activities to manage macroeconomic risk. The exposure of these enterprises to international commodity prices is often the most easily identified. Also, frequently the enterprises are part of a multinational firm and may need little incentive or training to be able to use financial hedging instruments effectively. The use of such instruments in these enterprises will be along the lines discussed by Masuoka in chapter 4. In these cases, the only other party that might be affected by the risk management activities of the enterprise is the (national or state) government through the effect on the variability of tax revenues.[32]

The larger firms in developing countries have been approached by the market makers regarding their interest in longer-dated instruments. Although risk factors related to the country put some constraints on the use of such instruments, the integration of these firms in international markets makes it relatively easy for them to overcome problems of creditworthiness.

Smallholder Producers and Commodity Consumers

Many developing countries that export or import commodities have markets made up of a large number of producers and consumers, each of which is too small to make economic use of instruments to manage commodity risk. This is the case for most of the countries exporting agricultural commodities and for many countries importing foodstuffs. In most cases the private sector is the preferred location for risk management, because it will be guided by strong incentives to use these instruments effectively. Competition among private exporters, for instance, will often lead to domestic prices that are as stable as possible for individual producers. The private sector will, however, be able to accommodate the needs of consumers and producers for risk management only when the appropriate institutional and regulatory (especially, the legal) framework is in place.[33] The public sector should be the location for a risk management unit only when there is a need to coordinate overall management of external exposures and borrowing, or when there is a large state enterprise, such as a state oil company. In some cases the most efficient option is for an institution—either existing and already involved in stabilization efforts or newly created—to undertake the external risk management and to serve as an intermediary in passing the risk reduction that is achieved on to the final consumer or producer.[34] Generally, it is preferable to develop a risk management strategy from the bottom up, that is, to determine first what the private sector can accomplish in risk management for the benefit of the country as a whole and only then to analyze what the government's role in performing risk management may be. It is likely that one will then find that the most important role for the government is to correct some of the market failures or to remove its own policy-induced distortions.

Relevant here are chapter 8, by Myers and Thompson, and chapter 9, by Claessens and Varangis, on managing the price risks of imported oil in Costa Rica. Oil price risk in Costa Rica is first incurred by the state import and refining company, Refinadora Costarricense de Petroleo (RECOPE), before being passed on to consumers. The analyses show how RECOPE could use futures and options in a straightforward way to manage this price risk for the benefit of Costa Rican consumers, who are not in a position to use such instruments.

The most common use by the public sector of commodity risk management instruments and commodity price–linked finance will be in countries where the government is already operating stabilization schemes or where prices were previously controlled but are now free. Instruments to manage commodity risk could complement or be imbedded in price stabilization schemes, such as buffer funds, variable rate tariffs, and marketing board operations. However, it may not always be advisable to continue these schemes. This will be the case particularly in developing countries where controls on domestic prices are removed as part of a reform program.

Price Stabilization Schemes

Price stabilization schemes provide good opportunities for using financial instruments to manage risk and for linking internal and external management of commodity risk. For instance, Claessens and Coleman suggest in chapter 10 that Papua New Guinea could use commodity futures to hedge the intrayear price risks of the agricultural stabilization schemes. Governments whose revenues or expenses directly or indirectly (through taxes) depend on commodity prices through the performance of stabilization schemes could use similar techniques to hedge their exposures. For example, Claessens and Coleman propose that the Mineral Resources Stabilization Fund (MRSF) in Papua New Guinea enter into commodity swaps to lock in future commodity prices, and thus a stream of tax revenues, before tax revenues enter the general budget instead of putting funds into foreign reserves at times of high commodity prices and drawing them down in times of low commodity prices, as done at present.[35]

External and internal risk management can also be combined in schemes that have buffer funds and variable rate tariffs. These schemes usually attempt to stabilize domestic prices of a traded (imported or exported) commodity within a band around a central price or provide a minimum price guarantee or some other form of price insurance. Typically, schemes that have buffer funds are operated by the government, which thus assumes the risk of world prices, converted into domestic currency, moving outside the band. Financial risk management for such schemes could involve the use of commodity price options. This approach is suggested in chapter 3, by Larson and Coleman, for food price stabilization schemes that use a band system. Through variable tariffs, many governments limit the effect of international price changes on domestic prices of consumer goods. Larson and Coleman suggest that governments buy long-dated calls, exercisable at the upper limit of the price band within which prices are stabilized, and sell puts, exercisable at the lower limit of the price band. The call options provide insurance if international prices move above the upper band, and the puts restrict price declines to the lower limit of the band. Similarly, where governments provide minimum price guarantees for exports or maximum price guarantees for imports, they could lay off the risks incurred through buying put or call options.

Other possible users of commodity options and futures are marketing boards. Often these boards announce prices at which they will buy the crop or provide advance payments. Thus they effectively provide price insurance by guaranteeing a minimum price.[36] They could use long-dated put options to hedge themselves against world prices that fall below the level of the minimum price or advance. This strategy is suggested by Myers in chapter 6 and Claessens and Varangis in chapter 7 for the coffee sector in Costa Rica. The coffee cooperative there, the Federation of Cooperatives of Coffee Growers (FEDECOOP), could buy put options with an exercise price equal to the advance provided to the farmers. This action would effectively reinsure in the international market the insurance provided to the farmers. In addition, commodity futures could be used to provide farmers with a certain payment at a fixed price upon delivery of their crop, as opposed to the current practice of paying farmers after FEDECOOP sells the crop.[37] Simulations by Claessens and Varangis indicate that such risk management strategies would provide substantial benefits in risk reduction.

There are other situations in which instruments to manage commodity risk could aid domestic price stabilization. One situation could be a domestic institution or marketplace that performed a clearinghouse function for the hedging needs of domestic suppliers or consumers or both. Where gross domestic consumption is large in relation to exports or imports, such a clearinghouse might be able to match up domestic parties and thus provide substantial domestic hedging services. Where the country is a substantial net exporter or importer of the good—and where domestic prices are not insulated from international price movements—a substantial exposure to international price movements will remain. The clearinghouse might then be able to engage in external commodity risk management to hedge this residual exposure—in effect, on behalf of domestic individuals.

Such a function could be necessary in the case of Hungary and other Eastern European countries that are moving to a market-based system, as described by Anderson and Powell in chapter 14. Hungary has substantial comparative advantage as a grain producer, but its production and marketing system has been centralized and strongly integrated, leading to a disappointing performance. The Hungarian government has begun to move the grain sector from a system based on state monopolies toward a more competitive, market-oriented system in which there is complete freedom to produce, sell, and buy. As Anderson and Powell document, several problems need to be addressed to complete this transition. Foremost are the impediments to the ownership and management of farms and cooperatives, and the practices of grain merchandising.

As part of the reform, the Hungarian authorities have established a formal futures exchange in Budapest—the Hungarian Agricultural Commodity Exchange—that permits trading in grain futures, currently corn and wheat. Anderson and Powell discuss the benefits of the new exchange with regard to risk management, focusing on the indirect benefits. They argue that the availability of risk management tools that are market-based will likely reinforce the move to a more decentralized, market-oriented system in the grain sector in Hungary. At present, major features of the sector are vertical integration and high concentration, which manage the risk of price fluctuations by moving the risk along the chain. The futures exchange could allow for new entrants in some parts of the marketing chain because it would provide them with a way to shift and manage risks. Thus, the futures exchange could be procompetitive and improve the chances of the reform process. The price discovery function of futures markets could also contribute to reform.

The establishment of a domestic futures market does raise the question of what one expects its advantages to be in relation to existing international markets. There are two possible reasons for establishing a domestic futures market: (a) either no futures market exists elsewhere that trades the contract to which the country is exposed,[38] or (b) transaction costs in accessing existing futures markets need to be reduced. (Transaction costs are defined in the largest sense to include the costs of collecting information and the problems of dealing with time differentials.) Although the first reason involves completing the markets for managing commodity risk and would in itself thus be recommendable, it is not clear whether developing countries have a comparative advantage in this area when one considers capital and human resources. The second reason is more likely valid when domestic consumption is large in relation to net exports or imports. In such a situation, matching domestic consumers' and producers' risk management needs through a domestic market could be efficient. However, the increased linkages between international financial centers, for example, the introduction of Global Exchange (GLOBEX), a system managed by Reuters for linking exchanges worldwide, may make reducing transaction costs increasingly irrelevant. The wrong motivation for establishing a domestic futures market would be the existence of large basis risks between domestic and international prices if the basis risks are caused by a regulated domestic physical market or other policy-induced distortions.

Conclusions

The case studies reported in this book show that countries can benefit significantly from using financial instruments to manage the risk of changes in commodity prices. To date, developing countries have not used the full range of commodity price–linked market instruments, especially the innovations of commodity price–linked swaps, loans, bonds, and long-dated commodity options. This omission can be attributed to a lack of awareness of risk profiles, lack of knowledge as to the potential use of these market instruments for hedging risk exposures, the limitations of a country's creditworthiness, and also domestic legal, regulatory, and institutional structures.

For developing countries to benefit fully from these instruments, there needs to be further technical assistance; training and education to increase awareness in developing countries of their external exposures to market prices; and credit enhancement by third parties. In addition, developing countries should clarify and alter their institutional framework to allow access to these instruments by both the private and the public sector.

The initial efforts in the World Bank's program of technical assistance, operating so far in only a few countries, have shown that it is possible to improve quickly both the awareness of external exposures and the use of market instruments, including innovative instruments and techniques. Efforts in this direction, combined with the potential pace of innovation in financial markets, both international and domestic, offer promising prospects for further developments in the use of financial instruments to hedge external exposures.

Notes

1. Misallocation is a particular problem for many perennial crops with long lags in their production process, because the profitability of investments depends on the evolution of prices several years into the future. Given the large sunk costs, once the investment has been made, it is unlikely that production will be changed in the light of relative price changes.

2. A price series for raw sugar, dating back 350 years, has been compiled by the British sugar refiner Tate and Lyle. The price series shows several periods in which prices rose much more sharply than the booms experienced in the 1970s and early 1980s.

3. In response to the problem of highly volatile commodity prices and the large forecasting errors involved, the International Trade Division has begun to issue (for internal purposes) forecasts that provide for a range of possible future commodity prices with assigned probabilities of outcome. These probabilistic forecasts can be used, for instance, in project analysis to check the robustness of the economic value of the project to different possible price outcomes, or in scenarios for macroeconomic analysis.

4. On a practical level, many of the concepts and instruments for managing external risk and liability are similar for the different external risks. The necessary human skills may be able to be brought together in a single institution to deal with several external risks when an overall approach to external risk management and finance is pursued.

5. The collapse of the International Tin Agreement in 1985 and the International Coffee Agreement in 1989 was in large part caused by intervention prices being set too high in relation to underlying demand and supply—as can be seen by the sharply lower prices since the collapse. Free-riding by suppliers in the case of tin and by consumers in the case of coffee also contributed to the collapse.

6. For instance, when the scheme involves an intermediary—such as a marketing board, a trader, a processor, or another third party—that guarantees a price in local currency to the producer (at the beginning of the production year) or to the consumer, the intermediary takes on the risk of deviations in the international price from the guaranteed domestic price in the period between the time the guarantee was made and final sale or purchase. Where these intermediaries have been government-owned, losses as a result of intervention prices being too high (in the case of exports) or too low (in the case of imports)

will be passed on to the government budget and reallocated to other parts of the economy. Intermediaries are often used where there are many smallholder producers, for example, cocoa and coffee farmers.

7. Reserve management schemes can insulate the economy from international price swings by investing in reserves (held offshore) in periods of high export revenues and transferring these reserves back to the economy in times of low commodity export revenues. Gilbert observes that, in practice, many of the foreign exchange reserve schemes have not been very successful, largely because of a lack of fiscal discipline. Gilbert mentions Côte d'Ivoire and Nigeria as cases in which sterilization was limited by the premature exhaustion of the funds.

8. Even with prices set to reflect long-run world supply and demand, stabilization efforts can still mean that decisions about investment and savings are distorted. Smallholders, for instance, typically save and invest in periods of high prices; therefore, price stabilization can reduce their investment. In addition, official stabilization schemes can reduce the incentive to develop private storage, which in itself can be an effective stabilization mechanism.

9. See Stiglitz (1987) for some valid reasons for government intervention in agricultural markets.

10. Examples include a commodity price–linked bond with an option at maturity that gives the right to buy a certain amount of a commodity for a given price, or a swaption that gives the buyer the right to enter a swap agreement at a certain price.

11. Parties involved in gaining access to a futures exchange in the United States, for example, include the brokerage house, the exchange itself, and the Commodity Futures Trading Commission (CFTC). The brokerage house is directly responsible for the individual contract obligation. The exchange sets the minimum margins and position limits and maintains the clearinghouse functions. The CFTC sets general trading regulations, monitors positions and financial requirements, and investigates possible abuses.

12. The only likely differences between the requirements for a firm from an industrial country and a firm, parastatal, or government agency from a developing country would be the level of the required maintenance margin, which would be higher for a developing country, and the restrictions on the maximum amounts of futures contracts that can be used, which would be lower.

13. These transactions refer to finance with contractual obligations dependent in some fashion on the price of a commodity or a commodity price index. It is not a description of finance that creates a special claim on future commodity export receipts or other commodity receivables or that uses some form of commodity-related collateral.

14. Masuoka mentions some examples of commodity swaps that are combined with a conventional loan, one example being the financing package for Mexicana de Cobre, a copper mining subsidiary of Grupo Mexico. An example of the use of commodity price–linked financing by a developing country is that of the Algerian state-owned oil company, Sonatrach, which entered into a loan agreement linked to oil.

15. Basis risk is the risk that cannot be hedged, expressed as a fraction of the overall risk of the spot price. It can be measured as one minus the correlation coefficient between spot and futures prices. It increases if there is a mismatch between the final maturity of the instrument and the date the exposure occurs. Whether in the absence of basis risk there is exact equivalence between a rollover and a swap will depend on the price process applicable; full equivalence would hold if, for example, the price behaved like a so-called random walk over time. But few prices appear to conform to this pattern exactly. Dynamic hedging strategies can be employed to reduce the risk that arises when (short-dated) futures or options mimic the payoff structure of other (long-term) instruments for managing commodity risk.

16. Many of the commodity bonds issued have included an option feature. In that case, the investor may, in addition to its regular payments, have the option to buy or sell a predetermined quantity of a commodity at a predetermined price. The value of the attached option usually allows for a lower coupon than in the case of a conventional commodity bond.

17. The party that incurred a large opportunity cost in relation to selling on a cash or short-term contract basis had a large incentive to renege on the contract, and many of these contracts could not be enforced in an international context.

18. The market for shorter-term instruments to manage commodity risk has always been large and has historically been of the same order of magnitude (in terms of volume) as the markets for exchange rate and interest rate instruments.

19. Occhiolini also discusses the so-called Mexico Letter issued by the CFTC, which allowed Mexico, in the context of its debt restructuring, to issue bonds with detachable oil warrants, an action not allowed under normal CFTC rules.

20. For example, a ruling by the CFTC in the United States has allowed banks to engage in commodity-related financing.

21. One of the problems here is that the arbitrage between the financial and the physical asset becomes more complicated when the costs of storage and transportation are high.

22. Additionally, the staffing costs of administering market dealing could be considered a type of transaction cost.

23. For instance, in many countries the futures prices for commodities for end-of-the-crop-year maturity are often used by producers when making planting decisions.

24. The case of the grain sector in Hungary, described by Anderson and Powell in chapter 14, is illustrative in this respect.

25. Hughes-Hallett and Ramanujam (1990) point out that instruments for managing commodity risk hedge only against price risk, therefore leaving quantity risk, and that buffer stocks hedge against revenue risk. The authors show that, depending on the nature of the price and quantity shocks, using either commodity risk management instruments or buffer stocks is the most effective revenue stabilizer. They conclude that price hedging is the most effective revenue stabilizer for high-value commodities and buffer stocks for low-value commodities, largely because of the financing costs involved with buffer stocks.

26. Many of the required changes directed at enhancing the efficiency of the physical markets were necessary conditions for a well-functioning, financial, forward market for commodities. For example, the forward market required the creation of a complete regulatory and legal framework of ownership to allow for the transfer of goods without physical delivery, which is a sine qua non for risk transfer.

27. The inverse relationship between the dollar and commodity prices is often mentioned as an important factor in this respect. Empirical studies have documented that the elasticity between the dollar exchange rate and the commodity price is between -0.5 and -1.0.

28. An example may be the coffee sector in Brazil. The effect on export revenues of sharp drops in production as a result of frost is to a significant extent offset by price changes. However, because most developing countries are small producers in relation to the size of their respective commodity markets and are therefore price takers, the effect of price changes translates for most developing countries into one-to-one revenue changes and there is no offsetting effect to reduce the need for hedging price risks to hedge revenue risks.

29. Credit risk for commodity swaps is, in principle, similar to that for exchange rate and interest rate swaps. The magnitude of the credit exposure will depend on the volatility of the underlying price and will be different for each underlying price (exchange rate, interest rate, or commodity price). The limit that counterparty risk imposes on the use of swaps can be illustrated by the type of counterparties commercial banks accept for their currency swaps. Marked-to-market swaps—which operate very similarly to a futures con-

tract by requiring an adjustable margin—can reduce somewhat the credit risk problem. See the chapter by Masuoka.

30. However, the use of collateral and the creation of special, senior claims on exports in the case of state enterprises can create problems related to the negative pledge clauses found in many bank loan agreements (including the World Bank's).

31. Alternatively, a distinction can be made as to the degree by which countries are affected by commodity price shocks.

32. This does not imply that in such cases the enterprises should be allowed to use instruments to manage commodity risk without any supervision or control. On the other hand, it may be that existing capital controls or other restrictions preventing the use of such instruments will have to be removed. In these cases it may be necessary to change the regulatory and legal framework to allow this type of risk management while at the same time ensuring adequate control to prevent misuse.

33. Use by the private sector of instruments to manage commodity risk can reduce the government's need to use these techniques for hedging purposes. In Papua New Guinea, for instance, some of the mining companies are using risk management instruments to hedge their net revenues against changes in mineral prices. As a result, the tax revenues of the government are less sensitive to price changes.

34. Often, the institutional structure in the country needs to be made more transparent in order to place the responsibilities, control, and information functions related to risk management with the parties incurring the exposure. For example, because risk management practices often delink the economic ownership of a commodity from its physical possession, implementing such practices may require legal and institutional changes to ensure a proper system of ownership, custody and clearing, uniformity of documentation and inspection procedures, and registration. In Argentina, for instance, the verification of ownership of grain stocked in warehouses is rudimentary because there is no adequate system for providing warehousing receipts. This hinders spot trading and constrains the possibilities for risk management.

35. Another good example of this kind of activity is the Chilean Copper Income Compensation Fund (FEC). The FEC has an uncertain revenue stream because of fluctuating mineral prices, although its objective is to provide a stable flow of funds to the government budget. It could achieve this stability through the use of long-term commodity swaps, which would effectively convert its uncertain revenue stream into a certain stream. FEC would enter a copper swap for a (notional) amount equal to (a fraction of) the expected revenues from the copper producers, expressed in terms of pounds of copper, and receive a fixed dollar payment. This exchange would allow FEC to provide a more certain income stream for the general budget and ensure currency sterilization. Of course, an important consideration would be whether the copper producers themselves carried out any risk management, because that would alter the exposure of the government to copper prices. At issue here as well is the relationship between price and quantity movements and the effect of these movements on revenues. If the effect of price movements on revenues is offset by quantity movements, only a fraction of exports would be hedged.

36. Marketing boards often have monopsony power, in which case preannouncement of a price is not identical to a minimum price guarantee. This is true only when producers have alternative outlets for their produce that may offer a higher price.

37. For the most part, futures lead only to short-term, within-year hedging and will leave entities exposed to the risk of between-year fluctuations or basis risk if a futures rollover strategy is used.

38. The incompleteness of the market for risk management instruments is to a large extent a matter of basis risks: there will always exist some instruments that provide some limited hedging potential.

2

Domestic Price Stabilization Schemes for Developing Countries

Christopher L. Gilbert

Primary commodity prices are notoriously volatile. For agricultural food commodities, this volatility originates predominantly in supply disturbances (in particular, from the weather), whereas for industrial raw materials, the origin is largely demand disturbances (in particular, fluctuations in industrial demand in industrial countries). In conjunction with low short-run demand and supply elasticities, these disturbances give rise to sharp price variations. Price variability is smoothed by stockholding, but when stocks become low, prices can jump sharply (for example in the mid-1970s and, for metals, over the period 1987–89). A consequence of this asymmetry in stockholding behavior is that commodity price cycles tend to be characterized by flat bottoms and sharp peaks (see Deaton and Laroque 1992). For metals and tree crops, these price cycles are aggravated by investment activity in which, because of long gestation periods, high prices can generate subsequent long periods of excess supply and low prices. On the demand side, technological change can result in major and unanticipated shifts in demand, which can again result in long periods of excess supply or demand (as happened, for example, for metals in the first half of the 1980s).

Price variability translates directly and almost proportionately into variability in export revenues. This export variability impinges on developing countries in two important ways. First is the impact on the producers (farmers and wage-earning employees), who will suffer variability

The author is grateful to Ronald Anderson, Hans Binswanger, Wilfred Candler, Ronald Duncan, and John Nash for helpful comments.

in their incomes. There may also be similar effects on consumers if they devote a significant proportion of their budgets to a single commodity. Second is the impact on government, which will suffer variability in both its fiscal position (through variability in tax and profit receipts) and its exchange reserves. The impact on producers and consumers can be offset to the extent that they can lend and borrow freely, but long periods of low prices may exhaust their capacity to borrow. The impact on producers can also be offset through real exchange rate changes or progressive taxation or less formal arrangements that spread the effects of income variation throughout the economy, thereby diversifying the risk. The macroeconomic impact on government can similarly be offset if the government can lend and borrow freely on international markets.

Concerns about the effects of variability in export revenues have led to efforts to stabilize commodity export earnings through one or more of the following measures:

1. Stabilization of world commodity prices (monopolistic action by a large producer or producer cartel, or through an international commodity agreement)
2. Stabilization of producer revenues, given producer prices (through hedging on forward, futures, or options markets)
3. Compensatory arrangements to offset variations in revenues (by domestic income maintenance, or, at a country level, through compensatory finance schemes)
4. Stabilization of domestic producer or consumer prices or both, given world prices (through a variable export tax or a variable tariff, through the operation of a marketing board, or through domestic stockpiling).

The first three measures aim at insulating the economy from price shocks, either by stabilizing international commodity prices (the first measure) or by transferring risks to third parties. The transfer of risks would be accomplished either by hedging (the second measure) or by borrowing or lending (the third measure). The last measure aims at reducing the impact of commodity price changes on a certain domestic sector by forms of self-insurance or domestic diversification.

The major direction of international commodity policy in the 1970s was toward the negotiation of international commodity agreements (ICAS) under the auspices of the Integrated Programme for Commodities (IPC) of the United Nations Conference on Trade and Development. These negotiations became highly politicized, and there was a justifiable suspicion that the governments of many producing countries were seeking mechanisms to raise prices rather than to stabilize them. As a consequence, only a single new agreement (the International Natural Rubber

Agreement) emerged from these negotiations, bringing the total of agreements with economic clauses to five. The IPC program was further discredited by the poor performance of a number of the other agreements—particularly the International Cocoa Agreement, which has had a negligible effect on the market, and the International Tin Agreement (ITA), which collapsed dramatically in 1985. The collapse of the ITA, previously the most successful ICA, has effectively eliminated this approach to commodity policy from the international political agenda.[1]

Developing-country governments have continued to perceive commodity price variability as a problem. Compensatory finance schemes (the International Monetary Fund's Compensatory and Contingency Financing Facility and the European Community's Stabilisation of Export Earnings (STABEX) fund have had only minor impact, and there is some question as to whether they have been stabilizing. The result has been that primary producers in developing countries have been forced back onto their own resources to combat this volatility problem.

One approach that has been stressed is the use of financial derivative instruments (forwards, futures, options) to reduce revenue variability. It is suggested that producers could directly, via dealers, use these markets to offset their exposure to price risk or that, alternatively, government marketing boards or finance ministries could use these instruments, perhaps passing the benefits on to producers. There is no doubt that governments and parastatal trading organizations can potentially benefit significantly by hedging their risk positions over a short-term horizon (one that is less than a year), although they will wish to weigh the benefits against the costs. It is difficult, however, to extrapolate these benefits over a longer period, because a longer period would require a substantially greater financial commitment, and access to credit. It is notable in this regard that there is little long-term hedging by private sector organizations in industrial countries.

Futures and related markets make possible substantial reductions in the riskiness of committed decisions, but they do not in general reduce revenue variability; rather, they allow it to be fixed in advance. Furthermore, both access and credit problems will severely limit the extent to which small-scale producers in developing countries can make direct use of the longer-term derivative markets. I shall argue, however, that these limitations do not preclude arrangements whereby developing-country producers can benefit from the services offered by futures and related short-term markets.

Without access to longer-term derivative instruments, domestic price stabilization schemes become the remaining candidates for producer revenue stabilization over longer periods. More or less formal schemes of this sort have existed from 1945 onward, but agency or academic attention has been diverted from them to the small number of more prominent international schemes. The purpose of this chapter is to provide a guide through the various forms of domestic price stabilization schemes.

Justifications for Intervention

Although most problems having to do with primary commodities originate in the variability of commodity prices, there is no single paradigmatic way to characterize these problems. This reflects the differing nature of the production processes and price cycles for different commodities; the differences between countries with regard to size, export concentration, indebtedness, and other characteristics; and the different priorities of the governments of producing countries. For these reasons, a large variety of domestic price stabilization schemes are being and have been employed in different countries. This diversity makes simple statements relatively unhelpful.

It is too simple, for example, to appeal to the standard result in welfare economics that, under specified conditions, unconstrained competition will result in a Paretian allocation of goods and resources in which one agent's welfare level may be raised only at the expense of lowering that of some other agent. This result requires too much and therefore proves too little. It invites the response that because the specified preconditions manifestly fail to obtain even more evidently in developing than in industrial economies, there is everything to be gained and little to be lost from governments intervening in their economies for whatever objectives they favor. The last three decades of interventionist experience across the broad range of developing countries are much more eloquent in making the case that government interventions should rest on specifically argued cost-benefit analyses, which should, where possible, be quantified. This is not to prejudge the debate against intervention, but simply to acknowledge that, just as there is no general argument that governments cannot improve the functioning of the economy, there is equally no presumption that even well-intentioned interventions will have that effect.

On the other hand, it would be a counsel of despair to state that one needs to look at stabilization on a case-by-case basis. It is possible to identify a number of general paradigms and, furthermore, to analyze a set of issues that arise in stabilization exercises which are, in other respects, quite diverse.

An important case, which I analyze in the next several sections, is one in which the government's objective is the stabilization of earnings of small-scale producers of an export crop (although there may be cases where this could also apply to metals). In particular, this will apply to schemes that have buffer funds and to export marketing boards that exercise a stabilization function (described below). Such organizations often stabilize by relating producer prices to a moving average of past border prices. An alternative but more limited objective is to attempt to reduce the price risk associated with agricultural production. This may be done by offering forward contracts or floor prices to farmers. I suggest that this objective is more appropriate for annual crops and that consideration of stabilization schemes should be confined to crops with longer lead times (specifically, tree crops).

I next turn to schemes in which the government's objective is the stabilization of the consumer prices of traded goods, and the related topic of variable tariffs on imported commodities. In general, I find few economic arguments that can justify schemes of this sort.

An issue that arises in all of these schemes is whether stabilization authorities should also exercise a fiscal function. In discussing this question, I submit that optimal taxation arguments will in general support taxation of exports in countries where comprehensive income or (general) commodity taxation are infeasible, but that tax rates will typically be quite low. These considerations also relate to the questions of budgetary independence.

A different set of issues arises in the context of stabilization schemes for nontraded goods or for goods that are only traded occasionally or peripherally. For such commodities it will be natural to consider storage as the major stabilization instrument. I argue that in general it is preferable either to improve transportation links or to encourage private sector storage in these cases. By contrast, public sector storage will typically tend to inhibit private sector storage. However, if public buffer stocks are to be instituted, the commonly used approach of band stabilization is unattractive, and in particular the buffer stock authority should not make any commitment to defend a ceiling price. Frequently, however, public stockpiling is directed at food security rather than price stabilization, and this raises distributional issues.

All of this relates to small-scale production of agricultural commodities. Mining and oil extraction, by contrast, typically take place in large-scale enterprises that are often, at least in part, government-owned. In any case, there are often substantial rents that governments will wish to capture irrespective of ownership. I suggest that the issue here is not stabilization so much as the appropriate degree of risk sharing.

It will often be the case that fluctuations in the government's take from mining or oil extraction revenues will be large in relation to national income, and the same may be true of fluctuations in export earnings from some agricultural crops. In these cases problems associated with absorption can be substantial, particularly in countries where there are import and other price controls. These problems are the subject of the penultimate section of the chapter, where I indicate that failure to acknowledge them can undermine otherwise sensible stabilization programs. As I point out, there are also implications for debt management.

Stabilization of Producer Revenues

For stabilization of producer revenues, it is important to distinguish between annual crops and tree crops. In each case, the most important decisions are taken at the time of planting. Planting decisions for annual crops are made on the basis of expected prices. Prices at harvest that are higher than expected can have little effect, but prices will seldom fall so far as to make it unprofitable to harvest at all. (Nevertheless, possible variation in the intensity of effort may result in a small short-run response.) For these crops it is important that prices at the start of each harvest year give the appropriate incentives, because the "long run" is fairly short. Planting decisions for tree crops, by contrast, lead production typically by three to five years, and trees will be productive perhaps for the two or three decades that follow. Weeding, the application of fertilizers, and other maintenance processes do introduce some short- to medium-term price sensitivity, and "scrapping" may also be price-sensitive, but it remains true that planting is the time at which prices matter most. For tree crops, then, it is possible for producer prices to differ significantly from border prices over periods of several years without giving inappropriate incentives.

This discussion suggests that stabilization of producer revenues is only sensible for crops with long lead times, principally tree crops. I argue below that the appropriate objective for annual crops is instead the reduction of short-term uncertainty and that this implies a certain set of schemes.

The textbook argument for governmental intervention in commodity trade (see, for example, Newbery and Stiglitz 1981) asks us then to consider the position of small, independent, specialized producers of the commodity. Typically, these producers will be farmers producing a market crop, either annual or tree (but there are also producers who extract metals on a small scale, for example, producers who dredge alluvial tin). Specialization implies that fluctuations in the commodity price transmit to fluctuations in the farmers' incomes, and the small scale of production will imply that any crop variability will generally add to, rather than offset, the price variability. It is then suggested that this income variability will imply variability in consumption levels, which (on standard concavity arguments) will lower farmers' expected utility levels in relation to the situation in which the government stabilizes the commodity price.

Here, the government is asked to smooth the farmers' consumption streams. But because farmers are not myopic, one needs to ask why they cannot do this task for themselves by saving in years when revenues are high against the eventuality of poorer years to follow. A possible argument would be lack of adequate savings instruments, although in practice rural credit institutions do exist except where they have been suppressed. Nevertheless, these institutions may be considered unreliable. Second, a succession of bad years may exhaust savings, and farmers may lack the collateral to borrow except at punitive rates. On that argument, the government is able to use its superior credit status to offer a greater degree of consumption smoothing. But to the extent that governments smooth farmers' revenues by stabilizing prices, they also reduce farmers' incentives to save. In attempting to offset one aspect of the market, stabilization tends to suppress market responses.

This suppression of market responses is also evident in the standard argument that stabilization will introduce a welfare loss by divorcing prices from short-run marginal costs. When a price is stabilized, farmers lose the incentive to produce more at periods of high prices and less in periods of low prices. Consumers' marginal rates of substitution are no longer equal to the marginal rates of transformation, and costless welfare gains are forgone.

A response here is to argue that short-run supply elasticities in agriculture are very low. This argument suggests that, so long as the right long-run signals are given, the welfare losses from the suppression of short-run supply responses are minimal. Whether or not this is the case will depend on characteristics of the commodity (tree or annual) and on the mechanism that is adopted for determining the stabilized price.

A related issue is the extent to which producer prices should be stabilized. Because the concern is with producer revenues, any (negative) covariance between domestic production levels and border prices would imply that revenue would be stabilized by less than full-price stabilization. In general, however, the world price of a traded commodity will be nearly independent of production levels in any particular small country unless there is a common pattern in the disturbances affecting a significant proportion of world production.

The more important issue, therefore, is to balance the efficiency losses that occur when price departs from marginal cost with the risk benefits that occur through stabilization (see Mirrlees 1988). Making the right evaluations to bring about this balance is difficult. There are measures of farmers' risk aversion, but calculation of risk benefits also requires that we know how much insurance farmers are obtaining from other (mostly informal) sources. On the cost side, I have suggested that short-term efficiency losses from setting prices equal to long-run values may not be high for tree crops, but will be high for annual crops. But even for tree crops, this calculation will suggest a high level of stabilization only to the extent that one is confident about the level of long-run prices. Knudsen and Nash (1990a) quote with some approval the 50 percent stabilization target set by the Papua New Guinea cocoa buffer fund, but it is difficult to see this figure as anything more than a reasonable guess.

Buffer Fund and Marketing Board Schemes for Tradable Crops

By "tradable crop" I mean a crop for which there are clear border prices and for which, in the absence of government intervention, movements in domestic market prices would closely follow movements in border prices. This definition covers export crops and also commodities of which there is substantial domestic consumption and of which the balance between domestic production and consumption is exported or imported as required. It excludes crops for which, in the absence of intervention, domestic prices primarily reflect domestic market conditions, even if there is some element of international trade. I consider stabilization for nontraded commodities in a later section of this chapter.

Stabilization of domestic producer prices for tradable crops may be achieved either through variable taxation or by the creation of marketing boards that set the prices at which they purchase from producers. For reasons I shall discuss, the latter arrangement is more common.

In variable export taxation schemes, stabilization is achieved through progressivity of the tax rate, the result being that producers pay higher rates of taxation when prices are high. In many instances governments choose to tax primary exports as a significant source of revenue (see below), and the stabilization achieved through progression is a consequence of the perception that flat rate export taxation might impose too large a cost on producers in times of low prices, rather than a consequence of any desire for stabilization per se.[2] Nevertheless, the result can be a significant degree of stabilization of producer prices at the expense of destabilization of government tax revenues.

Buffer fund schemes are similar to variable tax schemes in their effects, but here the explicit intention is stabilization. In buffer fund schemes, a progressive rate of export taxation when prices are high is combined with progressive subsidization if prices are low. Surpluses from the periods of positive taxation are added to the buffer fund to be available to be paid out as subsidies when required. If the scheme is purely aimed at stabilization the objective would be that the buffer fund be in balance over the long term, although this requires an accurate estimate of the long-run price (see next section). However, if the agency aims to tax on average more than it subsidizes, the buffer fund may be combined with taxation for the purpose of increasing government revenue.[3]

Operation of schemes of this sort requires an effective mechanism for ensuring tax payments. In industrial countries producers can be required to make verifiable returns of their production, and it is therefore possible to issue tax demands and make subsidy payments on the basis of these figures. In countries where tax evasion is common, it may be easier for governments to stabilize producer prices by setting up marketing boards to act as monopsony buyers.

Stabilization of producer prices is only one of the motives that might lie behind the creation of export marketing boards. If the commodity is consumed domestically, stabilization of consumer prices may be another objective (see below). Governments may also wish to use their monopsony power to keep down prices to consumers or, more generally, may simply believe that they can use the marketing board to control production levels. Usually they will also wish to impose an implicit export tax by keeping producer prices beneath border prices.

Stabilization is achieved if producer prices are less volatile than border prices. This reduction in price volatility might be the result of the application of a progressive formula, as in export tax schemes, but more usually the reduction results simply from bureaucratic procedures for price adjustment. The standard mode of operation under monopsony is for the board to fix an official buying price that is announced before planting or sowing in the case of annual crops and before harvesting in the case of tree crops. This price is maintained for a specified period (typically around six months) during which the board guarantees to buy whatever is offered. The absence of a preannounced formula for determining producer prices results in uncertainty about future prices, detracting from the benefits of stabilization. In addition, monopsonistic buying can be effective only if the government can control smuggling (outward when the commodity is taxed, inward when subsidized). The ability to control smuggling will depend, in part, on the size of the country.[4]

Do marketing boards need monopsony powers, or can they coexist with the private sector? In principle, producer prices could be enforced through explicit export taxation, the consequence being that private sector dealers could only afford to offer the same price as the marketing board. But in that case, the board would be superfluous. This serves to underline the point that monopsonistic marketing boards are set up either because export taxation is unreliable—it may, in certain countries, be easier to monitor production than trade—or because governments wish to use monopsony powers for other purposes. It is therefore difficult to resist the conclusion that these monopsony powers are central to the operation of export marketing boards that set producer prices. I shall, however, discuss a different role for export marketing boards in later sections.

Other negative market consequences result from the operation of export marketing board schemes of this form. By offering a fixed price, the board suppresses intertemporal (specifically seasonal), intergrade, and interregional variability. The suppression of seasonal variability will be important only for crops that have a substantial premium for early or late harvesting or for off-season production, and in those cases it would be appropriate to offer a premium. Suppression of seasonal variability also discourages intraseasonal stockholding, and the government may find itself obliged to assume this role. The suppression of intergrade variability encourages producers to deliver the grade that is the least costly to produce, and this will generally be of low quality. Again, it is important to offer differentials. The suppression of interregional price variability is likely to be important in countries where domestic transportation is expensive, whether for distance or for other reasons. In such countries a uniform price will overencourage production in remote areas and discourage production in locations with low transport costs. A solution is to set a guaranteed price at one or more ports or strategic rail stations and to buy at other locations at prices discounted to reflect transport to the base point. These problems arise principally where there is an attempt to stabilize earnings from annual crops, and this reinforces the view that stabilization may be an inappropriate objective for these crops. Furthermore, the fact that the solutions to these problems are all likely to be imperfect does suggest that, where possible, it is preferable to set producer prices through variable taxes and subsidies rather than through monopsonistic purchasing.[5]

Moving Average Stabilization

Producer prices set by government export marketing boards variously reflect estimates of current and likely future market conditions, production costs, the size of the fund at the agency's disposal, and the government's revenue requirements. Allowing this degree of discretion tends to make long-term producer prices unpredictable, and it may also destabilize producer prices in relation to world prices if the government puts its revenue requirements ahead of producer needs and incentives. There is a strong implication, therefore, that producer prices should be set by a formula.

I have stressed above that considerations of efficiency require that the producer price which is set in a scheme that has tax subsidies or monopsony purchasing should give the appropriate "long-run" incentives, but that for annual crops the "long run" may be relatively short. It is therefore necessary to consider price setting separately for annual and tree crops.

A standard way to estimate long-run price levels is to use a moving average of past prices. This procedure reflects the belief that, because of changes in consumer tastes and production technology, price levels vary secularly as well as cyclically. The moving average procedure ensures that the stabilization price tracks the long-run price, albeit with a lag.[6] In forming a moving average, it is desirable to make adjustments both for exchange rate changes, which have been an important source of fluctuations in commodity prices over recent years (see Gilbert 1989, 1991), and for changes in purchasing power. Prices may be expressed in approximately currency-neutral terms by converting them into special drawing rights (SDRs). Possible deflators include those of the U.S. consumer price index or gross domestic product (GDP), but because commodity prices are determined in the long run primarily by costs, it is preferable to use a supply-side deflator, and a possible candidate is the U.S. producer price index.[7]

Stabilization about a moving average producer price is attractive for tree crop commodities,[8] but it is likely to impose large efficiency costs for annual crops (see Walters 1987). For these crops, efficiency requires that appropriate incentives be given at the start of each harvest year, and these incentives must take into account the stock and expected demand conditions in the year in question. For commodities that are traded on organized exchanges, the relevant futures price gives the required incentive. This fact suggests that either under a variable export tax scheme or under monopsony purchasing, domestic prices should be based on futures quotations. Futures prices vary considerably from year to year, however, and therefore "stabilization" around the futures price may not give a very substantial reduction in revenue variability. I take up this issue in the next section.

Marketing Board Schemes Aimed at Reducing Revenue Uncertainty

Successful stabilization of a commodity price about a moving average trend will reduce price variability and thereby reduce the uncertainty associated with future revenues. It is, however, possible to reduce uncertainty without significantly affecting price variability. This may be done by hedging—the producers sell some or all of their planned production forward at a price settled at the date the contract is made but with payment made on delivery. Equivalently, for commodities for which there are organized futures markets, producers may sell a future in the commodity and close out the transaction by buying back a future corresponding to the same delivery month when the production is sold in the normal way. Because forward and futures prices of storable commodities tend to move in line with cash prices, except at times of marked shortage, hedging by selling forward does little to reduce interyear revenue variability, but it does substantially reduce the uncertainty associated with these revenues.

Simple models fail to distinguish between the value of reduced consumption variability and the value of reduced consumption uncertainty. One cost of uncertainty comes through induced stress and worry, but economists' models focus instead on the costs of uncertainty in terms of inappropriate decisions. Consider a farmer who can choose between planting a crop the price of which is fairly certain, and an alternative crop, the price of which is expected to be higher, but which is much more variable. Risk aversion will result in the farmer's planting more of the safe crop than would be chosen simply on the basis of the relative expected prices of the two crops. If, however, the farmer can fully hedge the risky crop by selling production forward, the relevant comparison will be between the forward price of the risky crop and the expected price of the safe crop; the price variances are now irrelevant (Danthine 1978). The benefit from the reduction of uncertainty is the higher overall return.

Smallholder farmers in developing countries do not have access to organized forward or futures markets. If they are to obtain the benefits of predetermined prices, this must be through the actions of some intermediary. In fact, this is also generally the case in industrial economies. Very few farmers operate directly in the futures markets. Nevertheless they obtain the same service through dealers, for example, elevator companies in grains. The elevator makes a contract for forward delivery with a farmer at a small premium on the exchange price. The elevator then immediately offsets its risk position by selling the appropriate quantity of futures on the exchange. Essentially, the elevator retails forward contracts purchased wholesale from the futures market.

Although the same principles can apply in developing countries, few developing countries have had a domestic institutional framework that was liberal enough to allow the emergence of privately owned elevator companies. Nevertheless, this example of elevator companies in developed countries provides a model for the operation of export marketing schemes for annual crop commodities. At the time of planting, a marketing board can announce a price at which it is committed to purchase at the harvest date. This price would be based on the current futures quotation for the month at which the board would be able to deliver the quantities it purchases from the farmers. The board then sells futures corresponding to this delivery month to offset its risk position with the farmers with the intention of subsequently closing these positions out at the time it delivers to its normal customers.

There are variants of this approach depending on whether the marketing board has monopsonistic purchasing powers or whether sales to the board are voluntary, and depending on the form of the contract, if any, between the farmers and the board. In the case where the board is a monopsony purchaser, and will therefore wish to sell forward its entire expected cash purchases, this approach should allow it to purchase at a price (discounted from the relevant futures price) at the time of planting. However, this sort of monopsony scheme has all the disadvantages, discussed above, with monopsonistic purchasing in relation to export revenue stabilization, and it is an important advantage of schemes based on retailing futures prices that they be voluntary.

In a voluntary scheme, farmers would contract with the marketing board to deliver specified quantities of the crop as and when they chose to do so. The board would act exactly as the elevator company in the earlier example and offset its price exposure by selling futures to exactly match its forward purchase commitments. It follows that the price the board offers will vary as the harvest approaches, in line with variation in the futures price. The practical difficulty that the board faces in this voluntary arrangement is to ensure the farmers' performance. Farmers who have contracted to deliver to the marketing board will have an incentive to renege and deliver to the market if, at the harvest, spot prices are higher than the contracted futures-based price. Viability of a voluntary scheme depends on the marketing board's being able to enforce contractual commitments. Coffee marketing cooperatives and private exporters in Costa Rica, which are currently using this scheme, face some of these problems as it is not possible to enter domestically into legally binding, fixed price contracts (see further Claessens and Varangis, chapter 6). In many developing countries, reform of the domestic marketing system and changes in the legal code will therefore be necessary for these schemes to be viable.

It is relatively easy within a scheme of this sort to accommodate intra-seasonal variation in prices. The marketing board will be able to deliver early crops to consumers at an earlier date than the main crop, and this will imply that the forward price it offers for early crops should relate to an earlier future. In large countries, intraregional price variation will be more problematic, and I revert to this in a later section.

Futures-based forward pricing schemes are attractive where planting decisions for annual crops can be affected by the reduction in uncertainty. Such schemes are also attractive where there is small-scale production of metals, including production from scrap. The schemes may not be as useful for tree crops, because the investment decisions are made several years in advance; we saw that for tree crops, moving average stabilization schemes are more attractive (or, at least, less unattractive).

Floor Price Guarantees

Floor price guarantees, which are variants of forward pricing schemes, maintain volunteerism but do not give rise to enforcement problems. In these schemes, the marketing board offers a guaranteed price floor to farmers rather than a fixed price. It is possible for the board to offset its risk position in this case by purchasing an appropriate number of exchange put options. The attraction of the options approach is that the farmers will wish to exercise their options on the marketing board only in the event that the market price is beneath the guaranteed floor; it becomes irrelevant to whom they sell when the price exceeds the floor. The marketing board, however, will need to pay up front for the options it purchases, and so there is a question of how it raises this money.

As with the futures-based scheme, the options-based scheme may be universal, so that the guarantee is available to all farmers, or may be available only to farmers who contract to sell to the board. The latter arrangement would replicate a form of contract offered by elevator companies to North American grain farmers, and in this case it is natural for the option to be paid for by shading the price paid by the board to farmers when prices are above the floor.[9] Alternatively, if the price guarantee is available generally without prior contracting, it would be reasonable for the board to finance the purchase of options through a general tax on exports of the commodity. Note that the cost of offering a price guarantee that is significantly beneath the postharvest futures price at the time of planting (that is, an option that is deep out-of-the-money) may be comparatively small.

There are differences in the ways in which price floor guarantees reduce producer uncertainty by comparison with contracted forward prices. A forward price contract eliminates or substantially reduces the price risk faced by farmers and allows them to calculate more precisely the profitability of alternative production plans. Floor price guarantees work, by contrast, by eliminating the worst cases at the expense of giving a generally lower return. Price risk remains, and it will influence the farmers' decisions, but suitable floor guarantees will enable them to plan without worrying that financial viability is jeopardized.

Stabilization of Consumer Prices

Governments have also stabilized domestic prices of primary commodities to protect consumers from the effects of price fluctuations. In developing countries, these schemes appear to be even more common than schemes aimed at the stabilization of producer revenues.

There are two issues here. The first is whether consumers in general benefit from a reduction in price variability. The second is whether higher prices for essential food, or conceivably energy, might result in such a large fall in the standard of living of the poor that governments would wish to take action to keep this from happening. In this section I discuss schemes aimed at the stabilization of consumer prices of traded commodities, postponing the discussion of nontraded commodities to a later section.

Standard textbook arguments indicate that, in general, consumer benefits from commodity price stabilization are likely to be small and possibly negative. For food products, price variability originates predominantly on the supply side, from changing weather conditions. Waugh (1944) showed that in this circumstance, price stabilization reduces consumer welfare by preventing consumers from increasing consumption levels when harvests are good and reducing consumption levels when harvests are poor. The size of the welfare loss is proportional to the price elasticity of demand, and although food as a whole is likely to be inelastically demanded, this may not be true of individual food commodities. Hence, if the stabilized commodity does have reasonably close substitutes in consumption, there may be a significant loss from stabilization.

This leaves the question of what the risk benefits are from stabilization. A second textbook result shows that the size of this benefit is ambiguous and depends on the difference between the coefficient of relative risk aversion and the income elasticity of demand for the commodity.[10] Typically, food commodities are necessities, in the sense of exhibiting less-than-unit income elasticities, and so reasonable values for risk aversion indicate a positive risk benefit from stabilization. This positive risk will only be large, however, if the share of the commodity in total consumption is large. For such commodities there may be a case for price stabilization, but typically we should expect consumers to be more diversified than producers, and so the benefit from stabilization will be correspondingly small.

The small benefits link to the situation of the poor. The poor are likely to devote a much larger proportion of their budgets to food than other sections of society do and will also be more precariously situated within their consumption sets. Formally, this would indicate both a high budget share for food and a very high risk aversion parameter—implying a substantial risk benefit from stabilization. Thus, although there may be no general argument for stabilization in terms of consumer welfare, that case may be sustainable for the poorest groups in the economy. But to make this argument stick, one needs to show that there is no alternative sectorally oriented policy, along the lines of social security provision, that could achieve the same objectives as efficiently and at lower cost. An important consideration here is the universality achieved by price stabilization. By contrast, social security provisions will typically only attain partial take-up, particularly in poor countries with widely dispersed populations (see Newbery 1989).

If stabilization is to be justified on this basis, it does suggest a very specific set of schemes. For example, if we consider a subsistence crop that is at most only marginally traded, food security suggests that governments might maintain stocks for release in times of shortage. Alternatively, it may be cheaper to facilitate imports in these circumstances. But the benefits arise predominantly from the avoidance of very high prices, not from the reduction of variability over the entire range of the price distribution, so there is no general argument for moving away from market prices. Nevertheless, where poor consumers are heavily dependent on imported food commodities, it may be worth subsidizing imports in periods in which these prices become very high. The Deaton and Laroque (1992) model indicates that such periods are likely to be only occasional and of short duration.

Energy is the other sector where the size of budget shares may suggest an argument for price stabilization, although here the poor will not typically be major consumers. The Waugh argument will again indicate a stabilization loss from loss of substitution possibilities, but short-term elasticities will be low, so this loss will be small. But because income elasticities for energy are high, the risk benefit from stabilization will also be small. It is difficult, therefore, to see that the potential benefits would outweigh the administrative and other costs of setting up the scheme.

This discussion brings up a more general point. Arguments for stabilization, both on the producer and on the consumer side, frequently disguise implicit requests for subsidies. Subsidization of consumers is attractive to governments that rely on these groups for the maintenance of power. Subsidization of foods is often a way of shifting resources from the rural hinterland to the urban population, whereas subsidization of energy prices favors the relatively rich and also transportation interests. It is therefore important to be clear that the economic case for stabilization of prices to consumers is weak except for the single possible exception of the stabilization of the price of subsistence foods, where budget shares may be large and where very high prices may have unacceptable implications for the poorest groups. But in that case, an adequate policy is simply to cap these prices.

Variable Tariff Schemes for the Stabilization of Import Prices

Variable tariff schemes aimed at stabilizing producer prices of imported or import-competing commodities are symmetric with variable export tax schemes aimed at stabilizing producer prices of export commodities. The tariff drives a wedge between the domestic price and the world price of the commodity and, if desired, can smooth the domestic price in relation to the world price. We may consider two reasons why governments may wish to smooth domestic prices of imported commodities. The first is to protect consumers of the commodity from fluctuations in the world price; the second is to protect domestic producers from these fluctuations. I noted above that the benefits to consumers from stabilization are at most slight unless the policy is a substitute for social security provision. In general, therefore, variable tariff schemes must be justified in terms of the domestic production sector.[11]

Variable tariff schemes simultaneously divorce producer prices and consumer prices from world prices. Suppose, for example, that the tariff is set so as to make domestic prices proportional to a moving average of past prices, as considered above. Now, not only will producers of annual crops face inappropriate incentives at the time their crops are planted, but domestic consumers will face incorrect incentives as well. The efficiency losses may be considerable. When the world market is tight, for example, domestic producers will not face the incentive to increase production and domestic consumers will not be given the incentive to economize. Rather, these incentives will be delayed until subsequent years, when they will affect the moving average, but by this time the world market may be in surplus.[12]

Typically, we are thinking here of annual food crops. The arguments presented earlier suggest that efficiency can best be reconciled with the required degree of risk reduction through the government's offering forward pricing facilities or (as described above) a floor support scheme. Neither of these alternatives requires a tariff. Furthermore, the reduction in price risk offered to producers leaves consumer prices unaffected.

It is possible, however, to see one circumstance in which a variable tariff might be desirable. Governments might be anxious to offer some degree of price support in the form of a floor guarantee, but there might be no suitable traded instrument that the government could exploit to offset its risk position. The reason could be either that no exchange has found it profitable to offer a contract of this sort or that because of transport or grade differences, currently traded instruments offer only poor hedges for the price risk in question. It is possible to use a tariff to replicate the effects of this form of floor price guarantee if the tariff is introduced at a positive level only when border prices are very low. Note that this form of price support is without cost to the government because, in effect, domestic consumers are required to write the options. One might view this arrangement as a nationally negotiated swap between producers and consumers.

This discussion is able to offer little support for the operation of variable tariff schemes. They do not obviously benefit consumers, and the efficiency cost of the stabilization offered to producers is likely to be high. Reduction of producer risk is more effectively obtained through futures-based forward pricing or by offering price floor guarantees. However, the employment of a tariff solely in periods of very low prices may have benefits where there is no suitable market for offsetting the price risk associated with the offer of a floor price to domestic producers.

Taxation

Pure stabilization schemes directed at producers' revenues will be broadly neutral in terms of expected revenue, in that payments are made by the stabilization agency when the stabilized price is above the market price and received when it is below the market price. It follows that if the stabilization price is the long-run average price, the agency will break even in expectational terms.[13] As I noted in an earlier section, however, raising general government revenue is an important, if not the major, supplementary objective of many variable export tax and export marketing board schemes. In any case, once governments have set up a mechanism that divorces payments to producers from market prices, it will be natural for them to wish to use this mechanism for revenue purposes.

A straightforward way to rephrase the question of whether stabilization schemes should have a fiscal function is to ask whether it is appropriate for countries to impose export taxes. There are two reasons for wishing to tax exports. The first is the standard argument that, if a country has significant market power in a commodity, it can extract an element of monopoly profit by forcing the price above its competitive level. Although short-run demand elasticities might suggest that some countries have significant short-run market power, very few countries exporting primary commodities have significant sustainable monopoly power. In general, therefore, export taxation must rest on the second and commonsensical argument as a means of raising revenue.

Trade taxes as revenue-raising devices are advisable only in countries where it is difficult to tax incomes or expenditures or where any attempt to do this will result in substantial distortions between the market and nonmarket sectors. The reason for this is that trade taxes distort production and consumption decisions, whereas expenditure and income taxes distort only the allocation between goods and leisure, and the evidence suggests that these distortions are typically small. However, in many primary commodity–producing countries in which subsistence crops are produced on family farms, it will be difficult to tax either incomes (many of which would have to be imputed) or locally consumed output. In such countries it is common for governments to raise a significant proportion of their revenue from taxes on exports and imports. If exports are already taxed, the government can adapt that mechanism to serve the price stabilization function by making the taxes proportional to values rather than fixed in money terms (see above).

There is a significant literature on optimal indirect commodity taxation in developing countries.[14] The optimal tax rate on the commodity export will depend on considerations of both efficiency and distribution. Any tax that is not a lump sum will impose some efficiency loss; therefore, given the government's revenue requirement, one needs to balance the efficiency loss at the margin. Suppose that the government is also taxing imports of manufactured goods. Then, to a first approximation, the more elastic the supply of the export crop in relation to the demand for manufactures, the lower the export tax should be in relation to the tariff on manufactures. (Of course, considerations of general equilibrium may qualify this simple judgment.)

The appropriate elasticities here are long-run because the taxes may be expected to be permanent. Consequently, supply elasticities will typically be high, particularly if producers can switch to untaxed subsistence production. The high supply elasticities suggest that very high export taxes are unlikely to be optimal. On the other hand, because there is clearly also a welfare cost in taxing imported manufactures, commodity export taxes will be well above zero. Distributional considerations will modify the efficiency-based taxes in relation to the income position of the commodity producers compared with the rest of the community and will also take into account the impact of the export tax on general equilibrium. In general, the producers of export commodities are neither among the richest nor among the poorest groups, so the earlier judgment may not be substantially affected. Any precise advice must depend on a quantified model of the particular country.

The foregoing analysis would hold irrespective of the variability of agricultural prices. Allowing for price variability, one would expect relatively stable producer and consumer prices, the implication being that tax revenue, which is the difference between the two, might be quite variable (Newbery 1988). Historical experience suggests that it is nevertheless worthwhile to split the tax wedge into a tax component that is constant (or only slowly changing) and a pure stabilization component. The importance of doing so may be illustrated by referring to the adverse performance of the agricultural marketing boards of colonial and post-colonial Nigeria.

Over the period from 1947 until their reorganization on a regional basis in 1954, the colonial Nigerian export marketing boards, which covered cocoa, cotton, groundnuts, palm kernels, and palm oil, generated enormous surpluses (Helleiner 1964). Indeed, in this period only the palm oil board paid out any subsidies, and this in only two years. It is probable that initially the generation of these surpluses was accidental and arose in large measure from the commodity price boom associated with the Korean conflict. After 1954, when commodity prices were less favorable, the boards continued to generate surpluses, which they used to make substantial investments in regional development programs and also in some domestic private sector schemes. By this time, the fiscal function had in practice superseded the stabilization function as the main objective of the boards. As a consequence, the Nigerian schemes drew substantial criticism, particularly from academics (see, in particular, Bauer 1967), and have thus come to be regarded as providing a strong case against this form of intervention.

An important lesson from the colonial Nigerian experience is that the fiscal and stabilization functions of an export marketing board should be segregated. I explore mechanisms for doing this in the next section.

Budgetary Independence

Even in the absence of a fiscal function, export marketing boards will earn surpluses when the world price is above the (say, moving average) producer price and will spend these surpluses—perhaps to the extent of running deficits—when the producer price is above the world price. There is then a question of what happens to the surpluses and deficits. If an agency is able to keep the entirety of any surplus for future stabilization, stabilization will have no effect on the government's fiscal position. To the extent, however, that the government regards stabilization surpluses as part of general governmental revenue, stabilization will simply transfer uncertainty about producer revenue to uncertainty about the general level of taxation or governmental expenditure or both and will destabilize consumer welfare. The magnitude of these effects will depend on the variance of the commodity price, which will affect the variance of the fund surplus and the importance of revenues from the economy in the government budget.

I argued above that consumers may be sufficiently well diversified for fluctuations in the price of any particular commodity not to impose more than a small welfare loss. This will not, however, be true of taxation, and hence if the variability of the stabilization fund is significant in relation to the size of total consumer expenditure, it will be necessary to balance the stabilization benefit to producers against the costs imposed on the remainder of the economy.

One difficulty here is that governments may be tempted to regard government-controlled stabilization funds as free and allow them to be invested in activities that could not be justified at a market rate of interest.[15] If, however, a stabilization exercise can be justified in welfare terms, the degree of stabilization must be such that one dollar invested in stabilization obtains the same expected return as a dollar invested in an activity with comparable risk characteristics in the rest of the economy. In that case, the agency should be prepared to lend surplus funds either to the government or to the private sector at market rates, but it should not be obliged to pass its surplus directly to the government.[16]

Within this framework, any general fiscal function should operate through a steady rate of taxation. But to the extent that the agency's funds do count as part of general government revenue, a lower level of stabilization will result. I return to this issue below in connection with parastatal resource industries.

Stabilization for Nontraded Commodities

By a "nontraded" commodity I mean a commodity for which, in the absence of tariffs, export taxes, and any other form of governmental intervention or intermediation, domestic prices move substantially in relation to domestic market conditions rather than in relation to border prices. There may be some trade in commodities that satisfy this characterization, but it will tend to be either occasional (when price divergences become substantial) or peripheral (relating only to areas of the country close to borders or with particularly good access to transport). Nontraded commodities will typically have low value-weight or value-bulk ratios in relation to local transportation costs. Countries with substantial nontraded primary sectors are likely to be either large or landlocked or both. Because production must be largely for domestic consumption, we would expect these commodities to be predominantly food crops. In many countries rice would be a typical example of a nontraded commodity, because domestic production and consumption will be large compared with net exports or imports (see chapter 16). Perishable fruits or vegetables are often also nontraded.

Price stabilization for nontraded crops raises different issues and suggests different mechanisms by comparison with price stabilization for traded commodities. Border prices are at most only occasionally relevant, and futures prices will be poorly correlated with domestic prices even where quotations on comparable commodity specifications are available. Finally, in the absence of cross-border trade, stabilization must be consistent with domestic market balance, and so price-setting schemes will typically imply either rationing of consumers, if the price is set beneath levels that would otherwise prevail, or, in the converse case, rationing of producers.

In this section, I consider schemes whose objective is the stabilization of producer revenues. (Below I shall consider related schemes where the concern is with consumers.) The major market mechanisms that facilitate smoothing of producers' consumption streams are commodity storage and saving. These are complementary activities because producers will seldom have a comparative advantage in storage, and this activity in any case exhibits scale economies. Typically, therefore, storage is undertaken by dealers. When harvests are good, it will make sense to store the commodity against poorer harvests in the future. When farmers' receipts are high, it makes sense for them to save against lower receipts in the future. The storage activity will tend to make revenue distributions less variable than harvests, and saving will make consumptions less variable than revenues. This pattern suggests that if governments want to smooth producers' revenues, they should in the first instance consider doing this through improving access to credit and through facilitating storage.

Commodity storage is a risky activity because the return will depend on the next year's harvest. It is not possible to use markets to off-load this risk if the commodity is nontraded. Furthermore, storage requires access to credit, and if credit provision is poor or is rationed, the result will be low levels of storage. With incomplete markets, it is difficult to make statements about the optimality or suboptimality of this low level of private sector storage, but it is reasonable to suppose that governments might wish to see higher levels of storage.

If so, governments will have to choose between encouraging private sector storage or undertaking public sector storage. To assist the private sector, the government might provide subsidized modern warehouse space[17] or a direct subsidy for each ton stored, which would be equivalent to an interest rate subsidy. If public warehouses are provided, the scale economies associated with storage disappear, and farmers may feel prepared to undertake their own storage. A related policy is to improve transportation links with other countries, and in particular to ports, because doing so will enable risk pooling with neighboring countries and with the world market.

Public sector storage, by contrast, inhibits private sector storage. Indeed, public sector storage tends to imply that the public storage agency is required to carry part, perhaps even a very large part, of the stocks that would otherwise have been carried by the private sector. This is because the private sector holds stocks in anticipation of a capital gain, and this gain will be reduced by public sector storage, particularly if public sector storage suppresses intraseasonal price variation. Public sector stockholding programs will therefore be expensive, and the alternative of encouraging private sector stockholding is to be preferred.[18]

Buffer Stock Stabilization

Despite the general view expressed in the previous section that it is preferable to encourage private sector storage, it is nevertheless worth briefly examining the principles that should underlie the operation of a public sector storage program, if only because such schemes are likely to continue. Buffer stocks have been widely used to stabilize prices in international commodity agreements—specifically, in cocoa, natural rubber, and tin. The results have had mixed success: the International Cocoa Agreements were never sufficiently well financed to have significant market impact; the International Natural Rubber Agreements have stabilized prices with modest success; and the International Tin Agreement enjoyed a broadly successful stabilization history until the disastrous experience of the final agreement, ending in a spectacular collapse in 1985 (see Gilbert 1987 and Anderson and Gilbert 1988). This mixture of success and failure belies the view that it is not possible for an intervention agency to stabilize the price of a competitively marketed commodity, but at the same time it does not establish that this is either a sensible or a desirable policy.

Storage may be appropriate for a country only if the country is large in relation to the world market for that commodity or if the commodity is not significantly imported into or exported from the country. In the former case, by stabilizing national prices, the agency also stabilizes the world price, whereas in the latter case the national and world prices of the commodity are free to diverge. Very few developing countries will possess the market power to make it possible for them to stockpile in order to stabilize world prices. Where countries do have significant market power, they are likely to find it more attractive to take these actions in consort with other large producers.[19] I shall therefore restrict attention to nontradable commodities.

A country producing a nontradable annual crop commodity with harvests that are independent over time should relate carryover to total availability of the commodity (current production plus carryover from the previous period). The carryover is zero if availability is less than a critical value, which will generally be slightly greater than the "normal" harvest, and then rises slightly faster than linearly with availability. If supply is completely inelastic, the initial marginal propensity to store is around one-half. But if supply depends on last year's expected prices for this year's crop, the storage propensity may be substantially higher than one-half, because storage will depress the expected price for the next year's crop and thereby discourage planned production.[20]

A notable feature of this mode of operation is that it links the carryover to quantities (production plus lagged carryover), not prices. This carryover to quantities contrasts with frequently recommended price band rules that specify floor and ceiling prices. In price band schemes, the authority buys at the floor price, or in a range above the floor price, and sells at the ceiling price, or in a range below the ceiling price. The objective is to keep the price above the floor and beneath the ceiling.

The major differences between the optimal rule and the band rule are that the optimal rule treats the previous year's carryover symmetrically with the current year's production, whereas under the price band rule, if the price is between the ceiling and the floor, the previous year's carryover is still held even though there is no requirement to purchase further stocks. More important, price band stabilization is subject to speculative attack at the ceilings (see Salant 1983). If the private sector knows that the stabilization authority has insufficient stock to defend the ceiling, it will buy as much as possible at or below the ceiling price in the expectation of capital gain. By contrast, an authority operating the optimal rule would sell its entire stock at the market-clearing price in the event of a shortage and thereby capture the entire profits from stockholding. This response suggests that much of the benefit of the optimal rule can be obtained from a scheme in which the public agency defends a floor price but disposes of its entire stock in the following year, subject to the price then being above the floor.[21]

A well-designed buffer stock stabilization scheme should be profitable in accounting terms and be able to contribute to government revenues. Price band schemes, however, tend to dissipate potential profits by selling beneath market prices in times of shortage. This waste can be avoided by abandoning defense of a ceiling. But it is unlikely that a scheme would fail to make any accounting profit unless stabilization was undertaken at far too high a price. More problematic is whether the accounting profit will cover the opportunity cost of the resources employed in the operation. If private sector storage was already adequate, it follows that the public sector must be accepting a lower return and therefore, unless the government has a sufficient advantage in terms of access to credit, intervention will be socially unprofitable.

To summarize, although buffer stock price stabilization does not lead to any short-term inefficiency in production or consumption, there are likely to be severe inefficiencies in terms of discouraging private sector stockholding. In general, therefore, governments are better advised to encourage private sector stockholding than to attempt to displace it.

Food Security and Distributional Concerns

In many developing countries, particularly in Africa, governments choose to hold stocks for distributional reasons rather than for stabilization as such. There is no presumption that private sector storage is economically inefficient, although it may be, but rather there is a concern that not enough may be stored to meet the needs, as distinct from the demands, of the poorest groups in the country. In the event of a crop shortage that, because of transport costs, cannot easily be met from imports, there are two groups at particular risk. These are the landless poor (particularly the urban poor), who will have large budget shares for food, and peasant farmers who have suffered crop failure. The former group is vulnerable because if urban wages do not adjust in relation to food prices, the income effect of price rises will be marked. The latter group is vulnerable if they have no other sources of income. Extended family relationships can offer quite high degrees of insurance against specific risks, but where whole groups are affected in common, as with crop failure caused by rain shortage, or a rise in prices that affects all urban workers, these forms of insurance do not help. In countries where these situations are not infrequent, governments will have to provide assistance.

Food security programs should therefore be seen as a form of social security. The policy question is whether these objectives are best achieved through price-based (buffer stock) schemes or through direct provision of either food or money. The argument in favor of price-based programs is that, to the extent that they do stabilize prices, they do so uniformly for all consumers. But there are two problems. First, storage can alleviate food shortages only to the extent that the commodity is in store. It may be necessary to aim for a high level of "normal" stocks if reasonable supplies are to be offered to all consumers with high probability. Second, if crop failure results in a situation in which some groups of farmers have very few resources, a policy that merely makes food less expensive will do little to improve their situation.

The alternative is to target food supplies to needy groups by rationing. The advantages of this approach are twofold: the scheme can be substantially less expensive because the government is not obliged to reduce prices to the better off and rations may be allocated to groups with low purchasing power. The difficulties are practical and relate to the operation of the rationing system and to ensuring high take-up. There is no a priori reason for preferring either the price-based or the quantity-based approach. In the extreme case of famine, governments will wish to use all possible means, including accelerated imports and stock release, to increase access to food.

In various countries, food marketing boards[22] have been set up following the apparently successful example of, and sometimes under the wings of, export marketing boards. However, the modes of operation of the two kinds of boards are quite different. Export marketing boards buy for export and tend to hold stock for as short a time as possible because storage involves both deterioration and price risk, both of which can normally be reduced by storage in consuming countries or at terminal markets. Food marketing boards, by contrast, buy for domestic resale and are required to store the crop between purchase from domestic producers and sale to domestic consumers.

Very frequently, food marketing boards have been given legal powers of monopsony purchase and monopoly sale. These are virtually never enforceable, because output can always be diverted to the black market or, where transport allows, smuggled abroad. Monopsony purchase powers have been aimed at keeping purchase costs down in order to subsidize sales prices. To the extent that enforcement is successful, production is discouraged and the shortages that the schemes were set up to alleviate are aggravated. The consequence is that the boards have often experienced difficulties in purchasing at low prices and in certain instances have found it necessary to import higher-priced foreign produce to meet demand.

Even so, food marketing boards have tended to impose budgetary costs. One reason for this is that, through their concern with the living standards of urban workers, they have set sales prices at a low margin over purchase prices. Where there has been no allowance for intrayear price variation, these price-cost margins have been absorbed by storage costs.

African food marketing boards have tended to combine both price-based and quantity-based approaches to food security. Both because of the direct effect of low prices on consumption and because of the diversion of production, low prices have implied a need to ration consumption at these prices. Because in many African countries it is not possible to develop complicated methods for doing this, rationing frequently takes the form of giving privileged groups priority when stocks are released. Public sector employees, rather than the poor, have been the main beneficiaries of these policies (see Hesp and van der Laan 1985, p. 21).

If it is decided that food security is an important objective of government and that stockpiling is the best method of doing this, there are strong arguments for attempting to enhance market mechanisms rather than supplant them. As in the case of producer revenue stabilization (described above), the best approach to food security is the development of efficient transport so that the country can import from and export to other local markets or world markets and thereby gain stabilization through risk pooling. This policy should be complemented by encouraging private sector storage.

Revenues from Mining and Oil Extraction

Up to this point the discussion has focused on small- to medium-scale production of (typically) agricultural products. Metals and oil are in the main extracted by much larger-scale enterprises, and this larger scale crucially alters the nature of the stabilization problem. Risk reduction, at least with respect to the producing enterprises, may not be the major consideration. The presence of mineral rents, however, implies an element of taxation or public appropriation irrespective of the general desirability of export taxation, and risk sharing considerations may then suggest that the government's take should vary with revenues.

Production enterprises may be either in the public sector or in the private sector or have a mixed status. Consider first an enterprise with at least an element of private equity capital. In most developing countries private equity capital will imply overseas ownership, and we may suppose that the owners of the equity hold diversified portfolios. The standard model for pricing capital assets implies that only the nondiversifiable element of the enterprise's risk will have a positive price. In fact, betas (the risk-return ratio) for extractive enterprises are high, so a relatively high rate of return will be sought. But if investors can look forward to earning a rate of return of the required order, they will be happy to hold the enterprise's equity. Revenue stabilization would reduce these betas and therefore the required rate of return. An announced stabilization policy might therefore increase initial investment levels, and this might be justified through the existence of externalities. If this justification is valid, however, the same objectives would be attained by a straightforward investment subsidy, and considerations of risk aversion indicate that the subsidy would be preferred. There is therefore no case for revenue stabilization analogous to that described above for small agricultural producers.[23]

The situation is more complicated where profits accrue to the state, because here the equity holders are in effect the citizens. They will be incompletely diversified, the extent of their diversification depending on the importance of (the state's share of) the enterprise's profits in national income. In small and highly concentrated economies the same sorts of consideration regarding price stabilization will apply to the population as were adduced for small-scale agricultural producers. The analogy of small and highly concentrated economies to the issue of stabilization for small-scale producers may imply significant benefits from stabilization, although small size may also make stabilization more difficult to attain. But in larger and less concentrated economies, fluctuation in profits from a particular sector is unlikely to be a major source of fluctuation in national income, and the risk reduction case for stabilization will be relatively weak.

To the extent that crude petroleum or metal ores can be produced at long-run marginal costs that are beneath those of the industry as a whole, either because of high metal content, low impurity content, or favorable location, rents will accrue. Irrespective of legal titles, governments will be able to extract part of these rents, although they may have to compete for them with labor unions. Governments can extract rents either by levying profit taxes on privately owned enterprises[24] or by paying fees to managers to run the publicly owned enterprises. In the former case, we need to ask how profit taxes should vary with profit levels, and in the latter, we need to ask the same question with respect to management fees. The answer to either question will depend on both considerations of risk sharing and incentives.

One may see this issue as an application of principal-agent analysis. The government is the principal that wants to see the highest return on the resource-producing enterprise, but it cannot obtain this return except through the agency of the managers, who may also be the legal owners of the enterprise.

Furthermore, the government as principal only knows the declared costs, revenues, and profits of the enterprise and cannot easily judge potential profits. Considerations of incentives therefore imply that payments to management (that is, for the privately owned enterprise, profits after tax) should vary positively with the enterprise's profits. At the same time, considerations of risk sharing indicate that when both parties are risk-averse, both should bear part of the risk. In the case of a privately owned enterprise whose shareholders are well diversified, risk sharing will suggest that they should bear most of the risk. This larger risk bearing will also give the appropriate incentives for them to hedge. Here the profit tax should be related to long-term profitability. But in a nationalized enterprise with local management, the managers will be relatively undiversified, and considerations of risk sharing will imply that the government should assume the greater part of the risk. It follows that privatization of publicly owned resource enterprises is an effective stabilization policy.

There are also issues with regard to investment requirements. Because investment projects in mining and in petroleum extraction will typically have long lead times but be productive over a long period of time, expected rates of return may be little affected by current prices and revenues in the industry. It may be very difficult, however, for a parastatal organization to obtain investment funds in years when revenues are low. This suggests that parastatals should be allowed to keep part of their surpluses for future investment. The same sorts of issues arise, however, as were examined in an earlier section in connection with stabilization by export marketing boards. Even if a scheme is set up in such a way that its funds are extrabudgetary, it will generally be possible for the government to increase expenditures or reduce taxation on other accounts. In practice, therefore, government funds tend to be fungible, and the only guarantee that the impact of a fund will be sterilized is government commitment to the stabilization objective ahead of other objectives. This conclusion does not imply that arrangements to isolate stabilization funds are not worthwhile, but only that they cannot be expected to be watertight.[25]

Considerations of Absorption

Fluctuations in primary sector export revenues can often be quite large in relation to total GDP, in particular for countries with export concentration. Traditionally, commodity policy has been concerned with alleviating the problems caused either by volatility as such or by periods of very low prices. Academic work suggests that for storable commodities, market mechanisms cope reasonably well with surpluses but nevertheless allow sharp price increases in periods of shortage. These arguments link with a growing volume of empirical evidence for the view that there are major problems associated with the absorption of temporarily high export revenues in controlled economies. In such cases, commodity bonanzas can result in major economic disruption. A related concern is that governments may myopically extrapolate high revenues into the future and commit expenditure on this basis.

Private sector storage introduces a marked asymmetry into commodity price cycles because in years in which harvests are good, much of the surplus can be added to stock, whereas in years in which harvests are poor, destocking can only take place to the extent that stocks exist. The implication is that, compared with the no-stock scenario, private sector storage raises prices in periods of surplus, but stockouts limit the extent to which prices are reduced in periods of shortage. It follows (Wright and Williams 1982, 1991; Deaton and Laroque 1992) that commodity price cycles typically have long, flat bottoms interspersed with short, sharp peaks. It is these peaks that may cause absorption problems.

Absorption problems arise when fluctuations in earnings from a commodity are large in relation to national income. Note that upward spikes in commodity prices can quite easily result in a doubling of earnings for a period of one or two years. Because these spikes in earnings should be perceived as transient, it will generally be appropriate for the greater part to be saved. Furthermore, such a large boost to savings in a small domestic market will force down rates of return, and so one should expect a large part of the savings to be in overseas portfolio investments. Two sets of factors may inhibit investing overseas. First, as discussed above, if the earnings accrue to a parastatal organization, it may not be possible easily to insulate them from government expenditure. Second, if the saving is undertaken by private sector agents, suitable financial instruments may be unavailable, or overseas investment may be prevented by controls, or both.

The second problem has been documented most thoroughly with respect to the effects of the 1976–78 coffee price boom on the Kenyan economy (Bevan, Collier, and Gunning 1987). In Kenya at that time the government did not tax coffee revenues that accrued directly to smallholders. It seems reasonable to suppose that the smallholders correctly perceived the rise in the coffee price, which originated from frost in Brazil, as temporary and therefore aimed to save most of the revenue excess over normal levels. Lack of suitable financial instruments obliged saving at an aggregate level through the purchase of domestic capital goods, but because of import restrictions, the attempt to save largely forced up the price of these goods in relation to the price of domestic consumption goods. Most of the increased saving therefore resulted in higher prices, which collapsed at the end of the boom.

This sequence of events reflects particular institutional features of Kenya at that time. Nevertheless, the general features of this episode occur to a greater or lesser extent elsewhere and may actually be exacerbated where revenues have accrued in part to governments that have not always been able to take a long-term view. In these cases, the "first best" solution is liberalization, but liberalization may not always be easy within a short time horizon. In that case, price stabilization schemes have the potential of reducing the scale of the problem. To be effective, however, the surpluses accumulated by these schemes must be insulated from government expenditure, and their effects on the monetary base and on exchange rates must be sterilized.

The implications of failure to ensure exchange sterilization are more complicated and depend on the country's exchange rate regime. In standard Dutch disease models for industrial countries, the effect of windfalls on the balance of payments is felt through exchange rate appreciation or depreciation, leading, respectively, to crowding out or crowding in of the domestic production of tradables. These effects may also be dominant in developing countries with floating rates. If, however, a fixed exchange rate is maintained through import and exchange controls, the windfall, which we take to be positive, will be invested domestically, and this is likely to result in a rise in the price of nontradables, in particular, real estate and nontraded capital goods. This was what happened in Kenya.

Comparison of stabilization schemes for coffee revenues over the 1976–78 coffee price boom indicates the crucial importance of exchange sterilization for macroeconomic performance.[26] Cameroon, Colombia, and Côte d'Ivoire all operated coffee buffer funds in this period. In Cameroon, the government adopted a conservative fiscal policy and raised agricultural producer prices. Sterilization was achieved by holding fund receipts, in part abroad and in part in extrabudgetary accounts. Holding fund receipts enabled the government to achieve high rates of public sector saving. In Côte d'Ivoire, by contrast, much of the accumulated fund was spent on government investment that continued after the fall in prices, resulting in high external indebtedness. Here there was neither budgetary nor exchange sterilization, and the macroeconomic effects of the coffee boom were comparable to those in Kenya, which had no stabilization agency (Bevan, Collier, and Gunning 1987). Colombia provides an intermediate case. Revenue stabilization took place through the privately owned Coffee Federation. Because the Coffee Federation kept its own surpluses, there was full budgetary sterilization. Nevertheless, these surpluses were predominantly invested domestically, resulting in an acceleration of growth of the monetary base. The lesson from these experiences is that, for countries that are highly dependent on exports of a particular commodity, price stabilization is useful only to the extent that its effects on exchange reserves are sterilized.

For heavily indebted countries, debt repayment provides a straightforward mechanism for ensuring that sharp temporary rises in commodity earnings are sterilized with respect to both the government budget and the exchange rate. Use of these funds to retire debt reduces subsequent debt service payments and may also increase the country's access to international credit markets. However, because countries with heavy debt commitments may see an advantage in partially reneging on these commitments, it may be necessary for funds to be mandated for this purpose through an agreement with creditors or international agencies. By agreeing to funds to be mandated, governments are to some extent refunding their debt as call options on their commodity earnings written in favor of the creditor institutions. This form of obligation is relatively advantageous in that it reduces debt service obligations in normal times at the expense of increasing service commitments at just those times that high earnings are likely to give rise to absorption problems.

Conclusions

The notorious volatility of primary commodity prices cannot establish any general argument that developing-country governments should act to stabilize these prices within their borders. But at the same time, economic theory does not support the view that the stabilization of prices would never be advantageous. I have emphasized the diversity of the situations in which countries find themselves and the differences in the characteristics of commodity production across commodities and countries. This diversity is reflected in the wide variety of stabilization schemes that are or have been in existence. In order to gain some idea of the merit of these arrangements, I have examined a number of important paradigmatic cases.

The first was that of smallholder production of an export crop. Inadequacy or unreliability of credit institutions might justify government smoothing of producer revenues and hence consumption. This smoothing can be done by divorcing producer prices from border prices through a scheme of variable export taxes, through a buffer fund, or by setting up an export marketing board that is endowed with monopsonistic powers. It is important that the government control smuggling. It is desirable that producer prices be set on the basis of a moving average of past prices, although generally adjustments are less systematic. I suggest that the welfare costs of these arrangements may be small for tree crops, where production lead times are long, but that the schemes are inadvisable for annual crops, where it is important that appropriate incentives are given at the time crops are planted.

Instead, for annual crops, it is preferable to try to reduce price risk through marketing board arrangements rather than through the stabilization of prices. The marketing board can reduce price risk by offering forward delivery contracts to farmers at the start of the crop year. The marketing board should then offset its contracted price risk by using organized futures exchanges. By this means, the marketing board essentially stands as a retail intermediary between the farmers and an industrial-country exchange. It is possible for the marketing board to have monopsonistic powers, but these contracts can be made on a voluntary basis, although this does give rise to performance issues. A variant is for the board to offer a guaranteed price floor, offset by the purchase of put options, which can again either be general and financed through taxation or be part of a negotiated price package agreed to on a voluntary basis. These arrangements offer a greater or lesser degree of risk reduction, but because cash and forward prices move together, the arrangements do relatively little to stabilize interyear producer revenues. If the schemes operate efficiently, they will tend to be welfare-increasing because they substitute for missing markets.

It is also possible to produce arguments for the stabilization of consumer prices of imported commodities, something that can be done through the operation of variable tariffs. The arguments for doing so are comparatively weak because consumers tend to be better diversified than producers. Where budget shares are large, however, there may be a case for stabilizing the price of some imported foods as a substitute for social security policies if these cannot achieve high levels of take-up. This objective may be satisfied by putting a cap on the price of food imports. In practice, however, variable tariff schemes tend to be used as much to protect domestic producers as to offer stabilization to consumers. If protecting domestic producers is the objective, it is best to restrict the schemes to offering protection only if border prices are abnormally low.

A general issue that arises with all schemes relating to traded commodities is whether stabilization agencies should have a fiscal function. Optimal tax arguments indicate that where it is infeasible to implement comprehensive taxation of income, there should be some level of taxation on exports, but consideration of elasticities suggests that taxation of exports will typically be at a low level. A related issue is what happens to accumulated surpluses or deficits. It is important here that stabilization agencies maintain budgetary control of their own accumulated funds because otherwise instability in the primary sector is simply translated to the remainder of the economy. Of course, if the stabilized sector is small, this instability will be of little consequence, but the issue is important for countries with high export concentration. The implication is that taxation for general revenue purposes should be at a more or less constant rate, particularly where concentration is high.

A different set of issues arises when one turns to commodities that are at most traded only occasionally or peripherally. Here stabilization must be consistent with market clearing, and this suggests storage as the principal instrument. Public sector stockpiling is one possibility, but I suggest that in general it will be preferable either to encourage trade by improving transport links or to encourage private sector storage by, for example, providing modern warehousing facilities or even a storage subsidy. By contrast, public stockpiling will discourage private storage. If a policy of public storage is introduced, it is important that the storage agency avoid any commitment to defend a ceiling price, because a ceiling price simply transfers the profits from storage to private sector speculators. Instead, in each year the whole of the previous year's carryover should be released, subject only to the price being greater than the guaranteed floor price. Alternatively, the agency might use a storage rule simply based on the availability of the commodity.

Frequently, governments introduce public stockpiling of nontraded food commodities for distributional reasons, rather than out of a concern for stabilization. In these instances they are anxious to ensure that the needs of important groups (for example, urban workers) are satisfied even if harvests are poor. The experience with these food marketing boards has been poor. They have typically used their monopsonistic powers to hold down producer prices, and doing so has obliged them to ration sales, which have often been directed toward favored groups rather than those most in need. Even so, food marketing boards have imposed budgetary costs.

Another set of issues arises with resource extraction industries because such enterprises will typically be large and may be parastatal. In any case, governments will naturally wish to capture part of the resource rents. Here, risk sharing rather than stabilization becomes the issue, whether the risk sharing is between the host government and the overseas resource company or between the government and the management of the parastatal organization. In either case, it will be appropriate on principal-agent arguments for the government to assume some of the risk. But if the industry is owned by a foreign company, considerations of diversification would imply that the government's take should be much less variable than in cases where the enterprise is nationalized.

There is an important macroeconomic issue that relates to the primary sectors in a large number of contexts wherever export concentration is high. Private sector storage generates price cycles that may be characterized as having flat bottoms and occasional sharp peaks. In countries with high export concentration these sharp revenue peaks can produce substantial absorption problems if there are restrictions on imports or on overseas investment, because attempts to save what is perceived as a temporary boost to revenues can be frustrated by changes in internal prices. Liberalization is obviously desirable, but if this cannot be done quickly, it is important to ensure that the country's exchange rate and money supply are sterilized with respect to the boost in export earnings.

One way of achieving this in an indebted country is to require that occasional jumps in export revenues of this sort be used to repay debt.

A general issue that arises throughout this discussion is the tension between, on the one hand, attempting to remedy perceived defects in market mechanisms and, on the other hand, attempting to improve the functioning of markets. Arguments for stabilizing commodity prices are based on the premise that one or more groups in the economy suffer from the volatility of primary prices either because of uncertainty or because of the possibility of unacceptably low consumption levels. But a number of the stabilization schemes considered in this chapter tend to stifle the operation of market mechanisms, as seen in the following:

- Governmental smoothing of producer revenues reduces incentives for private sector saving and removes incentives for producers to respond to short-term fluctuations in prices.
- Monopsonistic purchase arrangements eliminate the role of the private sector in the commodity trade.
- Tariff schemes impose well-known welfare costs and are not generally conducive to production efficiency.
- Public sector storage of nontraded commodities tends to discourage private sector storage.
- Nationalization of resource extraction industries reduces the extent to which risk is diversified away from the economy.
- Import and investment controls reduce the ability of the macroeconomy to respond to commodity price shocks.
- Stabilization agencies may favor special interest groups; indeed, power and high salaries result in the agencies themselves becoming major interest groups.

The problems stated above do not imply that the policies connected with them should always be avoided. Nevertheless, a consideration that should always be taken into account is the extent to which a proposed scheme enhances or reduces the functioning of market mechanisms. On that score, the only arrangements discussed in this chapter that appear to be undeniably beneficial are marketing board schemes that offer forward pricing or floor price contracts for annual crops.

In general, in the area of commodity policy one is looking at the consequences of poorly developed (risk and forward transaction) markets rather than market failure. Efficient markets do not, however, spring into existence overnight, and governments and agencies may need to take steps either to develop new markets or to enhance existing ones. One may look forward to the time, which may be distant, when the private sector can take over price insurance functions assumed by the government. But at the same time, considerations of taxation and absorption will require that governments always be involved in the primary sectors of their economies, particularly where export concentration is high.

Notes

1. I discuss the performance of ICAs in Gilbert (1987). See also Anderson and Gilbert (1988) on the collapse of the ITA.

2. The Malaysian variable export tax scheme, discussed in Knudsen and Nash (1990b), provides one example.

3. Knudsen and Nash (1990a) describe the Papua New Guinea cocoa stabilization fund, which has this structure.

4. It is widely believed that a high proportion of Ghanaian cocoa was smuggled into Côte d'Ivoire during the period in the late 1970s when Ghanaian producer prices were very low. However, tree crops are generally almost entirely exported, so if stabilization schemes are confined to this sector, domestic consumption is not a major problem.

5. All of these features were evident in the rice marketing program run by a Peruvian parastatal organization. The organization, which was a monopsony buyer, stabilized both intrayear prices (forcing out private sector storage and suppressing off-season production in the jungle area of the country) and intragrade prices (thus encouraging low-grade production). Producers in remote regions were actually paid more than producers in areas close to consumption centers, penalizing production in areas where it was most required (see Nash 1984; Knudsen and Nash 1990a).

6. In fact, in the most simple model for a nonstationary price, the appropriate estimator of the long-run price turns out to be an infinite average with exponentially decreasing weights (for example, 1, $^1/_2$, and $^1/_4$). This gives a long-run price, π, defined by

$$\Pi_t = (1 - \gamma) \sum_{i=0}^{\infty} \gamma^i P_{t-1-i}.$$

An n-year moving average scheme may be justified as an approximation to this exponentially weighted estimate by setting the number of years in the moving average as

$$n = \frac{1 + \gamma}{1 - \gamma}.$$

Thus a value of $\gamma = {}^1/_2$ is roughly equivalent to a three-year moving average and a value of $\gamma = {}^2/_3$ suggests a five-year moving average.

7. It may be supposed that, in order to conform with the exchange rate index, a weighted average of deflators should be used. But using a weighted average of deflators is dangerous because the positive skew in the distribution of inflation rates over countries may lead to an average deflator's inflating at an unrepresentatively fast rate (see Gilbert 1990). It is therefore preferable to use a dollar deflator but to make a purchasing power parity correction to the exchange rate adjustment (see Gilbert 1989, 1991). Over the 1970s and 1980s, this adjustment was quantitatively unimportant.

8. Knudsen and Nash (1990a) discuss the use of a ten-year moving average by the Papua New Guinea cocoa buffer fund.

9. Although this does lead to the reemergence of enforcement problems.

10. Turnovsky, Shalit, and Schmitz (1980). The risk benefit is given as

$$benefit = w\,(\rho - \eta)\,\sigma^2$$

where w is the share of the commodity in total consumption, ρ is the representative agent's coefficient of relative risk aversion, η is the income elasticity of demand for the commodity, and σ^2 is the variance of the commodity price.

11. The government of El Salvador has established a variable tariff scheme in conjunction with imports of grains. The scheme is based on a price band. If world prices are beneath the floor price, tariffs will be increased to protect domestic producers from the full impact of these low prices, but if world prices are very high, tariffs will be reduced.

12. See Walters (1987) for an amplification of this view.

13. In expectational terms, agricultural producers' revenues will be somewhat higher if disturbances originate predominantly on the supply side (because the negative covariance of quantities and prices will be reduced), but will tend to be somewhat lower if disturbances originate on the demand side (when the covariance will be positive; see Massell 1969). It is also possible that stabilization will alter the long-run market-clearing (and hence stabilization) price (see Turnovsky 1976; Gilbert 1986). Gilbert (1986) argues that this effect will normally be to lower the market-clearing price, and Ghosh, Gilbert, and Hughes-Hallett (1987) reach the same conclusion empirically.

14. In relation to taxation of the agricultural sector, see, in particular, Newbery (1987, 1988, 1990) and Sah and Stiglitz (1987).

15. This was the case with the Nigerian regional boards (see Helleiner 1964).

16. Knudsen and Nash (1990a) note the budgetary independence of the Papua New Guinea cocoa buffer fund.

17. A possible difficulty is that private sector agents may worry about the security of stocks held in government warehouses. In that case, support would necessarily be indirect.

18. See Miranda and Helmberger (1988) and Wright and Williams (1991). These effects, however, are not uniform. A credible floor support price reduces the prospect of capital loss, but at the same time, if this support exceeds the price that would clear the market, there is no prospect of capital gain. Also, if the private sector anticipates a public stockout—for example, if the public agency is obliged to release stock at a trigger or ceiling price—in this circumstance the private sector will wish to hold the entire public stock to capture the expected capital gain, and a speculative raid will take place (see Salant 1983).

19. Collective action may give rise to producer cartels. It is also possible to interpret international commodity agreements as internationally sanctioned cartels in which consuming countries exert some moderating influence, and it is notable that successful agreements often rely on the influence of a dominant or large producer (for example, Brazil in the International Coffee Agreement and Malaysia in the International Natural Rubber and Tin agreements). Note that the International Coffee Agreement is based on export quotas and does not use a buffer stock but that Brazil and Colombia maintain large stocks (see Gilbert 1987).

20. See Gustafson (1958a, 1958b), Gardner (1979), Newbery and Stiglitz (1982), Wright and Williams (1982, 1991), and Gilbert (1988).

21. Schemes of this sort are discussed by Wright and Williams (1991, chapter 13).

22. The term was coined by Hesp and van der Laan (1985).

23. This argument requires qualification if the enterprise adjusts wages in line with output prices, because in that case we would need to consider the risk benefits from stabilization accruing to the nondiversified production workers. However, standard implicit contract arguments imply that it will be optimal for equity holders to bear most of the price risk. One should therefore expect to see wages varying relatively little.

24. If profits can be disguised, it may be necessary to substitute a revenue tax.

25. This is illustrated by the experience of the influential Chilean Copper Income Compensation Fund (FEC), set up in 1985 as part of the Chilean government's structural adjustment agreement with the World Bank. Because Chile is a low-cost copper producer, there is a high rental element in the financial surplus of the Chilean parastatal copper producer, Corporación Nacional del Cobre de Chile (CODELCO). Therefore CODELCO is able to make a major but highly variable contribution to government revenues. Under the FEC agreement, the Chilean government budgets for revenues from CODELCO on the basis of an expected price (the "reference price") for the following year. A price band is defined around the reference price. Over the period of operation of the FEC these reference prices have tended to be consistently low, with the result that in 1987 and 1988 the actual price was outside the reference price band. The scheme obliges the FEC to deposit a proportion of the excess revenue in the Central Bank. The scheme is not explicit about what should happen if prices fall beneath the price band, and it is unclear about what is intended for the surplus. A law predating the scheme required that Treasury surpluses be used to pay back domestic debt, and this is what has happened. Because debt repayment effectively amortizes the surplus, it appears prima facie that the surplus is sterilized with respect to the budget. However, during the campaign for the presidential elections in 1988 the government reduced the value-added tax from 20 percent to 16 percent, and it is arguable that they would have been less willing to do this in the absence of the FEC surplus.

26. This discussion is based on Balassa (1988).

3

The Effects of Option Hedging on the Costs of Domestic Price Stabilization Schemes

Donald F. Larson and Jonathan R. Coleman

Because prices of commodities are notoriously unstable, many countries, both industrial and developing, intervene in commodity markets in order to limit the range of price movements. International efforts in the form of commodity agreements[1] attempt to use the market power of major producers and sometimes consumers to stabilize global prices; other programs are unilateral and are designed to defend prices within national borders. Although the mechanisms are varied, a common characteristic of almost all such programs has been their eventual failure. The reasons for the failure of the various schemes are multiple, some related directly to the form of the stabilization program.[2] A constant strain on any stabilization program, however, is the stochastic component of commodity prices, which renders the financial—or, in the case of buffer stocks, the physical—exhaustion of resources a statistical eventuality.

From a simple simulation model described in this chapter, several results are derived. First, the simulations demonstrate that samples of prices generated by a lognormal random walk can exhibit remarkably different sample distribution characteristics. This is not a new result (see Wright and Williams 1990) but serves to emphasize that, as a practical matter, managers of stabilization funds must treat the future as unchartable even when expectations are rational, that is, even when market agents are fully aware of the deterministic and stochastic components of price movements. Second, the simulations demonstrate that price band stabilization methods, similar to those currently used in Chile and Papua

New Guinea, are fairly neutral in long-term effects, including efficiency losses, but that single-period income effects can be quite large. In addition, the overall "risk" benefits coming from reduced price variability tend to be small. Finally, the simulations demonstrate that hedging can reduce the risks to stabilization schemes themselves. The part of the chapter that describes these results builds on the results of chapter 15, by Coleman and Larson, on price stabilization schemes in Venezuela. In that chapter it is shown that by operating a stabilization scheme, the government transfers the risk of large price movements from producers and consumers to the government and taxpayers or, more particularly, to the financial or physical assets of some stabilization fund or buffer stock. In this chapter it will be shown how governments can reduce this risk by simple strategies that use hedging instruments to manage commodity risk. Simulations show that through hedging, governments can greatly reduce the variability of fund revenues and payments. Hedging, by limiting extreme payouts from the fund, can extend the probable life of the stabilization scheme. Hedging does not, however, offer immortality. These results are quite robust across a wide range of assumptions. In addition, the gains attributable to hedging are shown to be independent of the assumption that prices follow a lognormal random walk.

In building the simulation model, some broad assumptions needed to be made about the basic way in which the modeled market was to operate. These basic assumptions are maintained throughout the chapter. Included are the assumptions that the country is a price taker, that expectations are rational, and that the country attempts to limit domestic price movements through a price band mechanism that draws its financial backing either from general government revenues or from a special buffer fund.

Price Band Outcomes and Fund Revenues

Consider a price-taking country that hopes to stabilize domestic prices around some moving average of international prices. For such a country there are a total of nine possible states that are definable by the relationships between the price band and trade flows, and the price band and border prices. The price band may fall in a range in which the country would always be a net exporter. Or it may fall in a range in which the country would always be a net importer. Or it may straddle the point at which domestic supplies equal domestic demand. In addition, the border price may fall above the band, below the band, or within the band. In operating a price band program, price risk is transferred from the producers and consumers to the government or stabilization fund. The government fund can gain revenue or, because of payouts, lose revenue. In four of the nine possible states the stabilization mechanism would produce revenue; in two of the nine states the mechanism would generate a loss; and in three of the states there would be neither a payout nor revenues generated.

Figures 3-1 to 3-3 illustrate the three possible states if the country is a perennial exporter of the "stabilized" commodity. Prices P^u and P^l represent the upper limits and lower limits of the band that the government is committed to protect. These are known with certainty at any point in time. P^w is the ex post world price and represents a possible outcome. This price is not known with certainty, but corresponding price-hedging instruments are assumed to exist for which prices *are* known with certainty. Finally, expected quantities are derived from expected demand and supply functions. In figure 3-1 the border price (P^w) falls above the upper limit of the price band. In order to peg domestic prices at the top of the band (P^u), the government would impose an export tax equal to $P^w - P^u$. If producers correctly anticipate the prevailing domestic price, Q^s will be produced. At the prevailing price of P^u, domestic demand will be Q^d. $Q^s - Q^d$ will be exported, generating $(P^w - P^u) \times (Q^s - Q^d)$ in revenues for the government. Figure 3-2 illustrates the state in which the border price falls below the lower range of the band (P^l). In this case, the government must first impose an import tax equal to $P^l - P^w$ to prevent less expensive foreign supplies from filling domestic demand, then subsidize exports ($Q^s - Q^d$) with a subsidy payment equal to $(P^l - P^w)$. The

Figure 3-1. *Exporter Facing World Price above Band*

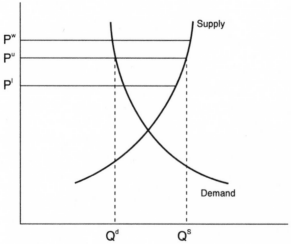

Figure 3-2. *Exporter Facing World Price below Band*

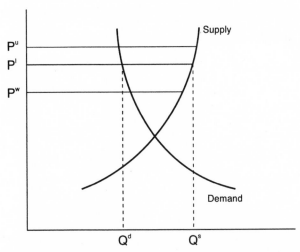

import tax will generate no revenues, and the net loss of revenues from the government or stabilization fund will equal $(Q^s - Q^d) \times (P^l - P^w)$. In figure 3-3, the border price falls within the price band; import and export taxes are set to zero, and the fund neither gains nor loses revenue.

Figures 3-4 to 3-6 illustrate the three importing states. In figure 3-4, the border price falls above the price band. The government must impose

Figure 3-3. *Exporter Facing World Price within Band*

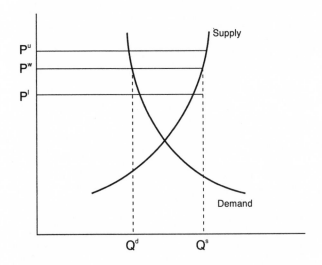

Figure 3-4. *Importer Facing World Price above Band*

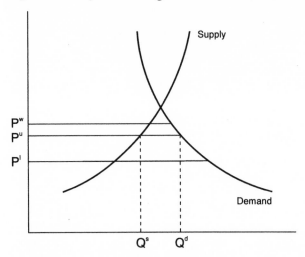

an export tax equal to $P^w - P^u$ to prevent domestic supplies from flowing to the more profitable export market. In addition, imports $(Q^d - Q^s)$ must be subsidized by a subsidy payment equal to $(P^w - P^u)$. In this state the fund loses $(P^w - P^u) \times (Q^d - Q^s)$. Figure 3-5 illustrates the importing case when the border price falls below the price band. The government imposes an import tax equal to $P^l - P^w$, which generates $(Q^d - Q^s) \times (P^l - P^w)$ in revenue for the stabilization fund. Figure 3-6 shows the state where the border price falls within the band, generating neither revenues nor losses.

Finally, figure 3-7 illustrates the case when the price band straddles the point at which domestic supplies equal domestic demand. When the border price falls above the upper range of the price band, the country will be a net exporter. To bring the domestic price in line with the price band (P^u), the government must impose an export tax equal to $P^w - P^u$, which generates revenues equal to $(P^w - P^u) \times (Q^s - Q^d)$. When the world price $(P^{w\prime})$ falls below the price band, the country is a net importer. The government imposes an import tax equal to $P^l - P^{w\prime}$ and collects revenue equal to $(P^l - P^{w\prime}) \times (Q^{d\prime} - Q^{s\prime})$. If the price falls within the band, the country may either import or export, but tariffs will be set to zero, and no revenues will be generated or lost.

Welfare Gains and Losses

By intervening in the domestic market, the government generates welfare transfers between consumers and producers as well as efficiency

Figure 3-5. *Importer Facing World Price below Band*

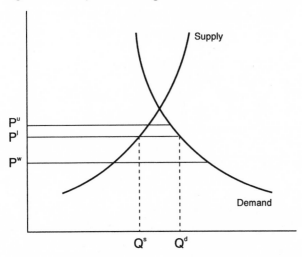

losses. These transfers occur for each period the government or fund manager intervenes and may have offsetting effects. In fact, one of the advantages of a price band mechanism is that the average effect on domestic prices is neutral (see chapter 15). In addition, by stabilizing the price component of producer income the program generates a stabilization benefit that occurs over the life of the program. Efficiency losses[3] and the monetary transfers between producers, consumers, and the gov-

Figure 3-6. *Importer Facing World Price within Band*

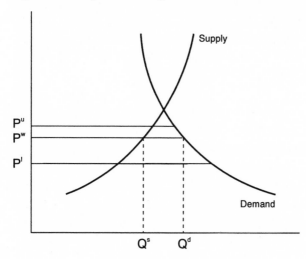

Figure 3-7. *Exporter or Importer Facing Domestic Price within Band*

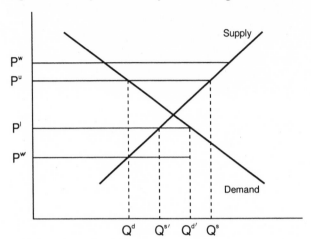

ernment are readily calculated by analyzing changes in the areas under the demand and supply curves, which are the traditional measures of consumer and producer surplus. Measurement of these changes gives a general indication of the welfare gains and losses for each period in which the government intervenes.[4]

Figure 3-8 illustrates the consumer, producer, and government surpluses generated by imposing an export tax on an exported good in order to lower domestic prices. Domestic prices fall from the border price of P to P' as the government imposes a tax equal to $P - P'$. Demand increases from Q^d to $Q^{d'}$, and supplies decline from Q^s to $Q^{s'}$. The government receives revenues equal to area d; producer surplus drops by an amount equal to the sum of areas a, b, c, d, and e; consumer surplus increases by an amount equal to areas a and b, leaving an efficiency loss equal to areas c and e. Generally speaking, consumer surplus is given by

$$(3\text{-}1) \qquad\qquad \Delta CS = -\int_{p}^{p'} D(p)dp$$

where P and P' are the original and alternative prices, respectively, and where demand $D(p)$ is a function of price. Producer surplus is similarly defined as

$$(3\text{-}2) \qquad\qquad \Delta PS = -\int_{p}^{p'} S(p)dp$$

Figure 3-8. *Income Transfers and Efficiency Losses under an
Export Tax*

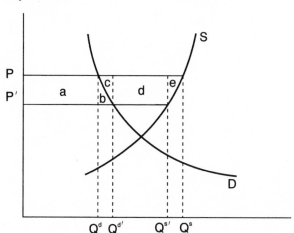

where supply, $S(p)$, is a function of price. The change in government
revenues is given by

(3-3) $\Delta GR = [S(p') - D(p')]\,[p - p'].$

The efficiency loss is defined as

(3-4) $EL = \Delta CS + \Delta PS + \Delta GR.$

The way in which income is transferred, or lost to inefficiencies, will
vary depending on the type of government intervention and will differ
from period to period as the type of intervention needed to defend a price
band changes with international price movements. In general, transfers
between producers, consumers, and the government stabilization fund
are likely to be offsetting. Inefficiency losses, however, are not offset and
are a general social cost incurred by operating a price stabilization program. Table 3-1 lists the income transfers associated with each of the nine
possible states that can occur under a price band scheme.

To the extent that producers prefer stable to unstable incomes, additional benefits accrue over the life of the stabilization program. These
benefits are based on the efficacy of the program in reducing income
variability by reducing the variability of the price component of producer
income.[5] Newbery and Stiglitz (1981) derived a quantifiable measure of
the value of the income stabilization achieved based on assumptions
concerning producers' relative aversion to risk. Assuming that producers
can be treated as a single aggregated agent whose utility can be repre-

Table 3-1. *Gains and Losses in Producer, Consumer, and Government Surpluses under a Price Band Stabilization Scheme*

Trade state and type of surplus	Changes in surplus as a result of border price		
	Border price above band	Border price within band	Border price below band
Exporter			
Consumer surplus	Gain	Neutral	Loss
Producer surplus	Loss	Neutral	Gain
Government surplus	Gain	Neutral	Loss
Importer-Exporter			
Consumer surplus	Gain	Neutral	Loss
Producer surplus	Loss	Neutral	Gain
Government surplus	Gain	Neutral	Gain
Importer			
Consumer surplus	Gain	Neutral	Loss
Producer surplus	Loss	Neutral	Gain
Government surplus	Loss	Neutral	Gain

sented by a von Neumann–Morgenstern utility function of income $U(Y)$, average benefits in relation to income are defined as

$$(3\text{-}5) \qquad \frac{B}{\overline{Y}_0} = \frac{\overline{Y}_1 - \overline{Y}_0}{\overline{Y}_0} - \tfrac{1}{2} R(\overline{Y}_0) \left[\sigma_{Y_1}^2 \left(\frac{\overline{Y}_1}{\overline{Y}_0} \right)^2 - \sigma_{Y_0}^2 \right]$$

where B is the money value of the stabilization benefits; Y_0 and Y_1 represent income without and with a stabilization program, respectively, and where a bar over a variable represents the variable's mean; σ_Y^2 is the square of the coefficient of variation (the ratio of the standard deviation to the mean) for income Y; and R is the coefficient of relative risk aversion given by

$$(3\text{-}6) \qquad R = -Y \frac{U''(Y)}{U'(Y)}.$$

The first term in equation 3-5 is a transfer benefit resulting from any change in the mean level of income, and the remaining term sign measures the benefit directly attributable to a reduction in the variance of income resulting from a reduction in the variability of price.

Producer Risk Versus Government Risk

By intervening at the border, a government operating a price band scheme commits its own resources to offsetting a portion of the range of international price movements. Consumers and, especially, producers gain a risk benefit because the risks associated with international price movements are transferred from individuals to the government. Generally, this scheme is assumed to produce a net gain in welfare because the government is assumed to be less averse to the risk associated with price movements than individual producers are. This assumption is consistent with one of the few empirical studies of risk aversion. Using games of chance in rural India to measure attitudes toward risk, Binswanger (1978) concluded that relative risk aversion tends to increase as the portion of wealth being gambled increases. To the extent that price movements result in the total resources of the government being less volatile in relation to producer incomes, a stabilization scheme and the transfer of risk should produce a flow of benefits.

Although it is self-evident, it should be noted that the derived benefits of a stabilization scheme flow only if the stabilization scheme remains operational. Mundlak and Larson (1990) have shown that changes in international prices tend to lead to changes in domestic producer prices, despite an ample number of programs designed to mitigate such effects. This result is more general, but consistent with the recognized failure of most stabilization schemes for international commodities. Wright and Williams (1990, p. 1) note that stabilization schemes ". . . almost never succeed for very long—and I do not mean long in the Keynesian long run. The founders easily survive the life span of the typical scheme, physically if not financially." The demise of two highly regarded stabilization schemes—for wool in Australia and for cocoa, palm oil, copra, and coffee in Papua New Guinea—emphasizes the fragile nature of stabilization programs. And when formerly successful stabilization programs do fail, it is unclear whether the benefits accumulated during the functioning life of the program outweigh the abrupt market reactions and the ensuing adverse effects as the mechanism crumbles.[6]

Stabilization programs can use discretionary rules to stabilize prices around some expert or legislated notion of the correct long-run prices or can use fixed rules to define the range in which prices should be defended.[7] Unfortunately, computer simulations demonstrate that extremely simple price movements, such as a lognormal random walk, can lead to extreme price distributions. Stabilization schemes that require the defense of unreasonable price levels will fail, and fail rapidly; however, there remains a great deal of uncertainty as to whether a "reasonable" price band can ever be defined. For example, Wright and Williams (1990) used computer simulations to demonstrate that a simple autocorrelated price mechanism can generate samples of 50,000 observations in which there remains a greater than 5 percent chance of improperly identifying a stationary mean by more than a standard deviation.

Rules can be used to generate a stabilization scheme that contains some feedback and therefore some adjustment mechanism. As the simulations in this chapter later demonstrate, however, the ability of the fund to remain liquid, given a limited borrowing capacity, is primarily a matter of luck. This is perhaps the most frequent reason why stabilization schemes fail. At the same time, the following lays out a strategy of hedging that can greatly reduce the variability of stabilization fund payouts and thereby help the fund manager survive small doses of bad luck.

Hedging Fund Risk

Of the nine possible states that can occur under a price band mechanism, only two create a liability for a stabilization fund, whereas four generate revenues (see table 3-1). In addition, the liability faced by the fund is limited; however, the limit may be quite large. Conversely, the potential for tax revenue is not bounded. Figure 3-9 illustrates the case for an exporter. The area above the price band and between the supply and demand curves is unbounded above and represents the potential area that could be used for financing a stabilization fund through an export tax. The area between the lower range of the price band and the demand and supply curves at P^l down to the axis represents the maximum payout from the fund for an exporter. The value of this area goes to zero, however, as the lower range of the price band falls to the point where supply equals demand. A similar situation exists for the other "liable" state, the case of subsidized imports.[8] For the exporter case, the maximum fund liability has the following characteristics as prices fall:

$$(3\text{-}7) \qquad \lim_{p^l \to p^m}(p^l - p)\,[S(p^l) - D(p^l)] = 0$$

where $S(p^m) = D(p^m)$.

For the case of the importer:

$$(3\text{-}8) \qquad \lim_{p^u \to p^m}(p^u - p)\,[S(p^u) - D(p^u)] = 0$$

where $S(p^m) = D(p^m)$.

For commodity markets in which options are available, the fund can further restrict the payout by buying options to hedge the fund's liability. Consider the following example. In period 1, producers, consumers, and the fund manager know what the price band will be but do not know the stochastic component of the international price. The fund manager does know the demand and supply curves of the relevant commodity. In period 2, the stochastic component, and therefore the international price, will be revealed, and the fund manager will have to defend the

Figure 3-9. *Potential Tax Revenue and Fund Payouts*

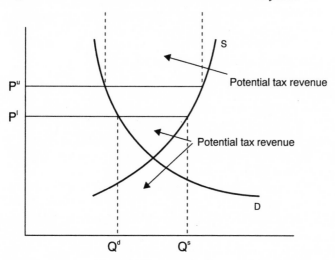

price band. To limit the potential payout from the fund, the fund manager, during period 1, looks at the range of prices covered by the band. If the country exports over the entire range of the band (see figure 3-2), the fund faces a liability only if the international price in period 2 falls below the lower range, that is, below P^l. Therefore, to hedge that liability, the fund manager hedges the quantity $S(P^l) - D(P^l)$ by purchasing put options at an exercise price of P^l for a delivery date corresponding to period 2. Should the border price actually fall below P^l, the added value of the put option would compensate the fund for additional outlays. The fund's liability is thereby limited to the purchase cost of the options.

In the case where the range of the price band implies that the country will be an importer, the fund is liable when the border price falls above the upper bound of the price band range (see figure 3-4). In this case, the fund manager can limit the fund's liability by hedging the quantity $D(P^u) - S(P^u)$ through the purchase of calls for an exercise price of P^u for delivery in period 2. Should the border price fall above P^u, the increased value of the call options would compensate the fund for additional payouts.

The value of the strategy will depend on the nature of the stochastic price element and the path of the resulting prices. Analytic answers may be derived that are based on the underlying parameters of the problem and the expectations about prices; but although results of such calculations may hold when samples are large, the properties when considering a small sample of prices are more important for a government operating a stabilization program.

Model Description: Production and the Price Band Mechanism

To calculate the benefits of a stabilization program as well as the effects of hedging on the fund risk that is a consequence of stabilization, the following computer simulation model was constructed. The model is designed to simulate a fairly simple set of actions for producers, consumers, and government officials operating in a price-taking country that has instituted a price band and uses import tariffs and subsidies to defend the band. The band operates for a single crop for which there are no close substitutes. To finance the enforcement of the band, the fund may freely borrow in simulation. The crop is annual and takes 120 days to mature. At the beginning of the period, farmers evaluate their expectations of the price they will receive for their crop and plant accordingly. Expectations are rational. International prices (p^i) are assumed to follow a lognormal random walk,[9] that is,

$$(3\text{-}9) \qquad\qquad p^i_t = p^i_{t-1} e^\epsilon$$

where ϵ is a random variable, normally distributed with mean $\mu - 1/2\ \sigma^2$ and variance σ^2. Equivalently, $\ln(p^i_t)$ is normally distributed with parameters

$$(3\text{-}10) \qquad\qquad E[\ln(p^i_t)] = \ln(p^i_t) + \mu$$

and

$$(3\text{-}11) \qquad\qquad \text{var}[(\ln(p^i_t)] = \sigma^2.$$

where var means variance.

When the government operates a price band, farmers are assumed to recognize fully the consequences of the band and to adjust their expectations of the domestic price (p^d) accordingly as the upper prices (p^u) and lower prices (p^l) given by the price band rules are known without error to the farmer.

$$(3\text{-}12) \qquad\qquad p^l_{t+1} \le E(p^d_{t+1}) \le p^u_{t+1},$$

Domestic production is a function of expected domestic prices, but total demand occurs 120 days later and is a function of actual domestic prices. Total demand therefore occurs after the random element has been revealed. Trade makes up the gap (positive or negative) between supply and demand. The demand and supply curves are assumed to be log-linear and are of the form

(3-13) $$\ln S_t = \ln(100) + e_s \ln(p_t^d)$$

and

(3-14) $$\ln D_t = \ln(100) - e_d \ln(p_t^d),$$

where e_s and e_d are constant supply and demand elasticities. The supply and demand elasticities used throughout the base run of the simulation were 0.8 and -0.5, respectively.[10]

The fund manager evaluates expected supply and demand, and therefore trade, at both the upper and lower levels of the price band. If, over the band, the country is exclusively an importer or exporter (that is, not a marginal trader), then the manager hedges the fund's liability: the manager buys puts at an exercise price equal to the lower level of the price band if the country exports at that price level, or buys calls at an exercise price equal to the upper level of the price band if the country expects to import the commodity. The quantity hedged is equal to the trade volume at the strike price. The prices of the options are calculated using the Black-Scholes option-pricing model and are based on expected prices, an annualized interest rate of 6.0 percent, and an expected coefficient of variation (CV, the ratio of the standard deviation to the mean) based on a five-period moving average calculation. Each option is held for 120 days. After 120 days the true price is revealed, as is domestic consumption and trade. Based on the revealed price, the manager liquidates the options if they have value, collects any relevant taxes, and pays out any relevant subsidies based on actual trade.

Simulation Results on Prices and Welfare Changes

The model described above was used to generate ten samples, each containing observations for 500 iterations. The simulations were dynamic within each of the samples; that is, at the beginning of each of the ten samples the international price was set to one, with a lognormal random walk generating prices for the next 499 observations in the sample. The fund manager started each sample with zero reserves, but could borrow freely. The manager operated a price band system with the upper and lower bands based, respectively, on 110 percent and 90 percent of a five-period moving average. Table 3-2 summarizes the settings for the control variables in the base simulation.

Table 3-3 summarizes some of the simulation results for the price

Table 3-2. *Settings for the Control Variables in the Base Simulation*

Variable	Setting
Sample size	500
Number of samples	10
Type of price movement	Lognormal random walk
Error distribution	Log of error is distributed $N(0, 0.01)$
Price expectations	Rational
Starting value of price	1.0
Initial value of stabilization fund	0.0
Initial volume of trading	Self-sufficient, 0 exports
Price band rules	Plus or minus 10% of moving five-period average
Option-pricing method	Black-Scholes
Period that option is held	120 days
Interest rate	6.0%
CV[a] used in option pricing	Based on moving five-period sample
Elasticity of domestic demand	-0.5
Elasticity of domestic supply	0.8

a. Coefficient of variation—the ratio of the standard deviation to the mean.

Table 3-3. *Summary Results for Key Price Variables across Simulated Samples for the Base Scenario*

Variable	Mean range across samples	Minimum value	Maximum value
Border price	0.20 to 13.77	0.02	49.18
Domestic price	0.20 to 13.73	0.02	47.61
Log of error	0.00 to 0.01	-0.36	0.38

Source: Authors' calculations.
Note: Results are based on a starting price of 1.0.

variables and reveals the underlying difficulties faced by the fund manager. (Full results of all simulations are given in Larson and Coleman 1991.) Even though the fund manager may understand the underlying price mechanism as well as the intricacies of the domestic market, the cumulative effects of random components can lead to very different price paths.

Recognizing a "reasonable" long-run price may be impossible and, even if possible, irrelevant in the "short run"—the short run in this case being 500 years.

Before turning to the question of how the fund is financed, it is perhaps best to consider how the stabilization program performs. Table 3-4 provides some summary results for three of the samples, and from these

Table 3-4. Summary Results and Welfare Effects for Selected Simulation Samples

Variable	Mean	Minimum	Maximum	CV
Sample 1				
World price	0.30	0.03	1.21	98.63
Domestic prevailing price	0.30	0.03	1.14	97.16
Consumer welfare change	-0.75	-28.14	23.86	-898.59
Producer surplus change, exclusive of risk benefits	0.02	-17.86	9.39	11,830.86
Government surplus change, without hedging	0.45	-16.76	20.53	1,125.37
Standard efficiency loss	-0.29	-6.08	4.70	-325.76
Producer income without stabilization program	22.28	0.65	127.47	136.97
Producer income with stabilization program	22.31	0.66	123.18	134.83
Sample 4				
World price	12.53	1.04	49.18	85.48
Domestic prevailing price	12.38	1.04	47.61	85.31
Consumer welfare change	1.96	-45.94	47.77	565.85
Producer surplus change, exclusive of risk benefits	-51.81	-2,495.25	2,299.26	-715.08
Government surplus change, without hedging	54.74	-3,421.58	3,337.53	884.98
Standard efficiency loss	4.89	-1,151.17	940.21	3,197.41
Producer income without stabilization program	5,532.67	104.19	33,974.97	124.33
Producer income with stabilization program	5,454.95	104.19	32,851.00	124.07
Sample 9				
World price	0.35	0.05	1.31	80.85
Domestic prevailing price	0.35	0.05	1.31	80.72
Consumer welfare change	-0.48	-32.32	25.07	-1,316.90
Producer surplus change, exclusive of risk benefits	0.18	-16.67	16.49	1,412.03
Government surplus change, without hedging	0.04	-21.79	16.87	11,228.17
Standard efficiency loss	-0.27	-8.65	3.54	-394.74
Producer income without stabilization program	25.29	1.04	148.73	125.04
Producer income with stabilization program	25.56	1.05	148.73	124.29

Source: Authors' calculations.

83

results several conclusions can be drawn. First, the information on domestic and border prices restates, in a slightly different way, the information contained in table 3-3 and supports the general conclusion that the random component of the price structure can generate very different sample price distributions. This is reflected in the differing ranges within samples and the varying means and CVs across samples. The second implication is that the average effects of the price band system on producer, consumer, or government welfare are small (less than 2 percent of average producer income), but that the single-year effects can be quite large (for example, multiple factors of average producer income). The price band system is able to reduce the CV of prices as well as producer income variability, but again, the average effects are quite small. The stabilization programs are roughly self-financing, but the year-to-year variation in revenues or payments is quite large.

Table 3-5 shows the extent to which producers benefited from the simulated stabilization program.[11] The results, which are expressed as a percentage of nonstabilized producer income, are quite revealing. Across all simulations, the value of the stabilization program to producers was exceedingly small. Although it can be argued that relative risk aversion changes at varying levels of income, it is clear that, on average, a very low tariff (for net importers) or export subsidy (for net exporters) would generate the same level of income benefits to producers as does a more complicated stabilization program. Across all of the samples, producers received a nonnegative net welfare gain (transfer benefit plus risk benefit) from the stabilization programs. Not all risk benefits were positive, despite the fact that the stabilization programs were successful in reduc-

Table 3-5. *Transfer and Risk Benefits to Producers from Simulated Stabilization Programs*
(percent)

Sample number	Transfer benefit	Risk benefit
1	0.13	4.00
2	1.07	−0.38
3	0.22	0.62
4	−1.40	3.70
5	0.15	2.94
6	0.39	2.65
7	−1.35	5.98
8	−0.23	0.64
9	1.05	−1.06
10	0.35	2.92

Note: Benefits are expressed as a percentage of nonstabilized producer income.
Source: Authors' calculations.

ing the variability of prices. But in the two samples that showed negative risk benefits, the reduction was so small that the adjustment for income changes (see equation 3-5) overwhelmed the small reduction in income variability.

Simulation Results on Fund Financing

Results reported in the previous section indicated that although the benefits of a stabilization program may be small, the programs tend to be self-financing and can generate substantial single-period income benefits. Results in table 3-6 show that borrowings are often needed to keep the fund in operation, but that the frequency and size of the borrowings can usually be reduced through hedging. Fund borrowings will not necessarily be eliminated by hedging, and the primary determinant of whether or not the fund must borrow heavily is luck. This fact is underscored by the great range of indebtedness the samples generated. In some cases the fund passed through the entire period with positive balances, whereas in other cases, the fund manager was forced to borrow the equivalent of the value of four years' worth of production.

What, then, is the value of hedging to a fund manager? Assuming that the government or agency administering the stabilization scheme has an aggregate utility function that can be characterized in the same manner as that of the producers, transfer and stabilization benefits derived from

Table 3-6. *Effects of Hedging on Borrowing by Stabilization Fund*

Sample number	Number of times fund borrows		Maximum debt as a percentage of average producer income	
	Unhedged	Hedged	Unhedged	Hedged
1	0	0	n.a.	n.a.
2	6	5	−3.31	−5.23
3	262	0	−130.89	n.a.
4	0	0	n.a.	n.a.
5	156	18	−73.76	−20.67
6	12	0	−43.91	n.a.
7	22	22	0.00	0.00
8	13	0	−0.54	n.a.
9	51	59	−170.34	−197.85
10	161	157	−392.01	−381.03

n.a. Not applicable.
Source: Authors' calculations.

hedging activities can be calculated using an identical approach. Define average government benefits from hedging as

$$(3\text{-}15) \qquad \frac{B^g}{\|\overline{T}_0\|} = \frac{\overline{T}_1 - \overline{T}_0}{\|\overline{T}_0\|} + \tfrac{1}{2}R^g(\overline{T}_0)\,[\sigma_{T_1}^2(\overline{T}_1/\overline{T}_0)^2 - \sigma_{T_0}^2]$$

where $\overline{T}_0$ and $\overline{T}_1$ are average net revenues (taxes minus subsidies) under a stabilization program with and without hedging operations; σ_t^2 is the CV associated with flows in and out of the fund; and R^g is the government's coefficient of relative risk aversion with respect to fund flows.[12] It is assumed throughout the remaining analysis that the government is unitarily risk-averse, that is, that $R^g = 1$. The hedging operation generates a pure transfer (positive or negative) that comes from the speculators taking the opposite position on fund option trades (the first term in equation 3-14) plus a "risk" benefit that comes from reducing the variability of the fund flows (the second term in equation 3-14). Both are expressed as a share of the average "unhedged" fund income.

The effects of hedging the fund revenues are reported in table 3-7. Because in many samples income flows that go into the fund are close to zero, the traditional measures of benefits, which are expressed as a percentage of income, take on very large values; however, it is clear from the large reduction in the CV of fund income that the hedging strategy usually reduces the variability of fund income flows. The income transfers that measure the simple value of the strategy are both positive and negative; the calculated values of the benefit of reducing the variability of the fund flows are all extremely large with regard to the average fund income.

Table 3-7. *Effects of Hedging on Fund Income and Fund Risk*

Sample number	Average fund flow		CV of fund income		Benefits as a percentage of fund income	
	Unhedged	Hedged	Unhedged	Hedged	Transfer	Risk
1	0.45	0.52	1,125	878	16	1,097
2	0.32	−0.21	942	1,240	−27	371
3	−0.93	1.97	−4,489	1,715	−310	35,822
4	54.74	86.21	884	477	58	1,089
5	0.03	0.13	18,129	3,506	345	424,956
6	0.28	0.37	1,795	1,187	32	3,915
7	12.77	26.77	2,130	902	110	4,810
8	7.52	44.86	6,100	853	496	56,600
9	0.04	0.02	11,228	17,786	−43	116,543
10	0.00	−0.04	n.a.	n.a.	n.a.	n.a.

n.a. Not applicable.
Source: Authors' calculations.

Although the benefits of the stabilization scheme in general may be suspect, the benefits of hedging an existing stabilization fund are clear and substantial under the assumptions made so far. The following scenarios are devoted to testing the robustness of these results under different assumptions.

Alternative Supply and Demand Equations

As discussed earlier, fund liabilities can exist only when the price band does not include the price at which the country would be self-sufficient. When the country is either exclusively an exporter or exclusively an importer over the range of potential prices, three possible cases can exist: one that is revenue-neutral, one that generates revenues for the fund, and one that taps the fund's resources. To test whether the simulation results reported earlier are sensitive to a change in the three possible cases, alternative scenarios were simulated. By shifting supply and demand intercepts, the simulation model was adjusted to simulate exporting and importing countries.

In practice, price band schemes are often based on nominal prices, because measures of inflation are frequently revised. At the same time, because the price band rules are often based on moving averages, current inflation enters the price band with a lag. Under such circumstances, the upper limit of the price band becomes more binding than the lower band. By adding a term for positive drift, the model was altered so that nominal prices would slowly rise throughout the simulation periods.

The effects of these simulations on producer welfare are reported in table 3-8. As in the base simulation, the net effects on producer welfare are all relatively small; however, the risk benefits are slightly larger (and all positive), especially for the case in which nominal prices drift upward.

Table 3-9 reports the effects on government welfare. Again, the results are consistent with earlier findings. Hedging the fund tends to generate quite large welfare gains to the extent that the government or fund agency is risk-averse. All scenarios generated positive risk benefits, but the transfer effects were mixed, depending on the luck of the draw. In the case of an upward price drift, the transfer benefits were all positive, because the government was able to tax more frequently.

Deterministic Price Movements

So far, the results have been based on the assumption that price movements drift randomly. This assumption is extreme in that behavioral forces inherent in supply and demand schedules have been ignored. In the

Table 3-8. *Producer Benefits from Hedging under Importer, Exporter, and Inflation Scenarios*
(percent)

Sample number	Importer case		Exporter case		Upward drift case	
	Transfer benefit	Risk benefit	Transfer benefit	Risk benefit	Transfer benefit	Risk benefit
1	−1.6	9.8	1.0	0.4	−2.0	5.8
2	−0.6	3.5	−1.1	4.9	−2.6	17.7
3	−10.0	3.9	−0.3	3.0	−2.2	6.1
4	−0.3	1.2	−1.5	5.3	−4.8	54.8
5	−0.6	2.6	0.4	5.7	−1.4	3.7
6	−1.2	5.1	−0.2	6.8	−2.0	12.6
7	−2.6	18.9	−0.9	5.4	−2.4	8.4
8	−0.4	1.6	−0.6	2.2	−1.1	2.0
9	−1.6	3.0	−1.9	9.7	3.7	73.4
10	−2.8	18.8	−1.8	8.9	−0.7	1.9

Note: Benefits are expressed as a percentage of nonstabilized producer income.
Source: Authors' calculations.

Table 3-9. *Government Benefits from Hedging under Importer, Exporter, and Inflation Scenarios*
(percent)

Sample number	Importer case		Exporter case		Upward drift case	
	Transfer benefit	Risk benefit	Transfer benefit	Risk benefit	Transfer benefit	Risk benefit
1	−442	65,453	−97	1,844	39	368
2	288	232,001	111	3,851	23	252
3	−10	2,983	1,454	915,127	53	526
4	−22	59,181	98	2,409	11	112
5	−19	4,917	−183	14,261	68	113
6	−30	1,108	442	52,823	35	563
7	24	698	148	4,976	31	280
8	50	32,654	199	6,719	87	1,921
9	−23	1,246	31	414	73	1,190
10	−12	1,462	34	660	237	11,372

Note: Benefits are expressed as a percentage of fund income.
Source: Authors' calculations.

following simulation an opposite but equally naive assumption is used, and the results are similar. Rather than facing a random walk international price, the price-taking country faces prices from a deterministic international commodity market consisting of supply and demand functions. International supplies are confounded by an additive random error. In general, economic markets are filled with both deterministic and stochastic components. Agents act on imperfect information about input prices and supplies, consumer income, and the prices of substitute and complement goods. As in any system, if the economic processes are complex enough, the system variables may have many of the characteristics that are normally associated with stochastic variables, even though they arise from a mixed stochastic-deterministic system. However, it is believed that results that are consistent under two extreme assumptions in simulation will prove robust in a more complicated reality that falls somewhere between the two models.

In the expanded model, equation 3-9 is dropped and replaced by three additional equations and two more variables—international supply (S^i) and international demand (D^i). D^i contains domestic consumption, given in equation 3-14, but, consistent with the price-taking assumption, domestic demand is small enough in relation to international demand that it can be safely ignored. The international demand schedule is assumed to be lognormal and is given by

(3-16) $$\ln D_t^i = \ln d_0 - e_d^i \ln(p_t^i)$$

where e_d^i is a constant international demand elasticity.

The supply equation is Nerlovian, implying a short-run supply elasticity different from the long-run steady-state supply elasticity and is given by

(3-17) $$\ln S_t = \ln s_0 + e_s^i \ln E(p_t^i) + l_s^i \ln S_{t-1}^i + v_t$$

where v is normally distributed $N(0, \sigma^2)$, e_s^i is the constant short-run price elasticity, and $e_s^i/(1 - l_s^i)$ provides the steady-state elasticity when $S_t = S_{t-1}$.

For simulation purposes, stock changes are set equal to zero so that

(3-18) $$S_t^i = D_t^i, \text{ for all } t.$$

Combining equations 3-16 and 3-17 into equation 3-18 yields

(3-19) $$\ln p_t^i = \frac{1}{(e_d^i - e_s^i)} [\ln(s_0/d_0) + l_s^i \ln S_{t-1}^i + v_t].$$

Noting that

(3-20) $$E\left[\exp\left(\frac{v_t}{e_d^i - e_s^i}\right)\right] = \exp\left[\frac{1}{2}\sigma^2\left(\frac{1}{e_d^i - e_s^i}\right)^2\right],$$

it follows that

(3-21) $$E(p_t) = \left(\frac{s_0}{d_0}\right)^{\frac{1}{\gamma}}(S_{t-1})^{\frac{l_s}{\gamma}} \exp\left(\frac{\sigma^2}{2\gamma^2}\right), \text{ where } \gamma = \frac{1}{e_d^i - e_s^i}.$$

In addition, because $D^i = S^i$ for all values of p, including the steady-state S^i,

(3-22) $\ln s_0 = (1 - l_s^i)\ln\delta_0$, since $\lim_{s \to 0} S^i(1) = D^i(1)$.

Table 3-10 summarizes some of the simulation results for the price variables under the deterministic model. Because of the feedback between international prices and international demand and supply, the range of values assumed by the price variables is much narrower than in the random walk simulations. Thus, given the extremely limited price volatility under the deterministic model simulations, producer transfer and risk benefits generated by further stabilizing the domestic price were essentially zero for most of the simulations. However, even though the stabilization programs themselves generated no real benefits, hedging the stabilization fund did prove to be a worthwhile endeavor.

Table 3-11 shows the effects of hedging on fund income and fund risk

Table 3-10. *Summary Results for Key Price Variables across Simulated Samples in a Deterministic Model*

Variable	Mean range across samples	Minimum value	Maximum value
Border price	0.99 to 1.02	0.62	1.55
Domestic price	0.98 to 1.02	0.73	1.33
Log of error	−0.01 to 0.01	−0.36	0.33

Source: Authors' calculations.

Table 3-11. *Effects of Hedging on Fund Income and Fund Risk under a Deterministic Pricing Model*

Sample number	Average fund flow (percent)		CV of fund income		Benefits as a percentage of fund income	
	Unhedged	Hedged	Unhedged	Hedged	Transfer	Risk
1	0.51	1.56	1,453	382	2	37
2	0.55	1.68	1,415	386	2	30
3	0.53	1.50	1,532	453	2	35
4	0.51	1.59	1,572	414	2	39
5	0.28	1.29	2,537	442	4	119
6	0.54	1.70	1,541	408	2	36
7	0.48	1.47	1,459	393	2	35
8	0.52	1.62	1,395	361	2	35
9	0.42	1.61	2,133	449	3	78
10	0.44	1.47	1,649	393	2	48

Source: Authors' calculations.

under the deterministic model simulations. The results on hedging funds are consistent with those reported earlier. Because the feedback of the deterministic pricing model leads to similar price scenarios under each of the simulations, the results on fund hedging are more consistent as well.

Conclusions

Casual observation leads to the conclusion that stabilization funds tend to be short-lived. Although it may be that some funds have failed because of poor management or unwarranted political interventions, the stochastic components of commodity prices can generate insurmountable difficulties for even the most expert managers. Price band schemes contain an element of information feedback and offer transparent rules—attributes that make such schemes preferable to many alternative mechanisms—but, although such stabilization schemes can have large single-year effects, the benefits to producers tend to be, on average, quite small. Benefits of similar size can be generated with very small import taxes or producer subsidies.

The simulation results demonstrate that if a stabilization scheme is adopted, the stabilization fund should be hedged unless the government is not at all neutral to the fund's financial failure. Still, hedged or unhedged, the fund will, with eventual certainty, generate a large debt because a statistically "rare" sequence of events must eventually occur. By hedging, the fund is more likely to survive in the short run.

Notes

1. McNicol (1978) documents seventeen major commodity agreements since the close of World War I.

2. See Knudsen and Nash (1990b) for a description of a wide range of stabilization programs.

3. Once the actual price is replaced by the expected price in the supply equation, efficiency losses need not be negative. This result comes from the fact that a price band can accidentally provide a domestic price that is closer to the actual prevailing price than the expected price is, generating a positive efficiency gain.

4. Only under very strong assumptions do ordinal monetary measures of consumer surplus correspond to unique measures of consumer welfare. However, for applied work there are few practical alternatives. See Just, Hueth, and Schmitz (1982, chapter 5) for a discussion of consumer surplus and applied economic analysis.

5. Potentially, there is a gain to consumers from stable prices (see Newbery and Stiglitz 1981, chapter 9); however, if consumption substitutes are readily available or expenditures on the good are small in relation to income, the benefits will be quantitatively small.

6. Akiyama and Varangis (1989) simulated the long-term effects of the International Coffee Agreement and concluded that the long-term production and price effects of the

agreement were small but that the short-run effects of the agreement's dissolution were large.

7. The Australian wool scheme was an example of the former and the Papua New Guinea stabilization programs examples of the latter.

8. In the importer case, total import tax revenues are bounded as well, but only by the nonnegativity condition on prices.

9. See Aitcheson and Brown (1957) for a discussion of expectations and lognormal errors.

10. In this stylized simulation, decisions are made and implemented once. In continuous time, managers may instead be more active, revising positions to lock in gains when possible or adjusting quantities that are hedged as new information on supply and demand become available.

11. For the purpose of evaluating the simulation benefits, the coefficient of relative risk aversion given in equations 3-5 and 3-6 was assumed to equal 1.5.

12. When the fund is hedged, the costs of purchasing the options as well as the revenues generated by exercising "winning" options are included in T.

4

Asset and Liability Management: Modern Financial Techniques

Toshiya Masuoka

For the past two decades, the world has experienced substantial volatility in interest and exchange rates and in primary commodity prices. The financial markets have responded with new market-based financial instruments, including forward, futures, option, and swap contracts. The market for instruments to manage commodity risk has developed more recently than that for managing currency and interest rate risk, and the number of corporations in the industrial countries that use commodity swaps, commodity-linked bonds, and the like has been increasing.

The concept of asset and liability management has been developed against this background. For financial institutions and corporations, asset and liability management includes those activities that attempt to control exposure to financial and other price risks. Basically, it aims at controlling the variability of future cash flows. Institutions and corporations examine the risk exposure of their assets and liabilities to future price movements to develop their risk exposure profile. Then, by entering into a set of financial transactions, they attempt to minimize any

The author is very grateful to Theo Priovolos for sharing information on commodity-linked instruments and their applications to Mexico and Algeria, Stijn Claessens for useful discussion on risk management theories and practice, and Jamil Baz for information on the financial technical assistance program carried out by the Treasurer's Office of the World Bank. The paper draws heavily on a report by Chandrasekhar and Castellanos, of the Treasurer's Office, for Chile's hedging operations with Eurodollar futures contracts.

As well, the author wishes to thank Stanley Fischer, Andrew Steer, Ajay Chhibber, D. C. Rao, Ronald Duncan, and Louis Hobeika.

unexpected decline in profits (net cash flows from operations) resulting from changes in interest rates, exchange rates, and commodity prices.

Although the importance of these activities has been broadly recognized in the industrial countries, applications to the developing countries have been limited. Because asset and liability management provides an opportunity to reduce the likelihood and effects of external shocks, it enables governments to put development planning on a more secure basis. It may therefore complement medium-term structural adjustment programs because risk management operations reduce the possibility of unanticipated deviations from initial projections in important economic variables.

This chapter provides an overview of (a) the concept of asset and liability management as it applies to a country and (b) modern financial instruments and the hedging activities that use these instruments. It then describes the concept of asset and liability management in developing countries and provides an explanation of the various financial instruments. To illustrate practical applications of these instruments, several examples of risk management activities in developing countries are then presented. That section also discusses some factors that limit the use of modern financial tools by developing countries and considers ways to overcome these factors.

Asset and Liability Management

General Concepts

In the industrial countries the techniques of asset and liability management were initially used by financial institutions to control unexpected downturns in net interest income[1] that were the result of changes in market interest rates. The techniques were later expanded to include the risks of changes in exchange rates and commodity prices and to make them applicable to other types of organizations.[2]

The main purpose of asset and liability management is to make the consideration of risk explicit in the planning process and to enable decisionmakers to control risk exposure. Any entity or investment project is bound to be exposed to price risks, and investment planning always involves assumptions about the movements of these prices. Many of the difficulties that developing countries suffered in servicing their debts in the 1980s reflect such implicit assumptions about future movements of interest rates, exchange rates, and commodity prices. Analysis of asset and liability management is designed to quantify as accurately as possible the sensitivity of an investment's performance to these price changes and to carry out appropriate hedging activities to alter the level of sensitivity.

Asset and liability management involves the following procedures:

1. Identifying an objective function (or a measure of an entity's performance)
2. Identifying and measuring risk exposure in relation to the objective function (or measuring the sensitivity of performance to unexpected changes in prices)
3. Deciding on an acceptable degree of risk exposure (or deciding on the degree of risk exposure to be hedged)
4. Choosing and executing hedging transactions.

The objective function is the quantitative measure of an entity's performance and is used for risk measurement. For a company, an objective function may be defined as net profit from operations. Net profit fluctuates over time because of various factors, including the company's investment strategy and competitiveness; exchange and interest rates; and commodity prices. The company then divides the possible fluctuations into two categories: those related to movements in financial prices and those unrelated to such variables. The first are called financial risks and can be hedged with financial instruments.

For a country, an objective function can be defined in a quite general way as well as in a more reduced, simple form. In several chapters in this volume a country's objective function is defined generally in terms of a social objective (for instance, in accordance with most economic theory, a utility function over the country's consumption) that the country will seek to maximize. Although a general definition provides a good theoretical base for identifying a country's risk exposure, more specificity is needed for practical applications. This and other chapters in this volume follow a simple approach, introducing specific targets. Examples of such specific targets in these chapters are a country's net foreign receipts and import costs (chapter 12), the foreign receipts of private coffee exporters (chapters 6 and 7), the costs of oil imports for a state oil company (chapters 8 and 9), and the budget revenues of a government operating a tariff-based price stabilization scheme (chapter 15).

Practical Asset and Liability Management

Here asset and liability management is defined as the management of a country's asset and liability structure to minimize adverse changes in future net cash flows arising from international transactions.[3] This definition implies that the country is risk-averse.[4] Any factor that generates inflows of cash is loosely defined as an asset, and any factor resulting in outflows of cash is viewed as a liability. Thus earnings on export activities are viewed as dividends on assets, or revenues from the sale of assets. By the same token, import activities are classified as liabilities. The cash flows can be analyzed in terms of the economy as a whole but can also be examined for subsectors, such as the government budget, the central bank's accounts, state enterprises, or private firms. Practically, cash flows to and from the country can be approximated through reclassifying items in the balance of payments data (for example, in terms of the composition of currencies and commodities). Alternatively, cash flows can be classified in two parts: external debt service requirements (cash required to service external debt on schedule), and the country's ability to service the debt (export earnings, and so on, net of import costs).

The practical objective function used should reflect the fact that asset and liability management involves smoothing the impact of shocks, favorable as well as unfavorable. Asset and liability management can protect against downside risk only in exchange for some current costs or by giving up some upside potential. This fact implies that the objective of asset and liability management cannot (directly) be to increase returns or lower costs; rather, it is a tool for better management, planning, and budgeting. As such, the practical objective function will simply be to achieve certainty. In this context, a statement by an official of the Finance Ministry in Mexico regarding its decision to hedge a significant fraction of Mexican oil exports is illustrative: "It is extremely important for us that investors know that, no matter what happens to the price of oil, the economic program is on for 1991. Regardless of what happens, we have got US$17 a barrel . . . and there's enough in the kitty" (Moffett and Truell 1991, p. C14).

The asset and liability structure can be changed directly, by changing the amounts of given assets or liabilities in the balance sheet (real diversification), and indirectly, through hedging instruments that change the characteristics of the returns on the assets and liabilities. For instance, a country can improve the risk characteristics of its assets and liabilities by holding an adequate level of foreign exchange reserves and borrowing in appropriate currency denominations, or by executing hedging transactions in futures and swap markets.

Risk Measurement

Two basic methods can be used to measure a country's risk exposure: measurement based on historical data, and measurement based on projections or simulations.

The first approach aims at extracting useful relationships between net cash flows and risk factors, usually by means of multivariate regression or vector autoregression analyses. The risk exposure with respect to each risk factor is then measured by the covariance between the cash flows and the risk factor in relation to variance of the cash flows (that is, the regression coefficient).

Put another way, the risk exposure is measured as the amount of change in the cash flow for each unit of change in financial prices. Although this approach provides a relatively convenient way of measuring risk, it does not take into account future changes in the country's economic structure. Preferably, one should attempt to predict and factor in future changes in the country's economic structure, changes which may drastically alter the country's risk exposure profile.

The second approach, simulation, extends the first approach by systematically incorporating future structural changes. It does this through projecting cash flows based on varying assumptions on future price and factor movements and changes in the country's economic structure. The statistical estimates of the variability of net cash flows with respect to changes in the prices of risk factors then represent the exposures. Although this approach is preferable, the quality of the analysis is largely dependent on the validity of assumptions about future events. Usually both approaches are carried out and results are compared in order to check plausibility and to illustrate the effect of future structural changes on risk exposure.

Important Rules for Effective Asset and Liability Management

Two important rules for achieving effective asset and liability management are the incremental hedge rule and the flexible hedge rule (see Toevs and Haney 1986).

INCREMENTAL HEDGE RULE. It should be noted that most countries undertake risk-hedging activities incrementally. Often adequate hedging instruments for achieving the desired asset-liability structure are not available to developing countries. Even if the instruments are available, the market for these instruments may not be very active. In this case, asset and liability management activities should aim to move risk exposure toward the best possible situation. In addition to a risk analysis that derives the desirable asset-liability structure, it is important to analyze the constraints on hedging transactions to reveal the best risk structure attainable under the circumstances. In addition, the risk analysis should identify the major factors contributing to the risk to enable decision-makers to carry out the most useful incremental hedging transactions.

Flexible hedge rule. Because there is no perfect asset and liability management model to measure risk exposure, estimates of risk exposure may turn out to be incorrect, and hedging activities already in place may become obsolete or even harmful. For this reason, flexibility in modifying or reversing hedging transactions is important. Modern techniques using such instruments as futures and swaps have significant advantages over conventional techniques, including adjustments to the currency composition and maturity structure of external debt, because the newer techniques can be changed almost on a daily basis.

Modern Financial Tools for Risk Management

This section explains the basic characteristics and mechanisms of financial instruments for risk management, focusing on the more recently developed financial instruments.[5] Table 4-1 gives an overview of these instruments.

Forwards, Futures, Options, and Swaps

Forward contracts. A forward contract is an agreement to purchase or sell a given asset at a future date at a preset price. At maturity, if the actual price (spot price) is higher than the contracted price, the forward buyer makes a profit. If the price is lower, the buyer suffers a loss. The payoff to the seller is the opposite of the buyer's.

Forward contracts are often used to hedge the risk of holding a certain asset or liability. This activity, called a "forward cover," involves the execution of a set of (reverse) transactions in both the spot and forward markets: if one holds (or purchases in the spot market) a certain asset, then, to execute the cover, the same amount of that asset is sold in the forward market at a prespecified price. When the forward contract matures, the asset is sold at the specified price. This enables the owner to fix the amount of revenue from the future sale of the asset at the time the contract is made, "locking in" the price.

For example, assume that an exporter's major market is in Germany and export revenues are denominated in deutsche marks. The exporter has taken out a $1 million[6] loan from a U.S. bank to be repaid in six months when the customer pays DM2 million for the delivered goods. The current exchange rate is 2 deutsche marks to the dollar. If the deutsche mark depreciates within the next six months (say, to 2.2 deutsche marks to the dollar), the exporter will face repayments on the loan that are larger than his receipts. The exporter can hedge the

Table 4-1. *An Overview of Financial Instruments to Manage Risk*

Instruments	Description	Advantages and limitations
	Financial instruments in general	
Forward	• An agreement to purchase or sell a given asset at a future date at a preset price. • Transactions are made mostly through brokers by phone and telex. • A typical use is for locking in a future price. • Contracts are available primarily for short-term maturities (up to one year).	• No cash transfer is needed at the beginning. Cash transfer occurs only at maturity. • Credit risk is involved. • Tailor-made contracts are available for specific hedging needs.
Futures	• An agreement to purchase or sell a given asset at a future date at a preset price. • Transactions are made in formal exchanges through clearinghouse systems. • Contract terms (amounts, grades, delivery dates, and so on) are highly standardized. • Profits and losses are settled daily, requiring daily cash flows. • Margin (collateral) money is required at the beginning. • A typical use is for locking in a future price. • Contracts are available primarily for short-term maturities (up to one year).	• Initial cash transfer is required for margin money. • Daily cash transfers are necessary. • Credit risk is minimal. • Tailor-made contracts are not available. • Markets are more active than forward markets for some contracts. • An original position can be closed or reversed easily and quickly.

(Table continues on the following page.)

Table 4-1 (continued)

Instruments	Description	Advantages and limitations
Option	• The right to purchase or sell a certain asset at a preset price on (or before) a specified date. • Transactions are made both through brokers by phone and telex and in formal exchanges. • A typical use is for setting a ceiling or floor for prices. • Contracts are available primarily for short-term maturities (up to one year).	• A buyer of an option contract can limit the maximum loss but keep open the opportunity to take advantage of favorable price movements. • A buyer has to pay a premium (cost of option) up front. • A buyer faces a seller's credit risk. (A buyer has the right; a seller has the obligation.) • Tailor-made contracts are available for specific hedging needs.
Swap	• An agreement to exchange specified cash flows at fixed intervals. • A series of forward contracts lined up on a schedule. • Transactions are made through brokers by phone and telex. • A typical use is for locking in future prices for a long period. • Contracts are available for medium- and long-term maturities (one to ten years).	• No cash transfer is needed at the beginning. • Credit risk is involved. • Tailor-made contracts are available for specific hedging needs.

Commodity-linked instruments

Commodity swap	• A swap contract on a certain commodity. An agreement to pay, at fixed intervals, a fixed amount of cash in exchange for a variable amount of cash or vice versa. The variable amount of cash is determined by the market price for a set quantity of a commodity. The fixed amount is based on a fixed price for the same quantity of the commodity. • Contracts are provided by international banks. • A typical use is for locking in a price of a commodity for the medium and long term. • No deliveries of physical commodities are involved. Transactions are purely financial, like the other swap contracts (see above for characteristics of swap contracts in general). • The markets are not very active.
Commodity-linked loan	• A loan in which interest or repayment amount or both are linked to the market price of a certain commodity. • A loan can be viewed as a combination of a conventional fixed rate loan and a commodity swap contract. • These loans are provided by international banks. • A loan can be regarded as effectively denominated in a commodity. • If used by a commodity producer, the credit risk of the loan is lower than that of a conventional loan. A producer can repay the loan even if the price of the commodity falls significantly.
Commodity-linked bond	• (Forward type) A bond in which coupons or principal or both are linked to the market price of a certain commodity. • (Option type) A bond to which the right to buy or sell a certain commodity at a preset price is attached. • These bonds are underwritten by international banks. • The bonds have been issued primarily on gold and oil. Some are available for silver, copper, and nickel. • (Forward type) Advantages and limitations are similar to those of commodity-linked loans. • (Option type) This type is often useful for commodity producers, to reduce the cost of financing.

exchange rate risk with a forward contract. The current forward rate for the six-month contract is 2 deutsche marks to the dollar.[7] The exporter purchases a forward contract to sell the DM2 million for $1 million at the end of the six months, thus locking in the amount of the export revenue at today's forward exchange rate.

This transaction shows two important characteristics of the forward contract (in addition to its use as a hedging instrument). First, no cash transfer occurs up front. The exporter is obligated to deliver the deutsche marks at maturity but pays no money up front except for transaction fees. Second, forward contracts involve a credit risk. Suppose the counterparty of the forward transaction fails to deliver the U.S. dollars at maturity. Although the exporter can then buy U.S. dollars for the deutsche marks in the spot market, the whole purpose of hedging fails. Because a forward contract is an agreement between two parties, credit risk or default risk has to be considered.

Forward markets for major currencies are liquid and efficient for transactions up to a maturity of one year. (For an overview of the liquidity of forwards, futures, options, and swaps for currencies, interest rates, and commodities, see table 4-2). Forward markets for major currencies have no formal exchanges. Transactions are made through brokers and dealers by phone and telex. This is also true for forward markets for interest rates.

Forward contracts for international interest rates are known as forward rate agreements (FRAs) and are liquid up to a year. The mechanism of FRAs is similar to forward contracts for currency: two parties agree to pay or receive a specified interest rate on a certain amount of money for the future period. For example, in a "3 × 6" FRA on $1 million at 6 percent,[8] two parties agree to receive or pay $15,000 ($1,000,000 × 6 percent × $3/12$) in interest for a period of three months starting three months from the date of the agreement.[9]

Forward markets for commodities are less liquid than currency and interest rate markets. The London Metal Exchange is one of the largest forward markets for commodities: aluminum, copper, lead, nickel, and zinc are traded on three-month maturities. Transactions are also made through brokers and dealers by phone and telex, as in forward and swap trading for currency and interest rates.

FUTURES CONTRACTS. Futures contracts are similar to forward contracts: the buyer of a futures contract agrees to purchase a specified asset at a specified price on a specified date. But futures contracts differ significantly in four ways. First, contract terms (amounts, grades, delivery dates, and so on) are standardized (see table 4-3 for examples of contract specifications). Second, transactions are handled only by organized

Table 4-2. *Liquidity of Markets for Forwards, Futures, Options, and Swaps*

	Currency	Interest rate	Commodity
Forwards			
Short-term	High	High	Moderate
Long-term	Low	Low	Low
Futures			
Short-term	Moderate	High	Moderate
Long-term	Low	Low	Low
Options			
Short-term	Moderate	High	Low
Long-term	Low	Moderate	Low
Swaps			
Short-term	Low	High	Low
Long-term	Moderate	Moderate	Low

Note: Here, a "liquid" market means a market where a counterparty to a transaction can be found easily and the transaction can be made quickly without changing the price of the instrument considerably. In a highly liquid market, a large transaction can be completed in a matter of minutes.

exchanges through clearinghouse systems. Third, profits and losses in trades are settled daily.[10] Fourth, futures contracts require depositing a small amount of "margin" money in the exchange as collateral. Through these arrangements, futures contracts significantly reduce the credit or default risk entailed in forward transactions. Liquidity is also better in many cases than it is for forward contracts because of the standardization of contracts.

Futures contracts cover the same hedging activities as forward contracts. For instance, as in the example given for a forward cover, the exporter can sell deutsche mark futures contracts instead of purchasing the dollars for the deutsche marks through a forward contract. The size of a deutsche mark futures contract traded in the Chicago Mercantile Exchange is DM125,000. To hedge the DM2 million revenue, the exporter needs sixteen futures contracts (DM125,000 × 16 = DM2 million) that mature in six months.[11] The price of the futures contract is quoted as $0.50 to DM1 (currency futures prices are quoted in dollars against another currency). Six months later, the gain or loss in the deutsche mark export revenue arising from changes in the exchange rate is offset by the cumulative loss or gain in the futures contracts.

The major differences from forward contracts are as follows: First, gains and losses are settled daily, requiring the transfer of cash to and

Table 4-3. Examples of Specifications for Futures Contracts

	Eurodollar futures (Chicago Mercantile Exchange)	Gold futures (Commodity Exchange, New York)
Contract size	US$1 million.	100 troy ounces.
Price quotation	Quoted in terms of a price index (100 minus rate of interest).[a]	Dollars per troy ounce.[d]
Settlement	In cash. Final settlement price at maturity is determined according to the London interbank offered rate (LIBOR) on three-month Eurodollar time deposits prevailing on last day of trading.	Physical delivery.
Deliverable grade	Not applicable.	Refined gold, assaying not less than 995 fineness, cast either in one bar or in three 1-kilogram bars and bearing a serial number and stamp of a refiner approved and listed by the exchange.
Delivery months	March, June, September, and December.[b]	The current month, the next two months, and February, April, June, August, October, and December.[e]

Last day of trading	Second London business day prior to third Wednesday of delivery month.	Third to the last business day of delivery month.
Minimum price change	1/100th of one percentage point.[c]	Price changes are registered in multiples of 10 cents per troy ounce.
Daily price limit	None.	$10 per troy ounce above or below closing price of preceding business day. Price limits do not apply to prices for current delivery month.

Note: Eurodollar futures contracts are also traded on the Singapore International Monetary Exchange (SIMEX), the London International Financial Futures Exchange (LIFFE), and the Tokyo International Financial Futures Exchange (TIFFE). The same contract specification is applied, except for some minor differences.

a. For example, the price index is quoted as 91.25 for an 8.75 percent interest rate.

b. Contracts maturing in each of these months are available up to thirty-five months out.

c. This means that the minimum price change in the price index is 0.01.

d. For example, the price is quoted as 400.00 (for $400) then 400.10, 400.20, 400.30, and so on.

e. Contracts maturing in each of these months are available up to twenty-three months out.

Source: Chicago Mercantile Exchange and Commodity Exchange.

from the exchange almost every day. Second, the exporter has to deposit margin money in the exchange. Third, credit risks are significantly reduced. Futures contracts are available for major currencies, interest rates, and commodities. For currencies, contracts are available in U.S. exchanges for Australian dollars, British pounds, Canadian dollars, deutsche marks, French francs, Japanese yen, Swiss francs, and European currency units—all against the U.S. dollar. Major futures contracts in U.S. exchanges for interest rates include U.S. Treasury bills, notes, and bonds; mortgage-backed securities; British gilts; and Eurodollar, Euromark, Eurosterling, and Euroyen deposits. Commodity contracts are available for gold, silver, and platinum and for such industrial commodities as aluminum, copper, lead, nickel, heating oil, propane, gasoline, and crude oil. Numerous contracts are also available for agricultural commodities. A list of selected commodity futures contracts traded in the U.S. exchanges is presented in table 4-4.

Table 4-4. *Selected Commodity Futures Contracts*

Commodity	Exchange	Contract size	Open interest[a]
Cocoa	CSCE	10 metric tons	49,482
Coffee	CSCE	37,500 pounds	31,016
Copper	COMEX	25,000 pounds	32,848
Corn	CBT	5,000 bushels	170,404
Cotton	CTN	50,000 pounds	44,467
Crude oil	NYMEX	1,000 barrels	262,959
Gold	COMEX	100 troy ounces	143,815
Silver	COMEX	5,000 troy ounces	88,700
Soybeans	CBT	5,000 bushels	100,617
Sugar	CSCE	112,000 pounds	167,624
Wheat[b]	CBT	5,000 bushels	52,486
	KC	5,000 bushels	134,705
	MPLS	5,000 bushels	9,970

CBT   Chicago Board of Trade
COMEX   Commodity Exchange, New York
CSCE   Coffee, Sugar, and Cocoa Exchange, New York
CTN   New York Cotton Exchange
KC   Kansas City Board of Trade
MPLS   Minneapolis Grain Exchange
NYMEX   New York Mercantile Exchange

Note: Table includes relatively liquid futures contracts traded on U.S. exchanges that may be relevant to developing countries.

a. The number of contracts outstanding as of December 9, 1989.

b. Wheat futures contracts on the CBT, the KC, and the MPLS differ in terms of deliverable grades of wheat.

Source: Commodity Futures Trading Commission (1989).

OPTION CONTRACTS. An option is the right to purchase or sell a certain asset at a preset price on (or before) a specified date. A buyer of the option owns the right to buy or sell and a seller (or "writer") of the option gives the right to a buyer. A number of technical terms are involved in options transactions:

- If an option gives the right to buy, it is a "call" option; if an option gives the right to sell, it is a "put" option.
- The asset on which the option is written is the "underlying" asset.
- The price at which a buyer of the option can buy or sell the underlying asset is called the "strike" or "exercise" price.
- If the right to buy or sell is exercised by the buyer, the option is "exercised."
- The date on (or before) which the buyer can buy or sell the underlying asset is called the "maturity" or "expiration."
- An option that can be exercised only on the expiration date is called a "European" option; one that can be exercised either on or before the expiration date is an "American" option.
- The price of the option is called a "premium." The buyer pays the premium to the seller at the time of contracting.

In the example given for a forward cover the exporter can hedge by buying a call option on U.S. dollars against deutsche marks (or, equivalently, buying a put option on deutsche marks) instead of using forward or futures contracts.[12] Suppose the exporter purchases a European put option on DM2 million with an exercise price of 2 deutsche marks to the dollar and a maturity of six months. The premium of this option is quoted as 1 percent of the contracted amount, that is, 1 percent of DM2 million, or DM20,000, which is $10,000 at the current spot rate of 2 deutsche marks to the dollar. If the deutsche mark depreciates to 3 to the dollar, the exporter will exercise this option to sell the DM2 million at 2 deutsche marks to the dollar and receive $1 million. If the deutsche mark appreciates to parity with the dollar, the exporter will instead sell the DM2 million in the spot market for $2 million, making an extra $1 million. If the deutsche mark is unchanged, the exporter will sell the DM2 million for $1 million by either exercising the option or trading in the spot market. The DM20,000 premium will have been paid at the beginning in any case.

Options have three characteristics that distinguish them from forward and futures contracts. First, unlike forward or futures contracts in which the future price is locked in, options contracts limit the maximum loss (equal to the premium paid up front), but leave an opportunity to take advantage of favorable price movements. Second, the buyer of an option has to pay the premium up front. This often requires a significant amount of cash at the time of purchase. Third, although the buyer of an option faces a credit or default risk by the counterparty, the seller does not. It is the seller who is liable, not the buyer.

There are liquid markets for options on currencies with short-term maturities. These options are traded both in formal exchanges, as futures, and informally, as forwards. Options on currency futures are also available on some exchanges (for instance, the Chicago Mercantile Exchange and the Singapore International Monetary Exchange). Long-term options on currencies are not actively traded.

Interest rate options also have liquid markets. There are two forms: options on interest rate–bearing securities (such as U.S. Treasury bonds) and options on interest rates themselves. The latter are known as "caps" (call options) and "floors" (put options), both of which are, in effect, a series of options maturing on different dates. For commodities, options on physical commodities and options on commodity futures are available only for short-term maturities. The most actively traded contracts are on gold, silver, and oil. Long-term options are traded over the counter primarily on gold, silver, and oil, but the markets are not very active.

SWAP CONTRACTS. A swap contract is an agreement to exchange, or swap, specified cash flows at fixed intervals. This means that a swap contract can be viewed as a series of forward contracts lined up on a schedule. For example, one party delivers a specified amount of a currency in exchange for another currency on every date specified in the currency swap. Returning to the example given for a forward cover, assume that the exporter and the German company agree on a long-term export contract in which the German company pays DM2 million for goods every six months over the next five years. Assume also that the exporter wants to lock in the dollar value of these revenues now. The exporter now enters into a currency swap contract with a U.S. bank. The U.S. bank agrees to pay $1 million every six months for the next five years to the exporter: the exporter agrees to pay DM2 million on the same dates when the bank pays the dollars over the five years. Thus, the currency swap contract is, in effect, a series of ten forward contracts lined up over the next five years. In interest rate swaps, two parties agree to exchange floating interest and fixed interest payments.

Swap contracts, therefore, have the same characteristics as forward contracts: no cash is required at the beginning[13] and there is credit risk. Markets for both currency and interest rate swaps have good liquidity. The maturities can generally be extended up to ten years. Transactions are made through traders and brokers. Swaps often accompany bond issues in Euromarkets.

Instruments to Manage Commodity Risk

COMMODITY SWAPS. Commodity swap contracts are the most recent development in the swap market. Markets for commodity swaps are not yet very active but have been growing. Swaps are available primarily for gold, silver, and crude oil. Copper, aluminum, nickel, zinc, and jet fuel can also be swapped, but the markets are thinner.

Commodity swaps are basically the same as currency and interest rate swaps. But a commodity swap is not exactly a series of commodity forward contracts. A commodity swap does not involve deliveries of physical commodities;[14] transactions are purely financial, as shown in the following example.

Assume that an oil producer wants to lock in the price of oil exports for the next five years, and will export 1 million barrels a year. The producer arranges the following commodity swap agreement with a commercial bank.

Commodity:	Oil
Amount:	The U.S. dollar equivalent of 1 million barrels of oil every year
Payor of fixed price:	Commercial bank
Payor of floating price:	Oil producer
Tenor:	Five years, with annual payments
Fixed price:	$17.00 a barrel
Floating price:	The average daily closing spot price of the North Sea Brent Oil Market over the year preceding each payment date
Settlement:	Netting-out.

In this example, the oil producer sells oil to the third party from time to time at the spot price, but the revenues for the next five years are effectively fixed at a price of $17.00 (see table 4-5).

Note that the oil producer has hedged its cash flows from oil sales. Even if the price of oil declines to, say, $8.00 a barrel, the producer's total revenues stay the same. The reduced risk may improve the producer's credit rating and thus lower the cost of financing working capital or provide access to new lenders. This point will be clear as we examine commodity-linked loans.

COMMODITY-LINKED LOANS. In these loans, interest or repayment amounts or both are linked to the price of a certain commodity or to a commodity price index. In a popular form of commodity-linked loans, interest and principal are paid in equal installments, the amount of which

Table 4-5. *Commodity Swap and Producer's Payoff on the U.S. Dollar Equivalent of 1 Million Barrels of Oil*
(millions of dollars except as noted)

Year	Oil price (dollars per barrel)[a]	Export revenue[b]	Commodity swap		OP's payoff	Settlement by "netting out"[e]	
			OP → CB (Floating)[c]	CB → OP (Fixed)[d]		OP → CB	CB → OP
1	18	18	18	17	17	1	0
2	16	16	16	17	17	0	1
3	12	12	12	17	17	0	5
4	10	10	10	17	17	0	7
5	8	8	8	17	17	0	9

OP Oil producer and exporter
CB Commercial bank
a. Hypothetical oil price per barrel during the year.
b. Producer's revenue from the export of 1 million barrels of oil at spot prices.
c. Calculated by multiplying 1 million barrels by a floating oil price.
d. Based on a fixed price of $17.00 per barrel.
e. Cash flows of the oil swap if the "netting-out" arrangement is used for settlements.
Source: Author's calculations.

is linked to the cash equivalent of a certain quantity of a commodity. In another popular case, only the interest payments are linked to a commodity price. In any case, a commodity-linked loan combines a conventional bank loan with a commodity swap. A commodity-linked loan or a conventional bank loan and a commodity swap will both yield the same financial results,[15] as seen in the following example.

A copper producer requires a $1 million capital investment to increase production capacity. But the success of the project depends on future copper prices. Copper is currently $1 per pound. If the expansion is financed by a bank loan, a decline in copper prices will adversely affect the producer's ability to repay the loan. The producer takes out the following copper-linked loan with a French commercial bank.

Lender:	French bank
Borrower:	Copper producer
Commodity:	Copper
Principal amount:	$1 million (equivalent to the value of 1 million pounds of copper at the current price)
Tenor:	Five years, with semiannual installments
Repayment schedule:	Ten semiannual payments of the U.S. dollar equivalent of 130,000 pounds of copper (multiplied by the reference price)
Reference price:	The average daily closing cash copper price in the London Metal Exchange over the six months preceding each repayment date.

The loan can be repaid regardless of the copper price over the next five years because the loan is effectively denominated in copper (see table 4-6).

The same result can be achieved with a conventional bank loan and a copper swap. The producer borrows $1 million from a U.S. commercial bank, to be repaid in ten semiannual installments of $130,000 over the next five years.[16] A parallel copper swap for 130,000 pounds with the French bank covers the fixing of the effective copper price received at $1 a pound, equal to the annual debt service.

With the $130,000 received from the French bank through the copper swap, the copper producer repays the loan semiannually. A floating amount is paid semiannually to the French bank in exchange for the fixed payment of $130,000. The financial result is the same as with the copper-linked loan.

COMMODITY BONDS. A commodity bond can be either a forward type or an option type. In the former, principal or coupons or both are linked to the price of a certain commodity or to a commodity price index.

Table 4-6. *Copper-linked Loan Repayment Cash Flows on $1 Million Lent When Copper Cost $1.00 a Pound*

Repayment period[a]	Copper price[b]	Cash to be repaid at end of the period[c] CP → FB
Year 1-1	1.05	136,500
1-2	0.92	119,600
Year 2-1	0.88	114,400
2-2	0.77	100,100
Year 3-1	0.90	117,000
3-2	1.02	132,600
Year 4-1	1.12	145,600
4-2	1.23	159,900
Year 5-1	1.07	139,100
5-2	0.91	118,300

CP Copper producer
FB French bank
a. Payments are semiannual; 1-1 denotes first half of year 1, and so on.
b. Hypothetical copper price per pound during the period.
c. Calculated by multiplying 130,000 pounds by the copper price for the period.
Source: Author's calculations.

If only the principal payment (redemption value) is linked to a commodity price, this bond is, in effect, a security in which a conventional bond and a commodity forward contract are combined. If the coupon payments are also linked to a commodity price, the bond is a combination of a conventional bond and a commodity swap. The forward-type bonds are often issued by commodity producers for risk hedging.

The option-type bond combines a conventional bond with commodity options. In this case, a holder of the bond owns the right to buy or sell a certain commodity at a certain exercise price in addition to a conventional bond. The option-type bonds are often used to lower the cost of financing (lower coupons) by attaching long-term options written on a commodity.

Consider an example in which a gold-producing developing country issues forward-type bonds in the Eurobond market in order to raise $50 million. The bonds are linked to the price of gold, which is $400 a troy ounce.

Issuer:	Gold-producing country
Face value of bond:	$1,000
Amount to be raised:	$50 million ($1,000 × 50,000 bonds)
Issue price:	$1,000 per bond
Maturity:	Ten years

Coupon payment: Annual payments of the dollar equivalent of 0.25 troy ounces of gold (multiplied by the reference price) per bond

Reference price: The average daily London morning fixing price of gold over the last year preceding each coupon payment date

Redemption: The dollar equivalent of 2.5 troy ounces of gold (multiplied by the reference price).

The 50,000 gold bonds carrying a $1,000 face value are issued. Thus, 12,500 troy ounces (0.25 troy ounces × 50,000) of gold are necessary for the annual coupon payment, and 125,000 troy ounces (2.5 troy ounces × 50,000) are required for redemption. Based on a current gold price of $400 a troy ounce, the coupon rate of the bond is 10 percent ($400 × 0.25 troy ounces = $100, or 10 percent of the face value).[17] The country can service the debt from gold exports regardless of the gold price over the ten years. Annual gold exports of 12,500 troy ounces, or approximately 390 kilograms, are necessary for coupon payments; 3.9 tons are required for redemption.

Bonds linked to commodity prices have been issued primarily on gold and oil, although some have been issued for silver, copper, and nickel.

The Importance of Financial Instruments in Risk Management

Forward, futures, option, and swap contracts are important for risk management activities in three respects. First, these instruments give governments flexible ways to hedge. Imagine that a country carries a floating rate debt with a five-year maturity but wants to hedge against the risk of rising interest rates only for the next nine months. It is difficult to find ways to accomplish this particular task other than using forward or futures contracts. These instruments are specifically designed to manage the risk exposure of the underlying assets or liabilities. By using these instruments the risk characteristics of the underlying assets (or liabilities) can be effectively altered without either renegotiating the terms and conditions of the existing debt or increasing the reserve holding at the central bank. In addition, a hedging activity with these instruments can be terminated relatively quickly because transactions to reverse the original position can be made easily. Second, these instruments provide active markets that would not otherwise be available for risk-hedging activities. For example, futures contracts provide active markets where short-term hedging transactions can be arranged in a matter of minutes. Swap contracts have added remarkable opportunities in long-term hedging activities. Third, these instruments, especially options, offer an unconventional risk profile. Options provide nonlinear risk exposure: one can limit the maximum loss but take advantage of favorable price movements. Imagine that an oil-producing country wants to hedge against declining prices of oil but wants to take advantage of any rise in prices. The country may not be willing to enter into a long-term sales contract at a fixed price but may be willing to purchase oil option (put) contracts. Options and the other instruments enable financial institutions to provide "financial engineering" services. That is, they can use sophisticated instruments designed to fit users' specific needs. The developing countries could take advantage of financial engineering to design appropriate instruments to suit specific risk management needs.

With an appropriate mix of commodity-linked schemes, developing countries can reduce the effects of external shocks and improve investment and project planning for economic development. Additionally, commodity-linked schemes may provide access to financial markets that would not otherwise be available. An improved ability to service debts improves a country's creditworthiness, which may lead to better financing terms (cheaper cost, longer terms) on commodity-linked as well as conventional types of financing.

Applying Modern Financial Techniques

Recent Examples in Developing Countries

Some developing countries have begun to use modern financial instruments.[18] Examples described below include Eurodollar futures contracts (Chile); currency and interest rate swaps (India and Thailand); currency options (India, Indonesia, and Turkey); a loan with a copper swap (Mexico); and a loan with oil options (Algeria).[19]

HEDGING WITH EURODOLLAR FUTURES CONTRACTS. The Central Bank of Chile uses Eurodollar futures to manage the risk of nominal interest rate fluctuations on dollar-denominated external debt. In 1988 and 1989, to reduce the uncertainty of its variable interest rate debt with commercial banks, the bank carried out short-term hedging operations with Eurodollar futures contracts on the International Monetary Market of the Chicago Mercantile Exchange.[20]

Chile's external debt carries considerable U.S. dollar interest rate risk. As of December 1987 about 83 percent of its total $18 billion[21] medium- and long-term debt consisted of variable rate loans, mostly tied to the six-month London interbank offered rate (LIBOR) (World Bank 1989). Of this amount, $13.8 billion is owed to commercial banks. About 90 percent of the total medium- and long-term debt is denominated in U.S. dollars. As part of the 1987 debt restructuring and financing package reached with a consortium of foreign banks, approximately $9 billion of debt was converted from loans tied to the six-month LIBOR to those tied to the one-year LIBOR. Interest rates were to be reset at various dates in February, March, and April 1988.

The Central Bank hedged about $1.5 billion of Chile's $9 billion debt, of which the Central Bank's direct obligations amounted to $3.5 billion. For the February and March reset dates, the Central Bank sold March 1988 Eurodollar futures contracts; for April 1988 it sold June 1988 futures contracts. The size of a Eurodollar futures contract is $1 million and the contracts are traded for three-month interest rates. To hedge against the one-year interest rate on the $1.5 billion debt, approximately 6,000 contracts, or $6 billion worth of three-month Eurodollar futures contracts, were necessary. Hedging every $1 million debt required $4 million Eurodollar futures (or four contracts) because a percentage point rise in a one-year interest rate results in four times as much increase in interest costs of the debt as a percentage point rise in a three-month interest rate (because the period covered is four times longer).

The sale of futures contracts was spread over more than three weeks. The Central Bank closed the position by buying back the contracts within a week of each interest reset date, for an effective LIBOR of 7.3 percent. The LIBOR would have been as high as 7.8 percent without the hedging. An initial margin of $1,500 per contract was required by the exchange. About $9 million in cash and U.S. Treasury bills was deposited for this purpose. The brokerage fee was $30 per contract (round-trip),[22] or approximately $180,000 (0.012 percent of $1.5 billion).[23] The Central Bank is said to have carried out similar hedging operations in 1990.

Several developing countries have occasionally used currency and interest rate swaps as well as currency options. India and Thailand have been frequently reported in finance journals as users of swap schemes, whereas India, Indonesia, and Turkey have used dual currency loans (loans with currency options).[24]

CURRENCY AND INTEREST RATE SWAPS. Currency and interest rate swaps are typically used in two ways: first, to hedge an existing risk by contracting a swap, and second, to obtain a desirable liability structure by contracting new debt and a swap at the same time. For example, a country may arrange a swap in such a way that the timing of cash flows in a swap matches the payment dates on the existing asset or liability. Or a country may borrow in one currency and enter into a swap transaction in which repayment cash flows are exchanged for another currency.

Thailand has used both types of swaps. The Ministry of Finance has arranged with U.S. and Japanese banks to exchange floating interest payments for fixed interest payments (or fixed interest payments for floating interest payments). In March 1988 the Ministry of Finance invited several U.S. commercial banks to bid for two (seven-year) U.S. dollar fixed-floating interest swaps of about $70 million. Although Thailand does not disclose its swap transactions, the country is known in the international financial community for this type of transaction.

Thailand also uses swaps with new borrowing. Thailand wanted to tap the deutsche mark and Swiss franc bond markets but preferred to repay part of the debt in another currency. In mid-1988 Thailand issued the first public Euro–deutsche mark bond for DM200 million and the first public Euro–Swiss franc bond for SwF200 million. The deutsche mark bond, managed by Commerzbank and Deutsche Bank, had a maturity of five years, with 5.75 percent annual coupon payments; the Swiss franc bond had a seven-year maturity with a 4.625 percent coupon. The deutsche mark and Swiss franc cash flows to service these bonds were partly swapped to achieve repayments effectively denominated in another currency (U.S. dollars). In another example, the Industrial Bank of Japan provided 13 billion yen in 1988 for the Electricity Generating Authority and the Petroleum Authority of Thailand, of which 8 billion yen was swapped for U.S. dollars to be effectively denominated in U.S. dollars.

Many Indian agencies and public sector firms, such as the Industrial Development Bank of India, the Export-Import Bank of India, the Industrial Credit and Investment Corporation of India, and Air India, have used swap transactions. It is estimated that swaps having a total worth of up to $1 billion were completed during 1988–90. These transactions include the following: yen fixed interest into yen floating interest, yen fixed interest into dollar fixed interest, and sterling fixed interest into dollar floating interest. Most of the swaps have reportedly only applied to the interest portion of liabilities.

DUAL CURRENCY LOANS. A dual currency loan is a loan with a currency option on the principal (or a part of the principal). There are three types of dual currency loans. In the first type, a loan is made in one currency, but the lender has the right to choose, at maturity, whether to accept the repayment of the principal in the original currency or in another currency at a prespecified exchange rate. From the viewpoint of the lender, this loan is a combination of a conventional loan and the purchase from the borrower of a currency option written on the principal payment. The second type involves a conventional loan and the sale of a currency option by the lender: the borrower has the right to choose the repayment currency at a prespecified exchange rate. In the third type, the borrower has the right to choose the currency of the loan at the time of drawing and has to repay in that currency.

Whenever the lender has the right to choose the repayment currency, the risk to the borrower tends to increase rather than decline: the borrower's cost may be less because of the sale of the currency option, but the borrower is open to loss if the lender exercises the option. For example, a $100 million dual currency (dollar–deutsche mark) loan requires the borrower to repay in deutsche marks if the currency appreciates above a set level. Unless the borrower can reasonably expect deutsche mark revenues that exceed the amount required to repay at maturity, the borrower is exposed to the risk added by the loan. This type of loan does not provide downside protection against exchange rate fluctuations. Nonetheless, many developing countries use dual currency loans of the first type, primarily because of the cost reduction derived from the sale of the option. The examples below describe several loans of the first type and one of the third type.

The Central Bank of Turkey frequently uses dollar–deutsche mark loans, because it can expect ample deutsche mark revenues from workers' remittances from Germany. Turkey agreed to a $100 million dual currency, syndicated loan in March 1988. The loan had a three-year maturity, with a deutsche mark option written on the $100 million principal. The premium from the sale of the deutsche mark option was used to reduce the cost of funding. As a result the loan carried a floating interest rate of 0.015 percent over LIBOR without any front-end fee. If it had been a conventional loan, the Central Bank would have paid 1.25 percent over LIBOR.

Air India and the Industrial Finance Corporation of India have also used this type of loan. In the case of Air India, a two-year deutsche mark option on $50 million was attached to a syndicated loan of $150 million. The option had an exercise price of about DM1.70 to the dollar and the option premium was used to pay the front-end fee. Accordingly, the loan carried a floating interest of 0.1875 percent over LIBOR for the first two years and 0.25 percent over LIBOR thereafter, with no front-end fee. The Industrial Finance Corporation of India used the same scheme with the Swiss franc as the second currency.

Indonesia used the third type (in which the borrower chooses the currency of drawing) several times for syndicated loans with Japanese banks. In October 1988 Indonesia contracted a 40 billion yen, Euroyen revolving credit facility for three years. In this facility, Indonesia could draw up to 40 billion yen or its dollar equivalent for three years. Once the loan was drawn down, it would become a conventional (yen or dollar) loan, with an eight-year maturity and a five-year grace period, and with a floating interest rate of 0.5 percent over LIBOR for the first three years and 0.625 percent over LIBOR thereafter. The front-end fee was 0.5 percent of the principal, and the commitment fee was 0.25 percent. The all-in cost was slightly higher than those of conventional loans because of the option feature. The loan gave the government an opportunity to choose the currency denomination of the debt over three years. Thus it provided Indonesia with an opportunity for better management of the external debt to avoid repeating the experience in servicing debt that was denominated in an expensive currency (yen).

A LOAN WITH A COPPER SWAP. Although the following scheme was used by a private company (in Mexico), it has significant implications for the management of country risk. A $210 million financing package with a copper swap was developed in 1989 by the New York branch of Banque Paribas for Mexicana de Cobre S.A. de C.V. (MdC), a copper mining subsidiary of Grupo Mexico (see Banque Paribas 1989). The syndicated loan, managed by Paribas, had a term of thirty-eight months and a fixed interest rate of 3 percent above three-year LIBOR (as determined by Paribas). The twelve equal quarterly payments started in December 1989. To eliminate MdC's copper price risk, a copper swap was attached to the loan, establishing a fixed price over the life of the loan for a portion of MdC's copper production. The proceeds of the loan were used to refinance the debt that was assumed when MdC went public and was acquired by Grupo Mexico in November 1988.

Because of the Mexican company's high credit risk, Paribas had to reduce the copper price risk and the payment risk. The copper price would directly affect MdC's earnings, and these earnings would have to be available for repayments over the life of the loan. To deal with the copper price risk, Paribas introduced a copper swap. The payment risk was covered by establishing an escrow account and a long-term sales contract with a copper user.

Paribas entered into a copper swap with MdC through its London branch. The scheme used is similar to the scheme described under "Commodity-linked loans" above. MdC agreed to pay Paribas an amount based on the floating copper price it received for its exported copper (the price being based on the daily prices for copper on the London Metal Exchange), and Paribas agreed to pay MdC an amount based on a fixed price for the thirty-eight-month term of the loan. Paribas's fixed payment amount under the swap was matched with the amount necessary for the periodic loan repayments. Thus, the copper swap enabled MdC to ensure that it had funds sufficient to repay the loan, regardless of the copper price over the following three years.

To mitigate the payment risk, a long-term contract with a copper user and an escrow account were established. SOGEM S.A., a subsidiary of

Figure 4-1. *Mexicana de Cobre–Paribas Scheme: Cash Flows with Regard to Loan Repayments*

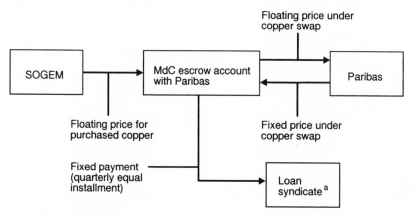

a. Paribas acts as the lead manager.

Société Generale de Belgique, agreed to monthly purchases of 4,000 metric tons of copper anodes for the period of the loan from MdC's "La Caridad" mining and smelting complex located in the northwestern Mexican state of Sonora. The amount contracted to be purchased accounted for about one-third of MdC's copper anode production. SOGEM promised to pay into an escrow account established by Paribas an amount based on the average price for copper on the London Metal Exchange. Under the copper swap agreement, Paribas paid the fixed payment amount quarterly into the escrow account and drew the floating payment amount. Finally, the quarterly repayments to the participants of the syndication were made from the escrow account. In this way, sufficient funds to repay the loan were secured through the escrow account. Figure 4-1 illustrates the entire scheme. The scheme, together with MdC's history of excellent operating performance and Mexico's favorable economic reform policy, made possible the first voluntary lending to Mexico's private sector in hard currency since 1982.

A LOAN WITH OIL OPTIONS. Algeria's state-owned hydrocarbon concern, Sonatrach, entered into a loan agreement with a syndicate of international banks in November 1989. The loan, coordinated by Chase Investment Bank, London, consisted of a $100 million conventional floating rate loan (with a seven-year maturity and a four-year grace period) and a series of oil option transactions.[25] With this scheme Algeria reentered the medium-term syndicated loan market at a significantly reduced cost. The agreement was for Sonatrach to pay an interest rate of 1 percent above LIBOR over the life of the loan. Without the scheme the cost would have been 3 to 4 percent above LIBOR. The proceeds of the loan were used to replace expensive (4 percent above LIBOR) short-term loans, thus reducing Sonatrach's cost of interest service.

To reduce Sonatrach's cost of funding, two special arrangements were added to the loan. First, Sonatrach sold Chase four call options written on oil.[26] By selling the options, Sonatrach reduced the cost of funding, just as Turkey did in the dual currency loan mentioned earlier. Oil options were used instead of currency options because oil is Sonatrach's major source of revenue. In this arrangement Sonatrach will have to pay Chase a certain amount of cash if the price of oil rises above a pre-specified ceiling (for example, $23 per barrel). This arrangement may not significantly increase Sonatrach's risk, because its revenue also will increase to cover this additional cost. In short, by selling the oil options Sonatrach traded some upside potential in its oil export revenue for an immediate reduction in the cost of funding. Sonatrach will pay 1 percent above LIBOR over the life of the loan except for this contingent obligation.[27]

The second arrangement was designed by Chase to form the syndicate successfully. To bring in other banks, Chase provided the syndicate with an opportunity for additional profits from oil price movements. Without this arrangement, the 1 percent margin above LIBOR from Sonatrach might have been too low for other banks to take part in the syndicate. Chase will pay the syndicate an additional interest margin above LIBOR if the price of oil rises above or falls below a prespecified price range. What the syndicate will receive is an interest rate from Sonatrach of 1 percent above LIBOR and an extra interest margin from Chase of 0.125 percent for a $1 move in the price of oil (if the price moves substantially). Note that this arrangement does not affect Sonatrach's payments: the extra margins are to be provided by Chase. The arrangement would have increased Chase's oil price risk, but Chase eliminated the risk through complicated transactions in the options market. Details of the arrangement are illustrated in figure 4-2.

Issues in Using Financial Instruments

Three major factors have impeded the use of financial instruments by many developing countries: the financial market's adverse perception of the countries' creditworthiness; the high cost of risk management instruments; and the lack of an institutional framework for risk management operations.

Figure 4-2. *Sonatrach-Chase Scheme: Option Transactions*

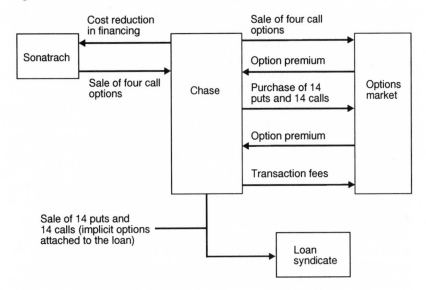

Forward, swap, and option contracts involve a consideration of the counterparty's creditworthiness. A forward contract exposes the counterparty to the risk of loss if the country defaults on its payment obligation during the life of the contract. The longer the performance period (the length of a forward contract), the greater the credit risk (Folkerts-Landau 1989). A swap contract essentially involves a series of forward contracts. In an option contract the buyer is exposed to the performance risk of the seller because the option seller solely bears the obligation to carry out the contract.

Active participants in the markets for these instruments—major international banks—generally have internal guidelines for handling exposures to country risk. These banks often prefer rationing access to charging a risk premium, depending on their perception of a particular country's credit risk. For a high-risk country, the banks allow no credit line for any transaction. They may set a small credit line for lending operations for a less risky country. If a marginally creditworthy country is interested in instruments such as forward, swap, and option contracts, the banks set credit lines for these instruments, within the limit of a total credit line.[28] Thus for some countries, use of these instruments depletes the credit line for funding operations. This banking practice has been effectively blocking many developing countries' access to the markets for these instruments.

A country's risk management efforts could supplement its macro-economic adjustment program by improving its creditworthiness. Risk management may be seen as a means of increasing a country's ability to repay its external debt. Commodity-linked financing could be a tool for a country to regain access to financial markets, because commodity-linked financing schemes contain a component to reduce risk—as shown in the examples from Mexico and Algeria.

In addition to commodity-linked schemes, other schemes have been developed by the financial market to alleviate credit risk, one scheme being marked-to-market swaps. Marked-to-market swaps, which have a component like a future, were developed by international banks to reduce the credit risk in conventional swap contracts. Under a marked-to-market swap a cash payment is made periodically (for example, every six months) to settle a gain or loss in the market value of that particular swap, just as a price gain or loss is settled daily in a futures contract. Therefore, the performance period can be shortened from the whole life of the swap contract (for example, five years) to the next settlement date of the swap (for example, six months).[29] This shortened performance period has significant implications for the banks' calculations of risk exposure.

The cost of risk management instruments may be an impediment to using them for countries that have already had problems in raising funds. Purchases of options, caps, and floors (the last two being a series of options) require a significant premium up front. Although the premium value of these instruments depends on the price volatility of the underlying asset, the exercise price, and other factors, it usually accounts for a significant portion of the amount of the underlying asset to be hedged.

The cost of a premium can be reduced by combining the sale of options with the purchase of options necessary for hedging risk. For example, if an oil-exporting developing country wants to buy options for hedging against a decline in the price of oil below $16 a barrel, it can buy put options on oil with an exercise price of $16 and at the same time sell call options on oil with an exercise price of, say, $24. A part or all of the premium cost for the put options can be recovered by the sale of call options. It is important to note, however, that the country effectively gives up a part of the upside potential of its future oil revenues by selling the call options. As described in the case of Algeria, the sale of call options implies trading future profit opportunities for the immediate revenue from option premiums. Therefore, proper risk assessment is critical when selling options.

Finally, risk management activities require considerable knowledge of these instruments and an appropriate institutional framework within which to carry out hedging operations. Considerable expertise is required in understanding the risk structure of the economy, identifying appropriate instruments, and making or supervising transactions. Setting up an appropriate institutional structure to undertake these tasks also requires a thorough understanding of the nature of risks and risk management instruments. Unfortunately, many developing countries lack the expertise for these operations. Substantial investments in information systems and human resources are necessary to train staff; to introduce adequate reporting, recording, monitoring, and evaluating mechanisms; and to establish internal control procedures.

Conclusion

The main purpose of asset and liability management is to make the consideration of price risk explicit and to enable decisionmakers to control risk exposure. The objective of a country's asset and liability management should be to minimize adverse changes in future net cash flows from international transactions; it is the variance of future net cash flows—or economic exposure—that should be hedged. By quantifying the sensitivity of a country's economic performance to changes in international prices, and by carrying out appropriate hedging activities to reduce risk, asset and liability management can reduce the adverse effects of external shocks and complement the country's development planning or structural adjustment process.

Recently developed financial products and techniques, including forward, futures, swap, and option contracts as well as commodity-linked schemes, can be used as hedging tools for a country's asset and liability management. These financial instruments provide flexibility, liquidity, and unique risk-hedging characteristics.

The applications described here illustrate how developing countries can use these techniques. The case studies from Mexico and Algeria, for example, show how a commodity-linked scheme can improve a country's creditworthiness and enable it to regain access to the international financial market. These and other cases that were presented provide an understanding of the costs and benefits of using modern financial techniques. By examining these cases, risk managers may see specific financial schemes that fit their country's needs.

Notes

1. Net interest income is the difference between the total revenue on interest-bearing assets and the total expense on interest-bearing liabilities. Net interest margin is also used as an objective function in asset and liability management. It is derived by dividing net interest income by interest-bearing assets or total assets.

2. In a financial institution's asset and liability management, primary attention is paid

to the "match" of the maturity structures of its assets and liabilities. If mismatches of maturities (interest rate repricing periods) between assets and liabilities exist, the institution is exposed to interest rate risks. Toevs and Haney (1986) present a good description of techniques that financial institutions use to control these risks—techniques such as the "maturity gap" method and the "duration gap" method.

3. External shocks may affect quantities as well as prices. Asset and liability management cannot eliminate quantity risks such as an export shortfall.

4. It is implicitly assumed here that the country does not take a view on the price movements of a particular asset or commodity and that it focuses on minimizing risk under the expected value of future cash flows.

5. This is not to say that these instruments are more effective in managing risks than the others are. Instruments may complement each other. For example, the short- and medium-term use of financial instruments may complement export diversification that has a long time horizon.

6. All dollar amounts in this volume are current U.S. dollars unless otherwise indicated.

7. For convenience and simplicity the spot and forward rates are assumed to be the same. Pricing theories and mechanisms of the financial instruments are not discussed here. There are numerous publications on these issues. Cox and Rubinstein (1985), Grabbe (1986), and Figlewski (1986) contain a good description with respect to both theory and practice.

8. The expression "3 × 6" (stated as "three against six") means the period starting three months from now and ending six months from now.

9. The actual market practice for settlements is different from that in this simplified case. In practice, two parties pay or receive the amount that is the difference between an FRA rate (6 percent) and a reference rate (the London interbank offered rate [LIBOR]) at the beginning of the agreed period (three months into the future), discounted by a three-month interest rate to reflect the value at the time of the agreement. Nonetheless, the financial effects are the same.

10. A futures contract is "marked to market" every day, using the closing price of the day (the "settlement price"). Profit or loss is calculated by using the settlement price, and the profit or loss is settled with clearinghouses daily. This feature prohibits the carrying over of large unrealized losses over a long period and thus reduces the risk of default.

11. Delivery dates of a futures contract are standardized in the contract specification to fall on a given day in several months of the year. Here, for simplicity the delivery date is assumed to coincide with the timing of the export revenue.

12. A call option on U.S. dollars (the right to buy U.S. dollars for deutsche marks) is a put option on deutsche marks (the right to sell deutsche marks for U.S. dollars). They are equivalent, except for the currency that is the underlying asset.

13. Some designs of currency swaps involve exchanges of cash at the beginning and/or at the end of a contract life to accommodate specific needs of users. Such cash exchanges do not, however, alter the essential nature of swaps mentioned in the text, because designs that include such exchanges can be regarded as combinations of a plain swap and cash flow transactions that occur at the beginning or end or both.

14. It should, however, be noted that the economic consequences are approximately equal to those of a series of forward contracts.

15. Legal implications are, of course, different between the two.

16. This means that the loan bears a fixed interest rate of approximately 10.42 percent a year.

17. The true yield to maturity on this bond should be calculated by using the forward rates for gold.

18. Some major oil-exporting countries, such as Saudi Arabia and the United Arab Emirates, have actively managed their cash reserves in international financial markets. This activity is not discussed here.

19. Precise pricing information is not available for some of these transactions, partly because the complete terms were not made public. Although some of the data given below may not be precise, they can be regarded as reasonably accurate.

20. The Treasurer's Office of the World Bank provided financial technical assistance for these operations. Also see International Monetary Fund (1989).

21. In this volume a billion is 1,000 million.

22. "Round-trip" means that the brokerage fee is charged when the sold (bought) contracts are bought (sold) back to close out the position, or when the contracts expire.

23. $30 × 6,000 contracts = $180,000.

24. See *International Financing Review* (various issues), *Euromoney* (various issues), and *Middle East Business Weekly* (various issues). See also World Bank (1990).

25. The International Trade Division of the World Bank provided Algeria with technical assistance for commodity-linked financing schemes.

26. The maturities of the four options are six, twelve, eighteen, and twenty-four months.

27. The scheme improved Sonatrach's creditworthiness by reducing the cost of debt service. But it did not provide direct protection against a decline in the oil price, because Sonatrach's repayments were not linked to oil prices on the down side.

28. However, the banks may raise the ceiling of a total credit line if they see the use of such instruments as improving a country's creditworthiness.

29. This chapter does not discuss details of the marked-to-market swap scheme. For theoretical and technical details, see Folkerts-Landau (1989).

5

Regulatory Aspects of Commodity-linked Finance: Implications for Developing Countries

Michael Occhiolini

Since the onset of the debt crisis in 1982, several articles in the economic literature have advocated the tying of developing-country debt repayments to fluctuations in commodity prices (see, for instance, Lessard 1986; Fischer 1989; Priovolos 1987; Besley and Powell 1989; Priovolos and Duncan 1991). A central point of these articles is that developing countries that export commodities can better match their debt service to their foreign exchange earnings by issuing commodity-linked financial instruments instead of raising capital through general-obligation loans.

Given the economic benefits, why have developing countries not participated more in these new financial markets? Clearly, a major reason is uncertainty about the creditworthiness of developing countries. Another reason, however, is uncertainty about the legal and regulatory implications of issuing such instruments in industrial countries' financial markets.

This chapter examines the legal and regulatory implications of a developing country issuing or using commodity price–linked financial

The author would like to thank Stijn Claessens for his useful help and guidance, along with Paul Gottlieb, Robert MacKay, Susan Ervin, and Ron Hobson for their helpful comments. The opinions expressed are the author's own and do not necessarily reflect those of the law firm of Wilson, Sonsini, Goodrich, and Rosati, P.C., where he is currently an associate.

instruments as a source of financing or as a method of hedging commodity price exposure. The chapter focuses mostly on the regulatory situation in the United States and to a much lesser extent in the United Kingdom.[1] Because the regulatory environment in the United States is extremely complex, the next section gives an overview of the three major U.S. regulatory authorities that have jurisdiction over the various types of commodity instruments.

The sections that then follow are structured around the three types of commodity price–linked instruments that are available: short-term, exchange-traded instruments; over-the-counter instruments; and capital market instruments (hybrids with futureslike components, hybrids with options, and trusts). The section on short-term, exchange-traded instruments examines whether there are unique requirements or restrictions for a developing country to participate in these instruments. The next section, on over-the-counter instruments, examines the trade option exemption and commodity swap contracts. These instruments are often used with capital-raising instruments. The first section on capital market instruments examines the implications of developing countries issuing hybrid financial instruments with embedded futureslike or optionlike components in the United States. A number of technical criteria must be met by such hybrid instruments, and examples are offered of instruments that would meet these criteria. The second and last section on capital market instruments describes the use of trusts. In particular, it describes the Phibro Energy Oil Trust, a trust of prepaid (crude oil) forward contracts.

The chapter then examines special exemptions, such as the Mexican Letter, which could have implications for developing countries that want to issue new-money instruments in the United States but fail to meet current CFTC requirements. The penultimate section gives a brief overview of the regulatory environment in the United Kingdom for commodity-linked finance.

An Overview of the U.S. Regulatory Environment

A number of regulatory agencies are involved in the oversight of commodity-linked financial instruments in the United States. Instruments such as commodity-indexed bonds, commodity swaps, and bonds with embedded commodity options combine elements from a variety of financial instruments that, historically, have been subject to separate regulatory control. As a result, there is often uncertainty as to which U.S. regulatory agency has jurisdiction over an innovative hybrid instrument.

It is important, therefore, to have a general understanding of the agencies that oversee financial instruments before describing the legal and regulatory implications of developing countries issuing commodity-linked instruments in the United States.

The Commodity Futures Trading Commission (CFTC), the Securities and Exchange Commission (SEC), and U.S. banking authorities are the three main bodies that regulate commodity-linked financial instruments in the United States. An instrument that is exempted from CFTC regulation is allowed to be issued in the United States but may still be subject to SEC or banking regulations. For example, a commodity-indexed bond exempt from CFTC regulation may still be subject to SEC registration requirements.

The Commodity Futures Trading Commission

As a result of the Commodity Exchange Act (CEA), the CFTC has exclusive jurisdiction over futures and commodity option contracts in the United States. Historically, Section 4 of the CEA has prohibited futures contracts not traded on, or subject to the rules of, a CFTC-regulated exchange. Section 4 has been modified, however, by the Futures Trading Practices Act of 1992 (the "1992 Futures Act"). The 1992 Futures Act grants the CFTC (for the first time) broad power to exempt certain instruments, including futures and options contracts, from the CEA if the CFTC finds that (a) the participant is an "appropriate person" as defined under the CEA and (b) the transaction will not have a material, adverse effect on the ability of the CFTC to enforce its regulatory responsibilities under the CEA.[2] The CEA's prohibition against off-exchange contracts does not extend to forward contracts, which are defined in the CEA as the ". . . sale of any cash commodity for deferred shipment or delivery."[3] The CEA does prohibit transactions involving commodity options that are not expressly authorized by CFTC regulations; with two exceptions (trade and dealer options), all commodity options have to be traded on an exchange.

For several reasons, the scope of the CFTC's jurisdiction has been the subject of debate. First, hybrid instruments combine elements of financial instruments that have traditionally fallen under separate and distinct regulatory agencies.[4] Second, an exception granted at one stage in the development of the instrument—when the instrument has a given set of attributes—may no longer be valid at later stages.[5] Third, terms like "futures" and "options" are not explicitly defined in the CEA, and disputes about whether a particular instrument is a future or an option can arise.[6] Finally, the authorizing legislation for the regulatory agencies is itself often unclear.[7]

The Securities and Exchange Commission

If a particular instrument is deemed a security, it must be registered with the SEC pursuant to Section 5 of the Securities Act of 1933, as amended (the "Securities Act"), unless there is an available exemption to registration, such as a private placement exemption. The Securities Act contains a very broad definition of "security," which is taken to include notes, stocks, bonds, debentures, and investment contracts. A developing country interested in issuing a commodity-indexed bond or note in the United States will, in the absence of an exemption, find itself subject to the registration requirements of the SEC.

The SEC allows for a number of exemptions from its registration requirements. Exemptions include U.S. government securities and municipal bonds, bank-issued or -guaranteed securities, short-term commercial paper, and private placements. SEC registration requirements in the United States are usually more extensive than registration requirements in other countries. Therefore, companies that do not need to access the U.S. capital market often decide to issue an instrument offshore to avoid the time and cost incurred for U.S. registration.

The SEC has adopted two measures to make it easier for foreign companies to access U.S. capital markets. The first measure, SEC's Rule 144A, reduces the need for qualified institutional buyers (QIBs), as defined in Rule 144A, to accompany privately placed securities with extensive protective documentation. (A QIB is a buyer that, acting for its own account or for the accounts of other QIBs, owns securities worth at least $100 million.) This rule makes the privately placed securities of foreign companies in developing countries more marketable by allowing later resale of such securities in the United States without registering these securities with the SEC. The second measure, adopted on May 2, 1990, as Regulation S of the Securities Act, provides a safe harbor from the registration requirements of the Securities Act for offers and sales of securities in offshore transactions by parties to a distribution of securities. Under Regulation S, foreign issuers are placed in one of three separate categories based on the amount of securities they plan to sell in the United States, and each of these categories has different offering and disclosure requirements.

U.S. Banking Authorities

The Board of Governors of the Federal Reserve, the Comptroller of the Currency, the Federal Deposit Insurance Corporation (FDIC), and state regulatory authorities regulate various aspects of banking activities in the

United States. The Federal Reserve regulates bank holding companies, the Comptroller of the Currency regulates nationally chartered banks, the FDIC regulates banks subject to federal deposit insurance, and authorities in the fifty states regulate state-chartered banks.

Banks sought and received permission to participate in matched and unmatched commodity price swaps, and as a result, banking regulations are particularly important for swaps. Banking authorities have generally resisted attempts by the CFTC to impose regulations on commercial banks participating in the swap market. The CFTC's decision to exempt certain swap contracts from CFTC regulation resulted in part from the recognition that banks are already subject to extensive regulation in the United States.

Banking authorities also supervise commercial bank compliance with capital adequacy requirements. Capital adequacy requirements for interest rate and currency swaps have been established under the Basle Accord, but capital adequacy requirements for commodity swaps have yet to be announced.

Jurisdictional Accord

In 1982 the chairmen of the CFTC and the SEC reached an agreement that attempted to clarify the jurisdictional boundaries of the two agencies. The agreement, known as the Shad-Johnson Accord, gave the SEC jurisdiction to regulate options on (a) securities (excluding certain securities exempted from the Securities Act), (b) certificates of deposit, (c) foreign currency, and (d) stock indexes listed on securities exchanges. The CFTC was given jurisdiction to regulate futures (and options on futures) on (a) exempted securities (except for municipal securities), (b) certificates of deposit, (c) options on securities not traded on national securities exchanges, and (d) indexes on securities.

The 1992 Futures Act modified the CEA[8] to incorporate some, but not all, of the provisions of the Shad-Johnson Accord. As a result, the CFTC does not have jurisdiction over any board of trade in which participants buy or sell any puts, calls, or other options on one or more securities (as defined in the Securities Act or the Securities Exchange Act of 1934 [the "Exchange Act"])[9] or index of securities.[10] However, the CFTC does have jurisdiction over any board of trade in which participants enter agreements (whether known as options, puts, calls, or other similar transactions) for future delivery of a group or index of securities, subject to the board of trade's meeting certain specific requirements.[11]

As a result of the 1992 Futures Act, the Federal Reserve System has the authority to establish margin requirements for stock index futures contracts (and options thereon). The CFTC, however, can still temporarily increase margin levels on any options or futures contracts subject to its authority.

Short-Term, Exchange-Traded Instruments

There are no special requirements for developing countries interested in purchasing or selling options or futures on commodity exchanges in the United States.[12] Like any customer interested in buying exchange-traded options or futures, the developing country must first choose a registered brokerage firm, referred to as a futures commission merchant (FCM), to handle its account. The FCM places the customer's orders for trading in designated contract markets. FCMs are subject to extensive CFTC and National Futures Association regulations, and they may or may not be members of an exchange. FCMs that are exchange members are subject to additional exchange regulations, but FCMs that are not must execute their clients' orders by clearing them through an exchange member firm.

When applying for an account, a customer must typically not only state the type of account desired but also make risk disclosure statements and provide confidential credit information and tax forms. A customer may be asked to make a disclosure statement for the purpose of establishing a noncash margin (one that would use U.S. Treasury bonds, for example, instead of cash). In addition, a customer may be asked to provide a hedge account representation letter (margin requirements are often less for hedged as opposed to speculative accounts) and a letter of transfer (if transferring an account from one FCM to another).

Requirements for Participation

All customers interested in participating in the futures or options market are required to establish an account with an FCM. For all open positions established on an exchange, the FCM is required to establish a deposit margin with the exchange's clearing department. The exchange sets the minimum margin requirements for both the FCM and its customers. The FCM can then charge the customer either the exchange-mandated minimum margin requirement or a higher margin requirement. There are no specific margin requirements unique to (entities in) developing countries; the margin requirement is privately negotiated between the (entity in the) country and its FCM (subject to minimum requirements). As a general rule, accounts established for hedging rather than speculative purposes have a lower margin requirement, because the hedged customer benefits from increases in the cash market price of the commodity, the increases offsetting any decline in the futures position or vice versa.

There are two types of margin requirements. An initial margin is required when the country first establishes (or increases) its position with the FCM. A maintenance margin is required when, as a result of adverse price changes in the futures contract, the amount on deposit falls below the maintenance levels established by the exchange. When this happens, the FCM issues a margin call to the customer that requires the customer to restore the amount on deposit to 100 percent of the initial margin level. The customer's inability to increase the amount on deposit in a "timely" manner can result in liquidation of its positions. Margin requirements vary between developing countries, and there is no guarantee that (an entity in) a developing country will be limited to paying the exchange-mandated minimum requirement. A number of factors may influence the FCM's margin requirement for a particular (entity in a) developing country: previous credit history; a history of meeting margin calls; the hedging or speculative position in the commodity; other positions with the FCM; the ability to wire funds; the location of the country (time zone); foreign exchange constraints; and net worth. As a result of these factors, the FCM may increase the initial margin requirement beyond the exchange minimum to cover more than a one-day market move.[13]

Meeting the Requirements

Most retail customers satisfy their margin requirements by a cash deposit. If a customer deposits cash to satisfy its margin requirements, the FCM may keep the interest on the deposit unless the customer negotiates to receive the interest payments. Most institutional and sovereign investors do not deposit cash for their margin requirements. Instead, they deposit U.S. Treasury bills, U.S. securities with maturities of (generally) less than one year, equities, letters of credit, gold warehouse receipts, and other U.S. governmental obligations. FCMs generally value these securities at 90 percent of par for margin requirement purposes. If a customer has a number of positions with an FCM, most FCMs will calculate an overall margin for the customer. In such a case, one futures position can offset other futures positions, and the FCM may require less margin.

One potential problem for developing countries interested in participating in the exchange-traded futures market is the possibility of daily FCM maintenance margin calls. Countries (or entities in these countries) that have severe foreign exchange constraints or complex foreign exchange controls may find it difficult to meet daily margin calls in a timely manner. One possible solution to this problem is for the developing country to deposit large sums of U.S. Treasury bills or letters of credit (accepted by some exchanges) that will safely exceed the expected price volatility.

Over-the-Counter Instruments

The two instruments discussed in this section are so-called trade options and swaps. These instruments are primarily risk management tools and are not independent sources for raising capital. However, they are often used with a variety of capital-raising instruments.

The Trade Option Exemption

Developing countries can offer off-exchange commodity options under the CFTC's "trade option" exemption. The trade option exemption allows an entity to offer ("write") a commodity option when the entity has a reasonable basis for believing that the offeree (purchaser of the option) is a producer, processor, commercial user, or merchant dealing in the underlying commodity of the option and is entering into the transaction for purposes relating to the offeree's business as such. Under the trade option exemption, sales to the general public are not allowed, and options can be offered only on nonagricultural products.

The Commodity Swap Contract

In a swap contract, two parties agree to exchange payments on particular cash flows at specified intervals.[14] A swap contract is essentially a series of simultaneous forward contracts structured to occur on a specific schedule. The structure of the swap arrangement can reduce default risk by combining forward contracts into a single legal document and by netting the payments in the swap contract (only the difference between the two sets of cash flows is paid to the other party).[15]

Estimates of the size of the commodity swap market vary greatly, but it is still much smaller than the currency and interest rate swap markets. The interest rate and currency swap markets together have been estimated at $1.5 trillion a year, whereas the commodity swap market was estimated to be about $10 billion in 1990 and about $40 billion to $50 billion in 1991 (Bank for International Settlements 1991). There are two reasons for the smaller size of the commodity swap market. First, commodity swaps are a more recent financial innovation than interest rate or currency swaps, and it takes time for markets to develop. The growth in the last two years would suggest that the market has passed its initial learning stage. Second, interest rate and currency swaps are in great demand by large institutional investors, who are more exposed to interest rate or foreign exchange fluctuations than to commodity price movements.[16] Thus, most experts do not expect the commodity swap market to develop on the same scale as the interest rate or currency swap markets.

The factors that make a particular commodity an attractive candidate for a swap include the following. First, the commodity must be subject to two-way price fluctuations. If the price of the commodity is expected to remain stable or to move only in one direction, producers and consumers have little incentive to enter into a swap agreement. Commodities that are heavily subsidized or subject to production quotas are less likely candidates for swaps. Second, there should be well-developed, liquid cash (spot) and futures markets. Financial intermediaries are more willing to enter swap arrangements in a market considered to be efficient, that is, not subject to price manipulation by any of the participants. A well-developed market will have the following characteristics: a reliable price index is available; the difference (spread) between bid and ask is small; determining payment if the contract fails to reach maturity is easy; and finding a counterparty to a given swap position is not difficult.

Geography plays a role in the pricing of a commodity swap, because different exchanges have prices based on different quantities and grades of a particular commodity.[17] For example, a producer of crude oil in Nigeria could find itself with a badly mismatched hedge if it entered into a swap contract based on a New York exchange index instead of on the price of crude delivered from Nigeria. Such mismatching would make settlement in case of default and early termination more complicated and less capable of standardization. The bid-ask spread in the commodity swap market can still be rather large.

U.S. Regulation of the Swap Market

The CFTC has issued two important regulations affecting the legal status of swap transactions. The first regulation is the policy statement issued on July 21, 1989, granting safe harbor from CFTC regulation to swaps that meet specified criteria.[18] The second and more important regulation is the final rule issued on January 14, 1993, exempting certain swap transactions from CFTC jurisdiction.

POLICY STATEMENT OF JULY 21, 1989. The policy statement issued by the CFTC on July 21, 1989, defines a swap as ". . . an agreement between two parties to exchange a series of cash flows measured by different interest rates, exchange rates or prices with payments calculated by reference to a principal base (notional amount)" (54 Federal Register 30695).

Although swaps were found by the CFTC to be instruments "possessing elements of futures or options contracts" (54 Federal Register 30694), the policy statement grants safe harbor from CFTC regulation to swaps meeting the following criteria:

- *Individually tailored terms.* The terms of the swap agreement must be individually tailored: the negotiations must be based on the credit risk of the parties involved in the transaction and documented in a contract that is not fully standardized. This requirement is designed to distinguish swap contracts from futures contracts, which are standardized and easily tradable on an exchange.
- *Absence of an exchange-style offset.* The swap agreement, absent default, can be terminated only by the consent of the counterparty. If a termination clause is inserted into the contract in advance, the formula for determining the termination price must be individually negotiated. Once again, this requirement is designed to exclude instruments that are readily tradable, that is, where the futures position can be liquidated by taking an opposite position (known as an offset).
- *Absence of a clearing organization or margin system.* The swap arrangement cannot be supported by the credit of a clearinghouse organization. In addition, the swap agreement cannot be based on a (futureslike) marked-to-market arrangement that eliminates the need for individualized credit determinations. In a marked-to-market arrangement, changes in the value of the financial instrument are settled daily.[19] Thus, swap agreements cannot involve payments from one account to another based on daily price fluctuations. But swaps can have collateralized credit arrangements by which the collateral payments are adjusted, based on certain specified events, if the collateral payments are pledged to, but not owned by, the secured party.
- *In party's line of business.* The swap agreement must be undertaken in conjunction with a party's line of business. This restriction is designed to prohibit public participation in swap agreements.
- *Not marketed to the public.* The swap arrangement cannot be marketed to the general public. As in the line-of-business criterion, this prohibition is based on the fact that most swap participants are large institutional and commercial organizations.

THE FINAL RULE ON SWAPS. As noted earlier, the 1992 Futures Act grants the CFTC broad authority to exempt certain financial instruments from the exchange-trading and other requirements of the CEA. In addition, the 1992 Futures Act requires the CFTC to act quickly to exempt swap agreements that are "not part of a fungible class of agreements that are standardized as to their material economic terms, to the extent that such agreements may be regarded as subject to the provisions of this Act."[20]

On the basis of this new statutory authority, the CFTC quickly issued proposed rules for the treatment of swaps on November 12, 1992, and then approved the final rule on swaps in January 1993. The final rule applies retroactively to all swap agreements occurring after October 22, 1974.

Under the final rule, officially cited as Part 35 of Chapter I of Title 17 of the Code of Federal Regulations, swap agreements subject to the CEA[21] are exempt from the CEA if they conform to specified terms and conditions.

First, the swap must fall within the following definition of a swap agreement:

> . . . (i) an agreement (including terms and conditions incorporated by reference therein) which is a rate swap agreement, basis swap, forward rate agreement, commodity swap, interest rate option, forward foreign exchange agreement, rate cap agreement, rate floor agreement, rate collar agreement, currency swap agreement, cross-currency rate swap agreement, currency option, any other similar agreement (including any option to enter into any of the foregoing); (ii) any combination of the foregoing; or (iii) a master agreement to enter into any of the foregoing.[22]

This definition is considerably broader than the swap definition used in the policy statement and includes a wide variety of existing and future swap arrangements having different financial characteristics. The broader definition increases the scope of the exemption and helps to secure the legal status of swaps in the financial markets. In addition, because the definition is the same as in the U.S. Bankruptcy Code,[23] it increases financial certainty by exempting the swaps from the automatic stay provisions of the Bankruptcy Code. Second, to qualify for an exemption under the final rules, the swap participant must be an "eligible swap participant." The definition of eligible swap participant (Part 35[2]) is, with a few minor modifications, the same as the 1992 Futures Act definition of "appropriate person." Eligible swap participants include banks and other financial institutions; corporations and other entities meeting specified financial criteria; governmental institutions at the state and national level; multinational institutions; and broker-dealers, merchants, and individuals in specified categories. Appendix 5-1 contains a more detailed list.

The determination of a swap participant's eligibility is made at the time the participants enter the transaction. Developing countries and other foreign entities benefit from the CFTC's adoption of the "eligible swap participant" definition instead of the "appropriate person" definition proposed in November 1992 because the adopted definition specifically recognizes that regulated foreign entities are eligible to participate in swap transactions. A swap participant that reasonably believes that a counterparty is an eligible swap participant may continue to rely on this belief absent information to the contrary.

The following terms and conditions must be met for the swap agreement to be exempt:

- *Eligibility.* (Part 35.2[a]) The parties must be eligible swap participants at the time of entering the swap agreement.
- *No standardization.* (Part 35.2[b]) The swap agreement "may not be part of a fungible class of agreements that are standardized as to their material economic terms."[24] Swap agreements in which the material economic terms of the swap are fixed and not open to negotiation will be subject to the CEA. As the material terms become fixed, the swap is more likely to be considered a futures contract that is subject to the exchange-trading requirement of Section 4(a) of the CEA. Material economic terms include, but are not limited to, contract provisions such as the notional amount of the swap, the interest rate, the maturity, or the payment dates of the swap contract. However, the final rule does not preclude the standardization of contract terms such as representations and warranties, covenants, and events of default. According to the CFTC, standardization of economic terms is a necessary, but not sufficient, condition for determining if the swap agreement is fungible.
- *Creditworthiness.* (Part 35.2[c]) The creditworthiness of the swap counterparty must be material in determining the credit terms of the swap contract. Therefore, the exemption is not available for swap agreements that are subject to a clearing system that eliminates the credit risk of the parties to the swap. The CFTC notes, however, that it will reconsider this restriction if and when a clearing system develops for swap agreements. This provision does not prevent parties from using margin arrangements to reduce credit risk.
- *No multilateral transaction facility.* (Part 35.2[d]) The swap cannot be traded through a multilateral transaction facility. A multilateral transaction facility is a physical or electronic market in which facility members make offers to all members, and a member can accept the offer simultaneously with another member's acceptance. This trading system is in contrast to a bilateral agreement between a single offeror and offeree.

The final rule on swaps does not affect the legality of swap transactions undertaken in accordance with the earlier policy statement. Congress did not want to affect the legality of securities-based swap transactions or other private swap transactions that comply with the Shad-Johnson Accord (that is, swaps that are not subject to the CEA and therefore are not subject to the final rule on swaps). As such, the CFTC has stated that swap participants can continue to rely on the earlier policy statement for new and existing swap agreements, including securities-based swaps.

Developing Countries and the Commodity Swap Market

There are no special regulatory requirements for a developing country interested in participating in a swap agreement. The developing country has to satisfy only the criteria outlined in the final rule on swaps. Collateral levels required by financial intermediaries are subject to individual negotiation and vary country by country and entity by entity. Financial intermediaries will usually require additional collateral payments if conditions change over the course of the agreement. In a number of situations, developing countries will have a significant market share in a given commodity market. As such, it is possible that the country could influence the price of the commodity in that market. There is no U.S. regulation that prohibits an entity capable of influencing the commodity price in a particular market from participating in swaps in that commodity. However, financial intermediaries are generally reluctant to enter into swap arrangements if the commodity market is subject to possible price manipulations. Because of the small number of financial intermediaries in the swap market, the market is currently relatively adept at controlling for this possibility.

Swaps, Banks, and Capital Adequacy Requirements

Banks are required to meet certain capital adequacy requirements for swaps (for interest rate and currency swaps, see Patrikis and Cook 1989). Swaps receive special treatment under the capital adequacy requirements because the bank is not exposed to the full face value of the swap, but only to the expected cash flows under the swap agreement, and banks treat swaps as items that are off the balance sheet. Capital adequacy requirements (as under the Basle Accord) are determined by a risk-based capital ratio; that is, certain designated capital is divided by weighted risk assets. Various financial items are assigned a risk category based on the type of entity legally obligated to the bank (obligor), the person guaranteeing payment to the bank, and the nature of the posted collateral.

Swaps, as items that are off the balance sheet, are given a risk weight based on the obligor. However, the risk weight for interest rate or currency swaps is not applied to the principal of the swap but to a "credit equivalent" amount. The credit equivalent amount is based on the bank's possible credit exposure to the swap arrangement. It is equal to marked-to-market exposure (current exposure) plus a percentage (credit conversion factor) of the principal of the swap (potential exposure). The current exposure represents the bank's current risk because of the swap, and the potential exposure represents any future liability the bank may face as a result of the swap. The credit equivalent amount for currency and interest rate swaps cannot exceed 50 percent of the value of the instrument. Swaps backed by collateral or other guarantees can receive a lower risk rate than can identical instruments without such guarantees.

The credit conversion factor varies according to the type of contract and the length of the swap's maturity. Exchange rate swaps have a higher conversion factor than interest rate swaps because exchange rates are generally more volatile than interest rates and often require an exchange of principal at maturity. Following this logic, the conversion factor for commodity swaps is likely to be at least as great as for exchange rate swaps. Commodity prices are highly volatile; moreover, banks have generally had less experience with commodity instruments than with exchange rate or interest rate instruments.[25]

The Regulation of Hybrid Financial Instruments

The previous two sections examined financial instruments that are used primarily to hedge commodity price fluctuations. The focus of this and the next two sections is on financial instruments containing commodity components that are used for raising capital. Hybrids are capital market instruments that combine equity, debt, or depository instruments.

The CFTC has issued three important regulations affecting the legal status of hybrid financial instruments. On January 11, 1989, the CFTC issued a statutory interpretation excluding hybrid instruments with futureslike components from CFTC regulation.[26] Later, on July 21, 1989, the CFTC issued a final rule regulating the treatment of hybrid financial instruments with optionlike components from regulation under the CEA.[27] Then, on January 14, 1993, the CFTC replaced these two different—and often confusing—regulations for hybrids with a single test: the Predominant Purpose Test of the final rule on hybrids (Part 34 of Title 17 of the Code of Federal Regulations).[28]

The Predominant Purpose Test does not affect instruments that were issued under the 1989 final rule, but it does supersede the 1989 final rule with regard to the issuance of all new hybrid instruments. Issuers may continue to rely on the 1989 "statutory interpretation," notwithstanding the Predominant Purpose Test of the new final rule on hybrids.[29]

The 1989 Statutory Interpretation: Hybrids with Futures-like Components

Under the statutory interpretation the CFTC allows hybrid instruments meeting certain criteria to be excluded from its regulation. An instrument that is excluded from regulation under the CFTC may still, however, be regulated by the SEC or one of the four banking authorities in the United States. The CFTC criteria for exclusion under the statutory interpretation are complicated. Instead of giving a broadly based exemption according to the nature of the instrument, the CFTC adopted specific technical criteria for each instrument. A major purpose of the criteria is to prohibit the sale of an instrument that is designed solely to escape the prohibition on off-exchange futures trading.

ELIGIBLE INSTRUMENTS. Hybrid instruments that are eligible for exclusion from CEA and CFTC regulations are certain debt securities; preferred equity securities; and demand, time, or transaction deposits that are marketed or sold directly to the customer and offered by a U.S. financial institution that is insured by a governmental agency or chartered corporation, or by an agency or branch of a foreign bank operating in the United States and licensed or regulated under U.S. laws.

Examples of instruments that are eligible for CEA exclusion under the statutory interpretation include a one-year note whose principal is indexed to the fluctuations in a specified foreign exchange rate; a time deposit that has its interest payment indexed to the price of gold; or a commodity-linked bond (say, in copper or oil) in which the interest payments are linked to fluctuations in the price of the commodity. Of particular interest to developing countries are commodity-linked bonds, in which the interest or principal payments, or both, are linked to fluctuations in commodity prices.

STATUTORY INTERPRETATION CRITERIA. In addition to corresponding to one of the categories of eligible instruments listed above, the hybrid must also qualify as a bona fide debt, preferred equity, or deposit instrument that meets the following criteria:

- The hybrid must be indexed to the commodity on no greater than a one-to-one basis.
- The hybrid must limit the maximum loss of the commodity-

dependent component to no more than the face value of the instrument.

- The hybrid's commodity-independent yield (for most instruments) must be no less than 50 percent and no greater than 150 percent of the estimated annual yield of a comparable nonhybrid instrument issued by a similar issuer and having a similar maturity.
- The hybrid's commodity component cannot be severable from the debt, preferred equity, or deposit portion of the instrument.
- The hybrid cannot require delivery of a commodity by way of an instrument specified in the rules of a designated contract market.
- The hybrid cannot be portrayed during marketing as having the characteristics of a commodity option or futures contract.

Below are the key elements of the six criteria.

The one-to-one indexing criterion. The one-to-one indexing restriction means that the change in the payment of the commodity-dependent component of the hybrid as a percentage of the commodity-independent component of the hybrid (whether the principal or coupon) must not be greater than the percentage change in the price of the commodity to which the bond is indexed. In other words, a 1 percent increase in the commodity price cannot result in more than a 1 percent increase in the commodity-dependent portion of the hybrid (calculated as a percentage of the commodity-independent portion of the instrument). The one-to-one indexing requirement must be met at each periodic payment. This requirement limits large variances in the instrument's return because of commodity price changes, thereby protecting investors from the possibility of large losses often associated with highly leveraged instruments.

The maximum-loss criterion. There are two basic ways to meet the requirement that the loss on the commodity-dependent payment cannot exceed the face value of the instrument.[30] The first way is to state explicitly as part of the terms of the hybrid that the loss on the commodity-dependent portion of the payment (whether principal or coupon) cannot exceed the commodity-independent portion of the payment. For example, the terms of an oil bond could state that the losses resulting from an oil price decrease could never reduce the indexed principal payments below the original face value of the bond. The second way to meet this maximum-loss criterion is through the design of the payoff terms of the instrument.

The commodity-independent yield (CIY) criterion. The yield on the commodity-independent component of the hybrid (with a few exceptions) must be no less than 50 percent and no more than 150 percent of the estimated annual yield of a nonhybrid instrument issued by a similar issuer and having a similar maturity. This criterion can be a difficult problem for developing countries. Because of their limited access to international credit markets, there may not be appropriate nonhybrid instruments to serve as a baseline comparison.[31] Another problem that arises in analyzing the CIY occurs when the underlying commodity is in backwardation. Backwardation occurs when the spot price of the commodity is greater than the forward (or futures) price, which indicates that the market expects the price of the commodity to decline. When a commodity is in backwardation, the issuer of the hybrid will have to increase the CIY on the instrument to offset the expected fall in the price of the commodity. However, in increasing the CIY to compensate for the backwardation, the issuer will be restricted by the upper CIY constraint of 150 percent.

Criteria for the nonseverable commodity component, delivery, and marketing. The requirement that the commodity component not be severable is designed to prevent off-exchange trading of futures or options. The commodity component of the hybrid cannot be traded separately from (or have a longer maturity than) the commodity-independent component of the hybrid. Allowing separate trading of the commodity component would conflict either with the CEA requirement that all futures trading be on an exchange or with the CFTC's regulations on options. The delivery criterion is designed to protect deliverable supplies designated for settlement of exchange-traded option or futures contracts from possible price manipulation or other interference. The marketing regulation is designed to protect the public from misleading characterizations of hybrids as futures or option contracts. The issuer of the hybrid is not allowed to market the instrument as having the "characteristics of a futures contract or commodity option" except when necessary to comply with securities registration or to describe the instrument's components.

The 1989 Final Rule: Hybrid Capital Instruments with Options

In July 1989 the CFTC published a final rule that exempted hybrids with certain option components from CFTC oversight. It is important to draw a distinction between this final rule on options and the statutory interpretation discussed in the previous section. The final rule is concerned only with hybrids that have commodity option–based payments, which the CFTC defines as "any commodity-dependent payment in which the commodity price indexing or referencing results in the indexing of payments for commodity prices either above or below the indexing price but not both."[32] Although the 1989 final rule has been superseded by the 1993 final rule as to the issuance of all new hybrid instruments, it still applies to existing instruments.[33] Appendix 5-2 contains a more detailed description of the old, 1989 final rule.

The 1993 Final Rule on Hybrid Financial Instruments

The new, 1993 final rule on hybrids, with its Predominant Purpose Test, greatly simplifies the CFTC's treatment of hybrid instruments and applies both to hybrids with futureslike components and to hybrids with optionlike components. The Predominant Purpose Test exempts from CFTC regulation hybrid instruments in which the value of the commodity interest (as determined in accordance with the rule) is less than the guaranteed return from the instrument. In other words, the hybrid is exempt from CFTC regulation if the value of the commodity-independent component of the hybrid exceeds the value of the commodity-dependent component of the hybrid.

In adopting the final rule on hybrids, the CFTC recognized that options, as the building blocks of financial instruments, can be combined to duplicate the payoffs associated with futures positions. The CFTC therefore abandoned the artificial distinction between the 1989 final rule and the statutory interpretation. For example, the combination of a long call option with a short put option at the same reference price duplicates the commodity price exposure received from a long futures position.

DEFINITION OF TERMS AND ELIGIBLE INSTRUMENTS. Part 34.2 of the new rule defines a hybrid instrument as an eligible equity or debt security or depository instrument (as defined below) that contains one or more futureslike or optionlike commodity components. The following instruments are eligible for exemption under Part 34.3:

- An equity or debt security as defined in the Securities Act[34]
- A demand deposit, time deposit, or transaction within the meaning of the U.S. Code of Federal Regulations[35] offered by an insured depository institution, credit union, or U.S. federal, state, or foreign bank.

This definition of eligible instruments is simpler and broader than the definition used in the 1989 rule and statutory interpretation.

ADDITIONAL PROVISIONS. The issuer must also meet four other Part 34 provisions for the hybrid instrument to be exempt from CFTC regulation. First, the hybrid issuer must receive the initial purchase price from the purchaser of the hybrid, and the holder of the hybrid must make any additional payments during the term of the instrument (the maximum-loss criterion of the statutory interpretation). Second, the hybrid instrument cannot be marketed as a futures or option contract. Third, the hybrid cannot provide for settlement in the form of a delivery instrument designated as such by a contract market. Fourth, the hybrid instrument must be issued in accordance with U.S. banking and securities laws.

The Predominant Purpose Test has to be applied at the time the instrument is priced. If the hybrid contains components that will eventually be severed from the instrument, these components must meet the Predominant Purpose Test at the time of issuance. The value of the commodity component of the hybrid is equal to the summation of the option premiums included in the instrument. The CFTC allows issuers to rely on a variety of analytical models (such as Black-Scholes) to price the instrument and to calculate the present value of the commodity options that are included. In determining the value of the commodity component, the issuer can rely on the method used to price the instrument or on a commercially reasonable method, such as the price of a futures contract. The issuer can also safely rely on an underwriter's calculations if the issuer reasonably believes that the hybrid meets the final rule requirements.

APPLICATION OF THE PREDOMINANT PURPOSE TEST. The Predominant Purpose Test requires that the net present value of the commodity-independent portion of the hybrid instrument be greater than the summation (in terms of absolute value) of all the net put and call option premiums associated with the commodity-dependent component of the instrument, that is:

$$\text{FACE VALUE}/(1 + r)^n > \sum [\text{abs (NET PUT)} + \text{abs (NET CALL)}].$$

As in the statutory interpretation, the value of the commodity-independent portion of the hybrid is calculated by using an interest rate for a similar nonhybrid instrument by the same or a similar issuer. Suppose the commodity-independent portion of a hybrid is a five-year bond with a face value of $1,000. If the issuer pays 8 percent for a similar, five-year, nonhybrid bond with a $1,000 face value, the net present value of the commodity-independent portion of the hybrid is $680.58. For the commodity-dependent portion of the hybrid, the issuer can then add to this bond any number of long or short calls, long or short puts, and caps or collars as long as these components, when added together, do not exceed $680.58. If, for example, a five-year, long-call option for gold with a premium of $68.00 is added to the bond, the hybrid instrument can easily pass the Predominant Purpose Test ($680.58 > $68).[36]

The issuer can also issue a second hybrid instrument with a long futures position by simply adding to the previous example a short put option. If the hybrid has the same strike reference price and premium for the put option as for the call option, the commodity-dependent portion of the instrument is $136, still clearly less than $680. (For purposes of the Predominant Purpose Test, the call and put premiums in the second example are added together; the CFTC believes that these premiums should not offset one another, because together the options add to the commodity price exposure of the instrument.)

Short calls and long puts can also be added to the second example to limit the upward and downward price exposure of the holder of the instrument. If a short call is added to cap the upward price exposure of the instrument, the premium paid for the short call is netted against the premium paid for the long call. The same calculation applies to the long put and the short put.

There can also be a number of identical put or call options in the same instrument. For example, if the hybrid contains an option to purchase 10 ounces of gold, the $68 premium for the option is multiplied by ten (the number of ounces of gold) to determine the commodity-dependent component of the instrument. Such a hybrid instrument would barely meet the Predominant Purpose Test ($680.58 > $680).

The Exemption of Capital Instruments from Security Registration

Commodity-linked instruments that are exempted or excluded from CFTC regulation under the final rule or statutory interpretation for hybrids are still subject to SEC regulation. Thus, their sale is either subject to Securities Act registration or offered under a private placement exemption or other Securities Act exemption. If the instrument is designed to be sold in small denominations to the general public, it will have to be registered.[37]

The Market for Capital Instruments with Commodity Components

According to market participants, the requirement of the old final rule that the commodity component could not be detached from the capital instrument limited the marketability of hybrid instruments in the United States. Bankers argued that there was no identifiable investor group to which the hybrid could be marketed, that the nonseverability of the commodity component limited the investor's ability to fully capture the value of the commodity to which the security was indexed, resulting in an insufficient market for nondetachable indexed instruments. Under the new rules, however, components of the hybrid may be detached as long as the components meet the Predominant Purpose Test when the security is issued. This may help to make hybrid instruments more marketable.

Since the summer of 1989 highly indebted countries, especially several Latin American countries, have seen some improvement in their ability to access international capital markets (World Bank 1992b). In June 1989

Mexico's Banco Nacional de Comercio Exterior sold $100 million worth of bonds in the Euromarkets. Since then, many other Mexican companies (among them, Nafinsa, Cemex, and La Moderna) have followed suit. A number of Venezuelan and Brazilian companies (for example, Petrobras) have also issued bonds in the Euromarkets. Because of economic reforms and debt reduction under the Brady Plan, confidence and interest in Latin American securities have also increased. Total capital inflows have increased to an estimated 3 percent of gross domestic product, up from 1 percent of gross domestic product during most of the 1980s. This increase has taken place not only through the issuance of new securities but also through foreign direct investment and direct portfolio investments into local stock markets. Other developing countries may be able to structure financial arrangements like the Mexicana de Cobre deal or offer hybrid instruments with commodity-linked features.

Trusts: The Phibro Energy Oil Trust

Another method for a developing country to raise capital is to participate in the creation of a trust in which the proceeds from the offering of the trust units are used to purchase a series of prepaid forward contracts from the developing country.

In August 1990 Salomon, Inc., established such a trust arrangement in offering the Salomon Phibro Energy Oil Trust (Phibro Trust). In the Phibro Trust, the proceeds from the offering of the trust units were deposited by Salomon in the trust in exchange for the trust units. On the date of the issuance of the trust units, the trustee (the Texas Commerce Bank National Association) used the proceeds to acquire a forward contract from Phibro Energy. The net proceeds from the offering of the trust units were an estimated $68 million. The trustee and Phibro entered into a forward contract that requires Phibro to deliver a quarter of a barrel of crude oil per trust unit (16 million units) in September 1995. The forward contract also benefits from an irrevocable, unconditional delivery guarantee from Salomon.

A single cash distribution will be made from the trust in November 1995. The amount distributed will be equal to the difference between the proceeds from the sale of the crude oil delivered under the forward contract and the trust expenses. Each holder of trust units will receive a quarter of the average per-barrel price at which the trust sells the crude oil under the forward contract, less a prorated share of trust expenses. Under terms of the arrangement, Phibro is required to act as a standby purchaser from the trust if, during the price period, the trustee does not receive a bid greater than the average daily settlement price less 10 cents a barrel. This requirement effectively limits downward price fluctuations from the price determined during the pricing period.

A similar type of trust arrangement could be used by developing countries that export oil or, to a lesser degree, by those that export metals. However, they may face a number of problems in establishing such a trust. According to market participants, one of the keys to the Phibro Trust was the Salomon guarantee. The developing country (with a higher credit risk) would therefore have to find an institution willing to guarantee the delivery of the forward contract. Market experts also believe that a developing country would have to schedule more payments during the life of the trust. That is, instead of one payment in five years, a developing country (with a higher credit risk) might have to offer a number of payments during the life of the trust. Finally, a requirement to repurchase the commodity at a baseline price (as in the Phibro Trust) could prove problematic for the developing country.

Special Exemptions: The Mexico, Venezuela, and Uruguay Letters

When a developing country wants to issue a commodity-linked financial instrument in the United States, it must determine if the instrument is exempt from CFTC regulation under either the trade option exemption, the new final rule on swaps, or the new final rules on hybrids. At times, however, a country may want to issue an instrument that does not fall within one of these exemptions. For example, a country may want to issue a commodity-linked bond in which the commodity component of the bond is detachable but fails to meet the Predominant Purpose Test at the time the hybrid instrument is issued. When the financial instrument does not fall under one of the CFTC's exemptions, the country can still request a case-by-case review by the CFTC.

In April 1990 the CFTC issued an order allowing Mexico, as part of its debt-restructuring agreement, to issue bonds having detachable commodity components known as recovery rights. The holders of the rights receive payments when Mexico's export receipts from its domestic oil production exceed a certain level. The order allowed the bonds and rights to be transferred only as a unit until July 1992, after which the rights could be traded separately. The payment under the right is equal to the product of Mexico's average oil export volume during the first four of the five months preceding the payment date and 30 percent of the excess over the reference price ($14 per barrel adjusted for inflation). This product is then multiplied by a fraction: the numerator of the fraction is the principal amount of eligible debt exchanged for bonds by the holder, and the denominator is the total principal amount of eligible debt. The payments under the rights are also subject to a payments ceiling of 3 percent of the debt exchanged. These bonds are privately placed in the United States and cannot be marketed to the general public. In granting Mexico the exemption, the CFTC found that the bond's detachable rights "would not be contrary to the public interest," because of the unique characteristics of the rights, the circumstances surrounding their issue, the public benefits of restructuring Mexico's sovereign debt, and the issuer of the units being a sovereign nation. Similar exceptions were granted to Venezuela and Uruguay in their 1990 debt-restructuring agreements, covering recovery rights based on oil prices and terms of trade, respectively.

Whether the exemptions granted to Mexico, Venezuela, and Uruguay will serve as a basis for future exemptions for developing countries interested in issuing (new-money) instruments linked to commodity prices is unclear. First, in these cases the detachable rights were part of rescheduling packages that had significant political support at both the national and the international level; a single (new-money) instrument issued by a developing country would generally be of less political importance. Second, the rights in the three cases were not designed to raise new money. Third, although exemptions were given in the three cases for detachable commodity rights, instruments that violate other criteria might be treated differently.

Conversations with CFTC officials suggest that they would consider requests for a public-interest exemption for developing countries interested in issuing new-money instruments that do not fall within existing exemptive relief categories. The CFTC's decision could be favorably influenced by arguments that a sovereign nation would be issuing the instrument, that there is a public-interest benefit in having developing countries return to international capital markets, and that the instrument is uniquely designed to overcome some of the marketability or credit constraints unique to developing countries. There is, of course, no guarantee that the instrument would be granted an exemption.

Regulations on Commodity-linked Instruments in the United Kingdom

Information on the implications of developing countries issuing commodity-linked financial instruments in industrial countries other than the United States is difficult to obtain. Much of the activity in over-the-counter commodity-linked instruments has happened in the less strictly regulated Euromarkets. The following provides a summary description—neither complete nor extensive—of the regulatory environment in the United Kingdom.

The Financial Services Act of 1986 (FSA) is the main legislative provision affecting investment in the United Kingdom. Unlike the United States, there are no FSA regulations applicable to specific categories of instruments, but the emphasis is on assuring that firms are "fit and proper" and that the exchanges comply with statutory requirements. Off-exchange transactions are not illegal but are subject to certain restrictions of the Conduct of Business Rules. Off-exchange transactions in futures, options, or swaps generally prohibit participation of an inexperienced private customer.

There are no regulations about margins and registration requirements that are specific to developing countries interested in purchasing exchange-traded futures, options, or swaps. As in the United States, margin requirements are individually negotiated between the exchange member and the client. The developing country may or may not be able to receive the minimum margin required under the exchange or clearinghouse rules. There are also no specific rules that would impose different registration requirements for developing countries.

The FSA does not impose any special requirements on developing countries interested in participating in the over-the-counter market. In the absence of an FSA exemption, a firm offering and selling over-the-counter instruments is subject to an FSA authorization requirement. There are no restrictions on developing-country participation in these markets under the FSA or the rules of the Securities and Investment Board (SIB). There are also no restrictions on developing countries issuing commodity-linked bonds or other commodity-linked securities except for general FSA authorization requirements when an exemption is not available. There is no instrument-specific regulation similar to the U.S. CFTC final rule on options or the statutory interpretation on hybrids.

There are two primary channels of regulation. Direct SIB regulation occurs when the firm is a directly authorized business, and indirect SIB regulation occurs when the firm is a member of a self-regulating organization subject to SIB review. The SIB focuses more on the participants in the markets than on the financial instruments themselves. Generally speaking, developing countries are not subject to special SIB requirements. Banks involved in investment business in the United Kingdom are overseen by the Bank of England.

Conclusion

Regulation in some industrial countries, especially the United States, has at times curtailed the development of the longer-maturity commodity-linked finance market. In some instances, this curtailment has been necessary, given the uncertain nature of the new instruments and their linkages with the cash market and exchange-trade instruments such as futures and options. In other instances, however, regulators have appeared either slow at adapting to these financial innovations or over-zealous in using concepts more applicable to their traditional areas of supervision.[38] As a result, the regulations, although appearing to serve their purposes, have a number of peculiarities, at least from an economic point of view. Some market participants believe that financial centers outside the United States are benefiting from the uncertainty surrounding the current U.S. regulatory framework, although there are no accurate data supporting this position.

The 1992 Futures Act and the new rules on hybrids and swaps are a response to the concern that U.S. financial markets have become less internationally competitive. Most market participants have responded favorably to the new regulations.[39] By granting the CFTC exemptive authority under the 1992 Futures Act, Congress has reduced the risk that a court would find swaps illegal because they violate the exchange-traded requirements of the CEA.

The final rule on swaps is a substantial improvement on the old CFTC regulations: the rule increases the legal certainty of swaps, offers a broader and more inclusive definition of swap agreements, allows swap contracts to provide for margin requirements, and provides for multi-lateral netting arrangements among participants. To receive an exemption, however, the material economic terms of the swap must still be negotiated and cannot be subject to a clearing system that eliminates counterparty risk from the agreement.

The new final rule on hybrids is also a substantial improvement. It eliminates the artificial and confusing distinction between the old rules and simplifies the criteria that a hybrid must meet to qualify for an exemption. To calculate the value of the commodity-independent component for the Predominant Purpose Test, a developing-country issuer may use Black-Scholes or other pricing models or may reasonably rely on an underwriter's calculation.

These regulatory changes should make it easier for developing countries to issue commodity-linked financial instruments in the United States. At the same time, the market for short-term instruments continues to remain accessible to developing countries and offers a wide variety of instruments for hedging risk. These short-term, exchange-traded products will become more attractive to developing countries as the maturity and liquidity of these instruments increases.

Appendix 5-1. Eligible Swap Participants

Under the January 1993 final rule on swaps (officially cited as Part 35 of Chapter I of Title 17 of the Code of Federal Regulations), a swap agreement that is subject to the CEA is exempt from the CEA if the participants are "eligible." Eligible swap participants, as defined in Part 35(2), are as follows:

- A bank or trust company
- A savings association or credit union
- An insurance company
- An investment company subject to the Investment Company Act of 1940 (the "Investment Act"), or a foreign investment company subject to similar foreign regulation, so long as the investment company was not solely formed to enter swap transactions
- A commodity pool operator subject to the CEA, or a foreign commodity pool operator subject to similar foreign regulation, so long as the commodity pool operator was not solely formed to enter swap transactions and has total assets exceeding $5 million
- A corporation, partnership, or other entity not solely formed to enter swap transactions and that (a) has total assets exceeding $10 million or (b) has swap obligations supported by a letter of credit or similar guarantee or (c) has a net worth exceeding $1 million and enters into the swap in connection with its course of business (for example, a business that uses specific commodity inputs) or (d) has total assets exceeding $1 million and enters into the swap to hedge a risk occurring in the course of business
- An employee benefit plan subject to the Employee Retirement Income Security Act of 1974 (ERISA), or a foreign employee benefit plan under similar foreign regulation, with total assets exceeding $5 million; or an employee benefit plan whose investment decisions are made by an entity subject to the Investment Act or by a commodity pool operator subject to the CEA
- Any federal or state entity in the United States, or foreign governmental entity, or multinational institution
- A broker-dealer subject to regulation under the Exchange Act (the broker-dealer, if an individual, is also subject to the asset test for individuals [see below] and to the investment company provisions)
- A futures commission merchant or similar foreign counterpart (the merchant, if an individual, is also subject to the asset test for individuals and to the investment company provisions)
- Any individual with total assets greater than $10 million.

Appendix 5-2. The July 1989 Final Rule on Hybrids

One example of a hybrid instrument subject to the 1989 final rule is an option attached to a bond that allows the holder to purchase five ounces of gold if the price of gold exceeds the (exercise, or strike) price of $400 an ounce. Another example is an instrument that has an adjustment to its principal only if the spot price of a specified commodity exceeds or falls below a certain exercise price. Embedded collarlike options with a ceiling or floor that is significantly out-of-the-money are excluded.

Definition of Terms and Eligible Instruments

The CFTC, under the 1989 final rule, defines a hybrid instrument as a "debt, preferred equity or depository instrument with a commodity-dependent payment that is not severable therefrom."[40] Instruments eligible for exemption under the final rule are as follows:

- A security that is registered in accordance with the Securities Act
- A security exempt from registration under the Securities Act (except commercial paper and certain types of insurance or annuity contracts)
- A security exempt from registration because it is issued or guaranteed by the U.S. government in some form
- Certain securities issued by a corporation
- Certain securities that are issued or guaranteed by a financial institution insured by the U.S. government (or a U.S. branch of a foreign subsidiary that complies with U.S. laws and regulations)
- An exempt security issued by an insurance company
- A security sold under the exempt transaction provision of the Securities Act
- Certain demand, time, or transaction deposits.

Final Rule Criteria

Each eligible instrument must meet four criteria to be exempt from CFTC regulations. First, the value of the option premium cannot exceed 40 percent of the price at which the hybrid instrument was issued. Second, the issuer must satisfy performance criteria designed to guarantee the ability of the issuer to meet its financial obligations under the hybrid. Third, the issuer cannot market the instrument as a futures contract or commodity option. Fourth, the hybrid cannot require delivery of a commodity through an instrument specified in the rules of a designated contract market.

Notes

1. Information about the regulatory environment in other major industrial countries (for example, France, Germany, Italy, and Japan) has proved much harder to obtain.

2. 1992 Futures Act, Section 4(c)(2). Section 4(c)(1) allows the CFTC to exempt finan-

cial instruments from the exchange-trading requirement of Section 4(a) of the CEA and other provisions of the CEA (except for Section 2(a)(1)(B), the partial implementation of the Shad-Johnson Accord) if the instruments meet the requirements of Section 4(c)(2).

3. Forward contracts are between commercial parties and contemplate delivery.

4. For example, a hybrid that consists of a bond (which would normally be under SEC regulation) with a futureslike or optionlike component (which would normally be under CFTC regulation) invariably results in confusion over which agency has primary responsibility for regulating the instrument.

5. For example, commodity swap transactions have become increasingly standardized over time, and market participants have shown interest in establishing clearinghouses and margin requirements. Some market participants argue that these changes make swaps more like futures contracts.

6. The lack of explicit definitions leads to disputes over whether certain contracts are futures contracts (and therefore under CFTC jurisdiction) or forward contracts (and therefore not under CFTC jurisdiction). In certain contracts (for example, in the North Sea Brent Oil Market), the distinction between futures and forwards is very difficult to delineate.

7. For example, recent legislation does not fully resolve the conflict between the CFTC's control over futures and the SEC's control over securities.

8. Section 2(a)(1)(B) of the CEA.

9. Section 2(1) of the Securities Act defines a security as "any note, stock, treasury stock, bond, debenture, evidence of indebtedness, certificate of interest or participation in any profit-sharing agreement, collateral-trust certificate, preorganization certificate or subscription, transferable share, investment contract, voting-trust certificate, certificate of deposit for a security, fractional undivided interest in oil, gas, or other mineral rights, any put, call, straddle, option, or privilege on any security, certificate of deposit, or group or index of securities . . . or any put, call, straddle, option, or privilege entered into on a national securities exchange relating to foreign currency, or, in general, any interest or instrument commonly known as a 'security,' . . ." (quoted in Jennings, Marsh, and Coffee 1992, p. 2). Section 3(a)(10) of the Exchange Act gives essentially the same definition, but says that the term "security" includes a "warrant or right to subscribe to or purchase any of the foregoing; but shall not include currency or any note, draft, bill of exchange, or banker's acceptance which has a maturity at the time of issuance of not exceeding nine months" (quoted in Jennings, Marsh, and Coffee 1992, p. 358).

10. Section 2(a)(1)(B)(i) of the CEA.

11. Section 2(a)(1)(B)(ii) of the CEA.

12. As a point of clarification, not all options are traded on commodity exchanges. Options on securities are traded on securities exchanges. Options on commodity futures, as well as some options on cash commodities, are traded on commodity exchanges.

13. According to conversations with CTFC officials and market participants. The minimum margin required by most exchanges is designed to cover a one-day market move based on historical price volatility.

14. See Masuoka (chapter 4) for more about the participation of developing countries in the swap market.

15. Financial intermediaries sometimes require their clients to post collateral for the swap or to provide additional guarantees or letters of credit.

16. Although there is clearly a relation between movements in all three rates.

17. Commodity swaps can also be priced off the cash market.

18. The CFTC terms this the "non-exclusive safe harbor treatment." It is more in the nature of a "no-action" position than an exemption. I will use the term "safe harbor" here. If the swap fails the criteria, it could still be granted an exemption based on a case-by-case review. Note that the CFTC chose to issue its statement on swaps as a policy statement instead of as a statutory interpretation. All things considered, a policy statement is less

forceful than a statutory interpretation or final rule. In fact, a policy statement has an uncertain legal stature.

19. As opposed to a classic forward contract, in which the instrument's change in value over time is settled once, at maturity.

20. The Futures Trading Practices Act of 1992, 102 Public Law 546, Title V, Section 502(c)(5)(B).

21. Not all swaps are subject to the CEA. Under the Shad-Johnson Accord, securities-based swap transactions or other private swap transactions are not subject to the CEA and are thus not subject to the new final rule.

22. Part 35.1(b)(1), cited in 25 Securities Regulation & Law Report 107 (January 22, 1993).

23. 11 United States Code (U.S.C.) § 101(55).

24. 57 Federal Register 53629; Part 35.2(b), cited in 25 Securities Regulation & Law Report 109 (January 22, 1993).

25. See Patrikis and Cook (1989) for a more detailed description of bank adequacy requirements.

26. 54 Federal Register 1139 (January 11, 1989), as amended. In 1990, the CFTC announced some minor modifications to the 1989 statutory interpretation to confirm the interpretation to the July 1989 final rule on hybrids with optionlike components (55 Federal Register 13582 [April 20, 1990]).

27. 54 Federal Register 30684 (July 21, 1989).

28. Part 34 of Title 17 of the Code of Federal Regulations, cited in 25 Securities Regulation & Law Report 115 (January 22, 1993).

29. 57 Federal Register 53619 (November 12, 1992); CFTC Final Rule on Hybrid Instruments, cited in 25 Securities Regulation & Law Report 108, note 2 (January 22, 1993).

30. Or the requirement that if the coupon is indexed, the loss on the commodity-dependent portion of the coupon cannot exceed the commodity-independent portion of the coupon.

31. See further Jordan, Mackay, and Moriarity (1990), who present a more detailed analytical discussion of this issue. The CFTC has since relaxed the 50–150 CIY requirement for some debt or deposit instruments and adopted new final rules for hybrid instruments.

32. 54 Federal Register 30692 (July 21, 1989).

33. 57 Federal Register 53619 (November 12, 1992).

34. See note 9 above for a definition of a security under Section 2(1) of the Securities Act.

35. 12 U.S. Code of Federal Regulations 204.2.

36. 57 Federal Register 53624 (December 12, 1992).

37. If the instrument does not involve sales to the general public but is offered as a private placement to a large institution, it could be exempt from registration under the Securities Act. It would still, however, be subject to antifraud, civil liability, and other provisions of federal securities laws, as well as to state securities laws and the rules of the National Association of Securities Dealers, Inc.

38. In addition, these financial innovations have led to controversies between the different regulatory bodies in the United States over which of them should regulate long-term commodity price–linked instruments.

39. Futures exchanges have strongly opposed the new regulations because they believe these rules have placed the exchanges at a competitive disadvantage in relation to the dealer markets ("Chicago Exchanges Oppose CFTC Swap/Hybrid Action," Reuters, January 14, 1993). Swap market participants, however, have applauded the legal certainty resulting from the new rules ("Swap Dealers Hail CFTC Swap Exemption Rule," Reuters, January 14, 1993).

40. 54 Federal Register 30692 (July 21, 1989).

PART II

Case Studies

6

Strategies for Managing Coffee Price Risks in Costa Rica

Robert J. Myers

Coffee is the most important crop grown in Costa Rica in terms of area cultivated, export earnings, and contribution to gross national product. Fluctuations in coffee prices therefore have serious (and sometimes disastrous) consequences for economic performance and the well-being of a large section of the population. These problems have been underlined by the collapse of the International Coffee Agreement, which precipitated a 30 to 40 percent decline in coffee prices.

Concern about coffee price fluctuations stems from many sources. One of the major problems is the risk implied for those producing and marketing the crop. The risk of price fluctuations makes planning difficult and leads to reduced profitability (or even losses) if price realizations are significantly below expectations. These problems could be overcome if a complete set of forward and contingent claims markets were available (Stiglitz 1987; Myers and Oehmke 1988; Myers 1992). Such markets would improve efficiency by facilitating the provision of credit, allowing contracting for future delivery of commodities, and promoting insurance of risks. Although the futures and options markets for coffee at the Coffee, Sugar, and Cocoa Exchange in New York (the New York Exchange) are used by exporters, transaction costs and information requirements make trading futures and options difficult and expensive for small growers and mills located in Costa Rica.

Costa Rica has a regulated system for marketing coffee. The system

The author would like to thank Steve Hanson for helpful comments and for constructing the return diagrams used to explain hedging positions.

has many goals, but for the present purpose it is important to note that the institutions and regulations have a significant influence on the distribution of coffee price risks. Basically, processing mills are required by law to operate on a fixed margin that ensures a "fair" distribution of returns to growers. Although there appears to be substantial satisfaction with this system, it has the effect of shifting most of the risks from price fluctuations back to the coffee grower. Some price risk is borne by mills and exporters, but this is generally small and exporters can hedge using the New York Exchange.

This chapter describes how price risks are distributed under the current marketing system for coffee in Costa Rica and suggests some alternative arrangements for improved risk management. One alternative is for processing mills to provide higher initial advances to coffee growers at harvest and then to hedge the resulting risk by buying put options on the New York Exchange. This approach has several advantages, not the least of which is that it would require only minimal adjustment to the current marketing system—a system that is widely perceived to be working well.

This chapter provides a brief description of the coffee sector in Costa Rica, outlines how price risks are distributed throughout the sector, and discusses some of the ways these risks are being managed. Some alternatives for improved risk management in the coffee sector are then proposed, and a futures trading strategy that could be employed by exporters is described. The penultimate section briefly introduces some issues surrounding commodity-linked finance; these are followed by the chapter's conclusions.

Coffee in Costa Rica

Costa Rica is a small country with a population of approximately 3 million, located in Central America between Nicaragua and Panama. Three mountain chains form rugged central highlands that run the length of the country, separating the Atlantic and Pacific coastal plains. The central highlands produce most of the coffee and are more densely populated than the coastal plains. Almost all of the coffee grown in Costa Rica is Arabica, although a small amount of Robusta is grown at low altitudes. Coffee is grown mainly at altitudes of 600 to 1,500 meters, where average annual temperatures are 16 to 20 degrees Celsius (de Graaff 1986). Some coffee, however, is grown at higher altitudes, even though there is a danger of frost damage. The optimum rainfall is 1,500 to 2,500 millimeters a year. Coffee can be grown under conditions of higher rainfall and humidity, but disease and weed control then become more problematic. Parts of the central highlands of Costa Rica are ideal for growing coffee, and these areas produce some of the highest-quality coffee in the world.

Coffee has played a leading role in the economic development of Costa Rica. Lacking mineral wealth and a large population that could be employed on plantations, Costa Rica turned to coffee as a cash crop for small farms in the central highlands. Once roads and railroads from the interior to harbor ports had been constructed, the production and export of coffee expanded rapidly. In 1988, coffee accounted for 24 percent of the total value of exports; the second biggest export, bananas, accounted for 19 percent (International Monetary Fund 1989).

Production

Coffee is grown on approximately 125,000 farms in Costa Rica. The farms range in size from less than 2 hectares to well over 100 hectares, the bulk of production coming from small farms scattered throughout the central highlands. Some of these farms produce coffee in monoculture; others have diversified, particularly into food crops such as maize and beans, but also into dairy products and sugarcane. Coffee is harvested mainly between November and February, and the official crop year begins on October 1.

Several important technological advances improved coffee yields during the 1960s. High-yielding smaller varieties of coffee were introduced, and planting densities increased markedly. More intensive production required higher levels of labor and modern inputs, particularly fertilizer, herbicides, and fungicides. Irrigation systems were introduced in some areas to improve the distribution of water and to reduce erosion. Despite these advances, however, coffee production in Costa Rica has remained labor-intensive; the rugged terrain largely precludes mechanized cultivation and harvesting.

Coffee is a perennial, tree crop and therefore requires a long-run investment in productive capacity. The yield depends on the age of the tree. There is little production in the first few years, then increasing capacity as the tree approaches maturity, and an eventual decline. This pattern has led to a "vintage-capital approach" to modeling productive capacity and supply response (Akiyama and Varangis 1989). Investing is clearly a risky decision: the returns are spread over many years, and future coffee prices are unknown at the time the investment decision is made. There is some scope for controlling variable costs by altering allocations of inputs, such as fertilizer and herbicides, in response to current economic signals. However, the only real disinvestment option when prices are low is to uproot the trees and plant something else, a practice that is itself risky because prices may improve quickly.

Production and yields of coffee in Costa Rica from 1960/61 to 1989/90 are shown in figure 6-1. A strong upward trend is evident in each series, reflecting increases in area planted as well as the technological improvements mentioned above. Currently, coffee yields in Costa Rica are among the highest in the world, and costs of production are among the lowest for countries producing high-quality coffee.

Marketing

After harvesting, the coffee cherries are transported to a mill, where they are processed and stored to await sale. Currently there are about 102 processing mills (*beneficiadores*), which handle all of the processing activities, from depulping, fermenting, and drying to curing and bagging.

Growers generally deliver their coffee within twenty-four hours after harvest to receiving stations (*recibidores*), located throughout the countryside. The receiving stations are run by the mills, and each mill has its own network of stations for accepting delivery of coffee. Growers are free to deliver coffee to whichever mill they choose, provided they have access to the mill's receiving stations and the quality of the coffee is acceptable to the mill. Some mills attempt to promote business by supplying growers with credit and inputs prior to the harvest.

After the processed coffee has been bagged, a certain proportion of the crop (currently around 11 percent) is required to be sold through the Instituto del Café de Costa Rica (ICAFE) for domestic roasting and consumption. ICAFE is a statutory body that regulates the Costa Rican coffee sector. The amount of coffee sold in the domestic market is controlled by ICAFE through a quota scheme which sets the proportions of each mill's output that can be sold on the export and domestic market. In recent years the quotas have been fixed according to Costa Rica's export quota resulting from the International Coffee Agreement. Coffee set aside for the domestic market is stained with a dye so that it cannot enter the export market. In practice, the very poorest quality coffee goes to the domestic market because of low, regulated domestic prices.

Exports of coffee are handled by about twenty-seven exporters who buy from the mills and sell to overseas roasters, located primarily in the United States and Europe. Exporters generally do not hold large inventories, so most of the storage that allows sales to be spread over the crop year is undertaken by mills. When exporters have made a sale they negotiate with mills and take delivery of the coffee in San José. Usually, the coffee is transported by rail to the Atlantic Coast and then by ship to

Figure 6-1. *Total Coffee Production and Yields per Hectare, Costa Rica, 1961/62–1989/90*

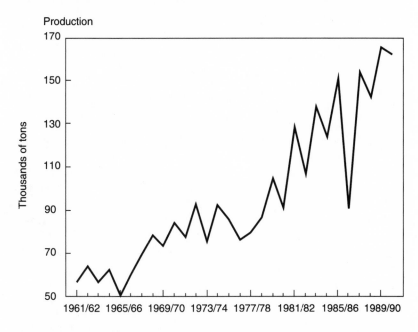

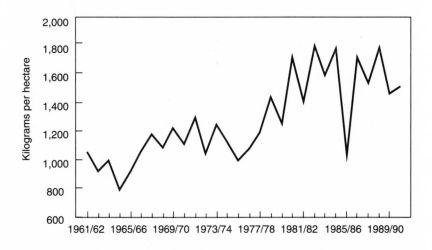

Source: U.S. Department of Agriculture, Foreign Agricultural Service, *Circular: Coffee* (various issues).

its final destination. Exporters may buy coffee from the mills before entering into an export contract if buying earlier is viewed as advantageous to their operation. In addition, exporters may provide loans to mills in advance of purchases in order to finance the milling operation and initial advances to growers.

There are two primary forms of business organization in the coffee marketing sector: private firms and cooperatives. Approximately 35 percent of the coffee mills are organized as cooperatives, and the rest are private firms. Some of the privately owned mills are vertically integrated with export operations and some with production activities as well. The cooperative mills have implemented their own form of vertical integration by organizing themselves into the Federation of Cooperatives of Coffee Growers (FEDECOOP), which exports coffee on behalf of the cooperative mills. Currently, FEDECOOP accounts for 35 to 40 percent of total exports.

The entire marketing system is regulated by ICAFE. Among its many responsibilities, ICAFE sets quotas, does quality testing, and ratifies all export contracts. ICAFE also plays a prominent role in pricing coffee and setting marketing margins.

Pricing and Taxation

The heart of the marketing system is that even though coffee is delivered to mills immediately after harvest, growers still legally own their coffee until the mill sells it to an exporter or local roasting firm. Therefore, instead of receiving payment in full on delivery, growers receive an initial advance, reportedly around 60 percent of the expected final price. As the marketing year progresses and more and more of the harvest is sold, mills make additional payments to growers at three-month intervals. The final payment to growers comes at the end of the crop year (October)—only after the entire previous year's harvest has been sold. Growers therefore receive an average, or pooled, price from the year's sales made by the mill they chose to deliver to.

Despite the regulated, pool-pricing system, there is considerable competition for business between mills. The reason is that each mill has its own pool price, calculated on the basis of the receipt from sales to exporters and local roasters. Furthermore, each mill is free to offer whatever level of first advance it wants. Thus, mills can compete for growers' throughput by offering higher first advances and by attempting to obtain higher coffee prices so that better final pool prices can be given. In practice, most competition reportedly takes place through the initial advance because most mills follow a typical pattern of diversifying sales over the crop year.

The price at which mills sell to exporters is negotiated freely between the two parties and therefore is not subject to direct control by ICAFE. This price, known as the *precio rieles,* is for coffee free on rail in San José. Although the precio rieles is not directly controlled, it does appear on every export contract, and these contracts must be approved by ICAFE. Thus, if ICAFE judges that there is an irregularity in the purchase price on an export contract (for example, that the price is out of line with market developments), the contract might not be ratified. The historical relationship between grower prices, the precio rieles, and international prices is illustrated in figure 7-3, in the next chapter.

The prices at which mills sell to domestic roasters are generally determined by auction, but the size of the domestic quota has a strong influence on the price levels realized. In practice, domestic prices have been considerably lower than export prices.

Once the precio rieles has been negotiated for a sale, the margin between this price and the grower price (on which the final, pooled price to growers is based) is strictly controlled. ICAFE calculates a minimum grower price by taking the precio rieles and subtracting (a) processing costs, (b) the return to the mill, and (c) a production tax. Algebraically, this can be expressed as

$$(6\text{-}1) \qquad P_g = P_r - C_m - \alpha(P_r - C_m) - \tau_p$$

where P_g is the grower price used to calculate the grower's final, pooled price; P_r is the price received by the processing mill (the precio rieles); C_m is the mill's processing cost per unit; τ_p is the production tax (currently zero) per quantity unit; and α is a fixed return to the mill (currently 9 percent of the difference between the precio rieles and processing costs, or 0.09). The mill can pay growers a price higher than P_g if it chooses, but doing so would lower the return to the mill. The price ultimately received by growers at the end of the crop year is a quantity-weighted average of all grower prices obtained by the mill on sales throughout the year. The mill must pay all of its growers the same price for coffee of comparable quality.

Processing costs, C_m, represent the mill's actual unit costs, but ICAFE determines a maximum cost allowance that depends on which of eight regions the mill is located in. If actual costs are above the maximum allowed by ICAFE, the mill can use only the maximum allowance to calculate grower prices. ICAFE also sets the mill's return and administers the production tax, which goes directly to the government. Currently, the production tax is at its lower limit of zero because coffee prices are so depressed. If prices rise, the production tax τ_p will rise according to the following schedule:

$$\text{If} \qquad P_x^* < 1.00, \qquad \text{then } \tau_p = 0$$
$$\text{if } 1.00 < P_x^* < 1.10, \qquad \text{then } \tau_p = 0.025 P_x$$

$$\text{if } 1.10 < P_x^* < 1.20, \quad \text{then } \tau_p = 0.05 P_x$$
$$\text{if } 1.20 < P_x^* < 1.30, \quad \text{then } \tau_p = 0.075 P_x$$
$$\text{if } \qquad P_x^* > 1.30, \quad \text{then } \tau_p = 0.10 P_x$$

where P_x^* is the export price, expressed in dollars per pound, and P_x equals eP_x^*, which is the export price expressed in colones, using the current exchange rate, e.

In addition to negotiating purchase prices with mills, exporters must negotiate selling prices with overseas buyers. ICAFE exercises little direct control over export prices, but, as mentioned earlier, export contracts do require ratification. The buying and selling operations of the exporter usually do not occur at exactly the same time: a sale is sometimes made before the coffee is purchased from a mill, and a purchase is sometimes made before closing the export sale. However, the time taken to complete the other side of a transaction is usually short (reportedly less than a month).

The relationship between the precio rieles paid to mills and the international prices received by exporters can be calculated by taking the export price (expressed in colones) and subtracting (a) exporter costs, (b) the return to the exporter (defined as a proportion of the difference between the export price and exporter costs), and (c) an export tax (currently 1 percent of the export price). The algebraic representation is

$$(6\text{-}2) \qquad P_r = e P_x^* - C_x - \beta(e P_x^* - C_x) - e\tau_x^*$$

where C_x is the exporter's per-unit cost in colones, β is the return to the exporter, and τ_x^* is the export tax revenue in dollars per unit quantity (currently 1 percent, or $0.01 P_x^*$).

Despite equations 6-1 and 6-2 having a similar form, there is an important difference between them. In equation 6-1, processing costs and mill returns are calculated and set by ICAFE. In equation 6-2, costs and returns depend on the trading decisions of the exporters and mills. In practice, exporter returns fluctuate over time in response to changing market conditions, but on average the returns are reportedly around 1.5 to 2.5 percent.

The first 1 percent of the export tax comprises ICAFE's operating budget. Any additional revenues raised over the first 1 percent go to the government. Currently, the export tax is at its lower limit of 1 percent because of depressed coffee prices. But if prices rise, so will the export tax, according to the following schedule:

$$\text{If} \qquad P_x^* < 0.95, \quad \text{then } \tau_x^* = 0.01 P_x^*$$
$$\text{if } 0.95 < P_x^* < 1.15, \quad \text{then } \tau_x^* = 0.01 P_x^* + 0.409(P_x^* - 0.95)$$
$$\text{if } 1.15 < P_x^* < 1.75, \quad \text{then } \tau_x^* = 0.1 P_x^* + 0.1(P_x^* - 1.15)$$

if $1.75 < P_x^* < 1.91$,   then $\tau_x^* = 0.16P_x^* + 0.125(P_x^* - 1.75)$

if $P_x^* > 1.91$,   then $\tau_x^* = 0.18P_x^*$.

Until recently, export prices were somewhat stabilized as a result of the International Coffee Agreement. The objective of the agreement was to keep a specified average of international coffee prices within a certain price band (since 1981, $1.20 to 1.40 per pound). Prices were regulated through a quota system in which producing countries agreed to reduce or expand exports (according to a specific set of rules) as prices moved to the upper or lower limits of the band, and consuming countries agreed to purchase according to their quota allotments. Under this system, producing countries achieved higher and more stable prices, and consuming countries gained price stability and furthered some of their foreign policy goals. Although there were problems, there is little doubt that the agreement stabilized prices, thereby reducing risks and facilitating investment planning in the coffee sector. However, the agreement now has broken down, and quotas are no longer operative. This turn of events has precipitated a significant drop in coffee prices and has added considerable uncertainty to the coffee industry.

The pricing arrangements discussed in this section have important implications for who bears the risk of price fluctuations in the Costa Rican coffee sector. The nature and incidence of these risks, and some potential strategies for mitigating them, are the focus of the remainder of this chapter.

The Incidence of Coffee Price Risks

Three main groups bear the risk of coffee price fluctuations in Costa Rica: exporters, mills, and growers. Others are also affected by coffee price volatility. For example, ICAFE's operating budget comes from the 1 percent tax on coffee exports and is therefore subject to considerable risk, and government tax revenues from coffee also fluctuate with coffee prices. Exporters, mills, and growers, however, are the main participants in coffee production and marketing, and this chapter concentrates on price risk management within these three groups.

Exporters

Because exporters often sell before they have made a purchase, or buy before they have made a sale, they are subject to the risk of adverse price fluctuations before they can complete both sides of a transaction. On the one hand, the time taken to complete the other side of a transaction is usually short (less than a month), and in this sense the exporters' risk exposure is not great. On the other hand, because exporters operate on large volumes and small margins, even minor unfavorable price movements can significantly affect their return.

For this reason, many exporters hedge their exposed spot positions on the New York Exchange. A very simple form of hedging might work as follows. An exporter buys coffee from a mill but does not yet have an overseas buyer. The exporter has a long spot position in coffee. To hedge the transaction, an opposite position is taken in the futures market (coffee futures are sold). Thus, if coffee prices fall (rise) before the overseas sale can be made, then losses (gains) on the spot position are offset by gains (losses) on the futures, and the overall return is hedged. If the exporter has sold coffee overseas before purchasing it from mills, then a similar set of transactions can be entered into, but this time futures would be bought rather than sold. The ability to undertake this type of hedging is beneficial to exporters because it allows them to operate on a small margin and provides the flexibility to exploit market opportunities without bearing an inordinate amount of risk.

Many of the private companies exporting coffee from Costa Rica make extensive use of the New York Exchange to trade futures and options. Up until mid-1989 FEDECOOP, however, did not trade coffee futures or options. Instead, it reportedly tried to match deliveries from member cooperatives to export sales with minimal delay as a means of reducing price risks. This strategy may have put FEDECOOP at a competitive disadvantage in relation to private exporters.

Since mid-1989 FEDECOOP has expanded into a range of "risk management" activities involving the use of futures and options markets for both hedging and speculative purposes. FEDECOOP now trades futures and options on its own account for coffee that has been purchased from mills at a fixed price, because it effectively "owns" this coffee. These transactions amount to approximately 60 percent of total FEDECOOP exports. For the remaining 40 percent, a risk management strategy would have to be negotiated with mills because they still effectively "own" the coffee. There would have to be agreement not only on the appropriate risk management strategy to implement but also on the distribution of the costs and benefits.

For export sales, FEDECOOP also has moved into "price fixing," or basis contracts whereby the purchase price is fixed at a specified margin (2 to 5 cents) below the price of a futures contract maturing after the agreed upon delivery date. The purchase price then varies over time with the futures price, but FEDECOOP can lock in a price (equal to the current futures price minus the agreed margin) with the overseas buyer at any time it chooses between the date of the initial agreement and the delivery date specified in that agreement. As we shall see below, this type of contract offers some particular advantages to both sellers and purchasers in terms of risk reduction.

Exporters face a potential risk that most other market participants do not: the risk of exchange rate fluctuations. Exporters typically buy coffee in local currency (colones) but sell in dollars and often obtain credit by borrowing overseas in dollars. However, even though there are no liquid futures or forward markets for the colón-dollar exchange rate, the Central Bank reportedly provides opportunities to lock in forward rates for those that desire to do so. Future sales can be "registered" at current exchange rates up to one year in advance of actual transactions. This effectively locks in the current exchange rate and eliminates exchange rate risk for the exporter.

Mills

Coffee processing mills currently face very little risk, because their margins and returns are strictly controlled by ICAFE. The aim of these controls is to ensure that growers receive a "fair" return on their coffee. Controls have an undesirable side effect, however, of transferring much of the risk from price fluctuations back to the growers. Nevertheless, there are four ways in which mills bear some risk.

First, the initial advance paid to growers is like a guaranteed minimum price, because mills cannot legally force growers to repay the advance. If subsequent sales do not cover the initial advance, the mill must incur the loss. Although this turn of events reportedly happened to some cooperative mills in 1987, it is usually avoided by making the initial advance a not-too-large proportion of the expected final price to growers (reportedly around 60 percent).

Second, if the mill sets initial advances to growers too low, or if it has a weak marketing performance so that its final price to growers is not competitive, it runs the risk of losing growers. The lower prices to growers hurt the mill by lowering throughput (thereby increasing per-unit costs) and by lowering total returns. These factors combine to put some pressure on mills to pay higher initial advances and achieve improved marketing performance.

Third, mills have to borrow to finance their first advance and other operating expenses. This finance is often provided by exporters, who may in turn borrow the money from overseas. Exporters reportedly are able to pass back to the mills some of the risk from exchange and interest rate fluctuations on these loans.

Fourth, the mill's return is fixed as a percentage of the difference between the precio rieles and mill's operating costs. Thus, fluctuations in the precio rieles lead to fluctuations in the mill's return per unit of output. This risk is small, because the mill only gets a small proportion of the price (currently 9 percent).

Clearly, the strictly controlled marketing system has meant that price risks faced by coffee mills in Costa Rica are minor. There is significant pressure, however, for higher first advances to growers, a change that would add significantly to the mills' price risks. Bigger advances would expose the mills to the risk of losses should realized grower prices fall below the initial advance. Without some means of hedging themselves against the effects of price declines, mills are understandably reluctant to undertake bigger advances.

Growers

When a grower delivers coffee to a mill, neither the price to be received for the current harvest nor price levels that might be achieved in the future are known. Growers therefore face difficult decisions about how to prepare for the next crop, even before they have been paid for the current one. The initial advance received at delivery acts as a guaranteed minimum price for the current harvest, but this initial advance is usually too small a proportion of the expected final price for the guarantee to be valuable. Thus, the grower is exposed to most of the risk of price decline over the year.

One way to think about the grower's risk exposure is as follows. First, there is the fixed initial advance, which is risk-free. Second, the grower receives an implicit call option on the coffee sold, with an exercise price equal to the initial advance. If the realized grower price for the mill turns out to be less than the initial advance, the implicit option expires worthless and the grower keeps the initial advance. But if the realized grower price turns out to be above the initial advance, the grower receives the difference between the realized grower price and the initial advance as an additional payment. This additional payment is the payoff on the implicit call option.

The implicit call option received on delivery of the coffee exposes the grower to considerable risk. The exercise price (initial advance) generally is low in relation to the expected final price, so there is a very high probability that the option will be exercised. This means that the option has little effect on the probability distribution of the final price to the grower; the implicit price guarantee in the initial advance to the grower does little to reduce price risk.

Figure 6-2 illustrates this argument. The distribution in the top panel represents the probabilities of various final prices to growers when growers receive no initial advance and are therefore exposed to the full

Figure 6-2. *Probability Distributions for Grower Prices under Alternative Initial Advances*

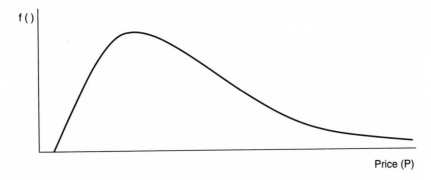

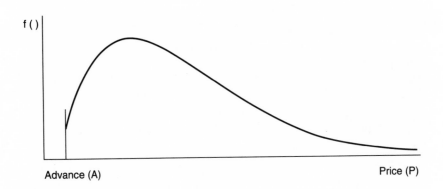

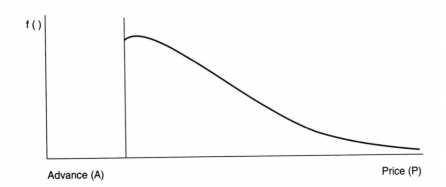

risk of price fluctuations over the crop year. This situation is equivalent to paying growers at harvest with a call option that has a zero exercise price and therefore will be exercised with a probability of one. The second panel represents the distribution of grower prices when growers receive an initial advance, A, plus a call option with an exercise price of A. The initial advance (exercise price) is so low, however, that there is little risk reduction and growers essentially face the same probability distribution as before. In the third panel, the initial advance is higher and there is a much smaller probability that the option will be exercised. In this case, the probability distribution of grower prices is truncated from below, which provides growers with significant risk reduction while still allowing them to participate in the gains if realized prices are higher than the initial advance.

A Proposal for Improved Price Risk Management

The easiest way to reduce grower price risk within current institutional arrangements is for mills to increase the level of initial advances to growers. As discussed in the previous section, increased advances reduce the probability that growers will exercise their implicit call option, thereby truncating the bottom part of the price distribution and reducing risk.

Other things being equal, a higher initial advance will always make risk-averse growers better off. This obvious result can be stated as follows.

Result 1. If growers are risk-averse, then their willingness to pay for a higher initial advance is always positive, other things being equal.

It should be clear, however, that higher initial advances to growers increase the risk exposure of the mills. The risk to the mill is that grower prices will fall below the level of the initial advance. In order to hedge, mills require an asset that pays off when prices fall below the initial advance. One such asset is a put option (the right, but not the obligation, to sell coffee at a price equal to a specified exercise price). When the price falls below the exercise price, the mill can exercise the put to offset the loss on its spot position.

To begin, suppose there is no initial advance, and growers must wait until their coffee is sold before receiving payment. In this case, the return per unit of coffee delivered to the mill at time t and sold at some later time, T, is[1]

$$(6\text{-}3) \qquad R_m(t, T) = P_{rT} - C_m - P_{gT}$$

where $R_m(t, T)$ is the return per unit of output for coffee delivered at time t, P_{rT} is the precio rieles received by the mill at time T, C_m is the average cost to the mill, and P_{gT} is the grower price used to calculate the final, pooled price to growers. The mill's return is the price received by the mill minus costs and payouts per unit of output.

The price to the grower is controlled by ICAFE and must satisfy

$$(6\text{-}4) \qquad P_{gT} \geq P_{rT} - C_m - \alpha (P_{rT} - C_m)$$

where α is the specified return to the mill set by law (currently 0.09). Assuming that equation 6-4 holds with strict equality, that is, that the mill extracts the maximum return allowable by law, then substituting equation 6-4 into equation 6-3 gives

$$(6\text{-}5) \qquad R_m(t, T) = \alpha (P_{rT} - C_m).$$

There is little risk to the mill, because it receives a fixed proportion of the difference between the precio rieles and operating costs.

Next, suppose there is an initial advance, which becomes an effective price floor. In this case, equation 6-5 becomes

$$(6\text{-}6) \qquad R_m(t, T) = \alpha (P_{rT} - C_m) - r_t A_t - \max (0, A_t - P_{gT})$$

where r_t is the interest rate on borrowed funds, and A_t is the initial advance to growers at time t. If the realized grower price (P_{gT}) is greater than or equal to the initial advance (A_t), then the last term in equation 6-6 is zero. In this case, the mill's return is basically the same as when there is no initial advance (except that there are additional interest payments on the first advance which must be accounted for). However, there is now some probability that the realized grower price will be below the initial advance $(P_{gT} < A_t)$. In this case, the last term in equation 6-6 equals $A_t - P_{gT}$, and the equation reduces to

$$(6\text{-}7) \qquad R_m(t, T) = \alpha (P_{rT} - C_m) - r_t A_t - (A_t - P_{gT}).$$

The mill must accept the additional loss $(A_t - P_{gT})$, if the realized grower price is below the initial advance. The next result follows immediately.

Result 2. Without hedging, and with other things remaining the same, increasing the initial advance will increase the risk surrounding returns to the mill.

To investigate hedging possibilities, consider a mill purchasing coffee put options on the New York Exchange. At time t the mill purchases the right, but not the obligation, to sell coffee futures contracts at the future time T for a specific price called the exercise price. If the price of coffee futures at time T turns out to be greater than or equal to the exercise price, then the right to sell at the exercise price is worthless and the option expires without being exercised. But if the futures price at time T turns out to be below the exercise price, the mill has the right to sell at the exercise price and buy at the lower market price. In this case, the option pays off the difference between the two prices.

The dollar value of the put option at time T can be written as

$$(6\text{-}8) \qquad\qquad V^*(T) = \max(0, K - F_T^*)$$

where $V^*(T)$ is the dollar value of the option at maturity, F_T^* is the futures price in dollars at time T, and K is the exercise price in dollars on the put option.

To buy the option, the mill must pay a premium, which is a market rate quoted on the New York Exchange. The mill's overall return on a unit of coffee purchased at time t and sold at time T is now

$$(6\text{-}9) \qquad R_m(t, T) = \alpha (P_{rT} - C_m) - r_t A_t - \max(0, A_t - P_{gT})$$
$$+ [e_T V^*(T) - (1 + r_t)e_t M_t^*]h_t$$

where e_t is the exchange rate at time t (in colones per dollar), M_t^* is the option premium in dollars, and h_t is the number of put options purchased per quantity unit. The last term in equation 6-9 represents the return on the put options.

Suppose there is a deterministic linear relationship between the futures price at T and the grower price in Costa Rica, also at T, both prices expressed in colones:[2]

$$(6\text{-}10) \qquad\qquad P_{gT} = \gamma + \delta e_T F_T^*.$$

The existence of a relationship like the one expressed in equation 6-10 is implied by the pricing functions described in equations 6-1 and 6-2 above. A serially uncorrelated stochastic error term could be added to equation 6-10 without changing the substance of the results that follow.[3] If the relationship between the futures price and grower price is not linear, a strategy of combining options and futures can be employed to mimic the grower price (see chapter 10, by Claessens and Coleman, where a combination of options and futures is used to hedge a nonlinear exposure to metal prices).

To hedge the mill's return, we seek values for K and h_t that counteract the effect of price declines. Consider what happens if the mill buys δ put options per unit of output ($h_t = \delta$) at an exercise price given by

$$(6\text{-}11) \qquad\qquad K = (A_t - \gamma)/\delta e_T.$$

For the moment, we assume that e_T is known at time t, but this assumption will be discussed further below.

There are two cases of interest. First, consider what happens when the grower price is greater than or equal to the initial advance ($P_{gT} \geq A_t$). Using equations 6-10 and 6-11, it follows that

$$\gamma + \delta e_T F_T^* \geq \gamma + \delta e_T K$$
$$F_T^* \geq K.$$

Thus, when $P_{gT} \geq A_t$, the implicit call option owned by growers is valuable at maturity, but the put options owned by the mill are not. The mill's return in this situation will be simply

(6-12) $R_m(t, T) = \alpha(P_{rT} - C_m) - r_t A_t - (1 + r_t)\delta e_t M_t^*.$

Second, consider what happens when the grower price is less than the first advance ($P_{gT} < A_t$). It should be clear that this also implies that $F_T^* < K$. Thus when $P_{gT} < A_t$, the implicit call option owned by growers is not valuable, but the put options owned by the mill are. The mill's return in this situation is

(6-13) $R_m(t, T) = \alpha(P_{rT} - C_m) - r_t A_t - (1 + r_t)\delta e_t M_t^*$
          $\qquad\qquad - (A_t - P_{gT}) + e_T(K - F_T^*)\delta.$

The mill incurs a loss because the grower price is below the initial advance, but it receives a payoff on the put options. Using equations 6-10 and 6-11, then

$$e_T(K - F_T^*)\delta = e_T[(A_t - P_{gT})/\delta e_T]\delta$$
$$= A_t - P_{gT}.$$

Thus, the mill's return reduces to

(6-14) $R_m(t, T) = \alpha(P_{rT} - C_m) - r_t A_t - (1 + r_t)\delta e_t M_t^*.$

Comparing equations 6-12 and 6-14 we have the following result.

Result 3. If the futures price in New York is linearly related to the grower price in Costa Rica at the maturity date on the option (if $P_{gT} = \gamma + \delta e_T F_T^*$) and the mill purchases δ put options on New York futures at an exercise price equal to $K = (A_t - \gamma)/\delta e_T$, then the return to the mill will always be

$$R_m(t, T) = \alpha(P_{rT} - C_m) - r_t A_t - (1 + r)\delta e_t M_t^*.$$

Thus, the mill is hedged and faces the same minimal risk as when there is no initial advance.

Result 3 is illustrated in figure 6-3. The mill's payoff without the put option decreases rapidly as P_{rT} falls below the value at which $P_{gT} = A_t$, because the mill is committed to paying growers at least A_t but is not receiving a price high enough to cover this advance. As the price moves above this critical value of P_{rT}, the mill's payoff increases by α for every

Figure 6-3. *Mill Returns with and without Hedging with Put Options*

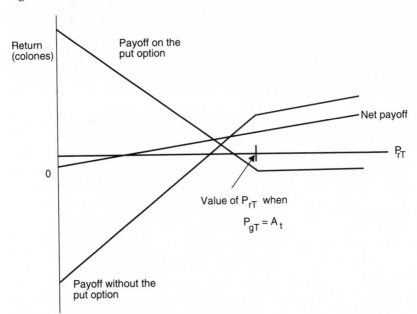

P$_{rT}$ Precio rieles, the price received by the exporter.

A$_t$ Initial advance to growers.

P$_{gT}$ Price received by the grower.

unit of increase in P_{rT}. With the put option, when P_{rT} is above the value at which $P_{gT} = A_t$, the option expires worthless and the payoff on the put option is a loss of premium. As P_{rT} falls below this critical value, however, the option payoff increases rapidly. The mill's net payoff therefore increases steadily by α for every unit increase in P_{rT} so that the large downside risk associated with the mill's exposed position has been hedged (at the cost of the put option premium).

The only differences between the mill's return with no initial advance and no put option, and the return with an initial advance but with the risk hedged by purchasing put options, are in (a) interest payments on the initial advance and (b) the cost of the option premium. The option premium can be viewed as an insurance premium for removing the risk of lower returns when the realized grower price falls below the initial advance. Of course, the higher the initial advance, the higher the exercise price on the option will need to be in order to hedge the risk. And the higher the exercise price, the higher the option premium. Thus the cost of hedging increases with the level of initial advance. Despite these additional costs per unit, however, a mill that offers higher initial advances will attract growers and increase throughput (at least initially), thereby raising total returns. Furthermore, the fact that risk is being effectively hedged could lower the cost of finance to the mill.

The distinction between cooperative and private mills does not seem to be crucial for implementation of an options trading strategy. Both types of mills are subject to the same pricing structure, and both could reduce grower risks by offering higher initial advances. Because of the pivotal role of FEDECOOP in the cooperative movement, however, there may be gains from centralizing the options trading activities of member cooperatives at FEDECOOP. Because FEDECOOP is vertically integrated, it might also be able to adjust its pricing formula more easily to account for the effects of options trading.

Before closing this section, a few comments on implementing the proposal for improved price risk management are in order. To calculate K and h_t (the appropriate exercise price and option positions), we need estimates of γ, δ, and e_T. The parameters γ and δ can be estimated using historical price and exchange rate data (Thompson and Bond 1987; Myers and Thompson 1989a). Alternatively, an estimate of these parameters can be obtained from the pricing relationships indicated in equations 6-1 and 6-2. Together, these equations imply that

$$(6\text{-}15) \qquad P_{gT} = \gamma + (1 - \alpha)(1 - \beta)P_{xT}$$

where $\gamma = -(1 - \alpha)(1 - \beta)C_x - (1 - \alpha)C_m - (1 - \alpha)\tau_x - \tau_p$. Assuming that F_T equals P_{xT} plus a constant basis at the maturity of the futures, and setting α at 0.09 and β at 0.02, the implication is that $\delta = 0.91$. The intercept parameter, γ, is (naturally) negative and can be calculated similarly by using data on costs and taxes.

A forecast of e_T, given information available at time t (along with knowledge of A_t and estimates of γ and δ), could be used to compute the appropriate exercise price for the puts. To the extent that this forecast is subject to error, it introduces additional risk into the mill's return. However, exchange rate risk is likely to be small in relation to price risk. Furthermore, the mills could presumably register their option trades with the Central Bank, thus locking in a forward exchange rate for any payouts received on the puts. Or a forward foreign exchange rate market could be developed. This would allow exchange rate risk to be hedged, and the forward rate would be used to calculate the appropriate exercise price.

A second aspect of implementation involves the length of maturities on the put options purchased by mills. The aim here should be to match the maturities on the options to the dates at which various portions of the harvest are to be sold. For example, if sales are to be spread evenly over the crop year, then option purchases should be spread evenly over existing maturities up to twelve months. If options do not exist for all of these maturities, a rollover hedging strategy is required. But if all of the crop is to be sold in the first six months, then all of the maturities on the options should be less than or equal to six months. As the crop is sold, the options should mature and be exercised (if valuable) at the same rate as the crop is liquidated, unless there has been a conscious decision to speculate on price movements.

Finally, implementation might begin cautiously by not raising initial advances to growers by too much until some trading experience has been accumulated. This would allow the exercise price on put options that are purchased to be kept low so that the option premiums would be inexpensive. After some trading experience has been gained, mills might begin increasing the initial advance, thereby providing greater price protection to growers but at the cost of paying higher premiums for the puts. Clearly, the cost of the puts will imply either lower average grower prices, lower average mill returns, or both. The benefits lie in reduced risk to growers.

The proposal for improved management of coffee price risk outlined in this section offers the promise of significant risk reduction for growers while still allowing them to participate in a rising market. Provided mills buy put options to hedge the risk associated with higher initial advances to growers, these benefits can be obtained without significantly adding to the risks of other participants in the marketing system. Furthermore, improved risk management can be achieved with only minor adjustment to the current system for marketing coffee in Costa Rica (see further the next chapter, by Claessens and Varangis).

Futures Hedging by Exporters

A simple futures hedging strategy for exporters, including FEDECOOP, might work as follows. A mill wants to sell processed coffee at time t. However, the exporter does not yet have an overseas buyer lined up. It is estimated that the coffee will be sold overseas at time T, which may be up to one or two months after t. If the exporter wants to pay the mill the precio rieles P_{rt} at time t, it will be exposed to the risk of an export price decline between t and T. To hedge this risk, the exporter could sell coffee futures.

Suppose that a futures contract on the New York Exchange matures at

T or sometime soon after T. Furthermore, there is a deterministic linear relationship between the export price that will be received by the exporter and the futures price at time T, both expressed in dollars:[4]

$$(6\text{-}16) \qquad P^*_{xT} = \zeta + \xi F^*_T.$$

The exporter wants to lock in a precio rieles of P_{rt} for the mill at time t and so immediately sells futures. The futures are bought back at time T when the coffee is sold overseas. Thus, the exporter's return in colones per unit of coffee purchased at t and sold at T can be expressed as

$$(6\text{-}17) \quad R_x(t, T) = e_T P^*_{xT} - C_x - (1 + r_t)P_{rt} + (e_t F^*_t - e_T F^*_T)b_t$$

where $R_x(t, T)$ is the exporter return per quantity unit for coffee priced at t and sold at T, C_x is the average unit cost of exporting, F^*_t is the futures price at time t in dollars, and b_t is the number of futures contracts sold (or purchased, if negative) per quantity unit. Without futures trading $b_t = 0$, and the exporter's return is clearly subject to the risk of a decline in $e_T P^*_{xT}$.

Now consider a strategy of selling ξ futures contracts per quantity unit at time t and buying the same amount of contracts back at T. In this case, b_t equals ξ, and substituting equation 6-16 into equation 6-17 gives the return as

$$(6\text{-}18) \qquad R_x(t, T) = \zeta e_T + \xi e_t F^*_t - C_x - (1 + r_t)P_{rt}.$$

The only source of risk in the exporter's return in this case is the term ζe_T, which is subject to exchange rate fluctuations. As discussed above, however, exchange rate risk will usually be small in relation to price risk, and the exporter can presumably lock in a forward rate by registering these transactions with the Central Bank. Thus this hedging strategy can be summarized as follows.

Result 4. If an exporter has a long spot position and the futures price in New York is linearly related to the export price at the maturity date on the future $(P^*_{xT} = \zeta + \xi F^*_T)$, then the exporter can sell ξ futures contracts per quantity unit to obtain a return:

$$R_x(t, T) = \zeta e_T + \xi e_t F^*_t - C_x - (1 + r_t)P_{rt}.$$

Thus, the exporter is hedged and only faces residual exchange rate risk.

Result 4 is illustrated in the return diagram of figure 6-4. The payoff without futures decreases steadily as coffee prices fall, because a purchase price has been fixed but the coffee has not yet been sold. However, the payoff on the futures position increases steadily as coffee prices fall, because the exporter has sold futures and can buy them back at the lower

Figure 6-4. *Return on a Long Export Spot Position with and without Hedging with Futures*

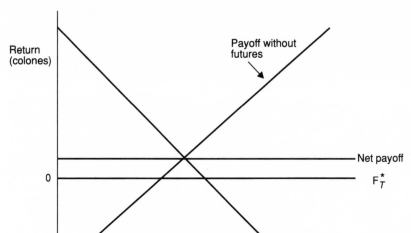

F_T^* Futures price at time T, in dollars.

price. The net return is fixed, assuming a forward exchange rate has been locked in.

An alternative possibility is that an exporter has an overseas buyer ready to commit to a purchase at time t but has no cooperative mills wanting to sell coffee at that time. It is estimated that the coffee will be available from the mills at time T, the delivery date on the export contract. But if prices move higher before the coffee is priced, the mills would expect to be paid the higher price. Thus if the exporter fixes the export price at time t, its return is subject to the risk of price increases before it can obtain the coffee.

A simple hedging strategy for this situation involves purchasing rather than selling futures contracts. Suppose that a futures contract on the New York Exchange matures at T or sometime soon after T. Furthermore, there is a deterministic linear relationship between the precio rieles and the futures price at time T:

(6-19) $P_{rT} = \lambda + \phi e_T F_T^*.$

Notice that equations 6-16 and 6-19 together imply a linear relationship between export prices in colones and the precio rieles. The concern in this case is with the relationship between the precio rieles and futures prices, because it is the precio rieles that is risky (and the export price fixed) when coffee is being sold short. The exporter enters the export contract at time t and immediately buys futures. The futures are sold back at time T, when the coffee is delivered to the overseas buyer. Thus, the exporter's return per unit of coffee sold at t and purchased at T is

(6-20) $R_x(t, T) = e_t P_{xt}^* - C_x - P_{rT} + (e_t F_t^* - e_T F_T^*)b_t.$

Without futures trading $b_t = 0$, and the exporter's return is subject to the risk of an increase in P_{rT}.

Consider a strategy of buying ϕ futures contracts per quantity unit at time t and liquidating them at time T. Then $b_t = -\phi$, and substituting equation 6-19 into 6-20 gives the exporter's return as

(6-21) $R_x(t, T) = e_t P_{xt}^* - C_x - \lambda - \phi e_t F_t^*.$

This return is known at time t, so hedging with futures has locked in a return and eliminated the risk of an increase in coffee prices. Thus we have the following result.

Result 5. If an exporter has a short spot position and the futures price in New York is linearly related to the precio rieles at time T (P_{rT} $= \lambda + \phi e_T F_T^*$), then the exporter can buy ϕ futures contracts per quantity unit to obtain a return:

$$R_x(t, T) = e_t P_{xt}^* - C_x - \lambda - \phi e_t F_t^*.$$

Thus the exporter has hedged by locking in a return at t.

A return diagram for this case would be similar to figure 6-4 except that the payoff without futures would increase as coffee prices fall and the futures payoff would decrease.

A final situation allows for the possibility that exporters might export using basis contracts. FEDECOOP has reportedly been moving into "price-fixing" contracts, and these contracts are essentially basis contracts. In a basis contract, the exporter enters into a contract to export coffee at a free on board price that is y cents under the coffee futures price maturing at time T, the delivery date on the export contract. The exporter is hedged at this point, even though the coffee has not yet been made available by the mills, because the sale price continues to fluctuate with changing market conditions.

Now suppose the mills start selling coffee. At time t the exporter buys coffee at a fixed precio rieles of P_{rt}. The exporter has a long spot position because the sale price on the export contract has still not been fixed. To hedge, the exporter could either fix the price on the basis contract or sell futures. In the latter case, the exporter's return per quantity unit in this case can be expressed as

$$(6\text{-}22) \quad R_x(t, T) = e_T(F_T^* - y) - C_x - P_{rt} + (e_t F_t^* - e_T F_T^*)b_t.$$

If the exporter undertakes a complete hedge by setting $b_t = 1$, the return per quantity unit reduces to

$$(6\text{-}23) \qquad\qquad R_x(t, T) = e_t F_t^* - e_T y - C_x - P_{rt}.$$

The properties of this hedge are summarized in the following result.

Result 6. If an exporter sells on a basis ("price-fixing") contract and completely hedges its long spot position ($b_t = 1$), then its return per quantity unit is

$$R_x(t, T) = e_t F_t^* - e_T y - C_x - P_{rt}.$$

Thus, the exporter is hedged and faces only residual exchange rate risk.

The exchange rate risk applies only to the margin, y, and so will be minimal. It could be eliminated completely by locking in a forward exchange rate with the Central Bank. The return diagram would be similar to figure 6-4.

Each of the hedging strategies investigated in this section could be undertaken with options instead of futures. That is, instead of locking in "fixed" prices with futures, options could be used to lock in a minimum selling price (or maximum buying price) while still allowing returns to increase if prices were to move higher (lower). However, because of the options premium, reserving the right to participate in favorable market moves is costly and, in the long run, should lead to about the same level of average return as the futures trading strategy.

To implement these futures trading strategies, exporters would need to know only the relationships between prices at different points in the marketing channel, represented by equations 6-16 and 6-19. Estimates of the parameters in these relationships can be made using econometric techniques on historical price data (Myers and Thompson 1989a). As discussed earlier, it is also possible to get approximate values from examining marketing margins and price differentials in the industry.

Commodity-linked Finance

Exporters reportedly borrow funds from both domestic and overseas sources in order to finance operations. Currently, this debt is mainly of the conventional type, having a fixed schedule of principal and interest payments at rates that may be adjusted at regular intervals. Because debt service obligations are not linked to performance (coffee price levels), exporters are exposed to financial risk. This section introduces a simple model that illustrates the risk management potential of commodity-linked finance, then discusses advantages of this mode of financing.

Suppose an exporter needs to borrow a certain amount at time t in order to finance operations until time T. A conventional loan is taken out and the principal plus interest must be paid in full at T. Net income over this time frame, excluding interest payments, depends on the price of coffee exports at T. Thus, total net income can be written as

$$(6\text{-}24) \qquad N(t, T) = I(P_{xT}) - r_t D_t$$

where $N(t, T)$ is the net income earned between t and T; $I(P_{xT})$ is the net income excluding interest payments; and D_t is funds borrowed at t. Income is clearly subject to risk because fluctuations in coffee prices lead to fluctuations in income, and debt service obligations are independent of income earned.

Now suppose that the exporter negotiates the following commodity-linked loan. The exporter takes out a loan of D_t and contracts to repay the lender either the fixed principal (that is, D_t) or the value of Q units of coffee at the reference price P_{xT}, whichever is greater. In return, the lender contracts to reduce the interest rate on the loan to offset the value of the option he is receiving. Assuming that the expected return on the commodity-linked loan and the conventional loan are the same, then the new interest rate on the commodity-linked loan will be

$$(6\text{-}25) \qquad r_t^o = r_t - \pi\{[E(P_{xT}|P_{xT} > D_t/Q) - D_t]/D_t\}$$

where r_t^o is the interest rate on the commodity-linked loan, π is the probability that $P_{xT} > D_t/Q$, and E is the conditional expectation operator. It should be clear that $r_t^o \leq r_t$ whenever $\pi \geq 0$.

These derivations imply the following result.

Result 7. If an exporter takes out a commodity-linked loan and provides the lender with the option of receiving at maturity $P_{xT}Q$ or the face value of the principal, whichever is greater, then net income will be

$$N(t, T) = \begin{cases} I(P_{xT}) - r_t^o D_t - (P_{xT}Q - D_t) & \text{if } P_{xT} > D_t/Q \\ I(P_{xT}) - r_t^o D_t & \text{if } P_{xT} \leq D_t/Q. \end{cases}$$

Thus, the exporter has partially hedged its income position.

Result 7 is illustrated in figure 6-5. If coffee prices turn out to be relatively low (if $P_{xT} \leq D_t/Q$), interest payments are less than with a conventional loan, and the option provided by the exporter is worthless. If,

Figure 6-5. *Income Streams with and without Commodity-linked Finance*

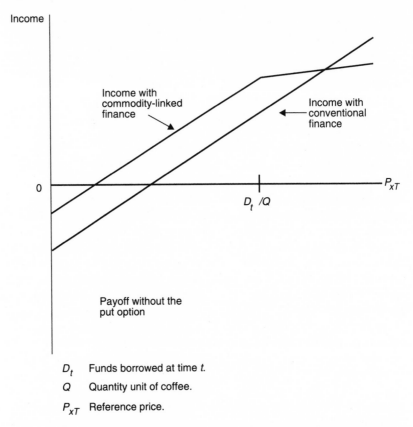

D_t   Funds borrowed at time *t*.

Q   Quantity unit of coffee.

P_{xT} Reference price.

however, coffee prices turn out to be relatively high (if $P_{xT} > D_t/Q$), the option is exercised and the exporter pays more to service its debt, but in this case it can afford to pay more. Commodity-linked loans reduce fluctuations in net income by linking debt service obligations to the level of earned income.

The loan illustrated above is a very simple example of commodity-linked finance. There are many others, including commodity-linked bonds, commodity variable rate loans, and swaps (Priovolos and Duncan 1991; Myers and Thompson 1991). This type of finance is beneficial because it combines the functions of raising capital and hedging risks. Risk management is on an ex ante basis rather than an ex post response to shocks that have already occurred, as is the case with conventional loans. By using commodity-linked finance, exporters and mills could conceivably improve access to overseas capital markets. They could also reduce financial risks, thus reducing borrowing costs and improving the efficiency of their operation. So far we have not seen any activity in coffee-linked finance, but this market may develop in the future.

Summary and Conclusions

Coffee price fluctuations imply considerable risks for those producing and marketing the crop. Growers currently bear most of the price risk because their initial advance (which acts as a guaranteed minimum price) is typically low in relation to the final price expected on the crop.

Mills could provide higher initial advances to growers and then hedge the resulting risk by buying put options on the New York Exchange. This strategy would truncate the bottom of the growers' price distribution at the level of the initial advance, thereby providing the growers with downside price protection while still allowing participation in the gains should prices rise. Under an option trading strategy, mills could, at the cost of an option premium, hedge the risk of offering higher initial advances to growers. Thus, downside price protection could be provided to growers at minimum cost without adding to the risk facing the mills.

FEDECOOP and private exporters could undertake option trading on behalf of the mills they purchase from, as well as trade futures and options on their own account. Exporters could also become involved in negotiating commodity-linked finance that combines the provision of capital with hedging, thereby reducing financial risks and lowering the cost of finance. These risk management strategies would make growers better off by increasing the level of first advances, thereby reducing risk, at little additional cost in terms of lower average prices. Whether or not it is worth paying for some of the costs of hedging is a question for Costa Rica to decide. This study indicates that the risk reduction would be substantial, the resulting implication being that hedging would have significant net benefits.

Markets for contingent claims are notoriously incomplete for developing countries that participate in international commodity markets. The lack of markets for contingent claims may be a reason for the powerful influence of government in the marketing system. Nevertheless, this study shows that innovative use of existing markets, and the engineering of new financial instruments that combine financial and hedging functions, may go a long way toward reducing risks and providing a more efficient marketing system.

Notes

1. For simplicity, the production tax is ignored. Including a production tax, however, would not fundamentally alter the following analysis, because of the way ICAFE controls marketing margins.

2. Equation 6-10 assumes a linear relationship between the New York price and the grower price. In practice, the trading decisions of and competition among the exporters will determine the exact nature of the relationship. The next chapter, by Claessens and Varangis, empirically investigates the relationship between changes in the New York spot price and the grower price and finds that a 1-cent change in the New York price translates into a 0.73-cent change in the final grower price.

3. See the next chapter for empirical estimates of the relationship between these two prices.

4. Linear relationships are entirely appropriate whenever the conditional covariance matrix of spot and futures prices is constant over time. Nonlinear models are required when this covariance is time-varying. Nonlinear relationships may be hedged by a combination of futures and options or by (dynamically) adjusting the hedging ratio β_t within the periods— or by using both these strategies.

7

Implementing Risk Management Strategies in Costa Rica's Coffee Sector

Stijn Claessens and Panos Varangis

In chapter 6 of this volume, Myers identifies the risks that coffee exporters, mills, and growers in Costa Rica face from movements in international coffee prices and presents a number of strategies that could be used to manage the risks. This chapter builds on the previous one by quantifying the risks and analyzing the benefits associated with the various strategies.

First, we present a quantification of the price risks for each party in the coffee sector. Second, we propose specific institutional changes that will facilitate and encourage the use of risk management techniques by mills and exporters for the benefit of themselves and the growers. Third, we quantify the benefits of four different strategies for risk management: the selling of futures by exporters, the selling of futures by mills, the buying of puts by exporters or mills, and the selling of physical coffee early in the crop year. Through simulations using historical and simulated data, we show that these strategies would have raised the dollar price of coffee by, on average, 1.5 to 2 percent. More important, these strategies would have significantly reduced the risks associated with movements of international coffee prices within a crop year.

This chapter was originally prepared for a presentation to the Board of Directors of ICAFE, San José, Costa Rica, on November 14–15, 1990. The authors would like to thank Robert Myers, Peter Hazell, Roberto Stewart, and the Board of Directors for their comments.

Figure 7-1. *Yearly Average Coffee Prices in New York and Costa Rica, 1957–90*

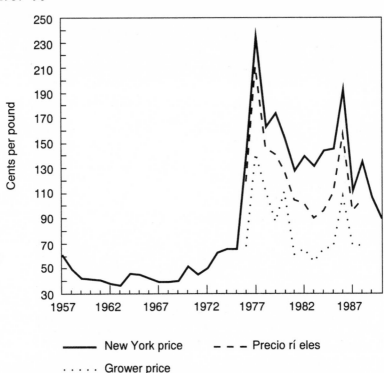

Source: For New York prices, International Monetary Fund (various issues); for precio rieles and grower prices, Stewart (1990).

Identifying the Risks

What Are the Magnitudes of the Price Risks?

Risks arise from both interyear and intrayear variability in coffee prices.

Interyear variability is shown in figure 7-1, which presents annual observations of prices, expressed in U.S. cents per pound, for the period 1957–90. Three sets of prices are plotted on the graph: the price on the New York Exchange, the *precio rieles* (the negotiated price at which mills sell to exporters), and the grower price. As shown in the figure, coffee prices have been quite volatile since the mid-1970s. The coefficient of variation (CV, the ratio of the standard deviation to the mean) of annual prices since the mid-1970s has been 28 percent.[1]

Figure 7-2. *Coefficient of Variation of New York Coffee Prices,*
1957–90

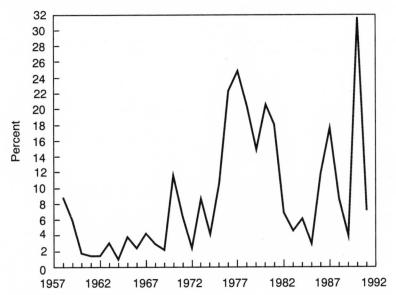

Source: International Monetary Fund (various issues).

Intrayear variability for the same period can be observed in figure 7-2,
where the intrayear CV is plotted. Intrayear variability has increased
since the mid-1970s, averaging about 14 percent since 1975. This period
includes years in which there were export quotas as well as years in
which there were none.[2] During several of the nonquota years the intrayear CV was considerably higher. For example, in 1989, a nonquota
year, the intrayear CV was 32 percent. Because it is likely that the International Coffee Agreement (ica) will not be reinstated shortly, Costa
Rica will be facing considerable intrayear price variability (perhaps on
the order of 25 percent).

The Allocation of Risks within the Current System

The allocation of risk in the Costa Rican coffee marketing system is
illustrated in figure 7-3. The three major players in the system are the
exporter, the mill, and the grower.

The exporter's price risk is associated with the period between the time
the coffee is purchased from the mill and the time a foreign buyer is
found, or between the time a sale is made to a foreign buyer and the

Figure 7-3. *Allocation of Risk in the Coffee Marketing System of Costa Rica*

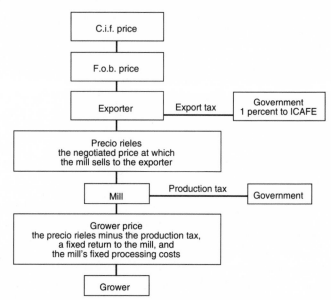

Note: The final, pooled price received by the grower at the end of the crop year is the quantity-weighted average of all grower prices obtained by the mill on sales throughout the year.

coffee is bought from the mill. If, during this time, the free on board (f.o.b.) price of coffee changes, the exporter absorbs all the movement, positive or negative. The average length of time between buying the coffee from the mill and exporting it is between a month and a month and a half. Because the exporter works on a relatively low margin (1.5 to 2.5 percent), potential profits can become actual losses if there is even a small adverse movement in the f.o.b. price.

The mill receives the precio rieles from the exporter, subtracts a fixed percentage margin and absolute costs, pays the production tax, and passes the rest on to the grower. The mill's exposure to risk is on two fronts. First, the profit margin in absolute terms depends on the level of the precio rieles.[3] Second, the initial advance paid to the grower entails risk. Legally, the mill cannot ask for a refund from the grower when prices fall. Thus, the higher the initial advance, the greater the risk the mill takes on. Currently, the advance paid to the grower is around 60 percent of the precio rieles, so the price has to fall within the crop year by more than 40 percent for the mill to incur a loss from this source.[4]

Nevertheless, in the past ten years such losses have been incurred twice—during the 1986/87 and 1988/89 crop years, when prices fell sharply because of the suspension of the ICA's export quota scheme. (In the second case, however, most of the coffee had already been sold.)

The grower bears most of the risk associated with the price fluctuations (see the chapter by Myers; Jaramillo 1989; Stewart 1990). The insurance is the initial advance, and the extent of this insurance is unknown until the coffee price is known, at the end of the season. The grower's risk is described further below.

Relationships between the New York Price, the Precio Rieles, and the Grower Price

Movements in the New York coffee price do not translate into equal movements of the final grower price for two main reasons, the first being the costs and returns of the two intermediaries—exporters and mills—in the Costa Rican coffee marketing system, and the second being the taxes levied by the government. On average, over the 1976–88 period the precio rieles (measured in dollars) has been about 81 percent of the New York price that includes cost, insurance, and freight (the c.i.f. price). The difference is accounted for by (a) the difference between the c.i.f. and f.o.b. prices and the exporters' costs, (b) the return to the exporters, and (c) the export tax. Exporters' returns have been between 1.5 percent and 2.5 percent, and the export tax has varied between 1 percent and 18 percent. However, the price difference is also dependent on the trading decisions of the exporters, which are heavily influenced by the stepwise operation of the export tax schedule (see the chapter by Myers). Within certain ranges of the New York coffee price, exporters are reluctant to raise the precio rieles, because then they would be paying a very high marginal export tax rate.[5] The notion that the precio rieles does not closely follow the New York price is historically confirmed: on a monthly basis a 1-cent change in the New York price resulted in only a 0.63-cent change in the precio rieles during the 1976–89 period.[6] The grower price during this period has been, on average, about 67 percent of the precio rieles. The difference is accounted for by processing costs, the return to the mill (currently 9 percent), and a production tax (currently 0 percent). The processing cost is fixed on a per-unit basis, and the other two are variable. It is estimated that over this period the fixed costs have averaged about 7 cents a pound and the variable costs about 27 percent. After deductions for the costs and returns of the exporters and mills and for the various taxes, the final price received by the grower during this period was, on average, about 55 percent of the New York price. As with the precio rieles, movements in the international coffee price do not translate one-to-one into movements in the grower price: a 1-cent change in the New York price translates into a 0.73-cent change in the final grower price. This difference implies that exporters and mills, and the government (in the form of tax revenues), absorb some of the international price fluctuations and that the current marketing system provides some, but limited, price insurance to the growers. The majority of the price risk—about 73 percent—is borne by the grower.[7]

Possible Approaches to Risk Management

The exporters' exposure, described above, can be hedged if the exporters sell futures at the time they negotiate the precio rieles, and buy them back when they sell the coffee to a foreign buyer. Thus, even without having a buyer at hand, exporters can effectively "lock in" an export price and thus reduce their exposure. Conversely, if exporters have a buyer but have not yet purchased the coffee from the mill, the purchase of futures will lock in the price. Futures can also be used to lock in prices for longer horizons based on planned future exports. For example, by selling futures in September that mature in March of the following year and which have a contract value equal to the amount of exports planned to be contracted in March, an exporter can lock in the price to be received for these March exports. Currently, many coffee exporters hedge their exposure by selling futures at the time the coffee is purchased from the mill.

To reduce the growers' exposure, Myers proposes that mills provide a higher initial advance to growers and hedge the resulting risk by buying put options on the New York Coffee, Sugar, and Cocoa Exchange. This strategy would provide the grower with significant downside price protection while allowing the appropriation of any gains from price rises during the year.

Possible approaches to improving the situation at the mill level are not as clear. In many cases there is some form of vertical integration between the mill and the exporter, and the mill's risk management operations cannot be separated from its other transactions with the exporter. It is our understanding, after conducting several interviews, that some mills use futures and options but not necessarily exactly in the sense of risk management. They mostly buy call options, at a premium that they consider to be acceptable, to take advantage of price increases. Strictly speaking, they speculate rather than hedge. A combination of buying calls and selling futures might be an acceptable risk management strategy. The improvement of risk management at this point of the marketing and distribution chain is discussed more fully in the next section.

Improving the Risk Management Environment

A key to improving the risk management environment lies in the role of the mill. The mill provides a service to the grower for a fixed fee (percentage of the price), as set by law, and never takes ownership of the crop. The costs that the mill is allowed to deduct from the price are also set by law. In other words, the difference between the precio rieles and the grower price is strictly governed.

There is some competition among mills on the basis of the average liquidation price paid for the previous year's crop.[8] This element of competition and the fact that in each region there are generally only two or three mills accessible to the grower create a certain type of behavior by the mills. Each mill, in setting its initial advance, looks at its competitor(s), particularly at the pattern of sales. A mill will sell, at about the same intervals, about the same quantities as its competition does, with the result that the mill's liquidation price at the end of the year will be very close to the competition's.

This behavior has two major implications. First, such a sales strategy may not result in a sales pattern that is most advantageous for Costa Rica. For example, according to Stewart (1990), the most advantageous sales pattern for Costa Rica to follow in terms of final price received would be to sell all of its coffee before May. No mill will do so, however, because of the fear that its competition, by sticking to the "traditional" sales pattern, would get a higher liquidation price if world coffee prices were to go up between May and September. As stated by a miller who was interviewed, "Even if the world price goes up to $10 a pound, nobody is going to sell more coffee than his competitor. Because if he does, and prices later go to $15 a pound and his competitor sells his coffee regularly, then the one who sold most of his coffee at $10 a pound will get a lower liquidation price and lose farmers."

Second, the current system provides no incentives to the mill to engage in risk management in order to give the grower a higher liquidation price, or a more certain price at the time the crop is delivered to the mill. Risk management is carried out only for the principal's benefit, and gains from these operations are not passed on to the grower. Mills and mill-exporters, because of their risk management expertise, but more important, because of the volume of coffee they handle, are better situated to perform risk management operations than growers are. For example, the Federation of Cooperatives of Coffee Growers (FEDECOOP), a cooperative that acts as a mill-exporter for its members, could provide risk management for its member growers on a systematic basis. As of 1990, however, even FEDECOOP's risk management operations were being done on an ad hoc basis, and it is not clear how the benefits from these operations trickled down to its member growers. (Since 1991, FEDECOOP has been engaged in more systematic risk management operations on behalf of its member farmers.)

Objectives of a Risk Management System and an Outline of Necessary Changes

A risk management system for the coffee sector in Costa Rica should have the following objectives, all of which can be realistically pursued.

- The system should provide the grower with more certainty about the final price (or less risk from falling prices). Price variations that occur after the crop is delivered to the mill and before the final payment is received should be hedged.
- The system should provide the grower with better cash flow so as to reduce the grower's borrowing requirements within the crop year. The grower should receive a higher initial advance.
- The risk management system should result in a minimal number of changes in the coffee marketing system, which is relatively effective as is. What is needed is to create incentives that will encourage the mill or exporter, or both, to manage risk for the benefit of the grower.
- The system should lay the foundation for price hedging across years.

Allowing exporters or mills, or both, to engage in risk management on behalf of growers would require a number of institutional changes. Some of these would need a formal (legal) framework. Others could be more easily instituted within the existing framework. The following five institutional changes are recommended.[9]

First, the current system should allow for a fixed price contract. That is, the grower and the mill should be able to have a fixed price contract so that when the crop is handed over to the mill, the grower will know its liquidation price. The contract could be implemented by the Instituto del Café de Costa Rica (ICAFE), the regulatory body for the coffee sector.

Second, on each marketing day ICAFE should announce a reference price in colones, basing the price on the spot price in New York adjusted for the difference between the c.i.f. price and the f.o.b. price, exporters' costs, and margins. The daily reference price would, after the same regional adjustments as are now made for each mill's costs and margins, serve as the basis for the fixed price contract between the grower and the mill.[10]

Third, growers should have a higher minimum advance, stated in colón terms and determined by ICAFE on the basis of the spot price in New York—again adjusted for the costs and margins of exporters and mills. The advance should be announced every market day along with the reference price. For the time being, the advance should be less than 100 percent of the reference price. The difference between the fixed price and the advance received by the grower upon delivering the crop to the mill should be an obligation of the mill to be paid at the end of the selling year, when the crop is liquidated. As is currently the case, the mill should pay no interest on the obligation. Over time (say, over a five-year period), the advance could be raised to 100 percent of the reference price, and the obligation and final payments at liquidation would disappear.

Fourth, domestic forward contracting of the precio rieles should be made possible and legally binding, allowing mills and exporters to agree on selling coffee forward at a fixed, domestic currency price.[11] Domestic forward contracting requires physical delivery at standard delivery points. Forward sales should be subject to verification by ICAFE, just as cash sales are now. ICAFE could reject the forward contract if, after adjusting for costs, the price were too far below the New York price for futures of the same maturity.[12]

Fifth, forward contracts on the colón-dollar rate should be made available, initially by the Central Bank and later by commercial banks, for up to one year. The rate should be determined in relation to the interest rate levels for dollars and colones.[13]

These suggested changes would not alter the basic structure of the Costa Rican coffee marketing system; rather, they would safeguard prices and income distribution. The main purpose of the changes would be to induce exporters and mills to manage price risk for the benefit of themselves and the growers. The grower currently bears the brunt of coffee price fluctuations but has little scope for managing this risk. The proposed changes would provide an effective domestic institutional and regulatory framework for allowing—but not requiring—exporters and mills to provide risk management for their growers. Costa Rica will stand to benefit most if, in the end, these risk management benefits are offered to the growers not as a result of formal requirements but as a result of competition among mills and exporters for the growers' business.

Implementing Possible Strategies

The above changes would allow for a range of risk management strategies that would benefit growers as well as all other parties. We have designed and tested four strategies that offer significant risk reduction benefits. Other strategies are possible and can be similarly analyzed and discussed. In analyzing these strategies we assume that the behavior of spot and futures prices does not change as the result of the introduction of fixed price domestic contracts and access to futures markets.

Strategy A: hedging by exporters. Under this strategy exporters sell futures contracts for December, March, July, and September that have contract values in accordance with their export sales pattern. Exporters are assumed to sell equal quantities of futures contracts for the volume of coffee they sell.[14] By selling futures, the exporters lock in a dollar price for the coffee, P_S. They then lock in a colón price for the coffee, P_c, by using a colón-dollar forward contract of the same maturity, assuming the Central Bank makes forward contracts available. Individual exporters then negotiate a forward precio rieles with a mill. Because the exporter faces a schedule of futures prices, the mill can choose from a schedule of forward prices the one that fits its needs in terms of its supply, storage, and production schedule. It is assumed that the exporter simultaneously negotiates the contract with the foreign buyer, sells the futures contract, and arranges the fixed price contract with the mill to minimize price exposure.

Because the mill knows the precio rieles, it knows which price to offer to a grower for a fixed price contract. The fixed price the mill offers will have to be in accordance with the spot reference price announced by icafe (see previous section). The mill is required to give a certain percentage (more than the current 60 percent) of this fixed price as an advance; the difference is paid by the mill to the grower at the end of the crop year. This arrangement is like that of the current system, but with two exceptions: the advance is higher, and the final liquidation payment is known. The mill seeks financing for the advance in the regular way (from a foreign or domestic bank or through the exporter).

Because the mill now has a fixed price contract, it needs to hedge and goes first to the domestic market to arrange a forward contract with an exporter.[15] The futures price in the New York Exchange is likely to be above the spot price (because of arbitrage and pricing relationships between the spot and futures price under normal market conditions); therefore, the domestic forward precio rieles is also likely to be above the spot precio rieles. The difference between the spot and forward precio rieles is collected by the mill (the mill paid the grower on the basis of the spot precio rieles) and is used to finance the higher advance to the grower. The legal system ensures that if the mill speculates on price behavior and goes bankrupt, the grower retains at least the advance payment.

The gain for the grower is a higher initial advance plus reduced intrayear price volatility. The mill has locked in its margins at an early stage and is able to offer growers a higher advance—an attractive competitive advantage.

STRATEGY B: HEDGING BY MILLS. The mill engages directly in selling futures in New York and using the colón-dollar forward market. This strategy bypasses the exporters, using the New York futures and the colón-dollar forward markets to lock in a colón price, which, after adjusting for costs and margins, can be the basis for a fixed price offer to the grower. Strategy B may need to be available in addition to strategy A to ensure competitive pricing by exporters. Large mills might prefer strategy B to strategy A, especially when they already know the New York market. For the grower, strategy B is equivalent to strategy A.

THE EFFECTIVENESS OF STRATEGIES A AND B. The effect these strategies would have had on coffee prices in Costa Rica from 1980 to 1988 is indicated in tables 7-1 and 7-2. The strategies have been simulated so that for different months of each year the following year's crop is sold forward using the five nearest futures contracts. The value of each of the five contracts is equal to the sales during the months surrounding the expiration dates of the contracts. For example, for the May contract, the contract value is equal to May and June exports.

Table 7-1 lists the effective price that could have been locked in at different periods for the prospective November–October crop. (November was chosen as the starting month, because most of the exports start then.) For example, the price locked in during the month of April 1980 by selling futures contracts for December 1980, March 1981, May 1981, July 1981, and September 1981 was 180.7 cents a pound. The last column of table 7-1 indicates the average price that was realized over the November–October season in each of the years by selling in the spot market (according to Costa Rica's actual exports). In 1980 (the crop year beginning in November 1980 and lasting through October 1981) the average realized price was 124.1 cents a pound.

By calculating the difference between the locked-in futures price and the average realized price, we can compute the gains and losses of this hedging strategy in relation to a no-hedging strategy. The results of such calculations, based on data in table 7-1, are shown in table 7-2. For example, the entry for April 1980 shows the difference between the futures price locked in in April 1980 and the realized price over the period November 1980 to October 1981. In this case, the hedging strategy (selling contracts in April 1980) would have resulted in a gain of 56.5 cents a pound (180.7−124.1) over the price that was realized without hedging.

Table 7-1. *Coffee Prices with and without Hedging, Costa Rica, 1980–88* (cents per pound)

Year[a]	Simulated locked-in price with hedging									Average realized price Nov.–Oct.
	Apr.	May	June	July	Aug.	Sept.	Oct.	Nov.	Dec.	
1980	180.7	192.0	180.5	147.9	141.6	132.7	128.2	121.4	125.1	124.1
1981	122.5	112.2	88.1	121.2	98.6	124.8	132.0	128.8	139.6	141.1
1982	—	—	120.4	109.5	115.5	132.4	131.8	132.0	126.5	130.1
1983	117.9	124.1	122.7	122.8	126.4	130.7	136.5	141.8	138.7	144.9
1984	139.2	142.9	138.3	134.0	144.8	134.3	136.1	136.5	137.9	140.1
1985	142.9	143.8	144.3	138.1	140.3	140.1	161.2	171.1	235.3	196.9
1986	247.3	209.7	179.4	183.0	200.0	194.7	170.6	151.1	137.4	116.6
1987	123.4	123.6	111.1	108.8	121.7	117.5	127.6	130.7	128.1	133.0
1988	137.3	136.9	131.4	124.1	122.4	131.6	124.4	123.1	151.4	120.2

— Not available, because futures contracts were not traded.

a. The year in which a future was sold or in which a crop year (November–October) began.

Note: The average realized price over the period 1980–88 was 138.5 cents a pound.

Source: Authors' calculations, based on data in figure 7-1; International Monetary Fund (various issues); and futures data from the Coffee, Sugar, and Cocoa Exchange, New York.

Table 7-2. *Simulated Effects of Hedging on Realized Coffee Prices, Costa Rica, 1980–88* (cents per pound)

Year[c]	Month-to-month gain or loss[a] by date of futures contract									Average gain or loss from a graduated hedging strategy[b]
	Apr.	May	June	July	Aug.	Sept.	Oct.	Nov.	Dec.	
1980	56.5	67.9	56.4	23.8	17.5	8.6	4.0	-2.7	1.0	25.9 (20.86)
1981	-18.6	-28.9	-53.1	-19.9	-42.6	-16.3	-9.1	-12.3	-1.6	-22.5 (-15.93)
1982	NA	NA	-9.7	-20.6	-14.6	2.3	1.7	1.9	-3.6	-6.1 (-4.68)
1983	-27.0	-20.7	-22.1	-22.1	-18.5	-14.1	-8.4	-3.1	-6.2	-15.8 (-10.90)
1984	15.0	18.8	14.2	9.9	20.7	10.1	11.9	12.4	13.7	14.1 (10.05)
1985	-53.9	-53.0	-52.6	-58.7	-56.6	-56.7	-35.6	-25.7	38.5	-39.4 (-20.01)
1986	130.7	93.1	62.9	66.4	83.5	78.1	54.0	34.6	20.9	69.4 (59.51)
1987	-9.6	-9.4	-21.9	-24.2	-11.3	-15.5	-5.4	-2.3	-4.9	-11.6 (-8.73)
1988	17.1	16.8	11.2	4.0	2.2	11.4	4.3	3.0	31.2	11.2 (9.35)
1980–88	13.8 (9.88)	10.6 (7.57)	-1.6 (-1.18)	-4.6 (-3.33)	-2.2 (-1.57)	0.9 (0.63)	1.9 (1.40)	0.6 (0.46)	9.9 (7.15)	2.8 (2.02)

a. Numerical gain or loss is calculated by subtracting the realized price from the simulated locked-in price; percentage gain or loss (in parentheses) shows numerical gain or loss as a percentage of the realized price.

b. Under the graduated hedging strategy one-ninth of the prospective November–October crop is sold forward, spread out over five futures contracts.

c. The year in which a future was sold or in which a crop year began.

Source: Authors' calculations, based on data in table 7-1.

The last column in table 7-2 refers to a graduated hedging strategy whereby, during the period April to December of each year, one-ninth of the prospective November–October crop is sold forward, spread out over five futures contracts. This column shows the gain or loss from such a strategy in cents per pound and as a percentage of the average realized price. For example, the entry 25.9 for 1980 indicates that hedging one-ninth of the crop during the months April through December 1980 would have led to an average gain of 25.9 cents a pound, or 20.86 percent over the average price that was realized without hedging during the crop year beginning in November 1980.

The bottom two rows of table 7-2 indicate the average of the annual gains or losses from hedging the crop in a particular month of the year during the 1980–88 period. For example, the 13.8 percent and 9.88 percent figures in the April column indicate that, on average, hedging the crop in April would have led to a gain of 13.8 cents a pound, or a gain of 9.88 percent over the average of realized prices during the period.

Table 7-2 shows that the hedging strategy would have produced small, positive gains for most months during this period. Only when the hedging was done during June, July, or August would there have been small losses. The rolling hedging strategy would have produced a small positive gain—on average, 2.8 cents a pound, or 2.02 percent of the average sales price.

The calculations shown do not account for the transaction costs involved in selling and buying. For a round-trip (selling and buying) transaction, these costs are estimated to be about $30 to $35 per contract or about 0.1 cent a pound (or 0.1 percent per dollar value of the contract). In addition, margin requirements have to be fulfilled by posting collateral with a broker. These collateral requirements are estimated to be about 10 percent of the dollar value of the contract. The collateral requirements can be satisfied by high-grade, interest-yielding securities, which means that the difference between the borrowing rate and the yield on the securities represents the net cost. This interest difference is assumed to be about 2 percent, implying that the collateral costs (per dollar of contract) are about 0.2 percent (10 percent of 2 percent). If these additional costs are incorporated, the gains are still positive—on the order of 1.5 percent of the average price in the case of the rolling hedge.

Even though this particular simulation resulted in gains in the average price from hedging, it is important to stress that one should not expect hedging to lead to higher net prices over long periods of time. Such an expectation would imply that the counterparty to the hedge would consistently lose money. The main objective to be achieved with hedging is risk reduction. In this case, intrayear price risk would have been eliminated.

The degree of risk reduction achieved can be calculated by using the results of table 7-1, as we do for the case of the rolling hedge. Hedging reduces the variability of the effective price received around the expected price. As a first, and good, proxy of the expected price, one can use the current spot price (one cannot reject the random walk hypothesis over this period). Use of the current spot price implies that one can calculate the risk reduction benefits as the ratio of the following two standard deviations:

(7-1) $$\mathrm{std}\,[(S_t - \overline{S}_t) - (F_t - \overline{S}_t)]$$

(7-2) $$\mathrm{std}\,(S_t - \overline{S}_t)$$

where std is the standard deviation (operation); S_t is the current spot price (which is equal to the expected price); $\overline{S}_t$ is the average realized price over the following crop year (last column of table 7-1); and F_t is the effective price locked in through futures contracts at time t (one of the first nine columns of table 7-1, depending on which month the hedge is initiated).

In the case of the rolling hedge, where in the months of April through December one-ninth of the exports for the period beginning in November and lasting through the following October are hedged, the results are as follows. Unhedged (equation 7-2), the standard deviation of cash receipts would have been 34.5 cents a pound. Hedged, it would have been 8.7 cents a pound. The risk reduction achieved by hedging would thus have been 75 percent. The hedge is not perfect, because of the basis risks and the fact that it is done on a rolling basis. Still, with a rolling hedge in place, only 25 percent of the world price risk would remain to be borne by the Costa Rican coffee sector as a whole.

STRATEGY C: SELLING EARLY. Figure 7-4 plots the average New York coffee price in each month of the year over the period 1957–90. The figure shows that prices in the first six months of the year (January through June) have historically been higher than the prices in the latter six months of the year. The higher prices in the early part of the year can be explained by the seasonal nature of demand and supply: in winter, demand in the North is high and the supply from countries in the southern hemisphere is small.[16] As a result, stocks are low and prices are relatively high. Because Costa Rica's harvest season is in the early part of the calendar year, it could benefit from selling earlier in the year (if this price pattern continues).

A comparison of simulations of sales evenly spread out over the first six months and sales evenly spread out over the whole year during the 1957–90 period indicates that, on average, the effective dollar price received would have been 2.33 percent higher under the strategy of

Figure 7-4. *Monthly Average Coffee Prices in New York, 1957–90*

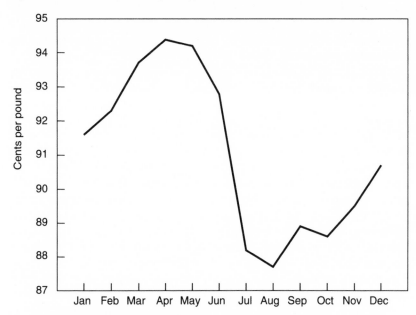

Source: International Monetary Fund (various issues).

selling early. Apart from the possibility of raising the average price received, selling early provides for earlier cash flow and lower storage costs and allows higher advances and earlier final payment.[17]

The advantages of selling early are recognized by some participants in Costa Rica's coffee system. However, the current arrangement by which mills buy coffee from growers on the basis of the average price received provides little incentive for early selling. Any mill aims to sell its coffee at a price that is no worse than that of the competing mill or mills (likely only one, but at most three). Selling early entails the risk of losing out on a possible price rise later in the year, thus achieving a lower price than the competition does and losing growers as customers. The "collusive" outcome among mills is to sell the crop gradually throughout the year and compete with each other on the basis of other, nonprice factors, of which credit is the most important.[18]

STRATEGY D: BUYING PUTS. The most important aspect of price risk for growers is the possibility of a sharp drop in prices during the year as a result of, for example, a large crop (as happened in 1978 and 1987, the years following the Brazilian frost and drought, respectively) or a breakdown in the ICA (as happened in 1989). A technique for managing this risk is to buy put options on coffee futures on the New York Exchange (see further the chapter by Myers). Doing so would provide price insurance, because the effective price received would not fall below the exercise (strike) price of the put.

We simulated a put option strategy for the years 1957 to 1990 as follows. In September of each year, we bought four put options spread out evenly over a period beginning in October of that year and ending the following September. Each put had a contract value of one-quarter of the year's total crop. The exercise prices of all four puts were based on the September spot price in the year in which the options were bought; that is, we simulated buying so-called at-the-money options. This strategy ensured that the effective price received over the October–September period would not fall below the September price and left the possibility of receiving higher prices open.[19] We calculated the premiums of the puts using the Black-Scholes pricing formula, a formula that is widely accepted in the financial industry and broadly confirmed by calculations on recently quoted prices of options (see also Kolb 1985; Labuszewski and Myhoff 1988a).

Figure 7-5 shows the net payoff of the put option strategy, where the net payoff is defined as the payoff of the put options at their maturity dates, discounted to September of each year, minus the premium costs of buying the put options. The net payoff is expressed as a percentage of the average spot price of coffee over the October–September period. As one can observe, in several years during the 1957–90 period the put option strategy would have led to large gains over the prices that were received without hedging. These gains would have happened in years in which coffee prices fell drastically, for example, in 1980, 1986, and 1988. In 1986 the strategy would have raised the effective price received (reduced the loss) by more than 50 percent.

As with all insurance schemes, in most periods the strategy would have resulted in a small loss, because the (put) premiums were paid but the insurance was not used or only a little used—that is, the puts were not exercised. Over the 1957–90 period the average premium for buying puts was about 2.4 cents a pound and the average gain from exercising the puts at maturity was about 4.2 cents a pound, resulting in an average net gain of about 1.8 cents a pound. This net gain meant that the put strategy would have increased the effective price received by approximately 2 percent.

The 2 percent average gain does not account for transaction costs, which are estimated to be between $30 and $35 per contract of 37,500 pounds (or about 0.1 percent of the current price) for a round-trip transaction. In general, it is to be expected that buying insurance would not,

Figure 7-5. *Simulated Gains and Losses from Using Puts to Hedge Coffee Prices in Costa Rica, 1957–90*

Note: Gains and losses reflect the puts' net payoff expressed as a percentage of the average spot price of coffee over the October–September period beginning in the year indicated.
Source: Authors' calculations based on spot prices from International Monetary Fund (various issues).

on average, result in gains, because otherwise the counterparty would, on average, make losses. The main benefit of the put option strategy is that it allows the mill to provide an advance to the grower equal to the spot price in September without being exposed to the risk of falling prices throughout the year and while still retaining the potential of passing on to the grower any increase in prices.

The Effect of Hedging on the Mill

The four strategies could be implemented by either exporters or mills. If the exporter were to execute the strategy, then the mill and the exporter would have to agree on a domestic forward contract with a fixed price (or with a price-sharing formula, in the case of the put option strategy). For that reason the proposals outlined above include the possibility of domestically binding forward contracts to be verified by ICAFE. The effect on the grower would be broadly identical under the first three options, and cash flows between the mill and the exporter would differ only with respect to who bore the transaction costs of futures trading. Under the fourth option, buying puts, the grower and the mill would have to agree on a formula for sharing the cost of the premiums and the possible payoffs. At the time of delivery the grower would receive the spot reference price minus the costs of buying the puts. At liquidation, the grower would receive the full gain if the price rose above the reference price (the exercise price of the puts). If the price fell below the reference price, the grower would not receive or owe anything at liquidation.

Under any of the four strategies, the mill would provide a higher advance to the grower. To analyze the effect on the mill of higher advances to the grower, including the effect of higher credit needs, we assume here that the mill executes the strategy. Currently, the mill provides an advance that is approximately 60 percent of the final liquidation price, makes some intermediate payments, and makes a final liquidation payment of about 34 percent. Raising the advance to 100 percent would result in a one-time increase in the credit needs of the mill of about 40 percent, because the final liquidation payment would be moved forward once by about one year. After the first year of adoption of the new strategy, the mill's credit needs would be no different than under the current system, because at the beginning of each crop year the mill would pay the initial advance and the final liquidation payment for the previous year (together, close to 100 percent).

In the first year of the new system the mill would have to obtain credit, either domestically or abroad, for the additional 40 percent advance. If the strategy of selling early were adopted, the mill would need this additional credit only for a short period: on average, the milled product would be sold within three to four months. The higher prices the mill could achieve by selling early (approximately 2 percent) would compensate for the cost of the additional credit.

If the mill were to sell the crop forward gradually over the year by using the futures market, it would receive payments gradually over the year, but would have paid the grower on delivery and thus have credit needs. However, the futures prices would under normal market circumstances be above the spot prices.[20] Because the mill would pay the grower on the basis of the spot price, the mill would collect the difference between the futures price and the spot price, which would compensate for the extra credit cost incurred in providing the higher initial advance.

Conclusions

Four risk management strategies to cope with the price risks faced by the Costa Rican coffee sector have been presented: hedging by exporters, hedging by mills, selling early, and buying puts. The purpose of the suggested changes is to provide incentives for the mills or exporters, or both, to assume and hedge some of the risk that growers presently face and are unable to manage effectively themselves. For the historical period sampled, all four strategies would have substantially reduced (by up to 75 percent) the intrayear risk associated with coffee price instability. And the strategies would have marginally increased (by 1.5 to 2 percent) the average price received by the growers. Effective implementation of these strategies would require several institutional changes in the Costa Rican coffee marketing system as well as the development of a market in forward contracts on the domestic currency.

Notes

1. The CV is just one measure of price instability. See Newbery and Stiglitz (1981) for other measures.

2. Allocation of country export quotas was the instrument used under the various international coffee agreements to exercise control over world coffee prices.

3. The percentage for profit margin and costs is around 10 percent, but effectively it is smaller because some costs are not allowed by law to be included in the deductible costs.

4. The advance is set with respect to the expected precio rieles. Stewart (1990) reports that mills set this advance at about 60 percent of the expected precio rieles.

5. This appears to have been the case at the end of 1990, when exporters were reluctant to raise the precio rieles (measured in dollar terms) above 0.95 cents, because the tax rate would have risen from 0 percent to 4.09 percent.

6. This result was obtained by regressing (ordinary least squares) the logarithm of the annual precio rieles, expressed in dollars, on the logarithm of annual New York prices, also in dollars, for the period 1976–89. The fit is poor: $R^2 = 0.36$.

7. This result is obtained by regressing (ordinary least squares) the percentage changes in the growers' annual prices, expressed in dollars, on the percentage changes in annual New York prices, also in dollars. $R^2 = 0.78$.

8. The liquidation price is the yearly sales-weighted average price a mill has obtained from selling its coffee, adjusted for fees, costs, and taxes.

9. The first three changes are to some extent substitutes: either the first two changes or the third change would be necessary to achieve the objectives.

10. ICAFE may announce several reference prices, one for each region in which allowances for mills' costs differ.

11. Currently, forward contracts are used for agreements only on the delivery of goods, not on price. The legal nature of existing forward contracts to deliver is unclear.

12. In addition to announcing a daily reference price, ICAFE could also publish daily New York futures rates, adjusted for exchange rates and costs. Such action would allow easy comparison and facilitate a competitive market in domestic forward contracts.

13. Possibly, forward contracts could be made available only if foreign financing is brought in or a futures contract is arranged for similar maturity. The arrangement of foreign finance or a future contract would need to be verified ex post.

14. The hedge ratio is thus taken as one. If the relationship between the spot price and the futures prices is not one-to-one, the hedge ratio would have to be adjusted.

15. The mill will always have the option of going straight to the New York futures exchange (see strategy B). This option will ensure competitive pricing.

16. The crop season of Brazil, the largest producer, is from July to June. Most of Brazil's crop comes on the market in the latter half of the calendar year.

17. Early selling may increase the variability of the average price received, because some of the risk reduction achieved by spreading out sales throughout the year is not attained. It would be advisable, therefore, to combine the early-selling strategy with a hedging strategy.

18. Some exporters sell early and cover themselves against the possibility of losing out on a future price rise by buying call options.

19. It can be shown that this strategy is equivalent to selling futures contracts and buying call options.

20. This relationship will hold because one can always simultaneously buy coffee spot, store it, and sell it in the futures market. For example, on November 5, 1990, the (weighted) futures price was 91.3 cents a pound and the spot price 84.9 cents a pound. This implies an effective basis of $91.3 / 84.9 = 1.076$ for six months, or a 15 percent annual rate.

8

Managing Oil Import Price Risk in Costa Rica: Strategies and Benefits

Robert J. Myers and Stanley R. Thompson

Virtually all of Costa Rica's petroleum-based energy needs are imported in the form of oil and gasoline. Indeed, petroleum products are a major import item, accounting for approximately 8 percent of total import expenditures in recent years. Some exploration is taking place, but so far it has not resulted in significant domestic production. Dependence on imported oil makes the Costa Rican economy vulnerable to oil price shocks, such as those that occurred in 1974, 1979, and 1990. Sudden increases in oil prices consume valuable foreign exchange and, if severe enough, can cause an economic slowdown or recession.

To help manage this price risk, and because of the strategic importance of the oil sector, the government of Costa Rica maintains strict control over the domestic petroleum market. A government-owned company, Refinadora Costarricense de Petroleo (RECOPE), has a legislated monopoly to import all petroleum-based products. RECOPE not only imports but also refines and distributes oil products. The company owns and operates port facilities and an oil pipeline that runs from coast to coast. It also engages in oil exploration and manages some coal developments used to generate electricity.

Despite its domestic monopoly powers, RECOPE is a price taker on world oil markets and so faces considerable risk from fluctuations in the price paid for imported oil. Some of this price risk can be hedged by using markets for oil futures and options. Currently, however, RECOPE does not trade in these markets and must therefore respond to increases in world

The authors wish to thank Steve Hanson for helpful comments and discussion.

oil prices either by requesting domestic price increases for petroleum products, by borrowing, or by running down financial reserves.

This chapter investigates RECOPE's potential for improving the management of price risk by trading oil futures and options on the New York Mercantile Exchange. A model is developed, and data on oil prices are used with the model to illustrate proposed hedging strategies for RECOPE. It is found that futures and options can reduce risk considerably, leading to improved planning and an increased capacity to absorb oil price shocks. The chapter by Claessens and Varangis, which follows, builds on these findings and provides more on the institutional background.

Oil Pricing and the Distribution of Risks

Domestic prices for electricity and petroleum products in Costa Rica are negotiated and set periodically by an energy pricing board, which consists of representatives from the government, energy consumer groups, and RECOPE. The board adjusts domestic prices approximately once a year, but sometimes more often and sometimes less. Since late 1990, domestic prices have been set according to an agreed formula covering periods of extraordinary international price movements. Essentially, the formula adjusts the domestic price up or down if the international price moves outside of a band determined by the trend in international prices.

Although the energy pricing board controls the prices RECOPE receives for petroleum products in domestic currency terms (colones), it obviously has no control over the prices RECOPE pays for imported oil and gasoline or exchange rates. An unexpected increase in world oil prices when domestic petroleum prices are fixed can put RECOPE in the position of having to finance the resulting losses. Similarly, an unexpected colón devaluation makes oil imports more expensive for RECOPE, thus putting additional pressure on profits. The risk of such adverse price movements is substantial, at least in the short run, because there is no direct link between domestic petroleum prices and fluctuations in world oil prices or the exchange rate.

RECOPE imports oil from various countries, including Colombia, Ecuador, Mexico, and Venezuela. However, the price selected as representative for spot market purchases is Venezuelan Tia Juana Light, quoted in dollars. Because most oil is traded in dollars, the colón-dollar exchange rate is the most relevant. Both of these series are graphed in figure 8-1 by using weekly data from March 1987 through May 1990. Prior to April 1989, the spot price series is relatively smooth because of imprecise reporting by the U.S. Department of Energy. Subsequent to this date,

Figure 8-1. *Spot Prices for Venezuelan Crude Oil and Dollar-Colón Exchange Rates, March 1987–May 1990*

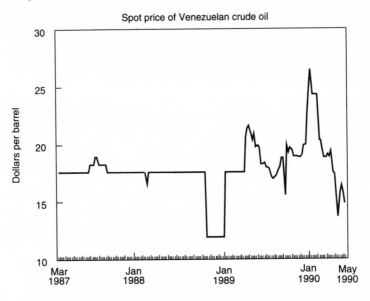

Spot price of Venezuelan crude oil

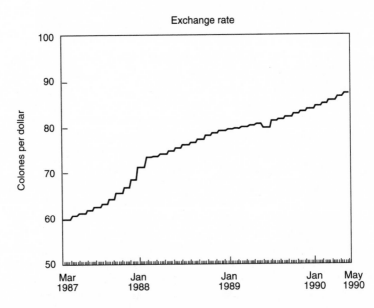

Exchange rate

Note: Beginning in April 1989, reporting of spot crude prices became more precise.
Source: For spot prices, *Oil and Gas Journal Energy Database*; for exchange rates, International Monetary Fund (various issues).

however, more precise reporting leads to a truer reflection of price volatility. It is evident that the price Costa Rica pays for imported oil fluctuates considerably: price increases occur in the third quarter of 1987, the second quarter of 1989, and the fourth quarter of 1989. The exchange rate appears much more stable and predictable, there being an almost continuous trend of colón devaluation.

When the energy pricing board sets domestic prices in colones over a planning horizon, it is exposing RECOPE to the gamble that the colón will not be devalued unexpectedly and that world oil prices will not increase significantly over the planning horizon. Futures and options markets can be used to hedge part of this risk, leading to improved risk management and planning. It is important to note, however, that futures and options trading will not eliminate the problems associated with a long-term increase in oil prices. Eventually, if prices do not fall back, domestic prices must be increased in line with world prices, and the economy must adjust to the higher oil prices. Oil-linked financial instruments such as swaps may be used to manage some of these longer-run risks (see Myers 1992). Hedging with futures and options can help cope with cash flow problems during the adjustment period. More important, hedging can enhance RECOPE's ability to plan by increasing the likelihood that anticipated cash surpluses from oil over a planning horizon will be realized.

The remainder of this chapter investigates how futures and options hedging could be implemented and what outcomes might be expected.

Hedging with Futures and Options

We begin by outlining a model that captures the main features of the problem. We then analyze hedging strategies—those that use futures and those that use options. Our empirical analysis reveals a good potential for RECOPE to hedge oil price risks by using either futures or options, or both.

A Model

In the model there is a planning horizon of n periods (for example, six months) over which the domestic price of petroleum products is fixed in domestic currency terms by the energy pricing board. For each period during the planning horizon, RECOPE's income (gross revenue minus oil import costs) is defined as

$$(8\text{-}1) \qquad\qquad Y_i = cg(Q_i) - P_i Q_i$$

where Y_i is the income in colones during period i; c is a $(1 \times k)$ vector of fixed domestic prices for petroleum products in colones; P_i is the import price of oil in colones during period i; Q_i is the quantity of oil imported and consumed during i; and g is a $(k \times 1)$ vector of production functions that transform oil into petroleum products. The sum of the incomes over the entire planning period is then

$$(8\text{-}2) \qquad\qquad Y = \sum_{i=1}^{n} Y_i.$$

For simplicity, discounting is ignored so that RECOPE is assumed to value income in different periods during the planning horizon equally. Discounting could be taken into account without changing the main results of the analysis that follows.[1]

Suppose that the quantity of oil imported and consumed in each period of the planning horizon can be predicted accurately at the beginning of the planning horizon. This supposition seems reasonable because the domestic price of petroleum products is assumed to be fixed over the planning horizon and demand can thus be assumed to be relatively stable. Furthermore, suppose that the amount of petroleum products produced per barrel of oil is determined by the physical characteristics of the refinery and known. Then gross revenues over the planning horizon are effectively known in advance, and the difference between actual and expected income in any period depends only on the difference between actual and expected oil prices:

$$(8\text{-}3) \qquad\qquad \Delta Y_i = -(P_i - P_i^*)Q_i$$

where ΔY_i is the difference between actual and expected income in period i, and P_i^* is the import price expected in period i, based on information available at the beginning of the planning horizon. Summing over the planning horizon gives

$$(8\text{-}4) \qquad\qquad \Delta Y = -\sum_{i=1}^{n}(P_i - P_i^*)Q_i.$$

ΔY is the net cash surplus (or shortfall) at the end of the planning horizon in relation to expectations held at the beginning.

The net cash surplus is risky because oil prices over the planning horizon are random variables. This is illustrated in figure 8-2, which shows the net cash surplus in period i as a function of realized oil import prices in period i. When the realized oil import price is below the expected price, the net cash surplus is positive because costs are lower than expected. But when the realized oil price is above the expected price, the net cash surplus is negative because costs are higher than

Figure 8-2. *Net Cash Surplus as a Function of Realized Oil Import Prices without Hedging*

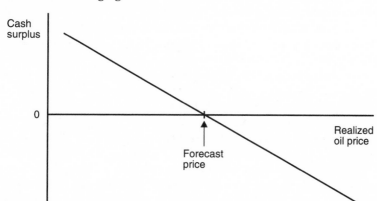

expected. The degree of risk depends on the nature of the probability distribution governing oil import prices and exchange rates. In what follows, the main objective of hedging is assumed to be the reduction of risk surrounding RECOPE's net cash surplus.

Hedging with Futures

RECOPE has a commitment to supply domestic petroleum products at fixed domestic prices over the planning horizon. This commitment exposes RECOPE to the risks of world oil price increases and colón devaluations. Now suppose that RECOPE tries to hedge these risks by trading oil futures contracts on the New York Mercantile Exchange. Futures contracts are legally binding commitments to deliver (if the contract is sold) or take delivery of (if the contract is bought) a given quantity and quality of a commodity during a specified future month. Delivery on contracts may take place anytime during the specified delivery month. However, by far the majority of futures contracts are offset by taking out an equal and opposite position before the delivery month arrives (sold contracts are bought back and vice versa). Because futures contracts are standardized and a clearinghouse acts as a third-party guarantor of all transactions, the offsetting position liquidates the trader's obligation. Therefore, the physical commodity need not change hands and can be marketed through normal channels.

RECOPE has a short spot position in oil because it has a commitment to satisfy domestic demand in each period of the planning horizon. To

hedge the resulting price risk, an asset is needed whose return is positively correlated with oil prices. Then, as oil prices go up and cash
surplus declines, the return on the hedging asset will increase to offset the
additional cost of higher prices to RECOPE. The purchase of futures contracts is a perfect example of such an asset. If spot oil prices rise over the
planning horizon, so will futures prices, and the profit from selling
futures contracts back at the higher price will help offset the extra cost of
importing oil. Conversely, if prices fall, then the lower costs of importing
oil will help to offset the loss on futures.

Assume the existence of futures contracts that can be delivered during
each month of the planning horizon. (Currently, the New York Mercantile Exchange trades crude oil futures contracts maturing in each month
over a horizon of approximately eighteen months.) Assume, as well, that
RECOPE purchases futures for each maturity at the beginning of the planning horizon and holds them (without adjustment) until they are
liquidated on the relevant maturity date. Further assume that the futures
markets are efficient in the sense that the expected return from holding
futures is zero.[2] Under these assumptions, RECOPE's cash surplus in
period i can be written as[3]

$$(8\text{-}5) \qquad \Delta Y_i = f_i X_i - p_i Q_i$$

where $f_i = F_i(i) - F_0(i)$, that is, the difference (in colones) between the
futures price for delivery in period i at time i, $F_i(i)$, and the same futures
contract quoted at the beginning of the planning horizon, $F_0(i)$; X_i is
the quantity of futures purchased (or sold, if negative) at the beginning
of the planning horizon for delivery in period i; and $p_i = P_i - P_i^*$, that is,
the difference (in colones) between the actual oil price in period i and the
price expected at the beginning of the planning horizon. The futures
prices, quoted in dollars, are converted to colones by using the exchange
rate applicable when the transaction takes place.

With futures, the net cash surplus at the end of the planning horizon
becomes

$$(8\text{-}6) \qquad \Delta Y = \sum_{i=1}^{n}(f_i X_i - p_i Q_i).$$

This cash surplus now has two random components: spot prices and
futures prices. The aim is to choose futures positions, X_i, for every
period to minimize the risk surrounding the net cash surplus.

The appropriate hedging strategy will depend on the relationship
between spot and futures price movements. The possibility that spot and
futures prices will not move together is called *basis risk*. Suppose there is

a simple linear relationship between unexpected oil price shocks in the spot and futures markets:[4]

$$(8\text{-}7) \qquad\qquad\qquad p_i = \beta_i f_i$$

where β_i is a parameter that may change for different periods over the planning horizon and is therefore indexed with an i. Equation 8-7 shows that some proportion, β_i, of any price shock in the futures market will transfer into an unexpected change in the spot price.

Substituting 8-7 into 8-6 allows the net cash surplus to be expressed as

$$(8\text{-}8) \qquad\qquad\qquad \Delta Y = \sum_{i=1}^{n} f_i (X_i - \beta_i Q_i).$$

If $X_i = \beta_i Q_i$ for all i, then $\Delta Y = 0$. Thus we have the following result.

Result 1. With no quantity uncertainty and in the absence of basis risk, $p_i = \beta_i f_i$; then a futures hedging rule, $X_i = \beta_i Q_i$, ensures that the net cash surplus is always zero.

This result is illustrated in figure 8-3. When the realized price in period i is above the expected price, import costs are higher than expected and the cash surplus from spot transactions in period i is negative. However, RECOPE has purchased futures as a hedge so that the higher costs are offset by profits on futures as the futures prices rise along with the spot prices. When the realized price in period i is below the expected price,

Figure 8-3. *Net Cash Surplus as a Function of Realized Oil Import Prices with Futures Hedging*

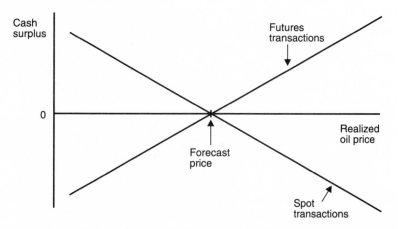

costs are lower than expected and the net cash surplus from spot transactions in period i is positive. But these gains are offset by losses on futures as a result of the unexpected price decline. In aggregate, the two effects cancel each other and the net cash surplus is always zero.

The problem with Result 1 is that it relies on a simple, deterministic linear relationship between spot and futures price shocks. Although spot and futures prices for oil obviously are closely related, we would not expect equation 8-7 to hold exactly at all times. Spot and futures prices may respond differently to the same piece of new information if it has different implications for current supply and demand versus future supply and demand. Thus there is basis risk.

Assume that the relationship between spot and futures price shocks is subject to a random disturbance:

$$(8\text{-}9) \qquad\qquad p_i = \beta_i f_i + u_i$$

where u_i is a zero mean, serially uncorrelated disturbance term. The random variable u_i represents the part of spot price shocks that cannot be predicted fully from observing movements in futures prices. The disturbance may occur as a result of exchange rate fluctuations or basis fluctuations (the changing relationship between spot and futures prices).

Substituting equation 8-9 into equation 8-6, the net cash surplus becomes

$$(8\text{-}10) \qquad\qquad \Delta Y = \sum_{i=1}^{n} [f_i (X_i - \beta_i Q_i) - u_i Q_i].$$

Thus, the hedging rule $X_i = \beta_i Q_i$ now results in a net cash surplus of

$$(8\text{-}11) \qquad\qquad \Delta Y = -\sum_{i=1}^{n} u_i Q_i.$$

The only remaining source of risk with this hedging rule is fluctuations in u_i. It can be shown that shocks to u_i represent uninsurable residual risk, which cannot be hedged using oil futures only. Thus we have the following result.

Result 2. With no uncertainty about quantity and in the presence of basis risk, $p_i = \beta_i f_i + u_i$; then the futures hedging rule, $X_i = \beta_i Q_i$, minimizes the risk surrounding the net cash surplus.

Because part of the fluctuations in u_i may be the result of exchange rate movements, it is possible that the residual risk could be reduced further if a futures or forward foreign exchange market were available (Thompson and Bond 1987). However, no formal forward or futures markets are currently available for the colón-dollar exchange rate; moreover, it is widely perceived that movements in this rate are easy to predict over short-to-intermediate time horizons.

Hedging with Options

When hedging with futures, the potential advantages of a decline in import prices are eliminated along with the disadvantages of an increase. A decline in import prices would be clearly desirable because it would reduce RECOPE's costs, thereby increasing income and net cash surplus. Hedging with options would allow RECOPE to participate in the gains if prices fall, while still providing protection against upward price movements (at a cost).

Suppose that the model outlined earlier is applicable, but that instead of trading futures, RECOPE can buy or sell call options on the New York Mercantile Exchange. An oil call option gives the owner the right, but not the obligation, to buy a futures contract for oil at a predetermined price called the exercise or strike price. If the futures price at maturity is higher than the exercise price, the option is valuable and will be exercised (because the owner can buy at the lower exercise price and sell at the higher market price). But if the futures price at maturity is lower than the exercise price, the option will expire worthless. Purchasing call options would allow RECOPE to lock in maximum prices for imported oil over the planning horizon (subject to basis risk) at the cost of the price paid for the options (the options premium).

Assume that there are call options on futures contracts for delivery during each month of the planning horizon. At the beginning of the planning horizon, RECOPE buys calls maturing in each period and holds them (without adjustment) until they are exercised (if valuable) on the relevant maturity date. Under these assumptions, the net cash surplus can be expressed as

(8-12) $$\Delta Y = \sum_{i=1}^{n} (v_i Z_i - p_i Q_i).$$

where $v_i = V_i(i) - V_0(i)$, which is the difference (in colones) between the value of an option maturing i in period at time i and the price of the option (that is, the option premium paid) when purchased at the beginning of the planning horizon, and where Z_i is the quantity of call options purchased (or sold, if negative) that expire in period i.

The value of the option at maturity will be either zero or the difference between the expiring futures price and the exercise price on the option, whichever is greater. Thus we have

$$(8\text{-}13) \qquad\qquad V_i(i) = \max[F_i(i) - K_i, 0]$$

where K_i is the exercise price on the option. The initial price of the option, $V_0(i)$, is whatever market price RECOPE pays at the time of purchase. Prices in dollars are converted to colones by using the relevant exchange rate.

It is assumed that RECOPE has the "safety first" objective of putting a ceiling on the effective price it pays for imported oil, the ceiling for each period being the futures price on contracts with that maturity date, quoted at the beginning of the planning horizon, $F_0(i)$. Thus, if $P_i > F_0(i)$, RECOPE effectively pays the lower expected price, $F_0(i)$, but if $P_i < F_0(i)$, RECOPE gains by paying the lower realized price, P_i.[5]

Assume that the simple deterministic relationship between spot and futures price shocks represented by equation 8-7 holds. Substituting equation 8-7 into equation 8-12 then gives

$$(8\text{-}14) \qquad\qquad \Delta Y = \sum_{i=1}^{n} (v_i Z_i - f_i \beta_i Q_i).$$

Three separate cases are examined.

First, suppose that all of the realized futures prices turn out to be greater than the exercise price, that is, that $F_i(i) > K_i$ for all i. Then equation 8-14 can be written as

$$(8\text{-}15) \quad \Delta Y = \sum_{i=1}^{n} \{F_i(i)[Z_i - \beta_i Q_i] + F_0(i)\beta_i Q_i - K_i Z_i - V_0(i)Z_i\}.$$

Furthermore, suppose that the exercise price on options maturing in period i is chosen to equal the futures price on contracts with the same maturity date, quoted at the beginning of the planning horizon, that is, that $K_i = F_0(i)$. Then equation 8-15 becomes

$$(8\text{-}16) \qquad \Delta Y = \sum_{i=1}^{n} \{[F_i(i) - K_i][Z_i - \beta_i Q_i] - V_0(i)Z_i\}.$$

Now consider the hedging rule $Z_i = \beta_i Q_i$, that is, buying $\beta_i Q_i$ calls with an exercise price equal to $F_0(i)$. For this rule, equation 8-16 reduces to

$$(8\text{-}17) \qquad\qquad \Delta Y = -\sum_{i=1}^{n} V_0(i)Z_i.$$

Net cash surplus is not sensitive to positive price shocks that send oil prices above their anticipated levels. However, the cost of this price protection is the option premiums paid, as defined in equation 8-17.

Second, suppose that all of the realized futures prices turn out to be less than or equal to the exercise price, that is, that $F_i(i) \leq K_i$ for all i. In this case, the options are worthless at maturity, and equation 8-14 becomes

$$(8\text{-}18) \qquad \Delta Y = -\sum_{i=1}^{n} [f_i \beta_i Q_i + V_0(i) Z_i].$$

Using the same hedging rule ($Z_i = \beta_i Q_i$) and with K_i equal to $F_0(i)$, equation 8-18 reduces to

$$(8\text{-}19) \qquad \Delta Y = -\sum_{i=1}^{n} [f_i Z_i + V_0(i) Z_i].$$

Because K_i was chosen to equal $F_0(i)$ and $F_i(i) \leq K_i$ for all i, f_i in equation 8-19 is negative and ΔY increases as $F_i(i)$ falls further below $F_0(i)$. Thus, RECOPE obtains a higher net cash surplus as oil import prices fall. However, the cost of the option premiums must be subtracted to get the final net cash surplus.

Third, it could be that some options are exercised, that is, that $F_i(i) > K_i$, but that other maturities expire worthless, that is, that $F_i(i) \leq K_i$. In this case, RECOPE participates in the gains in periods when futures prices are lower than the exercise price but has limited its losses when futures prices are higher than the exercise price.

These findings can be summarized in the following result.

Result 3. With no quantity uncertainty and in the absence of basis risk, $p_i = \beta_i f_i$; then an options hedging rule, $Z_i = \beta_i Q_i$, with exercise prices, K_i, chosen to equal current futures prices, $F_0(i)$, puts a floor under the net cash surplus.

This result is illustrated in figure 8-4. When the realized price in period i is above the expected price, costs are higher than expected and the net cash surplus from spot transactions is negative. In this case, the purchased call options are valuable, and the gains from options trading offset the spot market losses. In aggregate, losses are limited to the value of the option premiums. When the realized price is below the expected price, costs are lower than expected, and the net cash surplus from spot transactions is positive. The options expire worthless, but the option premiums still reduce the net cash surplus. The aggregate effect is represented by the dotted line, which shows a positive net cash surplus at low realized prices and a floor under cash surplus losses at high realized prices.

Figure 8-4. *Net Cash Surplus as a Function of Realized Oil Import Prices with Options Hedging*

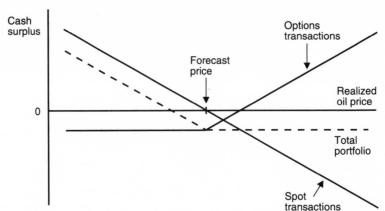

Result 3 relies on a simple deterministic linear relationship between spot and futures price shocks. However, we can allow for basis risk by using equation 8-9, which incorporates a random disturbance into the relationship between spot and futures prices. Substituting equation 8-9 into equation 8-12 gives

$$(8\text{-}20) \qquad \Delta Y = \sum_{i=1}^{n} (v_i Z_i - f_i \beta_i Q_i - u_i Q_i).$$

Consider the same hedging rule ($Z_i = \beta_i Q_i$) that was suggested for the deterministic analysis of Result 3, and again have K_i equal to $F_0(i)$. As before, there are three cases to consider.

First, suppose that all realized futures prices are greater than the exercise price, that is, that $F_i(i) > K_i$. Then it can be shown that under our hedging rule,

$$(8\text{-}21) \qquad \Delta Y = -\sum_{i=1}^{n} [u_i Q_i + V_i(i)Z_i].$$

The only difference between this and the deterministic case is the existence of basis risk, represented by u_i. However, the additional basis risk is uninsurable when using only the options market and therefore does not change the options hedging rule.

Second, if all realized futures prices are below the exercise price, that is, if $F_0(i) \le K_i$, the options expire worthless. In this case, and under our hypothesized hedging rule, it can be shown that the net cash surplus is

(8-22) $$\Delta Y = -\sum_{i=1}^{n} [f_i Z_i + u_i Q_i + V_0(i)Z_i].$$

Because f_i is negative, ΔY increases as oil prices fall. Thus, RECOPE participates in the benefits from falling prices, at the cost of the option premiums and at the risk of adverse basis movements.

Third, when some options are exercised, that is, when $F_i(i) > K_i$, but others expire worthless, that is, when $F_i(i) \le K_i$, then RECOPE participates in the gains when futures prices are lower than the exercise price but has limited losses when futures prices are above the exercise price. The only difference from the deterministic case is the presence of the residual basis risk, which cannot be insured using oil options only.

Similar to the deterministic case, these findings can be summarized in the following result.

Result 4. With no quantity uncertainty and in the presence of basis risk, $p_i = \beta_i f_i + u_i$; then an options hedging rule, $Z_i = \beta_i Q_i$, with exercise prices, K_0, chosen to equal current futures prices, $F_0(i)$, puts a floor under the net cash surplus, subject to basis risk.

We now turn to the estimation and implementation of these hedging rules.

Empirical Implementation

The key issue in the empirical implementation of both the futures and the options hedging strategies is how to estimate the parameters β_i for $i = 1, 2, \ldots, n$. These parameters define the relationship between spot and futures price shocks over different time horizons, thereby providing the proportion of imported oil that should be hedged with futures or options in each period, under the hedging rules derived above. An exercise price must also be chosen for options, but the hedging rules derived above suggest using the current futures price (that is, the one that exists at the beginning of the planning horizon), which is readily observable. Of course, other strategies for choosing the exercise price are also possible.

To estimate the β_i parameters, consider once again the stochastic relationship (equation 8-9) specified between spot and futures price shocks. For convenience, this relationship is rewritten as

(8-23) $$p_i = \beta f_i + u_i \qquad i = 1, 2, \ldots, n$$

where p_i is the cash price shock, which is equal to $P_i - P_i^*$, and f_i is the futures price shock, which is equal to $F_i(t) - F_0(t)$. As before, u_i is random disturbances to cash prices, which are uncorrelated with shocks to futures prices.

Equation 8-23 is in the form of a regression equation. Obtaining time-series data on p_i and f_i for each i, we can run a set of n regressions and use the slope coefficients as an estimate of the optimal hedge ratio, $\beta_i = X_i/Q_i$ or $\beta_i = Z_i/Q_i$. A likelihood ratio could be used to test whether the β_i are different for different i or whether the same proportion of imported oil should be hedged at every maturity ($\beta_i = \beta$ for $i = 1, 2, \ldots, n$). If the residuals from these regressions are autocorrelated, then a generalized approach to estimation will be required (see Myers and Thompson 1989a).

For purposes of illustrating implementation of the hedging rules derived above, the planning horizon is assumed to be six months, broken down into six monthly periods ($i = 1, 2, \ldots, 6$). Monthly periods seem a reasonable basis for projecting import quantities and consumption needs and for carrying out other planning activities. Furthermore, futures contracts for oil mature at monthly intervals. It must be remembered, however, that hedges placed for any particular month would need to be unwound gradually as the oil is imported during that month. Hedges are assumed to be placed in futures or options maturing the month following the month in which the oil is actually being imported. For example, oil imported in January is hedged in the February contract. This is to avoid problems of trying to liquidate futures and options positions during the delivery month. Data limitations precluded using a longer planning horizon in this application. However, longer planning horizons can be incorporated easily if additional data become available.

Weekly data on spot prices for Venezuelan Tia Juana Light were obtained from the *Oil and Gas Journal* Energy Database. Simple averages of these weekly prices are used as the monthly price. Data from April 1989 to May 1990—a total of fourteen monthly observations—were collected. Data prior to April 1989 were not used, because of imprecise reporting by the U.S. Department of Energy (see figure 8-1). Monthly exchange rate data published by the International Monetary Fund were used to convert the spot prices from dollars to colones. Because of the very short sample period, the following results should be regarded as an illustration of the method rather than a definitive estimate of futures and options trading rules for RECOPE.

Preliminary investigation of the data indicated that spot price movements in colones could be adequately represented by a model of the form

$$(8\text{-}24) \qquad P_t - P_{t-1} = \gamma + \epsilon_t$$

where γ is a constant and ϵ_t is a serially uncorrelated error. This is a random walk with drift and indicates that the best predictor of future spot prices is, up to a constant term, the current spot price:

$$(8\text{-}25) \qquad\qquad P^*_{t+i} = P_t + \gamma i.$$

The implication is that hedging rules for imports i months ahead can be estimated as the slope coefficient, β_i, from regressions of the form

$$(8\text{-}26) \quad P_{t+i} - P_t = \alpha_i + \beta_i [F_{t+i}(t+i+1) - F_t(t+i+1)] + u_{it}$$

for $i = 1, 2, \ldots, 6$ (see Myers and Thompson 1989a). The relevant data on futures prices are simple monthly averages of daily data on twelve different futures contracts as reported in the *Wall Street Journal* from April 1989 to May 1990. Prices were converted to colones by using the colón-dollar rate.

Results from estimating these hedging regressions are reported in table 8-1. The slope estimates $\hat{\beta}_i$ are interpreted as the proportion of imports i months ahead to be hedged using futures or options of the appropriate maturity. For example, $\hat{\beta}_2 = 1.49$ indicates that if an amount of oil Q_2 is going to be imported two months from now, then $1.49 Q_2$ futures contracts (or $1.49 Q_2$ call options with an exercise price equal to the current futures price) maturing three months from now should be purchased and held without adjustment. The futures or options positions would be liquidated as the imported oil for the relevant month, Q_2, is purchased and priced. Futures or options positions for all months over the planning

Table 8-1. *Estimated Optimal Hedge Ratios for a Six-Month Planning Horizon Using Colón Prices*

Parameter	Months ahead					
	$i = 1$	$i = 2$	$i = 3$	$i = 4$	$i = 5$	$i = 6$
$\hat{\alpha}_i$	-58.72	-143.16	-249.20	-366.64	-352.70	-339.97
	(-1.35)	(-3.03)	(-4.55)	(-5.44)	(-4.04)	(-3.25)
$\hat{\beta}_i$	1.28	1.49	1.93	2.31	1.97	1.76
	(2.78)	(4.99)	(6.65)	(7.38)	(5.77)	(4.93)
$\overline{R^2}$	0.43	0.62	0.78	0.89	0.81	0.77

Test of $\beta_i = \beta$ for all i

$\hat{\beta} = 1.84$ $\qquad\qquad F(5, 51) = 1.07$ $\qquad\qquad$ p-value $= 0.39$

Note: Numbers in parentheses are t-values, and p-value is the probability of obtaining the given F-value when the null hypothesis is true. Equation used: $P_{t+i} - P_t = \alpha_i + \beta_i [F_{t+i}(t+i+1) - F_t(t+i+1)] + u_{it}$.

horizon are taken out at the beginning of the horizon and held until the price on the corresponding spot position is fixed.

The $\hat{\beta}_i$ estimates range from 1.28 for hedging imports one month ahead to 2.31 for hedging imports four months ahead. However, an F-test on the equality between coefficients at all maturities indicates strong support for the null hypothesis that hedge ratios are the same, irrespective of maturity (table 8-1). The restricted estimate is $\hat{\beta} = 1.84$ at all maturities, indicating that the amount of futures or call options bought should be approximately 1.84 times the amount of oil to be imported, to hedge the short spot positions. R^2 results show that a substantial proportion of the variation in spot prices can be explained by the price movements of futures, indicating good hedging potential.

The same hedging regressions were also estimated using spot and futures price data in dollars, without conversion to colones. These regressions were done to determine how sensitive the results are to exchange rate effects. The results, which are reported in table 8-2, are similar to those obtained in table 8-1 using colón prices. Exchange rate movements therefore have little effect on the appropriate hedging strategy.

It may seem odd that hedging positions are so large in relation to the quantities of oil imported. However, the reason for this can be seen in figure 8-5, which shows levels and changes for spot and nearby futures prices. Spot prices are clearly more volatile than nearby futures, indicating that additional futures or options contracts have to be taken out to

Table 8-2. *Estimated Optimal Hedge Ratios for a Six-Month Planning Horizon Using Dollar Prices*

| Parameter | Months ahead | | | | | |
	$i = 1$	$i = 2$	$i = 3$	$i = 4$	$i = 5$	$i = 6$
$\hat{\alpha}_i$	−0.66	−1.57	−2.58	−3.67	−3.46	−3.30
	(−1.49)	(−1.44)	(−3.76)	(−5.80)	(−3.78)	(−2.98)
$\hat{\beta}_i$	1.23	1.44	1.88	2.28	1.89	1.67
	(3.03)	(4.08)	(5.68)	(8.06)	(5.36)	(4.39)
$\overline{R^2}$	0.41	0.59	0.76	0.88	0.78	0.72

Test of $\beta_i = \beta$ for all i

$\hat{\beta} = 1.78$	$F(5, 51) = 1.03$	p-value $= 0.41$

Note: Numbers in parentheses are t-values, and p-value is the probability of obtaining the given F-value when the null hypothesis is true. Equation used: $P_{t+i} - P_t = \alpha_i + \beta_i[F_{t+i}(t + i + 1) - F_t(t + i + 1)] + u_{it}$.

Figure 8-5. *Spot and Nearby Futures Prices for Oil, April 1989–May 1990*

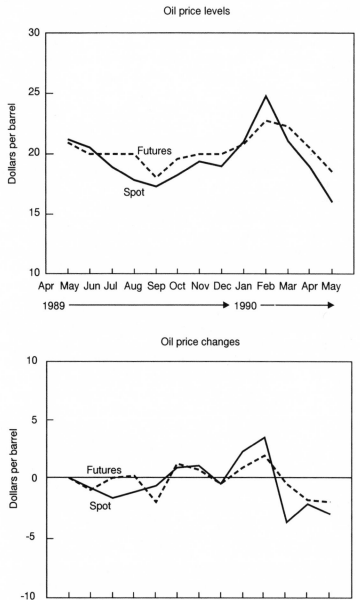

Oil price levels

Oil price changes

Source: Authors' calculations.

protect against spot price increases on a given quantity of imports. For example, if spot prices increase by twice as much as futures, then futures positions will need to be double the spot position to provide maximum risk reduction surrounding the cash surplus. Thus, hedge ratios greater than one are to be expected from estimates using this data set. Given the very small sample period used in this study, these estimates should be interpreted with caution and are best viewed as an example of how the hedging procedure can be implemented. A considerably larger sample would be required before confident estimates of the optimal hedging strategies could be derived.

To provide an example of how these hedging strategies might work, we simulated the recommended futures hedging strategy over a six-month planning horizon initiated in November 1989. (The performance of options hedging could also be simulated, but this would have required the collection of additional data on option prices. Thus, we simulated only the futures performance.)

The likely results from futures hedging over this planning horizon can be obtained from figure 8-5. At the beginning of the planning horizon, in November 1989, spot prices were around $19 a barrel and had been fairly stable over the previous six months. Thus, it might be expected that prices would remain around the $19 mark for the following six months and that domestic prices would be set accordingly. In fact, prices climbed steeply in December 1989 and January 1990 to around $25 a barrel. Spot prices continued to be above expected (in November 1989) levels until April and May, the last two months in the planning horizon, when they returned to normal levels. Without hedging, RECOPE would have experienced large negative cash surpluses over the first two to three months of the planning horizon, leading to a negative net cash surplus at the end of the planning horizon. With hedging, the negative cash surpluses on spot positions would have been offset by gains on futures, and the net cash surplus at the end of the planning horizon would have been improved.

These conjectures are borne out in the simulation results reported in table 8-3 for colón hedges and table 8-4 for dollar hedges. The first column in these tables shows the difference between actual and expected spot prices over the planning horizon. The second column shows the difference between futures prices when positions are liquidated, and the oil is imported, and futures prices at the beginning of the planning horizon, in November 1989. The remaining three columns report cash surpluses per barrel imported under three different futures hedging rules: no hedge, the constant coefficients hedge (hedge ratios restricted to be constant for all maturities), and the variable coefficients hedge (hedge ratios allowed to be different for different maturities).[6]

Table 8-3. *Oil Futures Hedging Performance for a Six-Month Planning Horizon Beginning in November 1989, in Colones per Barrel*

Month	$P_i - P_i°$	$F_i(i+1) - F_0(i+1)$	ΔY, per barrel		
			No hedge	Constant coefficients hedge	Variable coefficients hedge
Dec. 1989	233.2	104.5	-233.2	-40.9	-99.4
Jan. 1990	571.5	301.0	-571.5	-17.7	-123.0
Feb. 1990	289.7	282.0	-289.7	229.2	254.6
Mar. 1990	151.8	157.3	-151.8	137.6	211.6
Apr. 1990	-68.8	10.0	68.8	87.2	88.5
May 1990	-57.0	48.4	57.0	146.0	142.2
Total			-1,120.4	541.4	474.5
Average			-186.7	90.2	79.1

Table 8-4. *Oil Futures Hedging Performance for a Six-Month Planning Horizon Beginning in November 1989, in Dollars per Barrel*

			ΔY_i per barrel		
Month	$P_i - P_i^*$	$F_i(i+1)$ $- F_0(i+1)$	*No hedge*	*Constant coefficients hedge*	*Variable coefficients hedge*
Dec. 1989	2.76	1.11	-2.76	-0.78	-1.39
Jan. 1990	6.71	3.27	-6.71	-0.89	-2.00
Feb. 1990	3.39	2.92	-3.39	1.81	2.10
Mar. 1990	1.72	1.28	-1.72	0.56	1.20
Apr. 1990	-0.86	-0.59	0.86	-0.19	-0.26
May 1990	-0.73	-0.30	0.73	0.20	0.23
Total			-12.99	0.71	-0.12
Average			-2.17	0.12	-0.02

Without hedging, the cash surplus is large and negative over the first four months of the planning horizon and slightly positive in the last two months. Under both constant and variable coefficient hedges, the negative cash surplus from spot transactions is offset by profits on futures, and the overall net cash surplus changes from being large and negative to slightly positive.[7] Thus, futures hedging would have been successful at offsetting the losses from the run-up in oil prices that occurred in January 1990.

A number of caveats to these results are required. First, this example is for one particular period, and similar results will not always be obtained. In particular, profits on futures will only occur during periods when prices are increasing, and there will be losses when prices are falling (when the cash surplus from spot transactions is rising). Hedging can reduce fluctuations in cash surpluses but generally does not lead to higher average surplus levels.

Second, hedging does not completely eliminate fluctuations and produce a net cash surplus of zero over every planning horizon. Because of basis risk, the net cash surplus will continue to fluctuate from period to period, but at a reduced rate. The important point is that futures hedging reduces the uncertainty surrounding the net cash surplus to a minimum level, and the remaining basis risk cannot be reduced further by using only the futures market.

Third, the results might have been different if options had been used for hedging rather than futures. With options, the negative return on futures during April and May 1990 might not have materialized, because options need not be exercised when the futures price is below the exercise price. Offsetting this, however, are the option premiums that would have had to be paid at each maturity month over the planning horizon.

Fourth, the simulation was run within the data sample used to estimate the optimal hedge ratios. Thus, the results likely overestimate the performance of actual, operational hedging because, in reality, RECOPE will not have access to future price realizations when estimating optimal hedge ratios. An out-of-sample simulation would provide better information on actual hedging performance, but this type of simulation was not attempted here because of limited data.

Fifth, the costs of putting the hedges in place has not been taken into account. But, as noted in the chapter by Claessens and Duncan, the transaction costs for futures and option hedges are in general small. Other costs involve the provision of margins. The chapter by Claessens and Varangis provides specific estimates on the costs of margins in the case of RECOPE and finds these to be small as well. The most important "costs" in the eyes of the operators may be the opportunity costs of losing out on paying lower oil prices when having locked in a fixed price. But these costs will, on average, be compensated for by the gains from having locked in a low price when oil prices rise.

Discussion

One problem with the hedging of risks over longer planning horizons is the lack of liquidity on futures and options traded at longer maturities. For example, futures contracts traded at twelve or more months to maturity often have very low volume, and options usually are not traded at all at maturities beyond about six months. However, this problem can be easily overcome by using rollover hedging.

A rollover hedge is undertaken by hedging the entire import quantity over the planning horizon, $Q = \sum_{i=1}^{n} Q_i$, in a nearby futures contract. As imports are purchased, the appropriate proportion of the hedge is lifted. Then when the maturity date arrives on the nearby future, the remaining hedge position is simultaneously liquidated in the expiring contract and retaken in another nearby maturity. As imports occur, positions continue to be liquidated until the maturity date arrives again, at which time the remaining positions are rolled over into another nearby future. The process continues until the end of the planning horizon.

It can be shown that without discounting and transactions costs, the optimal hedge ratio for rollover hedging using the i month ahead maturity is β_i, from the equation

$$(8\text{-}27) \qquad\qquad p_i = \beta_i f_i + u_i.$$

Of course, the hedge ratio β_i is now interpreted as the proportion of total remaining imports over the planning horizon to be hedged in the futures or options contract maturing i months ahead. The relevant β_is have already been estimated in tables 8-1 and 8-2. Rollover hedging can avoid the problem of low volume on futures and options with distant maturities, at the cost of additional transaction costs and possibly increased basis risk.

In the analysis of the previous section, we have focused on risk management using either futures only or options only, but not both. The question arises as to whether some combination of futures and options could lead to improved performance. Lapan, Moschini, and Hanson (1991) have shown that as long as futures prices and option premiums are perceived as unbiased (as above), options are redundant instruments and all hedging will take place in futures. This conclusion provides a rationale for ignoring combinations of futures and options hedging.

Another question that arises in the estimation of optimal hedge ratios is whether the optimal hedge is constant or varied over time. Myers

(1991) and Baillie and Myers (1989) have found strong evidence of time-varying optimal hedge ratios in a number of commodities, although they did not study oil explicitly. The results are mixed concerning the extent to which hedging performance suffers from the assumption of constant hedge ratios when the ratios actually change over time. For some commodities there is little reduction in performance, whereas for others the reduction is substantial. Time-varying optimal hedge ratios could not be investigated in this study because of data limitations. In future work, using an expanded data set, this issue should be addressed thoroughly.

Conclusions

Oil price fluctuations imply considerable risk to Costa Rica's government-owned oil company, RECOPE, because domestic prices are generally fixed in colón terms over a planning horizon, but international prices, which must be paid to import the oil, may increase rapidly in response to changing world market conditions. Futures and options hedging can help manage this risk by reducing fluctuations in RECOPE's net cash surplus over a planning horizon. Hedging would thus facilitate the company's ability to plan and adjust to changing economic conditions.

In this chapter we designed and estimated hedging strategies using both futures and options. We found estimated hedge ratios to be greater than one because spot prices were more volatile than futures prices over the sample period used. Simulation results indicate a potential for substantial reductions in the riskiness of RECOPE's net cash surplus as a result of futures hedging. Additional empirical work is required to obtain improved estimates of an optimal hedge ratio and to put into operation the hedging strategy that has been outlined. The following chapter, by Claessens and Varangis, provides some further empirical work by investigating the benefits of hedging for different types of imported oil and by providing suggestions for making institutional changes in the Costa Rican oil sector.

Notes

1. The main difference would be that with discounting, hedging in distant futures contracts would be reduced slightly as a result of the risk of short-run payouts as futures are marked to market (paid) each day.

2. This assumption is for convenience and allows attention to focus exclusively on the hedging characteristics of futures trading.

3. Daily gains and losses on futures price movements must be marked to market at the end of each trading day, but the formulation here implicitly assumes all payments are made

when the contract expires. Of course, the two approaches are formally equivalent in the absence of discounting and exchange rate fluctuations.

4. Linear relationships are entirely appropriate whenever the conditional covariance matrix of spot and futures prices is constant over time. Nonlinear models are required when this covariance is time-varying. Nonlinear relationships may be hedged by a combining futures and options and by (dynamically) adjusting the hedging ratio β_t within the periods. The implications of time-varying optimal hedge ratios are discussed further in the penultimate section of the chapter.

5. This "safety first" objective may be inconsistent with behavior by RECOPE that minimizes variances or maximizes expected utility (see Lapan, Moschini, and Hanson 1991). However, the objective is simple and pervades much of the literature on hedging with options (see, for example, Overdahl 1986).

6. See tables 8-1 and 8-2 for these estimated hedge ratios.

7. If the dollar hedge is undertaken, the net cash surplus under the variable coefficients hedge is also slightly negative (see table 8-4).

9

An Oil Import Risk Management Program for Costa Rica

Stijn Claessens and Panos Varangis

Oil imports in Costa Rica have accounted for approximately 9 percent of total import expenditures in recent years. However, in periods of relatively high oil prices, such as during the early 1980s, oil imports accounted for around 20 percent of the total import bill.[1] The volatility of international oil prices as well as the dependency of Costa Rica on oil imports for its energy needs exposes the economy to large risks.

This chapter builds on the previous one by expanding on the number of crude oils that can be hedged and including more information on the institutional background of the oil sector. The purpose of the chapter is to examine how risk management techniques can be applied to Refinadora Costarricense de Petroleo (RECOPE, Costa Rica's state-owned oil company) and to estimate the potential gains from using these techniques. In the chapter we first discuss the internal market structure for hydrocarbons and related products, focusing on the mechanisms by which domestic prices are adjusted for international price movements and the historical experience of domestic price adjustment. Then we identify and discuss the nature of RECOPE's oil price exposures. After that we analyze possible risk management techniques for each of the exposures identified and address the internal and external constraints on the implementation of these techniques.

The authors would like to thank Ali Riazi of RECOPE and Mudassar Imran of the World Bank for their valuable comments. They would also like to thank Robert Myers for his helpful suggestions.

The Internal Market Structure

Domestic prices for electricity and petroleum products in Costa Rica are set periodically by an energy pricing board. There are two types of internal price changes: the extraordinary and the ordinary. The extraordinary change is relatively recent and was put into effect on August 27, 1990. The ordinary change is based on earlier laws.

The *extraordinary change* is based on a "formula of automatic adjustment," which is calculated as follows:

$$A = \frac{[(P \times e) - (P_0 \times e_0)] \times E}{P_0 \times e_0}.$$

In the formula, A is the percentage change in the domestic price for electricity and petroleum products; P is the last fifteen-day average of the weighted average price for imports of crude oil and derivatives;[2] e is the current exchange rate; P_0 is the weighted average price used at the last change; e_0 is the exchange rate used at the last change; and E is the proportion of total expenditures for the importation of crude oil and derivatives to total sales, according to the current budget of RECOPE. Note that A applies to all products across the board; that is, all products increase or decrease in price by the same percentage with each extraordinary change. The formula triggers price changes only if abs $[(P \times e)/(P_0 \times e_0) - 1] > 0.05$, where abs is absolute value.

According to this formula, every day RECOPE calculates the previous fifteen-day average of international crude and derivative prices and compares it with the weighted average price that triggered the last change. If the difference is more than 5 percent, a change is triggered. The following time-axis summarizes the process of extraordinary price changes. Note that the fifteen-day average is calculated on the basis of international prices, not on the basis of prices actually paid by RECOPE.

Days	$-X$	-15	0	$+21$
Date	A	B	C	D

Date	Activity
A	Last fixing of domestic prices, X days before new fixing.
B	Beginning of fifteen-day period over which the average of international prices is calculated,[3] using the cocktail from the last fixing.
C	Triggering of automatic, extraordinary price adjustment mechanism.
D	Adjustment of domestic prices (on average, three weeks after C).

Under the *ordinary change,* domestic prices are changed as a result of developments in international oil markets and in RECOPE's investments and financial and operational costs. The stated objective of the ordinary request is to cover the costs of RECOPE and include a sufficient profitability so that RECOPE can compete internationally and develop its investments. The ordinary request is usually considered once a year, during the first trimester.

In the case of ordinary price changes, domestic energy prices are set with many different objectives in view. Recently, price stability and the operational profitability of RECOPE have been the main concerns. Until 1989, all price changes were ordinary price changes.

The establishment of the extraordinary price adjustment mechanism has led to a significant reduction in RECOPE's exposure to oil shocks. Whereas before RECOPE could adjust domestic prices only incompletely and with a lag, now it can pass on international price changes more quickly and completely. However, Costa Rica's overall exposure to oil price shocks has not changed, because the extraordinary price adjustment has shifted oil price risk from RECOPE to the Costa Rican consumer.

The working of Costa Rica's price mechanism can be observed from a historical series of domestic and import prices for several products. Table 9-1 records the imports of RECOPE, and table 9-2 presents the coefficients of variation for domestic and import prices.[4] Over the 1981–89 period, 57.4 percent of colón-dollar exchange rate fluctuations were passed on to domestic prices for gasoline. The comparable figure for diesel was 52.4 percent. Only 29.1 percent and 27.7 percent of international price fluctuations were passed on to domestic gasoline and diesel prices, respectively. Furthermore, as table 9-2 shows, domestic prices for both diesel and gasoline were more stable in colón terms than were import prices in dollar terms; when converted into dollar terms, domestic prices for diesel and gasoline were even more stable.

These observations indicate that the Costa Rican energy pricing system achieved a great deal of stability in terms of domestic colón prices, in spite of large fluctuations in international prices (in colón terms). However, in order to achieve that stability, the markup—the percentage of domestic prices over the import price—was made very variable. The variability of the markup meant that RECOPE was stabilizing energy prices for the rest of the Costa Rican economy even while its operating margin was quite volatile.[5] However, the domestic price stability achieved was not necessarily a benefit to the Costa Rican economy as a whole: because the profits and losses of RECOPE form part of the general government budget, the effect of international oil price movements was not avoided by the Costa Rican economy but rather reallocated through the general budget.

Table 9-1. RECOPE's Crude Oil Imports by Type and Origin, 1986–90
(millions of barrels)

Type and origin	1986	1987	1988	1989	1990[a]
Bachaquero (Venezuela)	0.00	0.18	0.14	0.20	0.10
Caño Limón (Colombia)	0.00	0.26	0.72	0.25	0.00
Istmo (Mexico)	1.53	1.24	2.15	1.90	0.32
Lagotreco (Venezuela)	2.09	2.22	1.08	2.46	1.71
Olmeca (Mexico)	0.00	0.00	0.00	0.00	0.16
Oriente (Ecuador)	0.63	0.43	0.49	0.00	0.26
Orito (Colombia)	0.25	0.24	0.00	0.00	0.00
Tia Juana (Venezuela)	0.15	0.01	0.00	0.00	0.00
Total	4.65	4.59	4.59	4.82	2.55

a. January–November only.
Source: RECOPE.

Table 9-2. Coefficients of Variation for Domestic and Imported Fuel
Prices, 1981–89
(percent)

	Gasoline	Diesel
Domestic (colones)	22.64	25.12
Domestic (dollars)	16.68	19.37
Import (dollars)	27.78	28.10
Markup[a]	35.14	47.32
Exchange rate (colones per dollar)	34.11	34.11

Note: The coefficient of variation is the ratio of the standard deviation to the mean.

a. Markup is the percentage of the domestic price over the import price, or $(P^*/P - 1) \times 100$, where P^* and P are the domestic price and the import prices, respectively, both expressed in dollars per barrel.

Source: World Bank estimates based on prices furnished by RECOPE.

Risk Management Problems

On the basis of RECOPE's operating procedures and domestic price adjustment mechanisms, three types of risk management problems can be distinguished: transaction, internal price adjustment, and long-term.

Transaction Risks

Transaction risk refers to transaction exposure. The following time-axis illustrates the problem RECOPE has in managing this risk.

Days	−(50–20)	−(20–15)	0	+30	+(38–40)
Date	A	B	C	D	E

Date   *Activity*
- A   Production program decided on by RECOPE; shipping contracted.
- B   Payment (in colones) by RECOPE to the Central Bank.
- C   Loading (bill of lading) and setting of price.
- D   Payment to the seller (by foreign bank).
- E   Return of excess payment (in colones) by the Central Bank to RECOPE.

RECOPE decides on its program of production (whether to run the refinery and which mix to produce), based on expected demand, prices, and market sentiment, on the tenth day of every month. At this time it makes an assessment of the future prices of the different crudes and refined products. It then decides which crudes and refined products to import and contracts with its suppliers. Five days later the suppliers confirm availability, the contract is finalized, and RECOPE agrees with the supplier of the crude (or refined product) to take delivery. RECOPE then contracts with independent shipping companies for loading the different crudes at the different ports. After the shipping contracts are signed (A), a minimum of fifteen days elapses before the ships are loaded. The loading (C) therefore does not happen until twenty to fifty days after RECOPE decides on its production program (A).[6] The price to be paid for the crude is set at the international spot price prevailing on the day of loading and is stated on the bill of lading.

Approximately fifteen to twenty days before the date of the bill of lading, RECOPE transfers to the Central Bank the sum expected on the bill of lading, adding 10 percent for possible variations in oil prices and exchange rates over the fifteen- to twenty-day period (B). The Central Bank then arranges a letter of credit with a foreign bank to be used for payment on the date of lading. The letter of credit is cashed about thirty days after the bill of lading, when payments are made to the seller (D). About eight to ten days after the letter of credit is cashed, excess payments (the difference between the actual payments and the expected payments plus the 10 percent) are returned by the Central Bank to RECOPE in colones (E).

From the time the ships are contracted (A) to the time the excess payments are received (E), RECOPE is exposed to two types of risks: exchange rate risks and oil price risks. RECOPE faces exchange rate risks because of the possibility that the colón-dollar exchange rate will depreciate. If the colón depreciates between dates A and D, RECOPE's foreign currency payments at time D will be more in colón terms than expected and it will receive back less of the 10 percent variation margin. Likewise, if the colón depreciates between dates D and E, RECOPE will receive back less of its excess payments. RECOPE faces oil price risks because it has to decide to order supplies (A) twenty to fifty days before the price to be paid is determined (C). If oil prices increase during this period, RECOPE will have to bear the extra expense, because it cannot change or cancel its order except at a very high cost.

Internal Price Adjustment Risks

The mechanism for adjusting domestic prices to international prices exposes RECOPE to several forms of internal price adjustment risk. First, whenever there are extraordinary price movements, there is, on average, a three-week lag in the adjustment of domestic prices to international prices (although domestic prices tend to be adjusted upward more slowly and downward more quickly). Second, domestic price adjustment is limited in several ways: (a) in the case of extraordinary adjustments, only international price changes of more than 5 percent can be passed on, that is, RECOPE has to absorb all the oil price risks that occur when the price is within a band 5 percent above and below the previous fixed price; (b) all domestic prices have to be adjusted equally, whereas international prices may not have changed equally; and (c) the price adjustment is based on internationally quoted prices, not on prices actually paid by RECOPE. Third, changes in the colón-dollar exchange rate can adversely affect the difference between RECOPE's import costs and the domestic sales price in the 5 percent band. Even though the formula used in the case of extraordinary price movements adjusts for exchange rate movements, RECOPE incurs foreign exchange risk during the three-week period between the time the extraordinary change is triggered and the time the domestic price is actually changed.

Similar exposures exist under ordinary price changes. These domestic price changes generally occur once a year; sometimes differ by product; and allow for price adjustments to ensure RECOPE satisfactory margins. In contrast to the situation under extraordinary change, however, the lag between international and domestic price adjustments can be quite long, especially because past profitability is used to determine margins for the next fiscal year. Also, as noted above, the ordinary adjustment process leads to incomplete passing through of international prices and exchange rate movements to domestic prices and thus increases RECOPE's exposure. The exact nature of the ordinary exposure is difficult to determine, because the process by which domestic prices are adjusted is not completely known.

Long-Term Risks

If RECOPE wants to maintain a normal profit margin in the long term, it cannot avoid passing on a permanent oil price change or exchange rate change to the domestic market. When international price changes are passed on, they will then no longer affect RECOPE. They will, however, still affect Costa Rica's economy as a whole through variable domestic prices for petroleum products, with possible adverse consequences on production and growth. As the main provider of petroleum products, RECOPE may find it in its (political) interest to manage price risk for the benefit of the Costa Rican economy.

Risk Management Techniques

For each of the three risk management problems described above, a different risk management strategy is applicable. The following three risk management strategies complement each other. They also form a logical sequence for RECOPE to follow: first manage transaction risks (that is, short-term risks), then internal price adjustment risks, and finally long-term risks. It should be noted at the outset, however, that the application of risk management techniques to hedge internal price adjustment risk is not as strong as for the other types of risks.

Hedging Transaction Risks

The twenty- to fifty-day transaction exposure to oil price risks could be managed by using oil futures or options on oil futures. RECOPE has a short position in oil because it has a commitment to satisfy domestic demand and domestic prices that cannot be adjusted instantaneously. To hedge the resulting price risk, RECOPE could purchase oil futures, an asset whose return is positively correlated with oil prices. Then as oil prices go up, the return on the futures would increase to offset the additional cost of higher import prices (see the detailed description of both futures and options by Myers and Thompson in chapter 8).

For example, assume that it is March 1991 and RECOPE is planning its purchases. RECOPE decides to buy 10,000 barrels of crude oil in two months (that is, in May 1991) at the spot Mexican (Istmo) price. RECOPE then buys ten futures contracts of 1,000 barrels each, maturing in two months.[7] The price of the May 1991 futures contract is quoted at, say, $18.50 a barrel. Between initiating the futures contracts and closing them out, transfers of cash to and from the margin account held by a broker are required almost every day because of gains and losses in the futures contracts. Two months later, a gain or a loss in the import cost of the crude arising from the fluctuation of the Istmo oil price is offset by the cumulative loss or gain in the futures contracts. (The offset may not be exact because of basis risk, that is, the possibility that the futures price will move differently than the import price—see further below.)

Although hedging with futures eliminates the disadvantages of import price increases,[8] it also eliminates the potential advantages of import price declines. The advantages to RECOPE of import price declines are reduced costs and therefore an increase in income and net cash surplus. To participate in the gains if prices fall while still providing protecting against upward price movements (at a cost), a good alternative is hedging with options.

RECOPE could buy call options at the date of arranging a vessel. The maturity date of the option would need to be as close as possible to the expected date of lading. For example, in the case that RECOPE contracted in January 1991 to purchase oil in one month's time, paying the then-current oil price, RECOPE would buy a call option with an exercise price of, say, $22 a barrel. On January 21, 1991, it would have paid a premium of $1.10 for this option. In the case that oil prices moved above $22 a barrel, the gain on the call option would be offset by the loss on the extra import cost, and the net price paid would be $22 a barrel plus the cost of the premium, that is, $23.10 a barrel. In the case of a lower oil price, the net price paid would be the low oil price plus the premium.

Call options are available with several exercise prices; the lower the exercise price, the more insurance RECOPE would obtain, but the higher the premium for the call option. Figure 9-1 plots the premium as a function of the exercise price for January 21, 1991, call options. As can be observed, call option premiums decrease as the exercise price increases.

The exercise price of the call option best suited to the needs of RECOPE would depend on the following two factors, among others.

The first factor would be the exact effect of higher oil prices on RECOPE's cash flows and profitability. Through sensitivity scenarios, RECOPE could determine a profile of cash flows and profitabilities under different oil prices. The profile would provide RECOPE with an indication of which oil price levels were profitable and therefore not in need of insurance, and which price levels were not profitable so that price insur-

Figure 9-1. *Option Premiums on West Texas Intermediate Crude Oil, January 21, 1991*

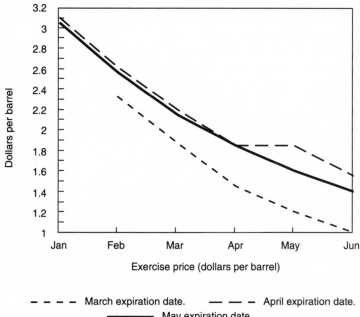

Source: *Wall Street Journal,* January 22, 1991.

ance would be needed. Price level insurance could then be obtained by buying call options with exercise prices equal to the level at which prices become unacceptable in terms of cash flow and profitability. For example, RECOPE could determine that prices above $25 a barrel lead to negative cash flows and that therefore call options with exercise prices of $25 a barrel should be bought.

The second factor determining the choice of options would be RECOPE's expectations about future oil prices. On the basis of its expectations, RECOPE might decide that a particular option is relatively attractively priced and therefore decide to buy it. It should be realized, however, that the prices for options already reflect market sentiment regarding future oil price movements and that options in general are fairly priced. It would thus be difficult to make profits consistently by buying certain options at certain times. In general, RECOPE's own price expectations would need to play a minor role in deciding whether to buy an option and, if so, which to buy.

So far, the costs of putting the hedges in place have not been taken into account. One cost is related to basis risk. Futures and options are available on the New York Mercantile Exchange (NYMEX), written on West Texas Intermediate (WTI). RECOPE, however, does not import a type of crude oil that is priced directly off of WTI; it imports most of its oil in the form of Istmo from Mexico (51 percent of all imports in 1989) and Lagotreco from Venezuela (39 percent in 1989; see table 9-1). RECOPE has also imported Bachaquero, Oriente, and Caño Limón crude oils consistently in recent years, although in smaller quantities. Some oil is bought on the spot market (more so recently), but this does not represent a large fraction of RECOPE's total import bill. Of the major crudes imported, Istmo, Caño Limón, and Oriente prices follow the WTI prices closely. Lagotreco prices have historically followed WTI much less closely, even though more recently the Lagotreco price has been closer to the WTI price. Bachaquero has a weak relationship with WTI. More important, WTI *futures* contracts and RECOPE's import prices do not move together perfectly. Because they do not, hedging with futures or options based on the WTI price would expose RECOPE to basis risks.

Basis risks can be accommodated by adjusting the *hedge ratio*, that is, the number of barrels worth of futures or options contracts to be bought as a fraction of the number of barrels of crude oil contracted to be shipped. Estimation of the hedge ratio for all given imported crudes was done here in accordance with the methodology outlined by Myers and Thompson (chapter 8) through estimating the regression[9] d log $(P_i) = a_i + b_i$ d log (WTI). In the regression, P is the spot crude oil price; i is Istmo, Lagotreco, Bachaquero, Oriente, or Caño Limón; a is the regression constant, and d denotes first differences. The slope coefficient, b, is the hedge ratio. The right-hand side variable of the regression is the difference between the price of the lagged second nearby futures contract and the price of the current first nearby futures contract, where both contracts are based on the WTI price and monthly averages of daily data are used. The left-hand side variable in the regression is the first difference in the relevant import prices. Data are for the period August 1986 to December 1990 and were obtained from RECOPE, NYMEX, and the World Bank. The results of the estimations are given in table 9-3.

Table 9-3 indicates that Istmo and Caño Limón oil import prices can be hedged using WTI futures contracts. The high R^2 with WTI futures prices shows that the basis risk is small (12 percent and 15 percent, respectively). Similarly, Oriente crude oil imports can also be hedged using the WTI contract. However, the basis risk is higher (23 percent). For the whole sample period, the weak relationship between Lagotreco and the WTI futures contract results in a relatively high basis risk (31 percent).

Table 9-3. *Hedge Ratios for the Regional Crude Oils and WTI, August 1986–December 1990*

Crude	Hedge ratio, b_i	t-statistic		R^2	Durbin-Watson statistic
		if $b_i = 0$	if $b_i = 1$		
Istmo	1.08	16.53	1.19	0.88	2.02
Lagotreco	0.85	10.73	−1.89	0.69	1.89
Lagotreco[a]	0.92	9.63	−0.84	0.78	1.84
Oriente	1.01	12.24	0.13	0.77	1.99
Caño Limón	1.05	15.03	0.73	0.85	1.99
Bachaquero	0.64	8.95	4.94	0.60	2.05
WTI (spot)	1.03	30.75	1.03	0.97	1.96

Note: Hedge ratios are the number of barrels worth of futures or options contracts to buy as a fraction of the number of barrels of crude oil bought.

a. Regression results for the subperiod August 1988 to December 1990.

Source: Authors' calculations, based on data from RECOPE, NYMEX, and the World Bank.

However, since August 1988, Lagotreco prices have followed WTI contract prices more closely, reducing the basis risk to 22 percent.

The hypothesis that the hedge ratio is equal to one is strongly accepted for Istmo, Lagotreco, Oriente, and Caño Limón. Because the hedge ratios estimated statistically are not significantly different from one, a hedge ratio of one for these four crudes, instead of the hedge ratio indicated by the regression, is therefore advised. A hedge ratio of one is also much simpler to implement, although with it the risk reduction benefits are somewhat smaller. Recalculating basis risk with a hedge ratio of one, we found that basis risk increased by 1.5 percentage points for Istmo, 0.6 percentage point for Lagotreco and Caño Limón, and 0.1 percentage point for Oriente. These are only slight increases in basis risk from the actual estimated hedge ratios and imply that RECOPE can still reduce its transaction exposure to these crudes by 77 to 86 percent. The relationship between the Bachaquero price and the WTI futures price is weaker, and therefore hedging Bachaquero crude oil imports is not advisable. The results for futures hold also for hedging using options based on the WTI futures contract, and thus a hedge ratio of one can also be used for options (see Lapan, Moschini, and Hanson 1991).

So far, the hedge ratios have been estimated for hedging physical barrels of oil. For hedging dollar expenditures, the hedge ratios can be obtained by estimating the slope coefficient, b_i, from an equation that has percentage changes in futures prices on the right-hand side and percentage changes in spot (import) prices on the left-hand side. This was done for all imported crudes, and the results are similar to the physical hedge ratios. The ratios were found to be not significantly different from one, but there was an increase in basis risk compared with the case of hedging physical barrels.

Hedging Internal Price Adjustment Risks

In the case of the extraordinary price adjustments, RECOPE has to absorb all price changes within a 5 percent band around the previous fixing price. To hedge against prices going up within this 5 percent band, RECOPE could buy call options having exercise prices at the previous fixing price and sell call options having exercise prices 5 percent higher than the previous fixing price. Doing so would completely eliminate the effect of upward price movements within the 5 percent band, but not outside the band.

The risk involved in the three-week time delay in domestic price adjustments during which RECOPE might not be able to pass on higher international prices could be managed by maintaining a portfolio of bought call options having short-term (one-month) maturities and exercise prices 5 percent above the previous fixing price. This portfolio would be rolled forward through time. If prices moved above the 5 percent band, the short-term options would compensate RECOPE for the higher import costs during the period when domestic prices had not yet been adjusted. Alternatively, RECOPE could use futures with short maturities to lock in prices, as done in the transaction hedge. RECOPE would then avoid premiums but give up the potential of lower import prices.

In the case of ordinary price adjustments, the price pass-through has been much more complex and erratic, which implies that it would be difficult for RECOPE to hedge internal price adjustment risks.

Compared with strategies for managing transaction risks and long-term risks, strategies for managing internal price adjustment risks offer the least benefits, given the extraordinary price adjustment mechanism. Although hedging strategies for internal price adjustment risks are possible in principle, they are not recommended for RECOPE. First, the strategies are quite complicated and would require an almost constant presence in the options and futures market, involving high transaction costs and large human resource commitments. Second, the strategies are not always in the interest of Costa Rica as a whole. For example, selling calls at an exercise price 5 percent above the previous fixing price would hedge part of RECOPE's internal price adjustment risks but would leave the risk of prices moving outside the 5 percent band unhedged, which would oblige RECOPE to pass this risk on to the Costa Rican economy. Therefore, RECOPE should not attempt independently to hedge the risk related to the internal price adjustment, especially with the extraordinary price adjustment in place. Instead, RECOPE should put its efforts into managing long-term price risk for the benefit of Costa Rica as a whole.

Hedging Long-Term Price Risks

As an initial strategy for managing oil price risk for Costa Rica as a whole, RECOPE could use longer-dated futures contracts. That is, it could buy a series of futures contracts with maturities varying from, say, one to six months. The amounts to be bought would reflect the anticipated imports of crude oils in each month. The hedges would be put in place twice a year or could be rolled forward during the year and thus cover overlapping periods. If this strategy were pursued, the short-term, transaction hedges would not be necessary (or at least would have to be modified).

One version of this strategy was simulated by Myers and Thompson (see chapter 8). We simulated the following strategy for RECOPE. In January and July of each year we had RECOPE lock in import prices over a six-month planning horizon[10] by buying six nearby futures contracts in amounts equally spread out over time. (If there were a seasonal pattern in imports, RECOPE would have to adjust the amount of futures bought for each month.) The nearest futures contract is not the most liquid, because of the physical delivery required. We therefore had RECOPE buy the second nearest contract until the seventh nearest contract. For example, in July of each year we had RECOPE buy equal amounts of September, October, . . ., February futures contracts. As the contracts approached their maturity month, we had RECOPE reverse them by selling an identical contract in the month before its expiration. For example, in August of each year we had RECOPE sell the September contract for that year. We assumed that RECOPE would buy and sell all contracts gradually throughout the month so that it would pay or obtain the average prices for the contracts in each month. This was to ensure comparability with RECOPE's cash transactions—we had data on average cash prices—which also took place gradually throughout the month.

We simulated eight six-month hedges, the first in July 1986 and the last in January 1990.[11] We used a hedge ratio of one, which was shown above to be a conservative, yet efficient, hedge ratio for short-term hedges. Table 9-4 reports the essential results.

The first five rows show the results of five different hedging programs for oil import prices—programs for Istmo, Lagotreco, Bachaquero, Oriente, and Caño Limón. The sixth row gives the results of a hedging program for the WTI spot price, and the seventh row (Istmo 90) reports a hedge that includes the last five months of 1990. The columns are as follows. "Cash" reports the average loss or gain RECOPE incurred over the

Table 9-4. *Simulated Results of Six-Month Hedging of Oil Import Prices in Costa Rica, July 1986–January 1990*
(dollars per barrel)

Crude	Cash[a]	S of cash	Net[b]	S of net	Risk reduction (percent)	S of monthly net
Istmo	−0.03	2.34	0.72	0.72	69.23	0.91
Lagotreco	0.17	2.32	0.92	1.50	35.34	1.81
Bachaquero	−0.03	2.39	0.71	1.09	54.39	1.46
Oriente	0.07	2.58	0.82	0.89	65.50	1.19
Caño Limón	0.04	2.53	0.79	0.74	70.75	0.97
WTI (spot)	−0.05	2.31	0.70	0.71	69.26	0.80
Istmo 90[c]	−1.48	4.64	0.41	0.91	80.39	1.11

S = standard deviation.

a. The average gain or loss over the price at the beginning of the period as a result of spot oil price movements.

b. The net results of hedging: the gain or loss on the cash position minus the gain or loss on the futures positions. The average gain on the futures positions was $0.75 a barrel, and the standard deviation of the gains was $2.06.

c. Hedging includes the last five months of 1990.

Source: Authors' calculations.

eight planning periods as a result of spot oil price movements in each planning period. For example, the entry −0.03 for the Istmo strategy reflects an average loss per barrel of 3 cents from buying Istmo at higher prices during the eight six-month periods. The table shows that, on average, the prices RECOPE paid over the planning horizons were not much higher than the prices in the months when the plans were started. "S of cash" reports the standard deviation of the unexpected higher or lower cash payments and is thus a reflection of the uncertainty in the spot market. For Istmo, for example, the standard deviation of unexpected spot prices was $2.34 a barrel. This table indicates the substantial price uncertainty over the planning horizons. "Net" represents the net results of hedging; the figure is thus equal to the gain or loss on the cash position minus the gain or loss on the futures positions. In the case of Istmo, the hedging strategy led to an effective oil price that was 72 cents lower than it otherwise would have been, resulting in a gain of 0.72. "S of net" indicates the riskiness of the net result: the standard deviation of the net gain or loss. "Risk reduction" indicates the percentage risk reduction achieved through using the futures. In the case of Istmo again, the risk reduction as a result of hedging was 69 percent. Finally, "S of monthly net" indicates the standard deviation of the monthly net gains and losses from unwinding the futures contracts and buying the crude imports. This standard deviation is different from that under "S of net" because the former shows a standard deviation of (forty-eight) monthly figures and the latter shows a standard deviation of only eight averages.

Table 9-4 indicates that Istmo, Oriente, and Caño Limón can be hedged very well over a six-month planning horizon. The results accord with those obtained for the short-term hedges, because these crudes follow the WTI contract closely. The average risk reduction for these three crudes is about 68 percent, similar to the risk reduction for hedging WTI itself and only slightly below the transaction hedge (which is 78 to 88 percent). The long-term hedges are worse for the other crudes because their price behavior over the period 1986–90 is considerably different from the WTI contract price behavior. Hedging these crudes with the WTI contract could be a problem. As reported above, since August 1988 Lagotreco has followed futures contracts more closely than it did before, so hedging Lagotreco with futures contracts has become possible. If hedging Lagotreco is done with futures, the risk reduction over the period August 1988 to December 1990 improves to about 58 percent.

The row for Istmo 90 reports a hedge that includes the last five months of 1990. The results improve because the hedge allowed RECOPE to avoid the increase in price volatility that resulted from the 1990–91 Gulf crisis. The average cash loss (− $1.48) is higher than the loss for the other crude oils, but so is the futures gain ($1.88). The result is a net gain of $0.41 a barrel over the whole period. This gain is somewhat lower than it would be if the second half of 1990 were excluded, because the hedge does not completely eliminate the effect of higher prices in that period. However, a much more stable price is achieved, and the relative risk reduction is also much higher—80 percent.

Figure 9-2 shows the gains and losses in the case of Istmo oil price hedges over the July 1986 to July 1990 period. It shows, on a six-month cycle, the gain or loss on futures, the gain or loss on cash, and the net gain or loss. It also shows the monthly gain or loss on futures. As can be seen, the net figures are much less volatile than the cash figures, because the gains and losses on futures offset the gains and losses on cash. The graph also shows that month by month there is more stability than there otherwise would be. The results for Istmo can be compared with those of Lagotreco, which, as shown above, had less favorable hedging results. As can be observed from figure 9-3, there is much more volatility in the net gain or loss of hedges for Lagotreco oil, a reflection of the fact that this strategy achieves only a 35 percent risk reduction for Lagotreco over the whole period, even though after August 1988 the risk reduction improves.

Other risk management techniques exist to hedge long-term risk (see Masuoka, chapter 4). The most applicable to RECOPE is the commodity swap. A commodity swap is essentially a series of commodity forward

Figure 9-2. *Average and Monthly Gains of Simulated Six-Month Hedges for Istmo Oil, July 1986–July 1990*

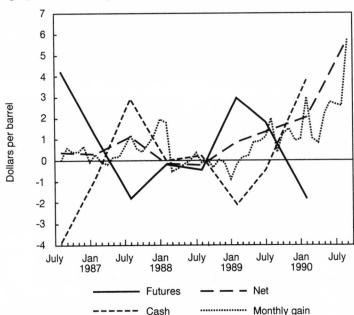

Source: Authors' calculations.

contracts but without deliveries of physical commodities, transactions being purely financial. RECOPE could use an oil swap to lock in the price of oil imports for, say, the ensuing five years, for all or a fraction of its imports (say, 2.5 million barrels a year, the lowest annual amount imported during the last ten years). The important point is that an oil swap would reduce RECOPE's probability of financial distress for its business. Even if the price of oil were to increase to, say, $40 a barrel, expenses would remain the same. The improved credit risk brought about by hedging might could lower the financial implications of financing RECOPE's working capital or give RECOPE access to new lenders.[12]

Considerations in Implementing a Risk Management Strategy

A number of changes must be made if the risk management strategies described above are to work in Costa Rica.

Figure 9-3. *Average and Monthly Gains of Simulated Six-Month Hedges for Lagotreco Oil, July 1986–July 1990*

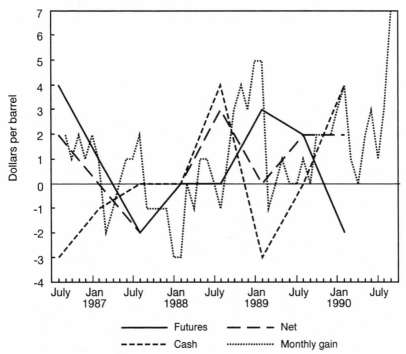

Source: Authors' calculations.

Cash Flow Implications

Under the present setup, one of the most important problems RECOPE would have in implementing a risk management strategy is the cash flow implication of margin calls on futures positions.[13] Maintenance margin calls can require a daily need for funds, depending on the daily fluctuations of oil prices.[14] There are several ways RECOPE could manage the cash flow problem. One way is take a stop-loss position: that is, for RECOPE to liquidate its position if RECOPE is long and prices fall below a certain level. Liquidation, however, would reduce the effectiveness of the hedge. Another way is to avoid margins by buying call options. Of course, options cost premiums.

Because futures are the instrument recommended for transaction hedging, we assessed the possible cash flow implications by simulating the

following futures position. At the beginning of each month we had
RECOPE buy 100 contracts of the second nearest futures contract. For
example, in January 1991, we had RECOPE buy 100 March 1991 contracts. One hundred contracts corresponds to 100,000 barrels per month
or, on a yearly basis, 1.2 million barrels, about half of RECOPE's annual
imports. We assumed that RECOPE would hold these 100 futures contracts through each month and then sell them at the end of the month.
RECOPE was thus faced with possible margin calls and margin
withdrawals.

The initial margin requirement on a single futures contract was $2,000
(the minimum dictated by the exchange), and the maintenance margin
was 75 percent of the initial margin, or $1,500. If prices were to fall and
accounts be resettled, RECOPE could face a margin call. If the account
were to fall below $1,500 per contract, RECOPE would have to bring its
account back up to the initial margin of $2,000 per contract. If, because
of a price increase, resettlement were to lead to a margin account above
$2,000 per contract, RECOPE could withdraw the surplus.

The simulations showed that the maximum margin call RECOPE would
have faced on any single day from July 1986 to December 1990 on a total
of 100 nearby futures contracts that were bought would have been
$400,000. This extremely large margin call would have occurred on the
eighteenth trading day of August 1990, when the futures price fell by $4
a barrel (from $30.91 to $26.91). The maximum withdrawal RECOPE
would have been able to make over this period would have been
$317,000 on the eighteenth trading day of October 1990, when the
futures price increased by $3.17 a barrel (from $31.08 to $34.25). It is
not surprising that RECOPE would have had the largest margin calls and
withdrawals in the fall of 1990, given the extremely large volatility in the
oil market during that period.

For all other months during the period July 1986 to December 1990,
the maximum call and withdrawal were considerably less. Figure 9-4
plots the maximum calls and withdrawals per contract for each month in
this period. (For 100 contracts the amounts need to be multiplied by
100.) The lower half of the figure shows the maximum call in each
month, and the upper half indicates the maximum withdrawal in each
month. The figure also indicates the average of the daily withdrawals
and margin calls in each month. As can be seen, the fall of 1990 was
exceptional in having the largest calls and withdrawals. During almost
all other months, the maximum withdrawal on any given day did not
exceed $1,000 per contract.

On average over this period, RECOPE would have been able to with-
draw money from its account as futures prices increased. The average
withdrawal per day per contract over the period July 1986 through

Figure 9-4. *Simulated One-Day Cash Flows per Futures Contract, Oil Sector, Costa Rica, 1986–90*

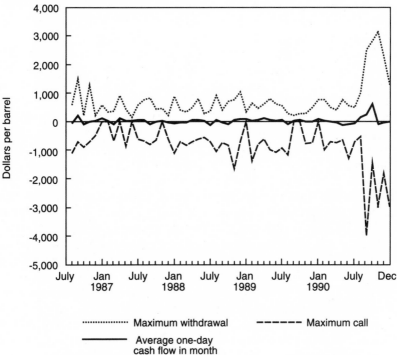

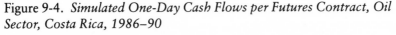

Source: Authors' calculations.

December 1990 would have been $28.44, or $0.028 a barrel. The largest average withdrawal over any month would have been in September 1990—$610 a day per contract(!)—because the futures price rose from $28.56 a barrel on the first of September to $39.51 a barrel at the end of that month, a gain of about $10 a barrel, or $10,000 per contract. The largest average margin call would have been in the month of June 1988— $122 a day per contract—because prices fell over that month from $17.72 to $15.16.

Overall, it can be concluded that margin calls and withdrawals would have been substantial and that RECOPE therefore would have needed access to funds on very short notice. We estimate that for 100 contracts, RECOPE would have needed access on an almost daily basis to at least $500,000—and preferably more—for possible margin calls. Of course, the need for funds for margin calls would not have represented a cost to RECOPE, because the negative cash flow effects of margin calls would have been offset by lower bills on oil imports in the future. The need for funds implies only that RECOPE's cash flow position would have fluctuated over time.

Institutional Changes

Risk management requires fast action, when situations demand it, and direct access to foreign exchange. Currently, the Central Bank obtains and handles foreign exchange for RECOPE's operations. This arrangement could lead to problems in obtaining foreign exchange to purchase futures or options and in maintaining a margin account. To solve these problems it would be necessary to establish a continuous, open line of communication between RECOPE and the Central Bank.

Ideally, a risk management program for RECOPE would have a high-level committee responsible for the general hedging plan, and a risk management unit within RECOPE responsible for working out the plan and executing it. The high-level committee would consist of staff from RECOPE, the Ministry of Mines and Energy, and the Ministry of Planning. It would discuss and outline the broad parameters of the hedging strategy and determine the cost of operating it. The risk management unit would consist of staff skilled in the use of risk management techniques. It would perform the hedging activities, such as day-to-day hedging operations and the monitoring of futures and options prices and open positions. The risk management unit would be in close contact with the parts of RECOPE that order the oil and deal with shipping. It would also form appropriate linkages between RECOPE and the Central Bank.

Some legislative changes would be necessary to allow state-owned enterprises, such as RECOPE, to participate in international financial markets. Currently, government-owned companies in Costa Rica are not allowed to use futures or options. This kind of legal and regulatory constraint hinders not only RECOPE, but also the access of the private sector to external hedging instruments.

Public Considerations

Oil importers should use futures and options not to achieve the lowest price but to guarantee a "reasonable" price and to reduce their exposure to oil price movements. A "reasonable" price is one that allows the importer to avoid losses in its operations, avoid cash flow problems, and guarantee a relatively stable price to the consumer. At times, hedging may imply "opportunity" losses compared with doing nothing (not hedging). But such losses do not represent costs, because, on average, opportunity losses and gains from hedging transactions balance each other. The main point is that hedging ensures risk reduction.[15]

Negative publicity could occur if RECOPE locked in a price for its oil imports for, say, six months ahead, only to find that oil prices fell. One remedy would be to use options to lock in a maximum price rather than futures to lock in a single price. However, options can be costly. One should then look for some mix of futures and options. Also, to ensure a broad consensus and an understanding of the possibility of opportunity losses, decisions regarding the general hedging strategy should be agreed on by several government entities, as recommended above.

The use of futures and options would require adjustments in the way domestic energy prices are set in order for the risk reduction benefits to reach the Costa Rican consumer. Ordinary price changes should be based not only on the international spot price, as is presently the case, but also on the locked-in price, the weights to be determined by the percentage of oil imports hedged. Likewise, the formula for the automatic adjustment in extraordinary requests should incorporate the effects of hedging by adjusting the price, P, in the formula to the weighted average of spot prices and the locked-in futures price, weights again being determined by the proportion of oil imports hedged. In this way, RECOPE could cushion the effects on the Costa Rican economy of transitory international oil price changes and smooth the effects of permanent oil price changes.

Conclusions

We have found that the basis risk between the WTI futures oil contract and four of the imported crudes (Istmo, Lagotreco, Oriente, and Caño Limón) is in the range of 12 to 23 percent and that the hedge ratio is not significantly different from one. The relationship between Bachaquero and WTI, however, is weak. We therefore recommend using WTI contracts to hedge Istmo, Oriente, and Caño Limón crude oil imports (and Lagotreco if the recent price relationship between WTI futures contracts and Lagotreco holds up). This result holds for either futures or options based on the WTI futures contract.

RECOPE faces three categories of risks: transaction, internal price adjustment, and long-term. Our simulations have shown that the potential gains in risk reduction as a result of hedging transactions risks are 75 to 86 percent for Istmo, Oriente, and Caño Limón crude oils (and for Lagotreco, if only the last two years of the study are considered). The potential gains from hedging long-term risks are about 70 percent for

Istmo, Oriente, and Caño Limón crude oils and less for the other crudes (about 35 to 50 percent).

The use of risk management techniques by RECOPE will require continuous communication between it and the Central Bank, an organizational structure to plan and manage the hedging, and legislative changes to allow it to engage in hedging. Hedging should aim to guarantee a "reasonable" price, not the lowest price. The use of options, or a mix of futures and options, could help to avoid price disparities that cause negative publicity. Formulas for the setting of domestic energy prices should be revised so that the benefits of risk reduction reach the consumer and therefore the economy as a whole.

Notes

1. The absolute annual value of oil imports (crude and products) ranged from $100 million in 1986 to $180 million in 1990.

2. The weights for crude and derivatives in the calculation of P are the proportions of crudes and derivatives in the "cocktail" used by RECOPE at the time of the calculation of the previous change.

3. Data on prices of crude oils and refined fuels are obtained from the on-line data base *Platt's Oilgram Price Report,* produced by McGraw-Hill.

4. Diesel and gasoline are featured in table 9-2 because they account for the major share of local hydrocarbon consumption and imports.

5. Part of the difference between domestic and import prices is explained by taxes, internal transportation costs, and margins for gas stations and RECOPE. Taxes are of three kinds: (a) a consumption tax of 13 percent, imposed on January 18, 1991; (b) a sales tax of 12 percent on RECOPE's total sales excluding transportation costs and gas station margins; and (c) specific taxes on gasoline, kerosene, liquified propane gas, and bunker fuel. Because of the lack of historical data, we can give figures only for 1990. In 1990, transportation costs were $1.07 a barrel, or 0.62 colón a liter; the average margin for the gas stations was 2.13 colones a liter; the specific taxes were 0.71 colón a liter (for gasoline); and the sales tax was around 3.55 colones a liter. After allowing for taxes, transportation costs, and gas station margins, domestic prices for gasoline and diesel were 59 percent and 36 percent, respectively, above import prices.

6. Fifty days is the longest time lag and occurs if, on the tenth day of a month, RECOPE decides to import crude to be delivered at the end of the following month.

7. For simplicity, the delivery date is assumed to coincide with the timing of the import costs.

8. Another disadvantage can be the unpredictability of the margin requirements; if spot prices drop, margin requirements increase. See further below.

9. See also Gemmill (1985), Kolb (1985), Labuszewski and Myhoff (1988a, 1988b), Overdahl (1986), and Thompson and Bond (1987) for descriptions of this methodology.

10. We chose this six-month hedging strategy because the nearby futures contracts were the most liquid of the contracts traded and a six-month horizon would allow RECOPE and Costa Rica sufficient lead time for adjusting domestic prices.

11. A July 1990 hedge would have to be a five-month hedge because daily January 1991 futures and cash prices were not available at the time of the study.

12. For reasons related to creditworthiness, RECOPE might have to put up some "collateral" to assure lenders of performance under the terms of the swap agreement. One way to do this is by using a marked-to-market swap that would operate in a manner similar to a futures contract. Other methods are also possible, such as escrowing some foreign exchange at a foreign bank.

13. This problem was identified in several interviews with officials from RECOPE as well as the Central Bank and the Ministry of Mines and Energy.

14. Note, however, that because margins can be put up by posting a U.S. Treasury bill or equivalent instrument, interest is not necessarily lost on margins.

15. Several oil-exporting and -importing countries have used futures to reduce the uncertainty of export earnings or import expenses (see, for example, Moffett and Truell 1991 on Mexico, Brazil, and Chile, and Laughlin and Falloon 1990).

10

Hedging Commodity Price Risks in Papua New Guinea

Stijn Claessens and Jonathan R. Coleman

Papua New Guinea faces substantial exposure to fluctuations in the prices of its major exports of primary commodities. Existing schemes to manage commodity risk provide limited protection against the impact of these fluctuations, have high cost, and, as demonstrated by recent events, are not able to provide protection over long periods.

In this chapter we argue that financial instruments available in developed capital markets are better suited to managing the external risks of Papua New Guinea than are its existing schemes and are less costly. This is especially true for mineral and energy price risks, for which financial instruments exist for hedging over long maturities. We demonstrate how Papua New Guinea could use these instruments to make the existing agricultural price stabilization funds more viable as well. For illustration, we develop a simple hedging strategy for the coffee fund.

The chapter begins by discussing Papua New Guinea's reliance on primary commodities and its exposure to the volatility of international commodity prices. We then describe existing commodity risk management mechanisms, and the effect of past commodity price fluctuations on economic stability is quantified. Then follows a general overview of risk management schemes and their costs and benefits, and we discuss some specific financial instruments applicable to Papua New Guinea for external risk management. Risk management strategies are then developed for the mineral and energy sectors and for the agricultural stabilization funds.

The authors would like to thank Ronald Duncan for his useful comments and World Bank staff working on Papua New Guinea for their contributions to this chapter.

The Importance of External Risk Management

External risk management is of primary importance to the Papua New Guinea economy. First, Papua New Guinea is highly dependent on the exports of primary commodities for foreign exchange earnings, government revenues, and employment. Second, Papua New Guinea is a price taker in the world markets of its major primary commodity exports. During the 1970s and 1980s these markets were highly volatile, with large intrayear and interyear fluctuations in prices. These price fluctuations were a major source of instability in the economy of Papua New Guinea. Third, Papua New Guinea's debt structure exposes it to both exchange rate and interest rate risks. Therefore, the use of management instruments to reduce these exposures to commodity, interest rate, and currency risk would be of considerable value.

The Importance of Primary Commodities to the Papua New Guinea Economy

The Papua New Guinea economy relies heavily on the strength of the export sector, which is composed mainly of mineral and tree crop exports (see table 10-1). Mineral and tree crop exports are crucial to the economy in earning foreign exchange, providing government revenues, creating employment, and servicing external debt. Papua New Guinea's major source of employment, however, is agricultural production. Within this sector, coffee and logs dominate, the importance of cocoa, copra, and palm oil having declined since the mid-1980s.

Table 10-1. *Contribution of Major Primary Commodity Exports to Total Export Earnings, Papua New Guinea, 1985–92* (percent)

Commodity	1985	1986	1987	1988	1989	1990[a]	1991[a]	1992[a]
Minerals	46.5	60.9	61.7	70.6	69.0	65.5	64.1	64.7
Gold	25.4	40.2	41.5	36.4	25.1	31.2	34.3	40.1
Copper	21.1	20.7	20.2	34.2	43.9	34.3	29.8	24.6
Nonminerals	53.5	39.1	38.3	29.4	31.0	34.5	35.9	35.3
Cocoa	7.5	6.3	5.3	3.5	3.8	3.2	2.6	2.6
Coffee	13.4	15.4	16.5	9.4	10.9	9.2	7.2	6.9
Copra	5.1	2.0	1.0	1.3	1.4	1.5	1.4	1.2
Logs	7.7	5.7	6.9	7.6	6.6	8.9	10.1	9.6
Palm oil	7.5	3.9	2.8	1.7	3.1	4.3	5.4	5.6
Other	12.3	5.8	5.8	5.9	5.2	7.4	12.2	9.4

a. Projections.
Source: Based on International Monetary Fund (1990, annex VII, table II).

Table 10-1 also shows that the composition of primary commodities is changing. In 1989 almost 70 percent of the total export earnings of Papua New Guinea were obtained from exports of gold and copper; the comparable figure in 1985 was less than 50 percent. The mineral sector is projected to continue to dominate in the early 1990s, contributing a little less than two-thirds of total export earnings in the 1990–92 period. Outside the mineral sector, logs and coffee contribute the most to export earnings. In 1989, coffee and logs contributed 10.9 percent and 6.6 percent, respectively; cocoa and palm oil 3.8 percent and 3.1 percent, respectively; and copra 1.4 percent. These proportions are forecast to remain fairly stable in the early 1990s.

The mineral sector makes a large contribution to government revenues through corporate income taxes, withholding taxes on dividends, and dividends from government equity in mineral projects. In addition, revenues come from import duties and payroll taxes paid by the mining corporations. In total, the mineral sector provided 20 percent of government revenues in 1989, and by the end of the 1990s the share is forecast to rise to more than 35 percent.

Although less important than the mineral sector, the agricultural sector makes a significant contribution to government revenues through direct taxation of company income, taxes on agricultural exports, and profits from government equity in agricultural projects such as oil palm estates. Revenues also come from taxes imposed on imported agricultural inputs, taxes paid by individuals earning agricultural incomes, and excise taxes levied on items such as fuel, beer, and cigarettes purchased with the incomes generated from agriculture. It is estimated that the contribution to total government revenues of the coffee sector alone is as much as 10 percent (see Brogan and Rewenyi 1987).

The mining sector generates few opportunities for employment in Papua New Guinea. Most of the capital used in the mines is technologically advanced and is imported. The two major mines, Bougainville Copper Limited (BCL) and OK Tedi Mining Company Limited (OTML), together employ only about 6,000 people (many of whom are expatriates), which is about 0.3 percent of the labor force. By contrast, agriculture, the most important source of employment, accounts for about 20 percent of the labor force, estimated to be 1.8 million in 1987.

Although the terms of trade have moved against the agricultural exports of Papua New Guinea since the mid-1960s, real consumption and investment have been maintained by overseas borrowing. As a result, external debt has increased dramatically, from less than $200 per capita in 1970 to more than $1,200 currently. The ratio of debt service to exports is now about 30 percent. In the 1988 government budget, interest payments alone made up almost 7 percent of total expenditures.

External debt servicing has been influenced by two external factors: international interest rates and cross-currency exchange rates. Movements in international interest rates have had relatively little influence on Papua New Guinea's debt service obligations compared with those of many other developing countries because a considerable part of Papua New Guinea's long-term debt (approximately 45 percent) is of a fixed-rate nature. Still, a change of 1 percentage point in the interest rate alters debt service by about $13 million. The influence of exchange rate movements on the level of debt measured in dollars has been large, however, because a significant part of Papua New Guinea's debt (approximately 60 percent) is in nondollar currencies. From 1985 to 1989 the absolute value of the currency valuation effect on debt stock has averaged about $72 million annually, or about 3 percent of the debt stock.

Fluctuations in the Value of Primary Commodities

The instability of export revenues from primary commodities is associated with fluctuations both in quantities produced and in prices. Indexes of the value, volume, and unit value of the major primary commodities of Papua New Guinea between 1985 and 1989 and projections for 1990 to 1992 are reported in table 10-2. Also reported in table 10-2 are the coefficients of variation (CVs; the CV is the ratio of the standard deviation to the mean), which provide a crude measure of instability.

The CV for the index of the value of mineral exports for the 1985–92 period is almost 20 percent, indicating that the export value is quite unstable. The value of copper exports is especially variable, the CV being 36.5 percent, whereas the CV of gold is 19.0 percent. Also, copper prices were highly unstable, recording a CV of 24.4 percent. The index of the value of nonmineral exports was more stable than the mineral index, the CV being 14.4 percent. The most important commodities, logs and coffee, reported CVs of 20.6 percent and 34.5 percent, respectively, both CVs being lower than the CVs for the other major commodity exports, except for gold. With the exception of gold and logs, the unit-value variability of each export commodity in the table is greater than its production variability. This difference reflects the high degree of instability of international agricultural commodities prices. Also of interest is the fact that the unit values of commodities have declined over the period, especially for coffee and cocoa.

The dependence of Papua New Guinea on primary commodities will increase with expected developments in the energy sector. Oil export earnings could amount to as much as a third of mineral export earnings by the year 2000, equivalent to 25 percent of total export earnings. With greater dependence on oil exports, the economy of Papua New Guinea

Table 10-2. *Indexes of Export Value, Volume, and Unit Value of Major Commodities in Papua New Guinea, 1985–92* (1990 = 100)

Commodity	1985	1986	1987	1988	1989	1990[a]	1991[a]	1992[a]	CV[b]
Value									
Minerals	68	95	86	131	128	100	96	111	19.3
Gold	78	132	122	141	98	100	108	145	19.0
Copper	59	62	54	121	156	100	85	80	36.5
Nonminerals	152	124	109	109	116	100	96	107	14.4
Cocoa	229	205	155	134	148	100	81	94	34.5
Coffee	139	169	164	123	144	100	77	84	26.3
Copra	327	133	67	104	117	100	91	91	59.9
Logs	83	65	71	116	90	100	111	121	20.6
Palm oil	167	93	58	47	88	100	122	143	37.2
Volume									
Minerals	81	115	104	136	118	100	108	129	14.5
Gold	72	125	115	124	102	100	110	149	18.8
Copper	90	105	94	146	133	100	106	110	16.4
Nonminerals	82	83	86	91	92	100	100	106	8.9
Cocoa	83	82	80	78	115	100	92	103	13.1
Coffee	68	64	76	87	87	100	87	90	13.7
Copra	135	150	131	117	104	100	88	88	17.9
Logs	87	90	93	114	95	100	112	118	11.0
Palm oil	70	78	72	48	76	100	118	129	29.3
Unit value									
Minerals	84	83	83	96	108	100	89	86	9.5
Gold	108	106	106	114	96	100	98	97	5.6
Copper	66	59	57	83	117	100	80	73	24.4
Nonminerals	185	149	127	120	126	100	96	101	22.3
Cocoa	276	250	194	172	129	100	88	91	39.9
Coffee	204	264	216	141	166	100	89	93	38.1
Copra	242	89	51	89	113	100	103	103	47.7
Logs	95	72	76	102	95	100	99	103	11.9
Palm oil	239	119	81	98	116	100	103	111	38.0

a. Projection.

b. Coefficient of variation (the ratio of the standard deviation to the mean).

Source: Based on International Monetary Fund (1990, annex VII, table III).

will open itself to risks associated with fluctuating oil prices. Recent events have been a reminder that oil prices are highly unpredictable, which suggests that management instruments to lower these risks will be of great importance in the future.[1]

Problems Created by Price Instability

The previous section clearly demonstrates that the instability of commodity prices, exchange rates, and interest rates has had, and will continue to have, a significant impact on Papua New Guinea's macroeconomy through its cash flow effects on export earnings and the burden of debt service. Volatile external prices affect not only contemporaneous cash flows, but also production and investment decisions. For Papua New Guinea, problems in developing the nonmining sector of the economy can, in part, be traced back to the heavy dependence on mineral exports and the volatility in mineral prices. In times of high mineral prices and high real exchange rates, the international competitiveness of the nonmining sector deteriorates and little investment occurs. However, in periods when mineral prices and the real exchange rate fall, the nonmining sector may still not develop, because investors realize the situation can easily reverse itself, rendering investments in the nonmining sector possibly unprofitable.

Existing Mechanisms for Managing Commodity Risk

Three main entities bear the risks associated with fluctuating commodity prices: the government of Papua New Guinea; private corporations that operate in commodity sectors; and the agricultural marketing boards for cocoa, coffee, copra, and palm oil. The exposure of these entities to commodity price risk, and the specific risk management schemes that are in place for each entity, are described below.

Management of the Government's Exposure to Mineral and Energy Price Risk

The Papua New Guinea government's exposure to mineral and energy price changes is affected by its participation in the Mineral Resources Stabilization Fund (MRSF) and the Mineral Resources Development Corporation (MRDC). The MRSF channels tax revenues to the government, and these tax revenues are affected by price changes. Through the MRDC, the government has an equity stake in mines and energy projects and is responsible for raising the funds necessary to finance the equity participation in new projects. This involvement also affects the government's exposure to price changes. Mechanisms set up by these two organizations to manage commodity risk have a further bearing on the degree to which the government is exposed.

Taxation and the mrsf. The structure of mineral resource taxation in Papua New Guinea reflects the authorities' objective of providing adequate incentives to producers while ensuring that the government is able to secure most of any windfall profits (see further Coopers and Lybrand 1989). The tax regime in place for both mining and petroleum projects places a heavy tax burden on the more profitable operations while minimizing tax requirements from marginal projects. Mining enterprises are subject to an effective tax rate of 46 percent. Highly profitable operations are subject to an additional profits tax, which can result in marginal rates of almost 65 percent. The additional profits tax on mining is payable when the project shows a return on investment above a specified rate. As a result of the additional profits tax, the government's revenues increase sharply in periods of high commodity prices. Petroleum projects are subject to a company tax rate of 50 percent. The additional profits tax for the petroleum industry is payable at a rate of 50 percent once the project has achieved a 27 percent nominal rate of return after income tax.

The mrsf was established in 1974 with the objective of reducing the impact of fluctuations in mineral revenues on the government budget. Under the legislation establishing the fund, all dividends in state shareholdings, company income taxes, and withholding taxes on dividends (identified above) from all designated mining operations must be paid into the mrsf. The assets of the mrsf are held by the Central Bank of Papua New Guinea, which invests them in securities abroad, primarily in the form of interest-bearing deposits and central bank securities. The surplus funds, managed by the Central Bank, constitute the country's main source of reserves.

Drawdowns from the mrsf are determined on the basis of recommendations submitted to the Board of Management of the mrsf. The general rule for withdrawal is that the amount to be drawn down should ensure that the fund is sustainable in terms of real purchasing power over the next five years (see also Guest 1987). The mrsf board is bound to make forecasts of future receipts for eight years ahead and (implicitly) forecasts of inflation five years ahead. The commodity prices implicit in the forecasts are not supposed to vary more than 10 percent from the historical moving average of commodity prices (20 years for copper prices, the preceding year for gold and silver).

In practice, the MRSF has operated with considerable flexibility, and a revision made to the MRSF Act in 1987 allows the government greater discretion than before. This revision, although providing greater flexibility in the use of mineral revenues, carries the risk of larger increases being allowed in drawdowns and expenditures in anticipation of future growth in these revenues. The contributions to and drawdowns from the MRSF have varied substantially over the past decade. The degree of stabilization the MRSF has provided over the 1980–88 period can be quantified by comparing the CV of its outflows (45 percent) with the CV of its revenues (56 percent). The figures suggest that very little stabilization of the government's budget has occurred by placing the MRSF between tax receipts and inflows in the budget; the relative reduction is only about 20 percent.[2] This result is to be expected, given the implicit use of the moving-average price with short time periods (one year for gold and silver) as an indicator of the future price and given the increased flexibility in the rules.

RULES OF THE MRDC. The government has followed a policy of taking an equity share in all major mineral projects. Although these investments have been characterized by a high degree of risk, there has been popular support for the principle that the government should maintain a share in the ownership and control of projects that exploit nonrenewable resources. The equity participation in new mineral projects uses the MRDC as the vehicle of ownership. In the case of mining projects, the government has reserved the right to take an equity share of up to 30 percent, although in most projects to date it has taken a 20 percent share.[3] For petroleum projects, the government reserves the right to take a 22.5 percent carried interest.

The MRDC has financed its equity participation in the different projects in a variety of ways, from deferred payback on future dividends—in which case the foreign investor effectively provides the financing—to loans obtained through external commercial borrowing (with a government guarantee).[4] More recently, the MRDC has relied on foreign financing. The MRDC receives its dividends on its equity stake and pays any excess of dividends over financing costs to the Department of Finance and Planning. The MRDC is exposed to commodity price risk because its expenses (interest and principal payments on foreign loans) are not dependent on commodity prices whereas its revenues are. The substantial level of government equity in new mines envisaged over the next few years will require large commercial loans from abroad. Estimated to amount to about $500 million in 1991 and 1992, these borrowings will greatly increase the MRDC's risk exposure.

Management of Private Corporations' Exposure to Mineral Price Risk

Foreign companies operating mines in Papua New Guinea are exposed to mineral price risks through the effects of price changes on the cash flow (dividend remittances and other transfer payments to the parent company) derived from the mines. Most foreign firms have put some risk management program in place to protect cash flow streams to the parent company against mineral price swings. An example is the use of long-dated instruments in the financing of a copper investment (see Priovolos 1991). It appears, however, that the risk management is done at the parent, offshore level, that is, that the net profit remittances received by the parent from the subsidiary are hedged at the offshore level, leaving export receipts and taxes exposed. Much of the mineral price exposure therefore appears to remain at the subsidiary level, leaving the Papua New Guinea economy exposed to fluctuations in the price of its main exports.

Risk Management by Agricultural Commodity Boards

Given the importance of agricultural commodity exports to the economy and the volatility of international prices of these commodities, stabilization schemes have been established in Papua New Guinea since the 1940s for the important export crops—namely, cocoa, coffee, copra, and palm oil. The four schemes are similar in design (see figure 10-1). A threshold price is determined equal to a ten-year moving average of free on board (f.o.b.) prices, adjusted for inflation. Then a buffer zone in which no bounties or levies apply is set 5 percent above and below the threshold price. When the current f.o.b. price is more than 5 percent above the threshold price, levies are imposed on producers at 50 percent of the difference between the threshold price and the current f.o.b. price. The levy revenues are paid into a commodity stabilization fund. When the current f.o.b. price is more than 5 percent below the threshold price, bounties are paid to producers at 50 percent of the difference between the current f.o.b. price and the threshold price. Bounties are paid out of the stabilization fund.

Until recently, the schemes were successful in stabilizing producer prices. However, in the mid- and late 1980s, commodity prices fell substantially in real terms, so that current f.o.b. prices were consistently below the threshold price. As a result, subsidy payments were made to producers over an extended period. These payments led to the eventual exhaustion of the cocoa, copra, and palm oil funds. The coffee fund was expected to run out in 1991. To prolong price support, the funds were

Figure 10-1. *Structure of Agricultural Price Stabilization Schemes in Papua New Guinea*

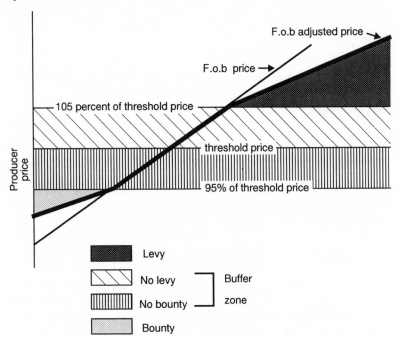

kept solvent through government financial contributions, commercial bank loans, and Stabilisation of Export Earnings (STABEX) transfers.

In response to these problems, the government decided in November 1989 to implement a number of interim measures that would provide support to the agricultural export sectors while a new approach to price stabilization was found. Instead of establishing a threshold price based on a long-run moving average, price support during the adjustment period is based on the difference between the estimated costs of production and the international price. The level of price support will decline over an adjustment period of three to five years, depending on the commodity. By the end of this period, producers will face international prices. The loans used to finance price support payments are to be repaid by the commodity boards from export revenues when the international price exceeds the support price.

The objective of these new measures is to give price protection to producers while they adjust to lower international prices. The rationale for this policy is that without such a scheme a significant proportion of the estate sector will go out of business. To the extent that supply has become uneconomical, it may be desirable that some estates go out of business. But a portion of the estate business may go out of business just because it experiences temporary difficulties in adjusting to a lower price. With price support as well as initiatives to improve productivity, such as extension and research, it is expected that the sectors will be able to adjust to lower prices, gain international competitiveness, and repay existing loans.

The Impact of Commodity Price Fluctuations on Economic Stability

Below are empirical estimates of the extent to which commodity price risk affects each of the following: tax revenues, the MRSF, and the MRDC and the private sector.

Tax Revenues

Historically, Papua New Guinea's total tax revenues have been very sensitive to variations in commodity prices. This sensitivity can be estimated by running the regression

(10-1) $$TR_t = \alpha + \beta P_{t1} + \gamma P_{t2} + \ldots + \text{ERROR}$$

where TR_t is the percentage change in tax revenues in period t, P_{ti} is the percentage change in the price of a relevant commodity (for example, copper or gold), α is the intercept, and β and γ are the sensitivities of tax revenues to the various relevant commodity price changes.[5] From these regression equations, the elasticity of tax revenues with respect to the copper price (both expressed in the annual percentage change in dollar value) over the period 1976–88 was about 0.25 (with a t-statistic of 3.3 and an R^2 of 0.56). The elasticity with respect to gold prices was about 0.18 over the same period, but not significant. A similar regression was done for export earnings. The elasticity of export earnings with respect to copper prices was about 0.18 (with a t-statistic of 1.37 and an R^2 of 0.135). The elasticity with respect to gold prices was about 0.738 over the same period ($t = 2.84$, $R^2 = 0.45$).[6]

These results suggest that the exposure of tax revenues to export prices is quite different from the relationship between export earnings and export prices in the case of the gold price, but similar in the case of the copper price. Because the average shares of copper and gold in export earnings over the 1976–88 period were about 25 percent and 30 percent, respectively, these elasticities also indicate that movements in volumes exported have partly offset the effects of price movements in the case of copper exports and exacerbated those movements in the case of gold exports.

The MRSF

Similar regressions were performed for the dividend stream on the government's share in the mining projects accruing to the MRSF. The elasticity for gold was 1.22 ($R^2 = 0.28$, $t = 2.06$) and that for copper 0.72 ($R^2 = 0.05$, $t = 0.77$). The regression coefficients for the annual levels of dollar dividends (in millions) on the level of prices for the period 1981–88 were 0.076 for gold ($R^2 = 0.43$, $t = 2.14$) and 0.0056 for copper ($R^2 = 0.42$, $t = 2.11$). Because the last regression is in levels, the coefficients measure the exposure of the dividend stream to prices and can be interpreted as the quantity of physical commodity "received" by the government each year. These quantities are equal to 2.56 tons of gold (converting ounces to tons) and 5,631 tons of copper (or 8 percent of gold exports and 2.5 percent of copper exports).

Regarding future price sensitivities, an internal World Bank report gives results for two scenarios: in scenario 1 the price of gold is 15 percent lower than in the base case, and the price of oil stagnates in real terms; in scenario 2 the price of gold rises in proportion to international inflation. The difference in the current account between these two scenarios is 7.5 percent of gross domestic product, and the difference in the fiscal balance is 6.7 percent of gross domestic product, both aggregates indicating the large sensitivity to international movements in the prices of commodities.

The MRDC and the Private Sector

Sensitivity scenarios regarding future prices can also be performed on the profitability and resulting tax revenues in the case of an individual mining operation. Such a scenario was done for a mine similar to the recently opened Porgera mine, which largely produces gold. Based on production estimates, costs of production, and current tax regulations, calculations were made to determine profits, tax receipts, and dividends paid abroad (the excess cash flow after subtracting the government's share) using different assumptions as to the price of gold.

Figure 10-2 plots the results for the present value of dividends paid abroad and the present value of gross receipts (tax receipts, royalties, and dividends) to the MRSF over the lifetime of the project. As one can observe, the present value of MRSF receipts is more sensitive with respect to the gold price than the present value of dividends paid abroad. As the gold price increases, the additional profits tax comes into effect and raises the present value of MRSF receipts relatively more than the present value of dividends. In regressing the present value of MRSF receipts on the gold price, the slope coefficient is around 2, but the slope coefficient of a regression of the present value of dividends on the gold price is only 0.75. Thus, the government is relatively (about three times) more exposed to gold price risks than the foreign investors are; foreign investors share less in the upside of a price increase, and the government shares more because of the additional profits tax.[7]

Risk Management Schemes and Their Costs and Benefits

Many different forms of commodity price risk management can be used by developing countries. We will discuss here the ones in use by Papua New Guinea.

Stabilization Funds

The principle behind the agricultural product stabilization funds and the MRSF in Papua New Guinea is that in periods of decline in commodity-related tax revenues the government draws on its reserves to finance its normal expenditures. The experience with commodity stabilization funds in other countries, however, has shown that these funds are seldom sufficient to sustain expenditures in times of prolonged downturns in commodity prices and that consequently the funds only insure against short-lived declines (see chapter 2, by Gilbert). Evidence is provided by the agricultural price stabilization schemes that are effectively depleted.

The Papua New Guinea agricultural stabilization schemes were originally designed to stabilize prices around the long-run average price. But because commodity prices are not stationary, the moving average of past prices is unreliable as an estimate of the long-run price, and the scheme is likely to fail. As reported above, the agricultural stabilization funds in Papua New Guinea were indeed exhausted following the persistently low prices of cocoa, coffee, copra, and palm oil during the late 1980s. Similar examples from other countries abound, such as the depletion of the stabilization funds for coffee in Côte d'Ivoire and for cocoa in Cameroon. So far, the MRSF is the only stabilization fund in Papua New Guinea that has performed successfully over a prolonged period. But the closure of the Bougainville copper and gold mine (BCL) has shown that even the MRSF can provide only very limited insurance against a major

Figure 10-2. *Sensitivity Scenario for a Gold Mine: Present Value of MRSF Receipts and Dividends Paid*

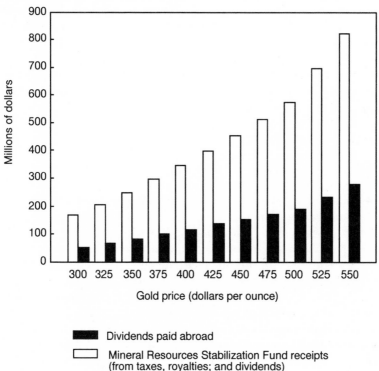

Gold price (dollars per ounce)

■ Dividends paid abroad

☐ Mineral Resources Stabilization Fund receipts (from taxes, royalties; and dividends)

Source: Authors' calculations.

shortfall in government revenues and that additional support for Papua New Guinea's balance of payments is sometimes necessary.

Adjusting the rules of a scheme will not prevent the funds from exhaustion over the long run unless the effectiveness of the scheme in stabilizing prices is drastically reduced. For example, historical data show that if the moving-average period had been shortened and the inflation adjustment eliminated from the Papua New Guinea agricultural schemes, the funds would not now be exhausted. However, although such changes would certainly reduce the frequency with which the stabilization funds are depleted, the tradeoff is that the price paid to producers would be less stabilized. Another way to modify the schemes so as to slow down the exhaustion of the funds would be to allow only 50 percent of the fund to be paid out as bounties in any one year. In this case, the fund would never become exhausted (although it could asymptotically decline to zero), but it would become progressively weaker in its ability to stabilize producer prices.

The agricultural schemes in Papua New Guinea have failed largely because of the difficulty of determining the long-term price which, in turn, determines the level of withdrawals. Funds in other countries have failed for this reason, but also because of lack of discipline in accumulating reserves in times of high commodity prices. The increased flexibility with respect to drawdowns from the MRSF thus raises some concerns about budgetary discipline.

Other Instruments

Papua New Guinea has benefited from the international commodity agreements for cocoa and coffee. However, most of the international price stabilization schemes, including those for cocoa and coffee, have collapsed in recent years because of a breakdown in cooperation among members or because of the exhaustion of support funds. Papua New Guinea has drawn funds from compensatory financing schemes (such as the STABEX and System for Safeguarding and Developing Mineral Production [SYSMIN] facilities and the Compensatory and Contingency Financing Facility [CCFF]), which can serve as risk management schemes. However, the availability of these compensatory financing schemes is limited and uncertain, as was shown following the closure of BCL. At that time Papua New Guinea had to make severe balance of payments adjustments because financing was not sufficiently available to compensate for the drop in export revenues.

Financial Instruments to Manage External Risk

The failure of international commodity agreements to stabilize prices on a reliable basis, and the possible drawbacks of compensatory agreements and domestic stabilization schemes, indicate the importance of using financial market instruments to manage commodity price risk. The most important financial instruments from Papua New Guinea's point of view are commodity futures, commodity options, commodity swaps, and commodity-linked finance (loans and bonds; see also Masuoka, chapter 4 of this volume). More specifically, forward contracts, futures contracts, and options could be used to eliminate price exposure over a short period (for example, one year) for agricultural commodities, and swaps could be used in the mineral and energy sector for price risk management over longer horizons. The possible nature and use of these short- and long-term hedging instruments in the context of Papua New

Guinea will now be further discussed. For the costs of each of these instruments, we refer to chapter 1, by Claessens and Duncan, and chapter 4, by Masuoka.

Commodity Futures

Suppose the Cocoa Marketing Board in Papua New Guinea wished to set a guaranteed price to producers for the coming season without incurring significant financial losses if international prices changed suddenly. Using historical export patterns, the cocoa board could predict fairly accurately the quantities of cocoa available for export during different months throughout the year. On the basis of these predictions, the board could then sell futures contracts at the beginning of the season for each of the delivery months in the coming year in proportion to the volume available for export in each of those months. The price guaranteed to producers at the beginning of the season could be set as the weighted average of the futures price, the weights being given by the export volume. As exports are sold at international prices throughout the year, nearby futures contracts (those closest to expiration) could be purchased (thus offsetting the original short position) at prices close to the international price. Such a strategy would eliminate intrayear price risk for the marketing board.

Commodity Options

Commodity boards could also use commodity options (on futures contracts). Say the Coffee Marketing Board wished to hedge the future price of its coffee sales by using options instead of futures or forward contracts. Suppose the board wished to sell 50,000 tons of coffee in six months time and wanted to receive a price of at least $2,000 a ton. In this situation the board could purchase put options giving it the right to sell coffee futures contracts at a price of $2,000 a ton. Say the premium quoted is $50 a ton, so that $2.5 million is paid to cover the entire 50,000 tons. If after six months the price is greater than $2,000 a ton, say $2,200 a ton, the board would not exercise the options and would receive $110 million in revenues. If, however, the price were to fall to $1,800 a ton, the board would exercise its options, enabling it to sell futures contracts at $2,000 a ton. The futures contracts could then be bought back at $1,800 (because the spot and futures prices are always equal at the expiration of the contract), resulting in a profit of $200 a ton. The board could then sell the coffee at the spot price of $1,800 a ton. The gain of $200 a ton on the futures contracts combined with the $1,800 a ton on the physical commodity would give an overall price of

$2,000 a ton and total revenues of $100 million. The coffee options would provide price insurance to the board, guaranteeing it at least $100 million in revenues in exchange for an insurance premium of $2.5 million.

Commodity Swaps

Assume that a Papua New Guinea copper exporter and a refining and fabricating company entered into a long-term export contract in which the latter agreed to buy 2 million pounds of copper every six months over the ensuing five years, paying the copper price current at each six-month interval. Assume also that the Papua New Guinea exporter wanted to lock in the dollar value of these revenues at the time the contract was signed. The exporter could enter into a commodity swap contract with a bank. Assume that the term for the swap is $1 a pound (indicative). The bank would agree to pay the exporter $2 million every six months for the ensuing five years. The exporter would agree to pay the value of 2 million pounds of copper using the spot price on the same dates the bank is due to make its payments. A "difference" check would settle the transaction every six months. Thus, the commodity swap contract—in effect, a series of (ten) forward contracts lined up over a specified (five-year) period—would lock in the price (at $1 a pound).

Commodity swaps and other long-dated risk management instruments involve credit risk to both parties of the contract because, depending on whether the prevailing market price is above or below the predetermined price, one party owes, or is due, the net amount. Papua New Guinea currently has a good credit standing, as reflected by the fact that it has sufficient access to private financial markets. Consequently, it should be able to use any of these financial risk management techniques. Given the increase in exposure of the Papua New Guinea economy to commodity price risk, the economy will increasingly depend on a handful of commodity exports for its growth and development. Therefore, commodity risk management should become an integral part of the Papua New Guinea government's economic strategy. We discuss in the next two sections some possible financial risk management techniques for the MRSF and agricultural stabilization funds. But before specific risk management operations can be implemented, Papua New Guinea will first need to establish a proper institutional framework and overall risk management strategy.

Because Papua New Guinea is not only exposed to commodity price risks but also to other forms of external risks arising from its financial liabilities and assets (that is, to exchange rate and interest rate risks), it is important that the links between different exposures are taken into account. First, movements in cross-currency exchange rates may offset or exacerbate movements in primary commodity prices, implying that the management of both commodity risk and exchange rate risk may need to be modified. Second, commodity prices can have an inverse relationship to quantities traded. Depending on the elasticity of supply and demand, the effect of price changes on export revenues or import expenses can be offset by changes in the quantity of goods exported or imported. Changes in quantity may reduce the need for hedging price risks as a way to hedge revenue or expense risks. Chapter 11, by Coleman and Qian, explicitly accounts for these interactions and estimates an optimal external debt portfolio.

Strategies to Manage Mineral and Energy Price Risk

As discussed above, the MRDC does not insulate the government budget from the risks associated with commodity prices, because the MRDC's liabilities (loans) and assets (dividend streams) are not matched. This discrepancy occurs because the MRDC's obligations on external loans (debt service payments) are independent of commodity prices, whereas its dividends are highly dependent on commodity prices. A matching between assets and liabilities over the long term can be made with either a commodity swap or commodity-linked finance.

For example, when the MRDC has an equity stake in a copper mine, its revenues are sensitive to the copper price. In that case, a copper swap can be used to convert copper price–sensitive cash flows into a certain cash flow stream that can be used to service obligations on conventional loans. As mentioned by Masuoka (chapter 4), this structure was successfully used by the Mexicana de Cobre copper mining company.

The notional amount of copper swap would depend on the sensitivity of the dividend stream to the copper price. Based on our earlier analysis, the annual value of dividends (and thus the MRDC's revenues) can be expressed as

$$(10\text{-}2) \qquad\qquad D_t = \alpha + \beta P_t$$

where D is the value of the dividends, P is the copper price, α is the copper price–independent portion of the dividends, and β is the sensitivity of dividends to the copper price. Graphically, the relationship is shown in figure 10-3.

In an earlier section the slope coefficient, β, was estimated to be about 5,631 tons. This figure implies that for every $1 change in the price per ton of copper, the MRDC's annual revenues change by approximately $5,631. This change is equivalent to the MRDC's receiving (having a long

Figure 10-3. *Sensitivity of the Dividend Stream to the Copper Price*

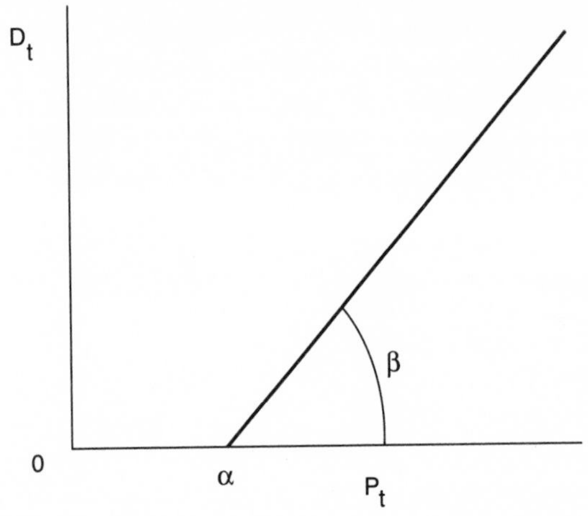

Note: D, dividend stream; P, copper price.

position of) 5,631 tons of copper annually, because the value of owning 5,631 tons of copper would change by an equal amount as a result of a price change.

The long position of the MRDC in copper can be hedged by a commodity swap. The swap would oblige Papua New Guinea to make annual payments equivalent to the spot value of 5,631 tons ($\beta \times P_t$, which is about $15 million at the current spot copper price) in exchange for receiving a fixed payment. The fixed payment would depend on conditions in the market for copper swaps and on the futures prices for copper, but for illustrative purposes a fixed price of $2,500 a ton can be used. The copper price–sensitive dividend stream would then be matched with the copper price–sensitive obligation on the swap. The net result would be a cash flow stream that is (largely) independent of copper price swings and that would thus, without any risk, be available to service conventional loans.

Commodity-linked loans can achieve the same result. Consider the case of the participation of the MRDC in a gold mine, for example, a mine similar to Porgera. Once the project comes on stream the dividend payments received by the MRDC will depend on the price of gold. It was shown above that for every dollar change in the price of gold, the present value of a dividend stream to the MRDC coming from a project like Porgera changes by approximately $80,000, or, equivalently, the annual dividend stream changes by about $8,000.[8] In order to hedge this risk, the financing of the equity participation by the MRDC should consist of an obligation whose servicing also changes by $8,000 for each dollar change in the price of gold and, for the remainder, a conventional loan. A gold loan could constitute the price-sensitive part. Gold loans stipulate payments in ounces of gold, and the costs of servicing the gold loan would thus vary one-to-one with the price of gold. In every period, the MRDC would want to owe 8,000 ounces of gold, because this obligation would vary in the same way as the dividend stream with gold price changes.

Assuming that interest rates on gold (gold fees) are between 2 percent and 3 percent, the MRDC could borrow between 250,000 and 400,000 ounces of gold. At current gold prices, this means that the MRDC could obtain between $100 million and $150 million in a gold loan. The remainder would have to be borrowed in a conventional dollar loan.[9] The combination of the gold-denominated and the conventional loans would hedge the MRDC perfectly.

Similar financial hedging techniques are possible for the MRSF. Currently, the reserves of the MRSF are invested by the Central Bank in relatively low-yielding, safe assets. This policy does not seem to provide Papua New Guinea with the best mix of return maximization and risk minimization. Even though using foreign exchange reserves provides a smoothing mechanism against income shocks, it does not involve diversifying commodity price risk. It is an expensive self-insurance scheme because the fund's asset returns are unrelated to commodity price movements and because it cannot sustain a prolonged decline in commodity prices. Furthermore, the fund ties up a significant amount of foreign reserves.

A better policy would be to manage reserves through commodity loans, commodity swaps, or short-term commodity hedging tools. Commodity swaps are the most suitable. Based on projected revenue streams that depend on the price of a particular commodity, the MRSF could enter a commodity swap with a foreign financial institution. (Altogether the MRSF should eventually enter several swaps, that is, separate ones for gold, copper, and oil.)

As an example, consider the MRSF's gold-dependent revenues. The MRSF received 42.5 million kina in total revenues in 1988. Based on the production numbers of BCL and on prevailing gold and copper prices, it is estimated that revenues related to gold mining amounted to about 30 percent of total revenues, or 12.4 million kina ($14 million) in 1988. This revenue stream depends on the gold price and is equivalent to the MRSF's holding a long position in physical quantities of gold. Using the 1988 gold price, this long position in tax revenues was equal to about

33,000 ounces of gold. Thus, for every dollar increase in the gold price, the annual tax revenues of the MRSF change by about $33,000, or the change in the value of 33,000 ounces of gold.[10]

The MRSF could now enter a gold swap with a foreign financial intermediary with an interest payment of 33,000 ounces of gold (with a notional interest payment of $14 million based on a spot price of $425 an ounce) in which it would effectively sell gold at a fixed price for, say, the next ten years. The size of the notional principal would depend on the current market gold fee; at a rate of 2 percent, the notional principal would amount to about 1,650,000 ounces, or about $700 million.[11]

In this way, at certain times the MRSF would pay the third party the equivalent value of 33,000 ounces of gold at the then-prevailing spot price—which would exactly offset the tax and dividend receipts it gets from the gold producer. In exchange, it would receive from the third party (commercial bank) a fixed payment of $X times 33,000 at each date (where X depends on the gold fee, the current spot price of gold, and the current interest rate), and the MRSF's tax revenues for the next ten years would be effectively fixed at $X times 33,000.

Swap transactions will not result in a perfect hedge because MRSF revenues do not depend linearly on the underlying price of the commodity, but rather in a nonlinear way on commodity prices, going up progressively when commodity prices rise. Considering the gold sector only, the dependence of the revenues paid into the MRSF can be represented as[12]

$$(10\text{-}3) \qquad R_t = \alpha + [\beta Q \times \max{(P_t - F, 0)}]$$
$$+ [\lambda Q \times \max{(P_t - M, 0)}]$$

where R_t is the revenue going to the MRSF, β is the effective corporate tax (the combination of the regular corporate tax rate, currently 35 percent, and the withholding tax, 17 percent, making a total tax rate of 46 percent), Q is the quantity exported, F is the fixed costs per unit for the producer (including depreciation allowances in the early years of the project), P_t is the gold price, and λ is the additional profits tax rate, which comes into effect when profits exceed a benchmark that is assumed to occur when prices, P_t, exceed the level M.

This exposure of revenues to gold prices can be hedged by using swap transactions (as outlined above) combined with long-dated options. Once the company has largely depreciated its fixed costs, that is, when $F = 0$, the swap transaction would involve a (notional) amount of gold equal to βQ, which would hedge the part of overall revenues that represents regular profit. This hedging would result in more stable streams to the general budget. In addition to the swap, the MRSF could sell a series of long-dated call options to a third party with exercise prices of M, for amounts equal to λQ and with maturities on which tax receipts are due in future years. The sale of the call options would give Papua New Guinea a premium income that could be invested in safe foreign obligations (for example, commercial bank deposits or Treasury bills or bonds) from which an annuity could be passed on to the government budget.

The gold swap would hedge the normal revenues from corporate taxes and withholding taxes on dividends, and payments on the swap would be matched with tax receipts at each maturity date. The options would hedge the additional profits tax. At the maturity date of the option, the commodity price could either be below the level M (at which point the additional profits tax would not be in effect) or above it. When it is below, the call is also out-of-the-money, and the MRSF would not be required to make payments to the third party. When the call is in-the-money, the payment on the call would be offset exactly by the tax revenue to the MRSF from the additional profits tax. Again, the transaction would result in converting a risky tax revenue stream into a certain yield on the invested premiums. These transactions are illustrated in figure 10-4. It can be seen that the net payoff is almost independent of the price of gold, being horizontal for almost all price ranges.

These transactions would enable the MRSF to largely lock in its revenues over a long period regardless of the gold price. They would also allow the MRSF to pass on a fixed stream of payments to the general budget and not have to rely on formulas based on expected prices or ad hoc decisionmaking.

The effects of using short-term commodity hedging instruments such as futures would be similar to those of using swaps. The following example illustrates the use of commodity futures to hedge current-year tax revenues against copper price risks.[13] At the beginning of the fiscal year, Papua New Guinea would sell copper futures contracts with maturities spread out over the year. The amount to be sold would depend on the sensitivity of the tax revenues to copper prices. The earlier analysis showed this elasticity to be about 0.25, which implies that Papua New Guinea would have to sell futures with a contractual face value equal to about 25 percent of anticipated tax revenues. The selling of copper futures contracts would reduce as much as possible the combined effect of price and quantity uncertainty on the next period's tax revenue.

Agricultural Stabilization Funds

In chapter 4, Masuoka indicated that for most agricultural commodities the markets for longer-term hedging instruments were not yet well

Figure 10-4. *Payoffs from Hedging Taxes by Using Swaps and Options*

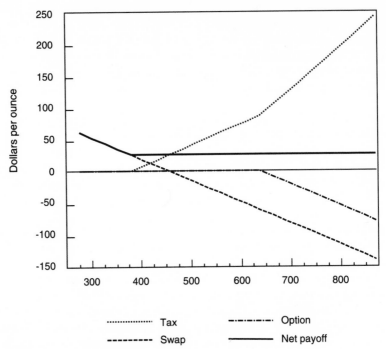

Note: The figure assumes that the profit tax will come into effect at a gold price of $400 an ounce and the additional profits tax at a price of $650 and ounce.
Source: Authors' calculations.

developed. For these commodities, however, the short-term hedging instruments are in general easily available. Below, we develop for the Coffee Marketing Board a hedging strategy that uses coffee futures traded in New York. Because the four agricultural stabilization funds have similar features, this kind of strategy would be applicable to the other three funds as well.

Although the prime objective of the coffee fund is to reduce the effects of sharply changing prices over time, substantial problems can be associated with sudden price movements within the year. These problems were illustrated with the breakdown in the International Coffee Agreement. The breakdown led to a decline in coffee prices, from $3,356 a ton in January 1989 to $1,515 a ton in December of the same year. The largest monthly decline was between June and July, when the price fell from $2,762 a ton to $1,942 a ton, a reduction of 30 percent.

Intrayear price risks can be hedged using futures contracts. A possible hedging strategy would work as follows. The Coffee Marketing Board offers producers a coffee price that is fixed for the entire year. This price is set at the beginning of the year and is equal to the weighted sum of the prices of coffee futures contracts that will mature at various months throughout the coming year. The weights are determined by the quantities of coffee available for export in the months between each contract expiration.

Say, for example, that in December 1988 the coffee board had wished to set a fixed price for the crop year 1989. There are five expiration months on coffee futures contracts (March, May, July, September, and December), and in December 1988 each had a price for delivery in these months in 1989. On the basis of historical export trends, the board could have predicted fairly well the proportion of the total exports available before each of these delivery months (for example, January, February, and March, 10 percent; April and May, 20 percent; June and July, 30 percent; August and September, 25 percent; and October, November, and December 15 percent). These proportions could have then been used to obtain a weighted price for the coming year.

Using monthly data from 1980 to 1989, we simulated this strategy, measuring the effect on intrayear variability by comparing the CVs of various price series. The results are reported in table 10-3 for the world price, the threshold price (ten-year moving average), domestic price A (the threshold price adjusted for subsidies and levies, calculated by using the world price), the fixed producer price (the weighted futures price), and domestic price B (the threshold price adjusted for subsidies and levies, calculated by using the fixed producer price instead of the world price and assuming that the price band followed the moving average). The intrayear CV of the world price is substantial, averaging 10.5 percent over the ten-year period. The instability in 1989 is clearly captured by the CV statistic, which reached 30.4 percent for that year. Domestic price A, which is based on the world price, also fluctuated sharply throughout the period. The results show that under the existing scheme the greater the intrayear variability of the world price, the greater the intrayear variability in domestic price A, even with subsidies and levies (see, for example, the figures for 1980, 1985, 1986, and 1989). In contrast, by using the futures contract to lock in an external price, the intrayear fluctuations in domestic price B are removed almost altogether. On average, the CV of the adjusted domestic price is 0.4 percent, which indicates that producers are almost entirely insulated from intrayear price instability.

The effect of this hedging strategy on interyear price variability is reported in table 10-4. The results show that the hedging program has little effect on interyear variability when compared with the effect of the

Table 10-3. *Effects of Hedging on Intrayear Price Variability for Coffee Papua New Guinea, 1980–89*
(percent)

	Coefficient of variation				
Year	World price	Threshold price[a]	Domestic price A[b]	Fixed price[c]	Domestic price B[d] (hedged)
1980	16.8	2.9	8.9	0.0	1.1
1981	6.2	2.0	4.1	0.0	1.0
1982	4.2	2.0	1.6	0.0	0.0
1983	5.5	1.4	4.7	0.0	0.0
1984	2.7	1.6	1.9	0.0	0.0
1985	11.2	1.5	7.4	0.0	0.7
1986	16.7	1.2	9.7	0.0	0.6
1987	8.3	2.5	3.9	0.0	0.0
1988	2.9	0.5	2.5	0.0	0.2
1989	30.4	1.4	16.0	0.0	0.7
Mean	10.5	1.7	6.1	0.0	0.4

a. Ten-year moving average.

b. Threshold price adjusted for subsidies and levies, calculated by using the world price.

c. Fixed producer price (the weighted futures price).

d. Threshold price adjusted for subsidies and levies, calculated by using the fixed producer price and assuming the price band follows the moving average.

Source: Authors' calculations.

stabilization fund. On average, domestic price A is $3,031 a ton, compared with $3,025 a ton for domestic price B, which is based on the fixed producer price. The stability of these prices is similar, the CVs being 10.8 percent and 10.2 percent, respectively. The impact of the hedging strategy on fund size is also shown in table 10-4. On average, the mean of the fund is larger with the hedging strategy than without it, but the variability of the fund is lower. This difference reflects the lower CV of the fixed producer price compared with the world price.

Our analysis shows that with a simple hedging strategy using futures contracts, the coffee board can fix the external price it faces for an entire year at a time. This stability can be translated into very stable within-year prices received by producers. The effect of implementing this strategy on interyear variability is very small, however. Interyear price risks may be managed by using futures with longer maturities or by rolling over futures.

Conclusions

Given the importance and benefits of risk management, Papua New Guinea should consider establishing a national financing and risk man-

Table 10-4. *Effects of Hedging on Interyear Price Variability for Coffee in Papua New Guinea, 1980–89*
(dollars)

Year	World price	Threshold price[a]	Domestic price A[b]	Fund size	Fixed price[c]	Domestic price B[d]	Fund size (hedged)
1980	3,466	2,444	2,955	68	4,106	3,275	73
1981	2,869	2,640	2,749	82	2,754	2,697	95
1982	3,088	2,840	2,964	87	2,733	2,733	96
1983	2,911	3,009	2,898	89	2,788	2,788	96
1984	3,189	3,173	3,157	91	3,033	3,033	97
1985	3,231	3,355	3,203	91	2,951	2,985	96
1986	4,295	3,541	3,897	104	3,939	3,740	100
1987	2,505	3,421	2,792	101	2,792	3,278	105
1988	3,013	3,257	3,019	90	2,926	2,930	105
1989	2,387	3,212	2,684	85	2,691	2,791	101
Mean	3,095	3,089	3,031	89	3,120	3,025	90
Standard deviation	504.1	334.9	328.7	9.4	481.6	308.6	9.6
Coefficient of variation	16.2	10.8	10.8	10.6	15.4	10.2	8.9

a. Ten-year moving average.
b. Threshold price adjusted for subsidies and levies, calculated by using the world price.
c. Fixed producer price (the weighted futures price).
d. Threshold price adjusted for subsidies and levies, calculated by using the fixed producer price and assuming the price band follows the moving average.

Source: Authors' calculations.

agement strategy, authorized, perhaps, by Papua New Guinea's National Borrowing Advisory Committee. Risk management of the MRDC's operations needs to be strengthened by establishing rules regarding not only the size of its participation in new projects, but also the type of external financing it uses (such as more commodity indexing features) and its risk management strategy.

In the past, the MRSF has been well managed, given the financial tools available. However, the MRSF would be well advised now to take advantage of innovations in international capital markets by using instruments such as commodity swaps to hedge tax revenues that are sensitive to commodity prices. Doing so would allow stable cash flows to be passed on to the general budget, independent of commodity price movements. Other techniques for managing commodity risk could also be introduced, such as commodity-linked loans and options.

With the expected expansion of the mineral and energy sector, Papua New Guinea should look for ways to reduce the potential for economic instability deriving from international commodity price fluctuations. Given its high international credit standing, Papua New Guinea is well placed to take advantage of new, longer-term financial instruments that are linked to the prices of commodities.

Notes

1. Historically, the CV of oil prices has been between 20 percent and 30 percent.

2. Guest (1987) derives the similar result that the MRSF has reduced the instability of mineral revenues by only 30 percent.

3. The participation of the various parties in Papua New Guinea (the national government, provinces, and landowners) in mining projects has been subject to internal policy debate. The expectation is that, in some form or another, the national government, provinces, and landowners will retain through the MRDC an equity stake in the mining projects.

4. Effectively, the Department of Finance and Planning has arranged the financing under its name and then passed it on to the MRDC.

5. See further Gemmill (1985) and Kolb (1985) on how to estimate these sensitivities.

6. Over a longer period the elasticity of export earnings with respect to copper prices is 0.54 (with a t-statistic of 2.97), and the elasticity with respect to gold prices is 0.64 (with a t-statistic of 2.11).

7. In terms of levels, the coefficient for the present value of dividends is about $80,000 for the government's share.

8. Notice that we measure here the sensitivity of the *present value* of the dividend stream and not the *annual* dividend stream. The present value of all future dividends will be more sensitive to assumptions about the future of the gold price than are the annual streams. Approximately, the difference will be the factor $1/(\text{discount rate})$.

9. Because the gold loan is likely to be in excess of the MRDC's financing needs, however, the remainder could be invested in conventional securities.

10. The earlier analysis of the gold mine indicated that the regression coefficient of the net present value of taxes (NPT) on the gold price was about 2. This result is confirmed in a

regression of the tax revenues paid into the MRSF on gold prices, the regression having a slope coefficient of about 0.23. Because the NPT is the discounted value of all future taxes, it will be more sensitive to the gold price by approximately the factor 1/(discount rate), or about ten.

11. Note that the notional principal amount is never exchanged between the two parties. Effectively, only interest payments are settled on a netting-out basis.

12. This example concerns the revenues after depreciation allowances have expired and the project generates a positive profit.

13. The actual transfers that mineral companies would make would be based on the current fiscal year's profits, which should—depending how far along one is in the fiscal year—be known with more certainty. The following year's profits, although transferred to the MRSF only at the end of the fiscal year in which the profits were made, would be determined within that fiscal year. Short-dated hedging instruments (say, up to twelve months) could thus be used within the current fiscal year to hedge cash flows that would not be occurring until the end of the following fiscal year.

11

Managing Financial Risks in Papua New Guinea: An Optimal External Debt Portfolio

Jonathan R. Coleman and Ying Qian

Throughout the 1980s, Papua New Guinea increasingly turned to external borrowing to finance its current account deficits. As shown in table 11-1, Papua New Guinea's indebtedness increased more than fourfold between 1980 and 1989. In contrast, the increase in debt was not matched by increases in gross domestic product and export earnings, which depended to a large extent on sales of a small set of agricultural and mineral commodities. Moreover, given the large fluctuations in the prices of primary commodities in international markets during the 1980s, Papua New Guinea's foreign exchange earnings from exports tended to be unstable.

In addition to the instability associated with fluctuating commodity prices, Papua New Guinea has faced financial risks associated with sharp movements of exchange rates. This is because a large proportion of its external debt is denominated in currencies other than U.S. dollars and because significant movements of the dollar in relation to other major currencies, in excess of interest differentials, have taken place in recent years. Thus, the currency valuation effect (that is, unanticipated deviations from interest rate parity—see below) on Papua New Guinea's external debt is considerable. Fluctuations in the level of debt stock measured

The authors wish to acknowledge the valuable suggestions of Takamasa Akiyama, Stijn Claessens, Ronald Duncan, Chris Jones, and Donald Larson.

Table 11-1. *Measures Of Debt, Output, and Trade, Papua New Guinea, 1980–89*
(millions of dollars)

	1980	1983	1986	1987	1988	1989
Total debt stock (TDS)	720	1,860	2,420	2,700	2,270	2,450
Total debt service	150	290	495	510	540	530
Gross national product (GDP)	2,460	2,220	2,450	2,940	3,320	3,650
Export earnings (EE)	1,090	950	1,190	1,400	1,720	1,670
Current account balance	−310	−380	−100	−370	−160	−200
TDS/GDP (percent)	29	84	99	81	68	67
TDS/EE (percent)	66	196	203	192	132	147

Source: World Bank data.

in dollars are likely to continue. This is because the volatility of cross-currency exchange rates is not expected to decline and the level of new borrowing by Papua New Guinea in currencies other than U.S. dollars will remain high, given the current pattern of international capital availability.

This chapter has three major objectives. The first is to analyze the two major financial risks faced by Papua New Guinea—exchange rate risk and commodity price risk—and to assess the extent to which these risks create serious problems in external debt management. The second is to present a rational expectations model—extending Myers and Thompson (1989b)—that solves for the optimal debt portfolio (including conventional debt denominated in different currencies, and commodity-linked bonds). The third is to compare the optimal debt portfolio (derived from the model) with Papua New Guinea's actual debt portfolio, and, on the basis of this comparison, to make some broad suggestions as to how the current debt structure might be altered in order to manage commodity price and exchange rate risks more effectively.

The chapter begins by discussing the risk exposure to commodity price fluctuations and to exchange rate movements. We then discuss results from a rational expectations model used to solve for the optimal portfolio of external debt. Finally, some conclusions are drawn.

Commodity Price Risks

In recent years copper, gold, coffee, logs, and palm oil have together accounted for more than 80 percent of total export revenues in Papua New Guinea. Furthermore, the contribution of these five major export

Figure 11-1. *Year-to-Year Changes in Export Prices, Papua New Guinea, 1969–88*

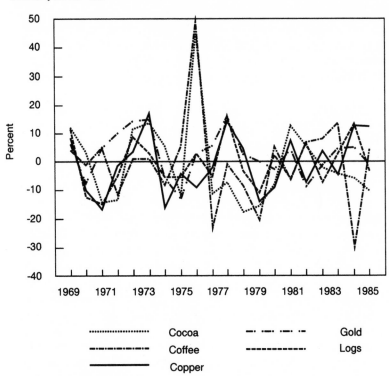

Source: World Bank data.

commodities to total export earnings has been increasing over time (see table 10-1 in chapter 10). This increasing dependence on the price and volume performance of a small set of commodities is likely to continue into the 1990s. For instance, the current mineral and petroleum expansion and exploration programs (see chapter 10) will lead to an increase in the dependence of Papua New Guinea on commodities for foreign exchange through crude oil exports.[1]

Figure 11-1 shows the annual percentage change in export unit values of Papua New Guinea's five major commodity exports. The coefficients of variation (CV, the ratio of the standard deviation to the mean) of these export unit values between 1977 and 1988 are as follows: copper 42 percent, gold 50 percent, cocoa 37 percent, coffee 34 percent, and logs 25 percent. Unstable export prices have resulted in unstable export revenues, which recorded a CV in excess of 27 percent during the 1980s. This high degree of instability, even by comparison with other developing countries, presents a significant problem in debt servicing and has an adverse effect on Papua New Guinea's ability to secure additional finance. Although the export performance of the country depends on the price and volume of a small set of commodities, the mix of imports has been more diversified and the unit values of imports have been relatively more stable.

Various instruments have been used by countries attempting to manage commodity price risk. Among these are (a) buffer stock schemes, commodity stabilization fund schemes, and macroeconomic policies; (b) financial market instruments such as futures, forwards, options, swaps, and commodity bonds; and (c) international commodity agreements and compensatory financing schemes. Papua New Guinea has extensively used instruments listed under (a) and (c) above to manage its risk exposure, with moderate success.[2] Claessens and Coleman (chapter 10) report that the financial market instruments listed in (b) above have not been used in Papua New Guinea.

Among the financial instruments associated with the primary commodities listed above, commodity-linked bonds have substantial potential for Papua New Guinea, which relies on commodity export revenues to meet its debt obligations. Commodity-linked bonds differ from conventional bonds in that coupon and principal payments are linked to a given quantity of a commodity. For example, a gold-denominated commodity bond might require coupon payments to be made annually, equivalent to the value of a prespecified quantity of gold, with the price set at some average daily price over the preceding twelve months. A decline in the price of gold leads to lower coupon payments, and vice versa, the result being that debt-servicing requirements are better matched with the ability to pay.

Foreign Exchange Risks

In addition to commodity price risks, Papua New Guinea is vulnerable to risks associated with exchange rate fluctuations.[3] The degree of exposure to exchange risk depends, to a large extent, on (a) the matching of the currency composition of net export earnings with the currency composition of net liabilities and (b) the effects on commodity prices of changes in exchange rates. On the basis of these criteria, the assets and liabilities for debt servicing in Papua New Guinea are potentially poorly balanced (see chapter 10, by Claessens and Coleman).

An appreciation of Papua New Guinea's currency, the kina, in relation to the currency of any country to which Papua New Guinea exports causes goods from Papua New Guinea to become more expensive. The higher prices can lead to a decline in Papua New Guinea's export revenues from this country as volume imported by this country declines. However, if Papua New Guinea borrows from this country, then debt-servicing requirements fall with an appreciation of the kina; consequently, the adverse effect of the appreciation may be diminished. As explained by Claessens (1992), for this reason Papua New Guinea should secure conventional loans denominated in the currency of those countries with which it has a positive trade balance. In addition, it should try to borrow from countries whose currencies move positively with the prices of the major exports of Papua New Guinea. Looking to the day when Papua New Guinea exports crude oil, perhaps Papua New Guinea should obtain loans from countries whose currency value is positively linked to the price of oil. An example would be the United Kingdom, because it exports oil. As the price of oil increases, the pound sterling tends to get stronger, leading to higher debt obligations in terms of the kina. However, as a result of the higher oil prices, revenues from oil exports also rise, allowing the higher debt repayments to be met. In contrast, lower oil prices tend to strengthen the yen, leading to higher yen-denominated debt repayment. Because repayment must be met by lower oil export revenues, the yen is a poor currency in which to borrow.

As demonstrated in table 11-2, Papua New Guinea's trade pattern and the composition of its currency debt are not well matched in terms of hedging risk. The most striking imbalance is in the shares of the dollar debt. If the dollar appreciates, Papua New Guinea's debt repayments will be higher without any significant offsetting effect of increased foreign exchange earnings from additional exports to the United States.

Estimation

Estimation of the optimal portfolio model, as described in appendix 11-1, is directly related to the vector autoregressive (VAR) process $A(L)y_t = \epsilon_t$. The VAR process predicts export revenues, commodity prices, and foreign exchange rates. More important, the conditional covariance matrix, Ω, of the error term, ϵ_t, provides Ω_{py} and Ω_{pp}. Furthermore, the parameter vector, γ, can be derived from coefficients of the VAR system as shown in equation A1-11. Table 11-3 presents the names of the variables in the model, and table 11-4 shows the results of the VAR regression. Only ordinary least squares (OLS) results are presented.[4] Table 11-5 presents the estimated covariance matrix, Ω, of the VAR system.

The stationarity of variables in levels was tested by using the standard set of unit root tests. When the Dickey-Fuller and augmented Dickey-Fuller tests were used, the unit root hypothesis for CP, GD, CC, CF, BP, and DM (see table 11-3 for definitions) was rejected at the 95 percent

Table 11-2. *Share of Exports by Destination, and Share of Public and Publicly Guaranteed Debt by Currency, Papua New Guinea, 1982–87* (percent)

	1982	1983	1984	1985	1986	1987
	Share of total exports					
Destination						
Australia	8.4	7.5	8.4	10.3	4.8	8.0
Germany, Federal Rep. of	26.9	25.7	21.3	30.0	34.4	27.2
Japan	34.0	35.3	29.3	22.5	25.6	28.5
United Kingdom	5.8	5.8	11.3	7.5	4.5	4.7
United States	1.8	2.2	2.7	3.9	3.3	2.1
Total	76.9	76.5	73.0	74.2	72.6	70.5
	Share of public and publicly guaranteed debt					
Currency						
British pounds	2.4	1.7	1.2	1.2	1.8	2.0
Deutsche mark	3.1	1.9	1.9	2.1	2.3	2.3
Japanese yen	3.4	3.0	8.1	12.9	14.5	16.2
Swiss francs	3.4	2.5	4.2	7.2	9.4	10.3
U.S. dollars	40.6	47.1	45.1	38.9	35.6	28.6
Total	52.9	56.2	60.5	62.3	63.6	59.4

Source: World Bank data.

Table 11-3. *Variables in the Optimal Portfolio Model*

Variable	Definition
XT	Total exports per capita (dollars)
CP	Price of copper (dollars per metric ton)
GD	Price of gold (dollars per metric ton)
CC	Price of cocoa (dollars per metric ton)
CF	Price of coffee (dollars per metric ton)
LG	Price of logs (dollars per cubic meter)
OL	Price of crude oil (dollars per barrel)
SF	Swiss franc–dollar exchange rate
DM	Deutsche mark–dollar exchange rate
BP	British pound–dollar exchange rate
JY	Japanese yen–dollar exchange rate
**L&	Lags of the variable ** in the order of &

Note: All dollars are constant 1980 U.S. dollars. All exchange rates have 1980 as the base year.
Source: Authors' calculations.

level; the test statistics for *SF*, *XT*, and *LG* were close to the critical values; and, in the case of *OL* and *JY*, the null hypothesis was rejected. However, when the Durbin-Watson tests of Sargan and Bhargava were used, the unit root null hypothesis was rejected for all variables. Therefore, all variables were assumed to be stationary.

Table 11-4. *Estimation Results for the Vector Autoregression Model (constant 1980 U.S. dollars)*

Total exports per capita

$XT = 108.6 + 0.50\ XTL1 - 0.035\ CFL3 + 2.75\ JYL2$
$(4.34)(7.666) (-14.82) (10.15)$

$ + 1.00\ LGL2 - 1.70\ OLL1$
$ (3.919) (-4.969)$

$R^2 = 0.99 DW = 2.34$

Price of copper

$CP = 1431.3 + 0.193\ CPL1 + 0.610\ CFL3 - 34.0\ SFL3$
$ (3.77)(2.28) (11.99) (-6.81)$

$ - 17.89\ LL2 + 0.215\ CPL3$
$ (-2.14) (3.322)$

$R^2 = 0.99 DW = 1.93$

Price of gold

$GD = 16903 - 0.16\ GDL1 - 2.84\ CCL1 + 0.72\ CFL1 + 32.12\ JYL1$
$ (10.92)(-1.70) (-10.65) (5.63) (3.58)$

$R^2 = 0.98 DW = 3.01$

Price of cocoa

$CC = 2878 + 0.45\ CCL1 - 8.82\ XTL3 + 0.122\ GDL1 - 25.09\ LGL1$
$ (13.29)(13.52) (-21.00) (8.23) (-16.11)$

$ + 19.06\ OLL3$
$ (6.77)$

$R^2 = 0.99 DW = 2.44$

Price of coffee

$CF = -14232 - 0.09\ CFL1 + 0.688\ CPL2 + 0.919\ GDL3 + 1.09\ CCL2$
$ (-4.07)(-0.50) (4.05) (6.19) (6.69)$

$ + 58.44\ SFL2$
$ (2.59)$

$R^2 = 0.94 DW = 1.62$

Price of logs

$LG = 37.27 - 0.195\ LGL1 + 0.009\ GDL1 - 1.03\ SFL1 - 1.60\ OLL1$
$ (1.90)(-2.21) (7.33) (-5.88) (-10.08)$

$ + 0.008\ CCL2$
$ (2.70)$

$R^2 = 0.99 DW = 1.46$

Table 11-4   *(Continued)*

Price of oil
$OL = 21.07 + 0.716\ OLL1 - 0.551\ OLL3$
          (1.89) (2.57)   (−1.59)

$R^2 = 0.55$ $DW = 2.72$

Swiss franc–dollar exchange rate
$SF = 88.70 - 1.02\ SFL2 + 0.959\ DML1 - 0.765\ OLL2$
          (3.51)(−3.81)   (3.70)   (−1.83)

$R^2 = 0.82$ $DW = 2.45$

Deutsche mark–dollar exchange rate
$DM = -22.04 - 2.44\ DML1 + 0.918\ BPL1 + 1.24\ JYL1 - 0.402\ BPL2$
          (−1.49)(−2.31)   (2.80)   (3.25)   (−2.39)

     $+ 0.659\ JYL2$
      (1.99)

$R^2 = 0.94$ $DW = 2.99$

British pound–dollar exchange rate
$BP = -156.6 + 1.15\ BPL1 + 2.70\ JYL1 + 0.364\ OLL1 - 3.61\ SFL1$
          (−2.22) (7.38)   (3.67)   (0.51)   (−3.33)

     $+ 1.78\ OLL2 + 2.56\ JYL2$
      (2.32)   (3.43)

$R^2 = 0.99$ $DW = 2.77$

Japanese yen–dollar exchange rate
$JY = 88.4 + 0.709\ JYL1 - 0.895\ DML2 - 0.99\ OLL2$
          (3.25) (3.63)   (−4.38)   (−2.30)

$R^2 = 0.90$ $DW = 2.67$

Note: Numbers in parentheses are *t*-values.
Source: Authors' calculations.

In order to specify the VAR equations, the SAS STEPWISE procedure was applied. It searches for the best-fitting model, allowing for degrees of freedom. It was assumed that exchange rates affect commodity prices, but not vice versa, except for the price of crude oil.

The seemingly uncorrelated regression (SUR) estimator was used to estimate the VAR system. Having obtained the coefficient matrix $(A[L])$ and the covariance matrix, we used equation A1-21 to compute the optimal quantity of commodity-linked bonds and the optimal foreign currency compositions. According to the theoretical model described in

Table 11-5. *Covariance Matrix of Residuals from the Vector Autoregression Model*

	XTR	CPR	GDR	CCR	CFR	LGR	OLR	SFR	DMR	BPR	JYR
XTR	7.17	-66.52	-110.33	-1.80	-245.44	-1.33	-1.13	1.31	3.40	-0.38	3.08
CPR	-66.52	6447.07	5992.51	222.75	3104.22	31.30	26.09	67.57	7.98	95.43	-47.34
GDR	-110.33	5992.51	26245.50	-932.91	14229.90	-2.66	-387.23	408.00	188.21	291.47	107.64
CCR	-1.80	222.75	-932.91	400.52	-1975.60	-6.07	87.14	-20.60	-14.86	-42.66	-52.20
CFR	-245.44	3104.22	14229.90	-1975.60	26851.10	109.68	-577.23	221.72	-43.65	188.47	171.50
LGR	-1.33	31.30	-2.66	-6.07	109.68	1.65	-3.17	1.42	-1.10	0.93	2.28
OLR	-1.13	26.09	-387.23	87.14	-577.23	-3.17	30.13	-13.94	-4.64	-10.35	-19.02
SFR	1.31	67.57	408.00	-20.60	221.72	1.42	-13.94	15.89	5.23	6.59	10.92
DMR	3.40	7.98	188.21	-14.86	-43.65	-1.10	-4.64	5.23	4.76	4.07	4.24
BPR	-0.38	95.43	291.47	-42.66	188.47	0.93	-10.35	6.59	4.07	9.45	8.01
JYR	3.08	-47.34	107.64	-52.20	171.50	2.28	-19.02	10.92	4.24	8.01	16.55

Note: ** *R* is the residual of variable ** from the VAR system.
Source: Authors' calculations.

the appendix, it is possible for the elements in the solution vector, b^*, to be positive or negative. Positive values of either commodity-linked bonds or foreign currencies indicate borrowing in these instruments (that is, commodity-linked bonds and conventional debt denominated in the particular currency). Negative values of commodity-linked bonds or foreign currencies indicate lending. However, it is highly unlikely that Papua New Guinea will be a lender in international financial markets, given its foreign exchange shortage, so the maximization problem was altered by adding a nonnegativity constraint, $b \geq 0$.

The nonnegativity constraint on commodity-linked bonds greatly complicated the maximization problem (the Euler equations in particular), making empirical estimation difficult.[5] However, an iterative method was used to impose nonnegativity without formally incorporating the $b \geq 0$ requirement into the mathematical formulation. This method was as follows. If, after the first round of calculation, any of the commodity-linked bonds were found to be negative in the optimal solution, they were dropped from the instrument list, and the redefined maximization problem on the remaining instruments was resolved. If more commodity-linked bonds on the remaining instrument list were found to be negative in the second-round solution, they were also eliminated and the previously discarded commodity-linked bonds in the first round were reinstated in the model. Iterations continued until all the commodity-linked bonds remaining in the model were positive.[6]

Although the financial instrument list changed in the iterative process, the VAR system specification as shown in table 11-4 did not need to change. The autoregressive process defined by equation A1-9 allowed the unused commodity-linked bonds (that is, the ones dropped from the list) to be treated as exogenous and included as state variables s_t in y_t. However, the matrixes Ω_{p^*y} and $\Omega_{p^*p^*}$ derived from the VAR covariance matrix presented in table 11-5 were respecified; accordingly, commodity-linked bonds were set to zero. The rows and columns of $\Omega_{p^*p^*}$ and Ω_{p^*y} corresponding to the dropped financial instruments were set at zero. In order to avoid singularity while inverting the matrix $\Omega_{p^*p^*}$, the diagonal elements were set to one before inverting this matrix and to zero afterward.

Results

The model was solved for 1988. Conventional debt in dollars was derived from the budget constraint given in equation A1-1 and under the assumption that no commodity-linked bonds were issued in 1987. Table 11-6 presents the estimation results of the optimal portfolio model. All

Table 11-6 Optimal Portfolio of External Debt per Capita, Papua New Guinea
(constant 1980 U.S. dollars)

Real interest rate (percent)	Cocoa-linked bonds	Oil-linked bonds	Swiss francs	Deutsche mark	British pounds	Japanese yen	U.S. dollars	Total commodity-linked bonds	Total debt
1	84.40	260.57	5.82	-1.86	151.59	14.06	261.00	344.97	775.58
2	82.49	247.77	1.46	-0.33	134.64	3.02	314.38	330.26	783.43
3	79.60	230.74	-2.91	0.84	115.03	-6.08	374.04	310.34	791.26
4	75.78	209.84	-7.14	1.57	93.34	-14.95	439.21	285.62	797.65
5	71.10	185.70	-11.11	1.85	70.30	-21.04	507.96	256.80	804.76
6	65.75	159.20	-14.68	1.66	46.78	-24.85	578.01	224.95	811.87
7	59.93	131.38	-17.77	1.06	23.66	-26.34	647.07	191.31	818.99
8	53.87	103.28	-20.32	0.93	1.72	-25.60	713.05	157.15	826.93

Source: Authors' calculations.
Note: Actual debt stock per capita in 1987 was $711.20. Per capita imports in 1988 were $436, and exports $378.

naming conventions follow the description in table 11-3. Results are presented for different real interest rates because the model does not have the feature of hedging against interest rate risk and because the real interest rate was assumed to be equal to the subjective discount rate. The last two columns in table 11-6 show the total commodity-linked bonds and the total external debt (including commodity-linked bonds and conventional debt).

The total imports, exports, and debt stock per capita for 1988 are also listed in table 11-6. Only bonds that are linked to cocoa and crude oil are found in the optimal portfolio. According to the results, Papua New Guinea should sell an amount of cocoa-linked bonds ranging from $54 to $84 per capita (in constant 1980 U.S. dollars), depending on the real interest rate. Furthermore, when oil exports are developed, a large share of the external financing should be obtained through sales of crude oil–linked bonds. The per capita value of oil-linked bonds ranges from $103 to $260 in constant 1980 dollars.

The foreign currency composition of the optimal debt portfolio is also presented in table 11-6. At low real interest rates, the optimal portfolio does not contain liabilities denominated in Japanese yen and Swiss francs, but includes liabilities denominated in British pounds. This supports the argument made earlier that Papua New Guinea should denominate its liabilities in currencies (for example, British pounds) that are positively correlated with its assets (for example, oil revenues). The negative signs for Japanese yen and Swiss francs suggest that Papua New Guinea should hold assets denominated in these currencies in its optimal portfolio. The deutsche mark does not play a significant role in the optimal portfolio. At high interest rates, total non-dollar-denominated debt declines, because the willingness to borrow declines. For example, conventional debt denominated in British pounds becomes less important in the optimal portfolio at high interest rates.

For clarity, table 11-7 presents the composition of the optimal portfolio in terms of total external debt. The first column of table 11-7 shows that the share of commodity-linked bonds ranges from 19 percent to 44 percent as the real interest rate declines from 8 percent to 1 percent. This emphasizes the important role that commodity-linked bonds can play in the external finance of Papua New Guinea. The second column gives the percentage for total net conventional debt. The third column gives the percentage of debt made up of Swiss francs, deutsche marks, and Japanese yen and shows that these currencies are not important to the external debt portfolio. The British pound's actual share is important when real interest rates are low. The proportion of dollar-denominated conventional debt is large when the real interest rate is high. However, this does not mean that dollar-denominated debt is the best liability for hedg-

Table 11-7. *Optimal Composition of Total External Debt, Papua New Guinea*
(percent)

Real interest rate (percent)	Commodity-linked bonds	Conventional debt	Combined SF, DM, JY[a]	British pounds	U.S. dollars
1	44.48	55.52	2.32	19.55	33.65
2	42.16	57.84	0.53	17.19	40.13
3	39.22	60.78	−1.03	14.54	47.27
4	35.81	64.19	−2.57	11.70	55.06
5	31.91	68.09	−3.77	8.74	63.12
6	27.71	72.29	−4.66	5.76	71.19
7	23.36	76.64	−5.26	2.89	79.01
8	19.00	81.00	−5.44	0.21	86.23

a. Swiss francs, deutsche mark, and Japanese yen.
Source: Authors' calculations.

ing risks. Rather, it shows that as the real interest rate increases, the hedging effectiveness of other instruments decreases because borrowing declines, while at the same time, the total debt stock carried over from the last period becomes larger. As a result, the proportion of dollar-denominated conventional debt in the optimal portfolio model has to increase in order to satisfy the binding budget constraint.

A comparison of tables 11-2 and 11-7 shows that there are significant differences between the optimal debt portfolio derived from the model and the one held by Papua New Guinea in the late 1980s. For example, the actual combined share of Swiss francs, deutsche marks, and Japanese yen in the debt portfolio was between 20 percent and 30 percent. In the optimal portfolio, their combined share is negative for almost all levels of the real interest rate. As shown in table 11-2, the British pound's share was only 2 percent in 1987, whereas in the optimal debt portfolio (table 11-7) the share is almost 20 percent at low real interest rates. Dollar-denominated debt shares in the optimal portfolio are consistent with the actual levels at moderate levels of real interest rates. As mentioned earlier, commodity-linked bonds are absent from the actual portfolio, whereas the optimal portfolio calls for a share of between 20 percent and 45 percent in these instruments.

To evaluate the hedging effectiveness of the optimal portfolio, it is necessary to examine its ability to reduce the variance of imports. Table 11-8 presents the variances of the expected future imports per capita under different real interest rates. These were derived using equation A1-24.

The first column in the table relates to the first term in equation A1-24, that is, to the variance of expected imports without external financing. The second column relates to the second term in equation A1-24, that is, to what can be interpreted as the contribution of optimally structured external financing to a reduction in the variance of expected imports. The third column shows the variance of expected imports that cannot be reduced through external financing. The fourth column is the ratio between the reduction in the variance as a result of hedging (column 2) and the variance that would occur without hedging (column 1), thus measuring the effectiveness of hedging in relative terms.

The results in table 11-8 show that the optimal portfolio of external debt can reduce uncertainty substantially. Between 37 percent and 64 percent of the variance of expected imports can be reduced by external financing that includes commodity-linked bonds and conventional debt (under various levels of the real interest rate). These percentages are equivalent to a 20 percent to 40 percent reduction in terms of standard errors or confidence intervals. It should be noted that the hedging effectiveness of all instruments other than conventional debt denominated in

Table 11-8. *Effects of an Optimal Portfolio of External Debt on the Variance of Expected Imports* (constant 1980 dollars)

Real interest rate, r (percent)	Variance of expected imports without optimal external financing	Reduction of variance through optimal external financing	Net [a]	Percentage hedged [b]
1	4,461.20	2,849.13	1,612.07	63.86
2	4,380.07	2,705.71	1,674.36	61.18
3	4,163.81	2,467.84	1,695.97	59.27
4	3,822.15	2,150.69	1,671.46	56.27
5	3,380.76	1,780.52	1,600.24	52.67
6	2,877.50	1,390.61	1,486.89	48.33
7	2,355.51	1,015.02	1,340.49	43.09
8	1,855.47	682.54	1,172.93	36.79

a. Variance without optimal financing (first data column) minus reduction achieved through optimal financing (second data column).

b. Reduction in variance as a percentage of original variance.

Source: Authors' calculations.

dollars is sensitive to the real interest rate. This can be seen from column 4 in table 11-8. The ratio that measures the hedging effectiveness falls by half when the real interest rate increases from 1 percent to 8 percent. This deterioration of the hedging effectiveness of the optimal portfolio coincides with the results reported in table 11-7, which show that the share of dollar-denominated conventional debt is more than doubled as the real interest rate changes from 1 percent to 8 percent. Because higher real interest rates lower the importance of conventional debt that is not denominated in dollars, and because dollar-denominated conventional debt does not make any contribution to reducing uncertainty (that is, to reducing the variance), it is to be expected that hedging is less effective at higher real interest rates.

A final issue is whether the model's optimal portfolio solution is robust to changing assumptions and model specification. However, with the VAR approach, which is equivalent to estimating the reduced form of a structural model, assumptions about model structure are irrelevant.

Conclusions

Papua New Guinea faces considerable financial risk associated with fluctuating commodity prices and exchange rates. This fact is borne out in an examination of the country's export earnings in the 1980s. The major primary commodities of Papua New Guinea—copper, gold, cocoa, coffee, logs, and palm oil—contributed about 90 percent of total export earnings over the period 1985–88, and the CVs of the prices of these commodities ranged from 25 percent for logs to 50 percent for gold. Overall, export revenues were highly unstable, the CV being 27 percent for the 1980s. Analysis of Papua New Guinea's trading pattern and the currency combination of the debt portfolio shows that these were not well matched. Furthermore, the value of debt when denominated in dollars was vulnerable to movements in cross-currency exchange rates.

To solve for the optimal debt portfolio of Papua New Guinea, a model was presented that allowed for the use of commodity-linked bonds as well as conventional debt denominated in different currencies. The hedging effectiveness of the debt portfolio was judged by the reduction in the variance of expected real imports. The model indicates that commodity-linked bonds can play a very important role in Papua New Guinea's risk management strategy. The proportion of commodity-linked bonds in the optimal debt portfolio ranges from 19 percent for a real interest rate of 8 percent to more than 44 percent for a real interest rate of 1 percent. The model shows that bonds issued with payments linked to the prices of crude oil (expected to become an important export) and of cocoa would substantially lower the variability of future imports.

The model also shows that Papua New Guinea's external debt structure is not well balanced to hedge the foreign exchange risk resulting from the existing composition of non-dollar-denominated liabilities. The actual debt portfolio contains an excess of liabilities denominated in Japanese yen and deutsche marks. British pounds, by contrast, are substantially underrepresented in the portfolio.

Appendix 11-1. Model for Optimal External Debt

The model used to determine an optimal hedging strategy for Papua New Guinea is that of aggregate consumer portfolio choice for a given output. It is an adaptation of the model presented by Myers and Thompson (1989a). In conformity with the model, Papua New Guinea is a small open economy with all its external debt issued by the government. The government has a utility function, $u(m_t)$, where m_t is the real value of imports of goods and services in period t. The utility function is assumed to satisfy the von Neumann–Morgenstern axioms, as well as $u'(m_t) \geq 0$ and $u''(m_t) \leq 0$.

For the current account to be balanced in each period, the value of imports and debt-servicing requirements must be matched by the value of

exports—unless there is borrowing. The government can borrow exter-
nally by taking out a conventional loan at a real rate of interest r. In
addition, the government can borrow by issuing commodity bonds that
mature in one period and require a payment at the beginning of the next
period equal to the price in the next period of the commodity to which
the bond is linked. Given these conditions, the government faces a budget constraint given by

(A1-1) $$m_t + (1 + r)(e_t' d_{t-1}^* + d_{t-1}^{us}) + p_t' b_{t-1}$$
$$\leq x_t + (e_t' d_t^* + d_t^{us}) + w_t' b_t$$

where

m_t is the real value of imports,

r is the real interest rate,[7]

e_t is the column vector of exchange rates of non-dollar-denominated
debt in units of real dollars per other currency $(e_{1t}, e_{2t}, \ldots, e_{mt})'$,

d_t^* is the column vector of conventional debt in each (non-U.S.) currency $(d_{1t}, d_{2t}, \ldots, d_{mt})'$,

d_t^{us} is the conventional debt denominated in real dollars,

p_t is the column vector of real prices of the underlying commodities
$(p_{1t}, p_{2t}, \ldots, p_{nt})'$,

b_t is the column vector of the quantity of bonds sold, denominated in
physical units of the commodity $(b_{1t}, b_{2t}, \ldots, b_{nt})'$,

x_t is the real value of exports, and

w_t is the column vector of real prices of the commodity bonds $(w_{1t}, w_{2t}, \ldots, w_{nt})'$.

Equation A1-1 can be rearranged as

(A1-2) $$m_t + (1 + r)d_{t-1}^{us} + [(1 + r)e_t', p_t'] \begin{bmatrix} d_{t-1}^* \\ b_{t-1} \end{bmatrix}$$
$$\leq x_t + d_t^{us} + [e_t', w_t'] \begin{bmatrix} d_t^* \\ b_t \end{bmatrix}$$

or

(A1-3) $$m_t + (1 + r)d_{t-1}^{us} + p_t^{*\,'} b_{t-1}^* \leq x_t + d_t^{us} + w_t^{*\,'} b_t^*$$

where

$p_t^* = [(1 + r)e_t', p_t']'$

$b_t^* = (d_{t-1}'^*, b_{t-1}')'$, and

$w_t^* = (e_t', w_t')'$.

The government also faces transversality conditions:[8]

$$(A1\text{-}4) \qquad \lim_{t \to \infty} (1 + r)^{-t} d_t^{us} = \lim_{t \to \infty} (1 + r)^{-t} w_t^{*\prime} b_t^* = 0.$$

The agent's problem is to choose a portfolio of commodity-linked bonds and conventional debt in different currencies to maximize the expected lifetime utility function

$$(A1\text{-}5) \qquad E_0 \sum_{t=0}^{\infty} \beta^t u (m_t)$$

subject to equations A1-1 and A1-4, where β is the subjective discount rate.

The associated Euler equations are

$$(A1\text{-}6) \qquad u'(m_t) - \beta(1 + r)E_t\, u'(m_{t+1}) = 0$$

and

$$(A1\text{-}7) \qquad u'(m_t)w_t^* - \beta E_t\,[u'(m_{t+1})p_{t+1}^*] = 0.$$

Solving this maximization problem requires that strict assumptions be placed on the form of the utility function, as well as on the probability distributions of prices and exports. Taking the approach of Myers and Thompson, a solution can be found by using the permanent income theory of consumption. The optimal import path can be defined as[9]

$$(A1\text{-}8) \quad m_t = \frac{r}{1 + r} \left[\sum_{i=0}^{\infty} (1 + r)^{-i} E_t\,(x_{t+i}) - p_t^{*\prime} b_{t-1}^* - (1 + r)\, d_{t-1}^{us} \right].$$

Equation A1-8 is not a decision rule because the $E_t\,(x_{t+i})$ terms cannot be observed. To retrieve it, $E_t\,(x_{t+i})$ can be expressed as a function of variables that the government can observe in period t. One procedure is to set up a vector, y_t, in which the first element is x_t. That is, $y_t = (x_t, p_t', s_t)'$, where p_t is a vector of commodity prices, and s_t is the set of other state variables useful for predicting future exports. The vector y_t is assumed to follow the autoregressive process

$$(A1\text{-}9) \qquad A\,(L)\,y_t = \epsilon_t$$

where $A\,(L)$ is a matrix polynomial in the lag operator and ϵ_t is a zero-mean, serially uncorrelated error vector, with covariance matrix Ω. The optimal projection of the future income stream through exports can be defined (see Hansen and Sargent 1980) as

$$(A1\text{-}10) \qquad \sum_{i=0}^{\infty} (1 + r)^{-i} E_t\,(x_{t+i}) = \gamma'\, y_t + B(L)\, y_{t-1}$$

with

(A1-11)
$$\gamma' = \phi A\left(\frac{1}{1+r}\right)^{-1}$$

and

(A1-12)
$$B(L) = \phi A\left(\frac{1}{1+r}\right)^{-1} \left\{ \sum_{j=1}^{q-1} \left[\sum_{k=j+1}^{q} (1+r)^{j-k} A_k \right] L^{j-1} \right\}$$

where ϕ is a row vector with a 1 in the first column and zeroes elsewhere.

Substituting equation A1-10 into equation A1-8 gives the operational decision rule

(A1-13)
$$m_t = \frac{r}{1+r} [\gamma' y_t + B(L) y_{t-1} - p_t^{*'} b_{t-1}^* - (1+r) d_{t-1}^{us}]$$

with imports as a function of observable variables. However, while this formula gives the optimal level of imports and therefore the optimal level of debt, it does not provide the optimal portfolio of conventional and commodity-linked debt.

To obtain the optimal debt portfolio, further derivations are needed. Rearranging the Euler equations (A1-6 and A1-7), and assuming that the expected real return on holding bonds is equal to the real interest rate, gives

(A1-14)
$$E_t\left[u'(m_{t+1})\left(w_t^{*'} - \frac{p_{t+1}^{*'}}{1+r}\right)\right] = 0$$

and

(A1-15)
$$E_t\left(w_t^{*'} - \frac{p_{t+1}^*}{1+r}\right) = 0$$

which imply

(A1-16)
$$\text{cov}\,[u'(m_{t+1}), p_{t+1}^*] = 0.$$

To calculate this covariance matrix, it is necessary to obtain an expression for $u'(m_{t+1})$. Following Myers and Thompson, a linear approximation of the first derivative of the utility function gives

(A1-17)
$$\text{cov}\,(m_{t+1}, p_{t+1}^*) = 0.$$

Leading equation A1-13 one period and computing the relevant covariance (equation A1-17) gives

(A1-18) $\text{cov}\left[\left(\dfrac{r}{1+r}\,[\gamma'\,y_{t+1} + B(L)y_t\right.\right.$

$$\left.\left. - p_{t+1}^{*\prime}\,b_t^* - (1+r)\,d_t^*]\right),\,p_{t+1}^{*\prime}\right] = 0.$$

Recognizing that $B(L)y_{t+1}$ is known at time t, the covariance expression is

(A1-19) $$\text{cov}\,[(\gamma'\,y_{t+1} - p_{t+1}^{*\prime}\,b_t^*),\,p_{t+1}^*] = 0.$$

Rearranging equation A1-19 gives[10]

(A1-20) $$\Omega_{p^*y}\,\gamma - \Omega_{p^*p^*}\,b_t^* = 0$$

where Ω_{p^*y} is the covariance operation between vector p^* and y, and $\Omega_{p^*p^*}$ is the covariance operation between elements in the p^* vector. Solving for b_t^* gives

(A1-21) $$b_t^* = \Omega_{p^*p^*}^{-1}\,\Omega_{p^*y}\,\gamma.$$

Although the optimal portfolios have been computed, it is important to determine whether the variance of real imports is reduced. Making such a determination is a way to evaluate the hedging effectiveness of commodity-linked bonds and conventional debt in different currencies. Leading equation A1-13 one period, the conditional variance of m_{t+1} at time t gives

(A1-22) $\text{var}\,(m_{t+1}) = \left(\dfrac{r}{1+r}\right)^2 l\,[\text{var}\,(\gamma'\,y_{t+1}) + \text{var}\,(p_{t+1}^{*\prime}b_t^*)$

$$-2\text{cov}(\gamma'y_{t+1},\,p_{t+1}^{*\prime}b_t^*)]$$

$$= \left(\dfrac{r}{1+r}\right)^2 (\gamma'\,\Omega_{yy}\,\gamma + b_t^{*\prime}\,\Omega_{p^*p^*}\,b_t^* - 2b_t^{*\prime}\,\Omega_{p^*y}\,\gamma)$$

Rearranging equation A1-20,

(A1-23) $$\Omega_{p^*y}\,\gamma = \Omega_{p^*p^*}\,b_t^*$$
$$b_t^{*\prime}\,\Omega_{p^*y}\,\gamma = b_t^{*\prime}\Omega_{p^*p^*}\,b_t^*.$$

Substituting equation A1-23 into equation A1-22,

(A1-24) $\text{var}\,(m_{t+1}) = \left(\dfrac{r}{1+r}\right)^2 (\gamma'\,\Omega_{yy}\,\gamma + b_t^{*\prime}\,\Omega_{p^*p^*}\,b_t^* - 2b_t^{*\prime}\,\Omega_{p^*y}\,\gamma)$

$$= \left(\dfrac{r}{1+r}\right)^2 (\gamma'\,\Omega_{yy}\,\gamma - b_t^{*\prime}\,\Omega_{p^*p^*}\,b_t^*).$$

Both of the terms in the lower expression of equation A1-24 are in quadratic form and, by definition, nonnegative. Therefore, if commodity bonds or non-dollar-denominated debt are unavailable (that is, if b^* is zero), then the variance of m_{t+1} is simply the first item in the expression. If commodity bonds and nondollar debt are determined by equation A1-21 and some of the elements in b^* are not zero, the second term in equation A1-24 is positive. Thus the conditional variance of m_{t+1} is always smaller.

Appendix 11-2. Derivation of Equation A1-8

Rewrite the binding budget constraint as

(A2-1) $m_t = x_t - (1 + r)d_{t-1} - p_t' b_{t-1} + d_t + w_t' b_t.$

Lead equation A1-1 one period, multiply both sides by $1/(1 + r)$ and take the expectation

(A2-2) $$\frac{1}{1 + r} E_t m_{t+1} = \frac{1}{1 + r} [E_t x_{t+1} - (1 + r) d_t - E_t p_{t+1}' b_t$$

$$+ E_t d_{t+1} + E_t w_{t+1}' b_{t+1}].$$

Assuming

$$E_t \left(w_{t+i} - \frac{p_{t+i+1}}{1 + r} \right) = 0$$

(A2-3) $$E_t \left(e_{t+i} - \frac{e_{t+i+1}}{1 + r} \right) = 0$$

$$i = 0, 1, \ldots, \infty$$

and summing equations A1-1 and A1-2 gives

(A2-4) $$m_t + \frac{1}{1 + r} E_t m_{t+1} = x_t + \frac{1}{1 + r} E_t x_{t+1} - (1 + r)d_{t-1}$$

$$- p_t' b_{t-1} + \frac{1}{1 + r} E_t d_{t+1} + \frac{1}{1 + r} E_t w_{t+1}' b_{t+1}.$$

Leading equation A1-1 two periods, multiplying both sides by $1/(1 + r)^2$, taking the expectation, and adding equation A1-3 gives

(A2-5) $$m_t + \frac{1}{1 + r} E_t m_{t+1} + \frac{1}{(1 + r)^2} E_t m_{t+2}$$

$$= x_t + \frac{1}{1 + r} E_t x_{t+1} + \frac{1}{(1 + r)^2} E_t x_{t+2} - (1 + r) d_{t-1} - p_t' b_{t-1}$$

$$+ \frac{1}{(1 + r)^2} E_t d_{t+2} + \frac{1}{(1 + r)^2} E_t w_{t+2}' b_{t+2}.$$

This operation is repeated an infinite number of times, and the transversality conditions are assumed.

$$(A2\text{-}6) \qquad \sum_{i=0}^{\infty} (1+r)^{-i} E_t m_{t+i} = \sum_{i=0}^{\infty} (1+r)^{-i} E_t x_{t+1}$$

$$- (1+r) d_{t-1} - p_t' b_{t-1}$$

Then, assuming the permanent income hypothesis,

$$(A2\text{-}7) \quad m_t = E_t m_{t+1} = E_t m_{t+2} = \ldots = E_t m_{t+i} = E_t m_{t+i+1} = \ldots.$$

$$i = 0, 1, \ldots, \infty$$

So the optimal import path can be found as

$$(A2\text{-}8) \qquad m_t = \frac{r}{1+r} \left[\sum_{i=0}^{\infty} (1+r)^{-i} E_t x_{t+i} - (1+r) d_{t-1} - p_t' b_{t-1} \right].$$

Appendix 11-3. Derivation of Equation A1-23

Redefine $y_t = (x_t, p_t')$. Thus the set of other state variables s_t is null. Rewrite equation A1-21 as follows:[11]

$$(A3\text{-}1) \quad b_t = \Omega_{pp}^{-1} \Omega_{py} \gamma = \Omega_{pp}^{-1} (V_{px}, \Omega_{pp}) \gamma = (\Omega_{pp}^{-1} V_{px}, I) \gamma = (\beta, I) \gamma$$

where V_{px} is the column vector of covariances between the unexpected export earnings, x, and the unexpected vector of prices, p; I is the identity matrix; and β is equivalent to the OLS regression coefficient of residuals of x on residuals of p', given as[12]

$$(A3\text{-}2) \qquad x_R = \beta' p_R = \beta_1 p_{R1} + \beta_2 p_{R2} + \ldots + \beta_n p_{Rn}$$

where x_R and p_R are the residuals from the VAR system (equation A1-9), which are the unexpected shocks in export earnings, commodity prices, and foreign exchange rates. Each element in the coefficient vector β indicates the amount of instantaneous hedge with commodity bonds or non-dollar-denominated conventional debt in response to unexpected shocks in commodity prices and foreign exchange rates. Because an unexpected change in price p_i by an amount p_{Ri} (where i is a commodity or foreign currency) results in a change in unexpected export earnings, x_R, by $\beta_i p_{Ri}$, it is possible to hedge the risk exposure by β_i amount of debt that is linked to p_i which experiences such an unexpected shock.

One can find similar formulations, such as β as the parameter estimates of a simple OLS regression, in other optimal portfolio literature (see Kroner and Claessens 1991). However, as suggested by equation A3-1, to derive the final composition of debt, β has to be adjusted by the vector of γ, which is defined in equation A1-11.

Rewrite equation A1-11 as follows:

$$(A3\text{-}3) \qquad R_t\left(\sum_{i=0}^{\infty} (1 + r)^{-i} E_t(x_{t+i}) \right) = R_t(\gamma' y_t + B(L)y_{t-1}) = R_t \gamma' y_t$$

where R_t is the "unexpected at time t" operator. $R_t \gamma' y_t$ can be further written as[13]

$$(A3\text{-}4) \qquad R_t \gamma' y_t = \gamma' y_{Rt} = \gamma_x x_R + \gamma_{p1} p_{R1} + \ldots + \gamma_{pn} p_{Rn}$$

where $y_{Rt} = (x_{Rt}, p_{Rt})'$, and $\gamma = (\gamma_x, \gamma_{p1}, \gamma_{p2}, \ldots, \gamma_{pn})'$, which can be considered as a vector of multipliers of unexpected shocks, x_R and p_R, to the permanent income of export earnings. Thus, as given by equation A3-1, the quantity of commodity bonds b_{it} that are linked to price p_{it} is

$$(A3\text{-}5) \qquad b_{it} = \gamma_x \beta_i + \gamma_{pi} \qquad i = 1, \ldots, n$$

The coefficient b_{it} has an interesting interpretation. Starting from equation A3-2, the unexpected shock p_{Ri} on price p_i can be hedged instantaneously by the amount of p_i-linked debt, β_i, because of the effect of the unexpected export earnings $\beta_i p_{ri}$ on x. However, shocks p_{Ri} and $\beta_i p_{Ri}$ continue to spill over into the permanent income of export earnings through the vector of γ. Thus, according to equation A3-4, the permanent income of export earnings is changed by $\gamma_x \beta_i p_{Ri} + \gamma_i p_{Ri}$. So the amount of price p_i-linked debt that can optimally hedge against the unexpected price shock p_{Ri} is $\gamma_x \beta_i + \gamma_i$.

Some implications can be derived through a decomposition of equation A1-22. First, it reveals the theoretical connections between the infinite horizon, rational expectations approach to the treatment of optimal debt portfolio analysis and approaches of the mean-variance type. Second, it provides econometric guidelines and insights into the empirical estimation process. For example, equation A3-2 can be estimated by OLS regression. However, if multicollinearity exists among price residuals—$p_{R1}, p_{R2}, \ldots, p_{Rn}$—which is most likely among groups of primary commodity prices or foreign exchange rates, the efficiency of estimating instantaneous amount of debts—$\beta_1, \beta_2, \ldots, \beta_n$—would be undermined, and the result for each individual β_i could be highly unstable. Therefore, the optimal composition of the debt portfolio could vary greatly for small changes in the model's assumptions and input. On the other hand, if some prices have been dropped to avoid the collinearity, the efficiency of estimating the remaining instantaneous debt is greatly improved without greatly reducing hedging effectiveness. Third, the vector multiplier γ shows that the effect on permanent export earnings of unexpected shocks in primary commodity prices or foreign exchange rates determines the optimal hedging strategy, not the instantaneous one. Intuitively, a positive shock in commodity price p_i will most likely bring a positive instantaneous rise in unexpected export earnings. But its effect on permanent export earnings is uncertain. It is possible for a positive shock in p_i to induce a decline in permanent export earnings, as in the case of Dutch disease. Thus the p_i-linked debt is not effective in hedging permanent export earnings.

Notes

1. Papua New Guinea's first oil project is likely to come on stream in the second half of 1992 and have a production profile that is heavily loaded at the front end.

2. The Minerals Resources Stabilization Fund was established in 1975 to prevent unstable mineral-based tax revenues from causing instability in the rest of the economy. However, Claessens and Coleman (chapter 10) show that the CV of outflows from this fund is only slightly lower than the CV of its inflows, indicating only moderate effectiveness in stabilization. Papua New Guinea has also operated commodity price stabilization funds for its major agricultural export commodities (that is, coffee, cocoa, copra, and palm oil). These funds were successful for many years and often cited as models of how effective well-administered schemes can be in managing risk. However, with the sharp fall in the prices of these commodities in recent years, these funds became depleted. New approaches to commodity price risk management for agriculture are now being sought.

3. Movements in cross-currency exchange rates can be expected to compensate for nominal interest rate differentials (uncovered interest rate parity), except for risk premiums (ex ante deviations from uncovered interest rate parity). However, ex post, deviations from uncovered interest rate parity are unobserved. Therefore, active currency management should be employed to reduce risks of ex post deviations through optimal currency composition. In the model developed here, all variables (denominated in nominal dollars) are deflated by Papua New Guinea's import price index (based on dollars). Thus the model measures the currency valuation effect in terms of units of imports.

4. The diagnostics for the SUR estimates (for example, R^2 and Durbin-Watson statistics) are not reported by the statistical package SAS for the individual equations in the VAR system.

5. A nonlinear programming package (for example, GAMS) can be used to solve this maximization problem with a nonnegative constraint. However, the solution tends to be highly unstable.

6. This approach is capable of producing an infinite loop in calculations. Fortunately, in the model tested for Papua New Guinea, the infinite loop did not appear, and the final solution was quickly located.

7. The model proposed here assumes that uncovered interest parity holds. Covered interest parity is not assumed, because long-term (more than a year) forward exchange markets do not exist.

8. This condition ensures that borrowing will not increase the present value of net wealth. This condition is used also in appendix 11-2.

9. A derivation and discussion of this equation is given in appendix 11-2.

10. For simplicity, subscript $t + 1$ has been dropped.

11. For simplicity, the superscript * has been dropped, because there is no essential difference in commodity prices and foreign exchange rates in the theoretical optimal portfolio model.

12. The VAR system acts like a filter.

13. For simplicity, subscript t has been dropped in the last part of the expression.

12

Commodity, Exchange Rate, and Interest Rate Risks in Colombia

Andrew Powell

Despite some diversification, Colombian exports remain relatively highly concentrated in primary commodities, in particular, coffee and petroleum products. Hence, there is a serious exposure to fluctuations in coffee and oil prices. In addition, Colombia's external liabilities have grown considerably—to almost $17.5 billion at the end of 1988—and debt service is projected to account for 57.6 percent of Colombia's exports of goods and services in 1990 (FEDESARROLLO, various issues). Debt is largely denominated in dollars, and much of the debt has been contracted at variable interest rates related to the London interbank offered rate (LIBOR). Colombia could therefore have a serious exposure to fluctuations in exchange rates and interest rates as well, with the result that changes in debt-servicing liabilities might not be matched by changes in debt-servicing capacity.

This chapter provides an overview of the commodity, exchange rate, and interest rate risks faced by the Colombian economy, in particular by those sectors of the economy that affect government revenue. The chapter also discusses techniques for managing these risks.

The chapter begins with a discussion of the risks faced by Colombia from fluctuations in world prices of coffee, crude oil, exchange rates, and interest rates. Next are discussed the potential objectives of risk management, the tools available to measure the degree of exposure, and some problems in analyzing the data available. This is followed by a brief

The author wishes to thank Theo Priovolos, Stijn Claessens, and Santiago Montenegro for useful advice and data.

discussion of the instruments that might be employed to manage the risks and to stabilize net revenue streams. The section that follows presents estimates of the degree to which Colombia is exposed to external risks and develops a framework for solving for the optimal composition of external debt. The penultimate section draws conclusions on specific hedging strategies and their implementation, and the final section provides a summary.

Exposure to Commodity, Currency, and Interest Rate Risk

The exposure of the Colombian economy and of the government in particular to movements in world commodity prices, exchange rates, and interest rates can be understood through a careful examination of the sources of these risks.

The Economy's Exposure

Historically, coffee has played a vital role in the Colombian economy. In 1986 coffee exports accounted for 51.5 percent of exports (net of oil imports) and for 3.1 percent of gross domestic product (GDP). There is also an association of the real coffee price with the real trade balance, as illustrated in figure 12-1. However, since 1986 the importance of coffee exports to the economy has declined. Coffee prices fell sharply when the economic provisions of the International Coffee Agreement were suspended. At the same time, the export volume rose only slightly, resulting, on net, in a decline in coffee export earnings. It is estimated that in 1990 coffee exports accounted for only about 22.3 percent of export earnings net of oil imports (FEDESARROLLO, various issues).

The relative decline of coffee in export earnings is also a result of the increase in petroleum exports. Until 1974, Colombia was a significant net exporter of petroleum products, but for twelve years after 1974 its petroleum trade balance was roughly constant or negative. Then, starting in 1986, production increased dramatically, largely as a result of the new Caño Limón field. Exports of petroleum and petroleum-related products rose significantly and were estimated to be 21.6 percent of total exports in 1990 (net of oil imports).

Colombia has borrowed heavily in international markets since 1978, as illustrated by the change in its long-term debt (figure 12-2). Servicing of Colombia's external liabilities is now a large drain on the country's resources, and estimates for 1990 are that debt service accounted for 57.6 percent of exports. It is projected that the ratio of debt service to exports will remain at this level through the mid-1990s. As of 1990 some

Figure 12-1. *Real World Coffee Price and Colombia's Real Trade Balance, 1970–88*

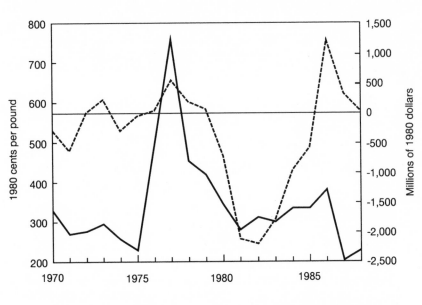

—— Coffee price (left scale).   ----- Trade balance (right scale).

Source: FEDESARROLLO (various issues).

50 percent of Colombia's long-term debt was on variable interest rate contracts.[1]

These statistics imply that Colombia has a serious exposure to commodity price and interest rate fluctuations. Fluctuations in coffee prices have indeed been an important source of fluctuations in the trade balance during the last twenty years (as shown in figure 12-1). Because more oil is exported than before, oil prices have also become a strong determinant of the external account. In addition, Colombia has an exposure to exchange rate movements. Two sets of exchange rates should be considered: the dollar against the peso, and the dollar against other major currencies.

The dollar-peso exchange rate is to a large degree a policy tool. Since March 1967 Colombia has explicitly maintained a crawling peg exchange rate policy. The stated objective has been to maintain a constant, trade-weighted real exchange rate for noncoffee exports. But Colombia's exchange rate policy has been interdependent with macro-

Figure 12-2. *Year-to-Year Changes in Long-Term Debt, Colombia,*
1970–87

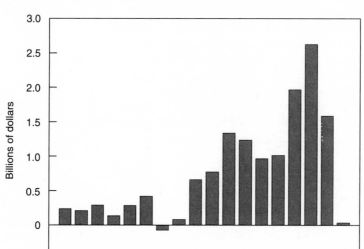

Source: World Bank (1992b).

economic and risk management policies as well. For instance, during the
coffee boom of 1976–78 the peso was allowed to rise in real terms as part
of a stabilization program. In the event of a deep fall in coffee prices,
however, the opposite policy is likely to be employed to stabilize peso
receipts.

An alternative to macroeconomic policies is the use of financial hedging instruments to stabilize foreign exchange revenues directly. These
instruments transfer risk abroad and hence lessen the impact of booms
and busts on the macroeconomy. Furthermore, the instruments operate
solely on the particular sector, whereas use of the peso exchange rate to
manage price risks affects the whole economy.

Movements in the exchange rates between the dollar and other currencies are clearly exogenous. The effects on Colombia are complicated
because of Colombia's trading pattern and the currency composition of
its external debt. To a large extent, the latter may be considered to be a
policy tool, so let us consider the pattern of trade first. Assuming that oil
and coffee exports are priced in dollars—note that this may not always
be the case, as, for instance, with Colombian coffee exports to some
European countries—a rise in the dollar may invoke a fall in the dollar

value of oil and coffee export earnings. Whether the value of these commodities rises or falls with respect to a basket of other goods depends on a complex set of relationships between supply and demand elasticities for these goods.[2]

Colombia can be characterized as commodity-dependent in terms of exports but less so in terms of imports. If both exports and imports are priced in dollars and the value of the dollar rises, one hypothesis is that import prices would rise in relation to export prices. The dollar prices of commodities may adjust downward faster than the dollar prices of other goods. Hence, Colombia would lose from a rise in the value of the dollar. The empirical results, given below, analyze this matter in detail.

The Government's Exposure

The government is exposed to commodity price, exchange rate, and interest rate risks through its institutional involvement in the coffee and oil sectors and through the effects that fluctuations in world commodity prices, interest rates, and exchange rates have on taxes, the trade balance, and ultimately the government budget.

Exposure to world coffee prices. The government's exposure to world coffee prices depends to a large extent on domestic marketing arrangements and, in particular, how these arrangements are altered when there are changes in the world coffee price. Here we give a brief account of recent and present policies under different world market conditions (for further details see Nash 1985 and Ocampo 1989).

Under the present marketing arrangements for coffee, producers can sell coffee to the National Coffee Federation or to private exporters. Nominally, the federation is a private body, but it operates very closely with the government, and its various committees have considerable government representation. Furthermore, the government has in the past assisted the federation through budgetary transfers to assist it in stabilizing the domestic coffee price for producers in relation to the world price. The federation sets a price at which it will buy, and this serves as a minimum price for each season. Effectively, the federation gives producers a put option on sales. The exercise price of the option is the minimum price offered by the federation, because producers are free to sell to private exporters that offer higher prices.

However, private exporters have rather limited freedom to offer higher prices. They must pay a retention tax, payable in kind, and thus a proportion of the coffee exported must be delivered to the federation. The retention tax accrues directly to National Coffee Fund, which is managed by the federation, and the tax is changed frequently, depending on world market conditions. Historically, the tax has been set so that about 45 to 48 percent of production is exported through private channels.[3]

Apart from the retention tax, both private traders and the federation are required to pay an ad valorem tax, which stands at the time of writing at 5.6 percent of the value of coffee sold. The receipts from the ad valorem tax are shared as follows: the central government gets 1.6 percent of the value of exports sold; the federation's departmental committees get 0.8 percent; and the National Coffee Fund gets 3.2 percent. Thus, in each year the federation either receives net funds from or transfers net funds to the central government, depending on its tax receipts and tax liabilities.

The three important potential sources of revenue for the federation are the profits or losses from its own purchases and sales of coffee; the retention tax; and the federation's net portion of the ad valorem tax. Each of these sources of revenue is affected by the world price of coffee, and the federation thus has three exposures. First, the federation's own purchases and sales expose it to the world price. This is a direct result of the federation's policy of stabilizing domestic prices relative to the world price. Between the time that the minimum price is set by the federation and the time the coffee is purchased from the farmer, and from that time to the time the federation sells the coffee at the world price, there is substantial uncertainty about what the federation's final net export revenue will be. Second, the value of the retention tax depends on the world price. The retention tax is adjusted upward as the world price rises, and because the tax is payable in kind, each ton of coffee delivered as payment is more valuable as the world price rises.[4] Third, the potential amount of ad valorem tax revenue is affected by the world price, because the ad valorem tax is expressed as a percentage of the value of exports. Whether the ad valorem tax results in a net cost to the federation or in a net revenue depends on the federation's share of exports. If the federation exports only a small amount of coffee, then it will pay rather little ad valorem tax and hence its share of the ad valorem tax revenue on all exports will exceed its tax liabilities. This will result in a net transfer from the central government to the federation. However, if the proportion of total coffee exported by the federation is large, the net transfer may be from the federation to the government. The three sources of revenue are obviously not independent of each other, nor is the net effect on federation finances a simple function of the world price of coffee. The net effect also depends on how taxes are adjusted in response to price movements. However, it is clear that a fall in the world price will seriously affect the financial position of the federation. If a stable real domestic price is maintained, losses will accrue from the federation's own purchases and sales. If the retention tax is adjusted downward—to maintain a constant amount of private exports—this will result in a loss of revenue. Finally, the total amount of the ad valorem tax raised will decline.

The exposure of the central government is much simpler to describe. The major source of revenue related to coffee is the ad valorem tax. Clearly, as world prices fluctuate, so too will the central government's share of the ad valorem tax. At the time of writing this tax is 1.6 percent of gross coffee export revenue. In addition, the central government is exposed to coffee prices through the net revenues it receives from, or pays to, the federation on account of the difference between the ad valorem tax and the retention tax.

EXPOSURE TO OIL PRICES. The Empresa Colombiana de Petroleos (ECOPETROL), a wholly state-owned company, is an active agent in the exploration, production, refining, transportation, and marketing of oil and gas. Private companies obtain rights to produce crude oil through contracts negotiated by ECOPETROL on behalf of the government.

ECOPETROL's exposure to oil prices is first through its own export and import activities. In 1987 ECOPETROL produced 79,500 barrels of petroleum a day and exported 71,100 barrels a day with a total export value of $456.6 million for the year. ECOPETROL also acts as an importer of petroleum products, mostly gasoline, which are sold at prices set by the government. Although ECOPETROL will gain from its own production and sales if world oil prices rise, this gain will, at least in part, be offset by a rise in the cost of imports, a cost that cannot be recovered if domestic prices are maintained.

ECOPETROL also has exposure through its concession and association contracts giving rights to private companies. Concession contracts have not been issued since 1974, but some contracts made before then remain valid. In terms of volume, association contracts are now the more important. Indeed, the development of the new Caño Limón field by private companies was largely through the medium of association contracts. In 1987, production under association contracts had risen to 243,700 barrels a day. Therefore, this discussion concentrates on association contracts.

Association contracts place the initial cost of exploration with the private company (the associate). If a commercial field is discovered, ECOPETROL reimburses some of the exploration costs to the associate and shares the investment costs, operating expenses, and production revenues.[5]

The system of association contracts gives ECOPETROL, and thus the government, considerable exposure to fluctuations in world oil prices. First, for all commercial fields under association contracts, 20 percent of the value of production is paid in the form of royalties, which are shared between the central government (8.5 percent) and municipalities and departmental committees (11.5 percent). Second, ECOPETROL receives 44 to 48 percent of the value of production (net of royalties), leaving the associate with 32 to 36 percent. Thus, as world oil prices rise and fall so, too, does the revenue to ECOPETROL and to the government.

EXPOSURE TO WORLD INTEREST RATES. Approximately 50 percent of Colombia's long-term external debt is contracted under variable interest rates, in particular, the U.S. dollar LIBOR. Thus, as world interest rates rise, total debt service in dollar terms increases.

There may be important interactions between interest rate movements and currency movements. For instance, if the dollar interest rate rises in relation to other interest rates, then, according to a popular theory of currency behavior, the so-called uncovered interest parity (UIP) theory, this would lead to a fall in the value of the dollar. Indeed, according to UIP, movements in currencies should exactly offset relative interest rate movements. In that case, the level of world interest rates alone would be important. However, this theory of exchange rate behavior has not been borne out by events; for instance, the rise of the dollar in the early 1980s was accompanied by relatively high dollar interest rates. In general, tests of UIP have shown that it is not a robust assumption. The possibility of ex post significant deviations from UIP thus implies significant exchange rate risks.

EXPOSURE TO EXCHANGE RATE MOVEMENTS. Since 1978 Colombia has contracted about $20 billion of external debt. Of this, 45.2 percent is in dollars, 36.5 percent in multicurrency liabilities (for example, liabilities to the World Bank), 8.2 percent in deutsche marks, and 5.8 percent in Japanese yen.

Two kinds of exchange rate movements are considered here: the dollar against the peso, and the dollar against other major currencies. The determination of the peso-dollar exchange rate is, to a large extent, a policy tool and beyond the scope of this study.[6] However, interactions with risk management policy may substitute for using the peso exchange rate as a tool to stabilize the domestic peso price of coffee in response to changes in the world coffee price. For example, the government may let the peso appreciate against the dollar when the world (dollar) price of coffee declines in order to maintain a high domestic coffee price. Indirectly, the government may thus be exposed to changes in the world coffee price as it needs to adjust its monetary and fiscal policies to achieve the desired peso appreciation or depreciation. Hedging shifts risks abroad, whereas stabilization through the exchange rate disperses risks throughout the domestic economy by way of the government's fiscal or monetary policies.

Exposure to movements of the dollar against other currencies depends on the currency that external government transactions are denominated in and how prices in such transactions change in response to movements in exchange rates. A more detailed examination of this issue is presented below.

Formulating the Objectives of a Risk Management Strategy

A risk management strategy should be based on careful analysis. This means asking the right questions and using empirical tools to measure exposures to various sources of risk. The foremost question is, what are the costs for the country concerned of volatile and unpredictable revenues and liabilities? Specifically, if in Colombia the processes that drive commodity prices, exchange rates, and interest rates were well understood and Colombia could borrow and lend freely (at a stable interest rate), there might be few or no costs from the volatility of prices; Colombia could simply borrow and lend to smooth net revenues. These conditions, however, are not realistic. The stochastic processes underlying commodity prices and exchange and interest rates remain controversial, and these prices are notoriously difficult to predict. This uncertainty creates a difficult planning environment and may lead to costly mistakes in macroeconomic management (see Powell 1989). In addition, there are asymmetries in international credit markets. Borrowing and lending rates are not equal for developing-country borrowers, and at times Colombia might find it difficult to borrow at any interest rate. Credit rationing may be the product of this uncertainty, because lenders will tend to reduce credit if defaults or reschedulings are thought likely. Revenue smoothing through the use of international credit markets will then be costly, if indeed it is possible.

The factors leading to Colombia's financial crisis of 1982 are illustrative. On the strength of the high coffee prices prior to 1980, Colombia borrowed heavily. From 1978 to 1982 Colombia contracted $4.09 billion of debt, whereas from 1970 to 1977 it had borrowed just $1.5 billion. During a two-year period starting in 1980 Colombia experienced a combination of adverse price movements. Coffee prices fell, the dollar rose strongly, and world interest rates increased. These price movements, together with important internal factors, were determinants of a financial crisis that culminated in a severe curtailment of foreign lending in the fall of 1982.

From this discussion we can formulate two possible objectives of a risk management strategy. The first is to reduce the variability of future net revenue streams. Reducing the variance of the future trade balance would create a more stable planning environment and lead to less dependence on the international credit market to smooth consumption. The second is to ensure that a crisis—like the one in the early 1980s—does not recur, that is, to protect against a particular scenario of adverse events occurring. This strategy could be thought of as maximizing the net revenue under worst-case conditions. These two objectives are interdependent, because protection against a worst-case scenario (for example, default) should lead to improved ability to borrow in the international credit market.

The above discussion highlights the main areas of risk. However, the statistics that have been presented do not give a precise idea of the magnitude of the risks. Neither do they give the optimal method for dealing with these risks in order to achieve possible objectives. Further analysis is needed. One way forward is by regression analysis to test the degree to which historical revenue and liability streams, such as exports and imports, have depended on important prices, such as commodity prices and exchange rates. In regression analysis it is necessary to ensure that a valid and consistent framework be used. For instance, it is likely that the objective of the policymaker is the stabilization of real net revenue streams, that is, real exports minus real imports. However, the financial hedging instruments that are available—and these are discussed in the next section—are often nominal and may offer limited hedging against real price shocks. Also, when dealing with a nominal series, it is quite possible that the time series involved may be nonstationary. To cope with this problem, the regressions can be estimated in first-difference terms in logarithms. The coefficients on the price series then correspond to the elasticities of the revenue or liability stream with respect to those prices and are natural measures of the exposures with respect to those prices.

What currency should be used for these analyses—local currency or dollars? This analysis is done in nominal terms in dollars because the domestic exchange rate is considered to be a policy tool. For analyses conducted in local currency, the results would be conditional on the historical exchange rate policy adopted. It was decided, therefore, that there would be more value in searching for results that were independent of the exchange rate policy.

Financial Instruments to Manage Commodity, Exchange Rate, and Interest Rate Risk

A wide range of instruments are available to manage commodity, exchange rate, and interest rate risks. Masuoka (chapter 4) describes the possibilities in detail. Some general remarks on the potential of these instruments in the case of Colombia are discussed in this section.

Futures and options contracts traded on exchanges may be appropriate for an institution such as the National Coffee Federation, which guarantees producers minimum prices before the coffee harvest but does not know the actual value of spot sales until well after the harvest. An important advantage of purchasing options rather than futures is that no margin payments are required.[7] However, the option premium is normally paid in advance. An alternative is to finance the purchase of a put option with the sale of a call option. One possibility here is to buy a put and a call for the same quantity of coffee but with different exercise prices. An out-of-the-money put could be financed by an out-of-the-money call. Financing the put this way would give price protection at the lower exercise price of the put but would imply a cap at the exercise price of a call. Alternatively, options could be written on different quantities so that an out-of-the-money put is financed by an in-the-money call, but with the call written on only a fraction of the quantity of the put. An entire spectrum of so-called zero-cost option strategies lie between these two extremes. All, however, require the sale of a call option, and for such sales, margin payments are normally required (at least on the call options in these examples).

An alternative to using exchange-traded options is to use over-the-counter options, that is, options that are negotiated with a counterparty. Because a dealer accepts the default risk on the options sold, these may not be available to developing-country institutions that do not have a good credit standing. These over-the-counter-traded options often have maturities well beyond the furthest exchange-traded option contracts (option-type deals have been negotiated with commodity-producing countries that go out as far as three to six years). However, given that the incentive to default on these contracts can be quite large, it is likely that the premium for such contracts will be high.

For longer-term exposures, vehicles with risk-sharing features may be appropriate for Colombia. Interest rate swaps and currency swaps have maturities of ten years or more, and these markets are very liquid. A less well-known instrument is the commodity swap, whereby a liability linked to an interest rate (say, the LIBOR) is swapped with one linked to a commodity price (say, the price of oil). Suppose that Colombia borrows in the international credit markets, at LIBOR, to finance the development of an oil production facility. Liabilities will then be related to movements in the LIBOR, but proceeds from the project will be dependent on the price of oil. In this case, a commodity swap to transform liabilities so that they reflect the price of oil would clearly reduce risks. Bonds with risk-sharing features have become popular in the financial markets of the Organization for Economic Cooperation and Development (OECD) countries. Bonds with payments tied to commodity prices can provide a hedge for a commodity producer (see further Masuoka, chapter 4). Financial markets offer a considerable variety of hedging instruments and great flexibility in their design.

To examine what an optimal hedging program might look like, we will consider in the next section a simple methodology discussed in Claessens (1988). Essentially, the objective is to derive the optimal composition of debt across different currencies and different commodity-contingent structures, given the currency-commodity correlations appropriate to Colombia.

External Exposures and the Optimal Composition of Debt

The exposure of Colombian institutions to commodity price, exchange rate, and interest rate risks can be estimated through regressions. Separate regressions were performed to show the degree to which external exposures affect the economy as a whole and the public sector in particular.

The Effect on the Resource Balance

A useful concept in the analysis of a country's exposure to commodity price and exchange rate risks is the resource balance: exports minus imports. The resource balance may be used either to pay debts or to build reserves. Stabilization of the resource balance is a useful risk management objective. To determine a country's external exposure to various world prices, it is tempting to construct, from historical data, a series for the resource balance ($R = X - M$, where R is the resource balance, X is exports, and M is imports) and simply regress this series against the prices in which one is interested. However, a more robust econometric procedure, which is employed here, is to regress both elements of the resource balance separately against the appropriate prices. Regressions are performed in first differences in logarithms. The commodity prices included are coffee and oil, and all values are expressed in dollars. A weighted index of the value of the dollar against other major currencies is also included. The regression results are as follows:

Exports
$$\Delta LX_t = 0.05706 + 0.32826 \, \Delta LCOFFEE_t + 0.10887 \, \Delta LOIL_t$$
$$\qquad (2.05) \qquad (3.91) \qquad\qquad\qquad (1.82)$$

$$\qquad -0.92929 \, \Delta L\$_t + 0.27157 \, \Delta L\$_{t-1} + \epsilon_t$$
$$\qquad (-4.41) \qquad\qquad (1.22)$$

$$R^2 = 0.75 \qquad \sigma = 0.0973 \qquad F(4, 12) = 8.76 \qquad DW = 1.71$$

Imports
$$\Delta LM_t = 0.02158 + 0.26814 \, \Delta LOIL_t - 0.10514 \, \Delta LOIL_{t-1}$$
$$\qquad (0.58) \qquad (3.70) \qquad\qquad (-1.06)$$

$$\qquad -0.62825 \, \Delta L\$_t + 0.38945 \, \Delta LM_{t-1} + \epsilon_t$$
$$\qquad (-2.35) \qquad\qquad (1.46)$$

$$R^2 = 0.64 \qquad \sigma = 0.1163 \qquad F(4, 12) = 5.25 \qquad DW = 1.99$$

where ΔL is the first difference in logarithms, X is exports, M is imports, *COFFEE* is the coffee price, and *OIL* is the petroleum price; $\$$ is the weighted value of the dollar against the yen, deutsche mark, and sterling where, when the index is increasing, the dollar is appreciating. The data period is 1970–88, and data sources include the International Monetary Fund's *International Financial Statistics* and the World Bank's *World Debt Tables* and commodity data base. An analysis of the residuals from the equations showed no evidence of serial correlation or heteroskedasticity and no evidence of serious correlation of residuals between the equations (*t*-statistics are in parentheses).

The regressions illustrate the significance of coffee prices as a determinant of export revenues. Oil prices appear with a positive sign, but the coefficient is insignificant. In the import equation, however, oil prices do appear as significant. Note that the value of the dollar has a negative sign and is significant in both equations. Because all prices and values are expressed in dollars, a rise of the dollar against other major currencies implies that the value of trade not denominated in dollars will decline in dollar terms unless prices adjust quickly. The negative sign indicates therefore that prices do not adjust instantly with changes in the dollar exchange rate. Note that this effect is independent of the effect that changes in the value of the dollar might have on coffee and oil prices that are expressed in dollars. The latter effect is already taken into account by including the prices for coffee and oil.

The conclusion from these regressions is that the elasticity of Colombian export revenues with respect to coffee prices is about 0.3. In other words, a 10 percent increase in coffee prices has been associated with a 3 percent rise in export values. The effect of petroleum prices is roughly equal on both the export side and import side. It should be noted that Colombia's export composition changed markedly over the period of the study. Petroleum exports were about 21.6 percent of exports (net of petroleum imports) in 1990, whereas in the earlier period Colombia was a net importer of oil. Coffee declined from an average of 45.3 percent of exports (net of petroleum imports) over the period 1970–88 to 22.3 percent in 1990.

The Effect on Public Institutions and Revenues

In this section we first consider the exposure of the National Coffee Federation to coffee price risks and then the exposure of ECOPETROL to oil price risks. Next, we consider the effect of coffee and oil prices on government revenue as a whole. Finally, we consider government revenue without including the National Coffee Fund.

THE NATIONAL COFFEE FEDERATION. The National Coffee Federation has provided valuable price stabilization for coffee producers in Colombia through the medium of the National Coffee Fund. The extent of price stabilization achieved can be judged from figure 12-3, which plots the real world price of coffee against the real internal price of coffee. It can be shown that both the variance and the kurtosis of the internal real price is lower than that of the world price. However, this internal price stabilization necessarily implies that the National Coffee Fund, and hence the federation, has a serious exposure to fluctuations in the world price of coffee. The exact nature of this exposure depends on the policy rules followed by the federation in changing the internal price as world market conditions alter. As discussed above, the National Coffee Fund (and hence the federation) is also exposed to fluctuations in the world price through its own net revenues received through the retention tax and the share of the ad valorem tax.

Figure 12-4 plots the surplus of the National Coffee Fund as a percentage of GDP and the ratio of the domestic price of coffee to the world price of coffee over the 1950–87 period. We can obtain a measure of the dependency of the real surplus on world coffee prices through the following regression analysis.

$$SUR_t = -350.10 + 1.132\,EXT_t + 10.55\,REXRATE_t - 8.392\,REXRATE_{t-1}$$
$$\quad\ (-2.736)\ (2.637)\qquad\quad (3.993)\qquad\qquad (-3.129)$$

$$R^2 = 0.367 \qquad \sigma = 115.2 \qquad F(3, 33) = 6.38 \qquad DW = 1.86$$

Figure 12-3. *Domestic Price of Coffee, Colombia, and World Price,*
1940–87

Index: 1975=100

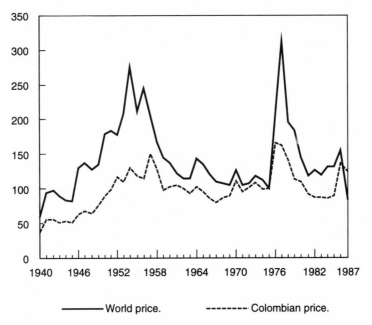

———— World price.   -------- Colombian price.

Source: Ocampo (1989).

where *SUR* is the surplus or deficit of the National Coffee Fund in real
pesos, *EXT* is the real world price of coffee, and *REXRATE* is the real
exchange rate for imports. All data are from Ocampo (1989). The sample period is 1950–87.

The regression results and figure 12-4 indicate that even though the
relationship is not straightforward, the surplus in the National Coffee
Fund is clearly dependent on the real world price of coffee. The relationship does not display great stability, however. The lack of stability may
be the result of changes in the amount of coffee exported and in the
policies of the federation (the federation will affect the surplus of the
fund through the level of the guaranteed domestic price of coffee in
relation to the world price of coffee). Future exposures will be dependent
on the policy rules adopted by the federation.

ECOPETROL. Here we consider the exposure of ECOPETROL to changes
in world oil prices. The dependence of the Generación Interna Neta

Figure 12-4. *National Coffee Fund Surplus and Ratio of the World Price to the Domestic Price of Coffee, Colombia, 1950–87*

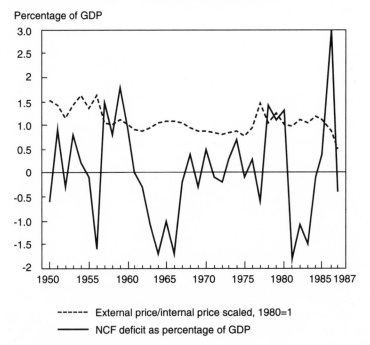

Percentage of GDP

------ External price/internal price scaled, 1980=1
——— NCF deficit as percentage of GDP

Source: Ocampo (1989).

Fondos (GIN, ECOPETROL's net internal revenues) on oil prices, in nominal terms, is defined by employing regression analysis. In this case, controlling for volumes produced, a stable relationship was discovered. The regression was estimated as follows:

$$\Delta LGIN = 0.035 - 0.318\,\Delta LGIN_{t-1} + 0.357\,\Delta LPETROL + 1.410\,\Delta VOL$$
$$\quad\;(0.03)\,(-1.84) \qquad\qquad (2.76) \qquad\qquad\quad (4.61)$$

$$R^2 = 0.68 \qquad \sigma = 0.1713 \qquad F(3, 12) = 8.37 \qquad DW = 2.18$$

where ΔL is the first difference in logs, *GIN* is defined as above, *PETROL* is the world petroleum price, and *VOL* is total production including that of ECOPETROL. The association and concession production figures are from Perry Rubio (1987, table 8). Data are from 1970 to 1987.

There is a significant dependence of *GIN* on oil prices with an elasticity of revenue with respect to price of about 0.4. As discussed above, this dependency comes about not only through ECOPETROL's own operations, but also through the workings of the association (and, to a lesser extent, concession) contracts.

GOVERNMENT REVENUES. First, we consider the effect of changes in the world price of coffee and oil on total public revenue. Regressions, using data from the national accounts over the period 1970–86,[8] were performed in first differences in logs, with amounts expressed in dollars. The results are as follows:

$$\Delta LREV_t = 0.075 + 0.129 \, \Delta LCOFF_t + 0.184 \, \Delta LCOFF_{t-1} + 0.083 \, \Delta LPETROL_t$$
$$ (2.76) \quad (1.44) (2.07) (1.467)$$

$$R^2 = 0.46 \quad F(3, 11) = 3.06 \quad \sigma = 0.093 \quad DW = 1.97$$

$$\Delta LRWNCF_t = 0.406 + 0.051 \, \Delta LCOFF_t + 0.184 \, \Delta LRWNCF_{t-1} + 0.087 \, \Delta LPETROL_t$$
$$ (1.09) \quad (0.63) (1.76) (1.60)$$

$$R^2 = 0.44 \quad F(3, 11) = 2.91 \quad \sigma = 0.084 \quad DW = 2.58$$

where ΔL is the first difference in logs, REV is total public sector revenue, $COFF$ is the world coffee price, and $RWNCF$ is public sector revenue without the National Coffee Fund.

The regressions indicate that revenue for the public sector as a whole was significantly dependent on world coffee prices. However, dependence on petroleum prices was not significant over this period. Furthermore, for the public sector net of the National Coffee Fund, the dependence on coffee prices on net revenues was also insignificant.

Calculating the Optimal Composition of Debt

In the above, the exposure of certain net revenue flows to international prices has been examined. An example of such a revenue flow is the Colombian resource balance. One way to stabilize the resource balance is to adjust the currency composition of debt, for example, by matching it to the trading pattern of the country or by borrowing in currencies that have tendencies to move with particular commodities. In the case of Colombia, however, it might be more beneficial to tie debt repayments to the movements of prices for commodities such as coffee and oil. A general framework for defining the optimal composition of debt, using the stabilization of Colombia's resource balance as an example, is discussed below.

Consider the resource balance as related to a set of commodity prices and effective interest rates as follows:

$$RB = \alpha_o + \sum_{i=1}^{r} \alpha_i P_i + \sum_{j=r+1}^{s} \alpha_j P_j$$

where RB is the resource balance, P_i represents the set of commodity prices, and P_j represents the set of interest rates. The sensitivities of the resource balance to these prices are thus represented by α_i, where $i = 1$, . . . , s. Although a number of these sensitivities may be exogenous, a number are endogenous. Claessens (1988) considers the case in which commodity quantities (and thus sensitivities) are exogenous whereas the amount of debt denominated in a particular currency (and hence the sensitivity of the resource balance to that currency interest rate) is endogenous. This approach can be generalized as follows: Say the sensitivity of the resource balance to p parameters (for example, a set of interest rates) can be thought of as endogenous. Let P_n be the $(1 \times p)$ vector of such parameters and let n be the $(1 \times p)$ vector of endogenous sensitivities. Say there are q parameters (for example, a set of commodity prices) that can be thought of as exogenous, and let P_x be the $(1 \times q)$ vector of such parameters and let x be the $(1 \times q)$ vector of exogenous sensitivities. Then the resource balance may be reformulated as follows: $RB = P_n n' + P_x x'$.

The optimal value for n can then be obtained by differentiating the expression for the variance of the resource balance with respect to the p endogenous variables. This results in p equations in p unknowns, which may be written in matrix form as $Bn = Ax'$, where B is the $(p \times p)$ variance-covariance matrix of the endogenous variables [that is, $B = \text{var} (n)$] and A is the $(p \times q)$ matrix of covariances between n and x [that is, $A = \text{cov} (n, x)$]. We can then solve for the optimal set of variables n as follows: $n = B^{-1} Ax$.

This provides a simple framework within which to answer questions concerning optimal debt composition. The framework is quite general and can be applied to a country as a whole or to a particular institution. Note that the framework allows for different variables to be considered as exogenous or endogenous. In this example, commodity sensitivities are exogenous and debt composition is endogenous.

The first problem is to put values on the sensitivities labeled α_i (that is, those that are exogenous). The coefficient estimates derived in the regressions above are natural candidates. However, Colombia's export composition has changed significantly in recent years; in particular, petroleum has become an important net earner of foreign exchange and will likely become even more important. Therefore, a range of sensitivities is used, varying from those estimated in the regressions above to those calculated from current projected values.

Two questions are posed for the analysis. The first is the question asked by Claessens (1988): if debt can be denominated in fixed interest rate contracts in dollars, deutsche marks, yen, and sterling or in dollars at LIBOR,[9] what is the optimal composition of debt? The second question posed is, if debt can also be made contingent on coffee and oil prices,

Table 12-1. *Optimal Composition of Debt under Various Elasticity Estimates for Colombia, 1970–88*
(percent)

Type of interest rate contract		Assumed elasticity of export earnings with respect to commodity price			
	Coffee	30.0	25.0	22.0	20.0
	Oil	0.0	15.0	22.4	25.0
		Optional debt composition with yen			
Dollars (LIBOR)		3	85	125	139
Dollars (fixed)		200	216	222	221
Sterling (fixed)		−200	−309	−360	−371
Yen (fixed)		−57	−82	−94	−96
Deutsche mark (fixed)		154	190	206	206
Total		100	100	100	100
		Optional debt composition without yen			
Dollars (LIBOR)		4	87	128	142
Dollars (fixed)		162	161	160	157
Sterling (fixed)		−171	−268	−312	−323
Deutsche mark (fixed)		105	120	125	124
Total		100	100	100	100
		Optional debt composition with yen and commodity-contingent financing			
Dollars (LIBOR)		0	0	0	0
Dollars (fixed)		−11	−48	−64	−66
Sterling (fixed)		0	0	0	0
Yen (fixed)		0	0	0	0
Deutsche mark (fixed)		0	0	0	0
Coffee-contingent		111	92	81	74
Oil-contingent		0	55	83	92
Total		100	100	100	100

Source: Author's calculations.

Note: A negative value indicates the accumulation of reserves by Colombia in the instrument in question.

what is the optimal composition of debt? The calculations made to answer these two questions are detailed in table 12-1, and the correlation matrix used for the analysis is presented in table 12-2 (the correlations were estimated for the period 1970–88).

A negative sign in table 12-1 implies that Colombia should invest in that particular instrument. The first panel of table 12-1 shows that most borrowing should be at fixed interest rates, especially U.S. dollar fixed interest rates, for all elasticity estimates. The share of fixed rate deutsche mark debt increases as the elasticity of oil export earnings is assumed to be higher. However, as oil prices become a more important determinant of export earnings, more debt should be at a variable interest rate,

Table 12-2. *Estimated Correlation Matrix for Table 12-1*

	Coffee-contingent	Oil-contingent	Dollars (LIBOR)	Sterling (fixed)	Yen (fixed)	Deutsche mark (fixed)
Coffee-contingent	1.0000					
Oil-contingent	0.5095	1.0000				
Dollars (LIBOR)	0.0976	0.7206	1.0000			
Sterling (fixed)	−0.6454	−0.5825	0.0079	1.0000		
Yen (fixed)	0.4783	0.4304	0.0978	−0.5332	1.0000	
Deutsche mark (fixed)	0.4993	0.4326	0.2107	−0.2518	0.7393	1.0000

Source: Author's calculations.

because the interest rate is positively correlated with the oil price. There is, however, a high correlation between the dollar-yen and dollar–deutsche mark exchange rates and hence a problem of multicollinearity in the results. This may account for the result that Colombia should borrow in deutsche marks and lend in yen (although these results are also supported by the work of Cartiglia 1989). Because the dollar-yen and dollar–deutsche mark exchange rates are highly correlated (having a correlation coefficient of 0.74), one of these rates should perhaps be excluded from the analysis. This is confirmed in the second panel, where yen lending is not allowed. Compared with the first panel, the share of deutsche mark debt drops significantly, roughly by the percentage of yen lending in the first panel, the result of the multicollinearity between the yen and the deutsche mark. The third panel of table 12-1 indicates an important result: commodity-contingent contracts are highly desirable for Colombia. If debt can be contracted on commodity-contingent terms, then all borrowing should be done on these terms and Colombia should lend at fixed interest rates. Note also that these results indicate that Colombia should lend in fixed interest rate dollars rather than borrow in dollars. These results are in sharp contrast to the actual debt composition of Colombia, which is heavily skewed toward dollars. Other analyses could be performed using this framework; it could, for instance, be applied to various Colombian institutions.

Hedging Strategies and Implementation

Before discussing possible hedging instruments and risk management strategies that might be employed by Colombian institutions, let us first summarize the conclusions of the analyses described above.

- Colombia's resource balance is highly exposed to coffee prices but not to petroleum prices. However, recent increases in petroleum production and exports and declines in coffee exports imply increased exposure to fluctuations in petroleum prices.
- Colombia's public sector revenue is exposed to coffee price fluctuations. However, the rise in the importance of petroleum production implies an increased exposure to world petroleum prices. If the National Coffee Fund is excluded, the dependence on coffee prices is reduced to an insignificant level.
- Marketing arrangements in the coffee sector distribute world price risks among various sectors. The National Coffee Fund plays an important role in this process and has a serious exposure to world coffee price changes.

- ECOPETROL is clearly exposed to world petroleum prices, both through its own activities and through the use of association contracts with private companies.

The most appealing solution to the risk management problems of the National Coffee Federation and ECOPETROL is for them to develop, respectively, coffee and oil hedging strategies. However, if this approach is taken, some attention should be paid to the question of overhedging. Oil and coffee prices are not perfectly correlated; the correlation coefficient between oil and coffee prices is 0.51 for the period 1970–88, implying that total exports are relatively less variable than coffee or oil exports alone. Hence, as in any standard portfolio problem, the public sector already has some gains from diversification. To exploit these gains, some planning is necessary.

Consider risk management strategies for the National Coffee Federation. As argued above, the federation in effect grants a put option with an exercise price set at the federation's minimum price. However, returns to the federation are affected by the changes in taxation as the world price changes. The minimum domestic price moves with the world price to some extent, although the domestic price is considerably more stable than the world price. The federation is thus exposed in two respects. First, once the minimum price is set, there is a strong exposure to world price movements between the time the federation buys at the minimum price and the time it sells at the world price. A hedging strategy to deal with this risk would be to purchase a similar put on, say, the New York futures exchange or to mimic a put option hedging strategy through selling coffee short and adjusting the hedge position as the world coffee price changes. The details of this hedging strategy would be affected by the way in which the taxation system might be used to stabilize federation revenues. Second, there is a longer-term exposure to coffee prices because the internal minimum price is not adjusted strictly with world coffee price movements. Given that long-term option contracts can be expensive and that constructing long-run futures positions might be risky because of rollover risks, the most appropriate method to hedge the risk of coffee price movements might be to denominate a portion of federation debt in the form of coffee-contingent securities (if this is possible).

Now consider risk management strategies for private exporters. Private exporters have exposure to two types of risks. First, the world price might move between the time a private exporter purchases the coffee and the time it sells the coffee on the world market. In this case, an appropriate hedging strategy would be to take a short position on a futures contract of a duration commensurate with the time lag involved. Alternatively, a private exporter could purchase a put option as insurance against a decline in the world price. Second, private exporters face a longer-term risk because, if world coffee prices decline and the federation is committed to maintaining a stable internal price in Colombia, the margin to exporters must decline. In other words, margins must to some extent reflect the world price. Again, the appropriate hedge is to take a short position in futures or to purchase put options. Or the exporter could seek some form of commodity-linked finance.

As for coffee producers, although they are insured to a significant extent at the minimum price offered by the federation, they may still have some risk. The federation does change the minimum price with world price movements. Hence, a longer-term hedge for producers might be appropriate. The most appropriate form of hedge might be through the credit market by using loans with interest rates or principal dependent on coffee prices. However, it might be more appropriate for the federation to keep internal prices even more stable in the face of world price movements and in effect perform the hedging operations on behalf of the producers.

ECOPETROL has the standard risks associated with a commodity producer. In addition, it carries risks arising from its participation in association contracts. For ECOPETROL's own activities, price insurance could be obtained through the purchase of put options or through selling futures contracts. Oil-indexed finance might also be an attractive proposition for ECOPETROL's own exploration and drilling. Exposure through the association contract is present only if a commercial field is discovered, after which ECOPETROL participates in the associated costs and revenues. This is analogous to ECOPETROL's owning a call option. The field is commercial if the world price of oil is above the unit extraction costs. Hence, either the field is not commercial (the world oil price is too low, given the reserves discovered) and the "option" expires worthless, or the field is commercial and ECOPETROL earns a share of the oil price minus the unit extraction costs for each barrel produced. If ECOPETROL wished to stabilize all its revenues, it could hedge the returns from the association contracts. Doing so would require some careful analysis of the success rate of associate exploration, but one possibility is that ECOPETROL could sell call options to hedge its own "call option," as described above.

Conclusions

The analysis indicates that Colombia's external debt composition is far from optimal. In particular, fixed rate dollar liabilities do not appear to have good risk-sharing characteristics, given the currency-commodity correlations appropriate to Colombia. LIBOR-denominated dollar debts become more attractive only as petroleum becomes a more important component of exports. However, all these results should be treated with caution. In particular, the covariances that are estimated may be unstable over time. Conducting the analysis over a different time period might give different results (see further Cartiglia 1989). A robust result is the value of commodity-contingent liabilities. Both coffee- and oil-contingent liabilities have large proportions in the optimal composition of external debt. The strong policy implication is that Colombia should attempt to link its debt-servicing payments to the outcome of commodity prices and in this way stabilize its resource balance.

Notes

1. The high percentage of debt having variable interest rates may reflect a short supply of fixed rate contracts. This may, in turn, be caused by an unwillingness on the part of commercial banks to be vulnerable to interest rate risk with a developing-country counterparty.

2. See Gilbert (1990) on the effect of exchange rate changes on commodity prices.

3. It is reported in Thomas (1985) that the price paid by private exporters tends to be slightly less than the federation's minimum price. The price is lower because the coffee sold to the private exporters tends to be of slightly lower quality than that sold to the federation, and the private exporters use the poorer-quality coffee to pay the retention tax.

4. It might also be conjectured that the amount of coffee exported by private traders increases as the world price rises.

5. The contracts are made more complex because, although an initial area of land is contracted to the associate, after a certain period of time ECOPETROL may claw back parts of this land. Thus, if a commercial field is discovered on one part of the land, then ECOPETROL may, after a certain period of time, conduct its own drilling operations on nearby land clawed back from the associate. The contracts appear to be designed to give ECOPETROL maximum benefit from the exploration skills of the private oil companies. The contracts certainly make ECOPETROL's own exploration risks very low.

6. To understand how government accounts are affected by a devaluation of the peso, it is necessary to distinguish between tradables and nontradables as sources of government revenues and expenditures. This is not a common distinction within the usual national accounting framework but is the natural distinction in all models concerning the effects of trade shocks, including the so-called Dutch disease models (see, for instance, Kamas 1986).

7. There is considerable flexibility in option purchases, because a selection of exercise prices is generally available. However, ensuring a higher minimum return (higher exercise price) means paying a higher premium.

8. I am indebted to Santiago Montenegro for assistance with the national accounts data.

9. Note that, in reality, variable interest (LIBOR) rates are also available in currencies other than the dollar. If uncovered interest parity (UIP) is correct, then borrowing costs in different currencies at variable interest rates should be equivalent. I concentrate here on the case of fixed interest rates in nondollar currencies.

13

Financial Risk Management in Sub-Saharan Africa

Stijn Claessens and Ying Qian

This chapter investigates the vulnerability of the forty-four countries in Sub-Saharan Africa to commodity price, exchange rate, and interest rate uncertainty. Although there are considerable differences among these countries, they do share a number of common characteristics: heavy dependence on primary commodity exports, heavy reliance on outside aid, large debt burdens (with large nondollar debts), poor infrastructure, and low levels of education (see further Husain and Underwood 1991). Because of these similarities the countries are studied in this chapter as a group.

The chapter identifies commodity price risk as the most significant external exposure of Sub-Saharan Africa. Countries in Sub-Saharan Africa are particularly vulnerable to commodity price changes, given both the large share of primary commodities in total exports as well as the large share of essential foods in their imports. It is concluded that financial instruments to manage commodity price risk would provide these countries with significant risk reduction benefits. Creditors would also gain from the introduction of commodity price–linked finance because it would reduce their credit risk.

To account for the possible interactions between external risks, an optimal portfolio of external financial instruments is estimated for Sub-Saharan Africa. It is shown that the risk-minimizing portfolio consists of only about 30 percent general-obligation loans and about 70 percent loans in which repayment obligations are indexed to the price of Sub-Saharan Africa's most important exports: cocoa, coffee, cotton, copper, and oil. This portfolio results in a reduction of the uncertainty of Sub-Saharan Africa's resources available for imports by about 90 percent. The risk reduction benefit of the optimal portfolio is fairly stable with respect to the commodities included and the time period over which the portfolio is estimated.

Financial instruments that are linked to the price of a commodity can achieve external diversification of risk. Many governments in Sub-Saharan Africa have adopted stabilization schemes for domestic prices of commodities. However, these schemes generally do not transfer the risk of price movements outside the economy. As a result, external price shocks are largely absorbed by the government's budget, through the stabilization schemes. Although commodity price–linked financial instruments can insulate these economies from external price movements, use of the instruments may require mechanisms internal to the country for allocating the benefits of external price risk reduction among the public sector, parastatals, and the private sector so that the final producer or consumer receives the benefits. This chapter does not discuss how to carry out this internal risk management, nor does it discuss any issues related to nonconvertibility or capital controls that may prevent the private sector from undertaking external risk management. The issue of internal transfer of external risk management is investigated in other chapters in this volume.

The chapter begins by discussing the major external exposures faced by Sub-Saharan Africa. The next section discusses issues related to risk identification and risk measurement. The risk exposures of Sub-Saharan Africa are then matched up with financial instruments available in the capital markets of developed countries in order to identify the optimal external liability portfolio for Sub-Saharan Africa. The concluding section offers some policy recommendations.

The Nature and Magnitude of the Exposures

Commodity Exposures

Sub-Saharan Africa faces large risks because of its relatively undiversified sources of export earnings. Exports of most countries in Sub-Saharan Africa are concentrated in a few primary commodities. Over the 1965–88 period five key commodities accounted for roughly 75 percent of the region's total exports (see table 13-1), and fish, iron ore, tea, timber, and tobacco accounted for another 9 percent.[1] Among thirty-five African countries for which export data are available for 1984–85, these ten commodities accounted for more than 80 percent of total exports in eight countries, more than 60 percent in nineteen countries, and more than 40 percent in twenty-five countries. The share of the single largest

Table 13-1. *Share of the Top Five Commodities in Total Exports of Sub-Saharan Africa, 1965–88*
(percent)

Year	Share of top five	Cocoa	Coffee	Cotton	Copper	Crude oil
1965	44.94	7.15	12.15	4.03	16.29	5.32
1966	50.34	6.55	12.65	4.30	20.96	5.88
1967	52.55	8.28	12.01	5.06	21.47	5.72
1968	52.81	8.64	12.94	5.17	24.00	2.07
1969	55.55	9.44	9.84	4.50	25.14	6.63
1970	59.98	8.38	11.59	4.52	23.62	11.86
1971	59.02	7.32	11.26	4.29	14.90	21.25
1972	58.78	5.98	10.03	3.85	14.24	24.68
1973	60.92	6.01	9.48	3.41	15.68	26.35
1974	73.10	4.92	6.44	2.33	12.85	46.56
1975	69.20	5.82	6.79	2.16	7.58	46.84
1976	69.22	5.12	10.02	2.65	7.03	44.40
1977	74.28	7.62	14.40	2.58	6.13	43.55
1978	72.00	10.96	12.89	2.19	5.96	39.99
1979	70.80	6.51	8.58	1.97	5.62	48.12
1980	75.81	4.41	6.60	1.52	5.15	58.13
1981	77.62	4.53	5.93	1.69	4.99	60.49
1982	86.72	4.80	8.02	1.54	5.12	67.24
1983	81.58	4.68	8.51	2.33	5.59	60.48
1984	81.46	5.23	8.11	2.67	4.63	60.81
1985	85.73	6.09	7.54	2.06	4.55	65.48
1986	71.82	7.51	13.60	2.60	5.42	42.69
1987	65.51	6.84	8.47	2.81	5.60	41.80
1988	40.71	3.68	4.21	1.33	2.96	28.54
Average	74.11	6.52	9.67	2.98	11.06	36.04
Standard deviation	12.45	1.74	2.67	1.16	7.25	21.02

Source: Authors' calculations, based on World Bank data.

commodity exceeded 50 percent in twelve countries and exceeded 30 percent in twenty-four of the thirty-five countries (see table 13-2).

This high degree of commodity dependence continues into the 1990s for most countries in Sub-Saharan Africa. For some the reliance on the leading commodity increased in the 1980s as production of other commodities fell because of increased competition from other regions, falling prices, and domestic disincentives. A few countries, such as Kenya, have diversified their composition of commodity exports but remain heavily dependent on primary products. Successful efforts to diversify significantly into intermediate and final export products have been limited to exceptional cases, such as Mauritius.[2]

Table 13-2. *Commodity Export Concentration in Sub-Saharan Africa, 1984–85*

Share of total exports (percent)	Number of countries in which ten key commodities have the indicated share	Number of countries in which the leading commodity has the indicated share
90	3	2
80	8	5
70	15	1
60	19	3
50	21	1
40	25	6
30	28	6

Source: World Bank data.

At the same time, world prices for Sub-Saharan Africa's main exports have been very volatile. During the last decade the annual volatility of an index of nominal prices for thirty-three primary commodities has been more than 20 percent. In figure 13-1 the annualized standard deviation of the monthly price changes during the previous twenty-four months is plotted for the period 1962–90. As can be observed, this standard deviation has reached levels up to 90 percent and has in recent years not been below 20 percent. Some primary commodities have experienced price changes that are not only large but also extremely rapid. Coffee prices, for example, fell by a third in the last three months of 1987 and again by 45 percent between April and August of 1989.

Commodity prices also tend to be highly correlated with each other; therefore, the export of several commodities does not present an effective diversification strategy. Table 13-3 lists the correlation coefficients between the prices of the top nine commodities in Sub-Saharan Africa and between these commodities and the World Bank's index of thirty-three primary commodity prices. Most of these correlations are significantly positive and quite high. Table 13-4 lists the correlations of the commodity prices deflated by the import price index for Sub-Saharan Africa.[3] With the exception of crude oil and logs, the real prices of the nine commodities are positively related to each other and with the general index.

Compounding the impact of volatile prices has been the fact that in the 1980s the trend underlying the volatile price swings has been downward. The real price index for thirty-three primary non-oil commodities,[4] also plotted in figure 13-1, has declined by 33 percent since 1980 and is now at its lowest level since World War II. Real crude oil prices fell by 60 percent between 1980 and 1989, reaching their lowest level since 1973.

Figure 13-1. *Price Volatility and Index of Prices of Primary Commodities, Sub-Saharan Africa, 1962–90*

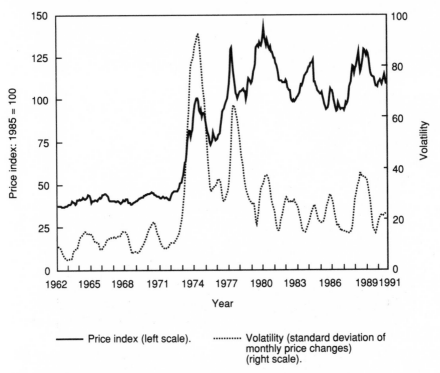

Price index (left scale). ·········· Volatility (standard deviation of monthly price changes) (right scale).

Source: International Monetary Fund (various issues).

Several international price stabilization schemes—for cocoa, coffee, and tin—have collapsed in recent years, and beverage commodities especially have seen a sharp decline in prices.

Although export prices for Sub-Saharan African countries have declined, the prices of imports for these countries have increased considerably. The higher prices of imports are in part a reflection of a worldwide increase in prices but in part also a result of factors specific to Sub-Saharan African countries, such as relatively small markets and limited access to competitive suppliers (see further Yeats 1990). As a result, Sub-Saharan Africa's terms-of-trade index in 1989 was approximately 25 percent below that of 1980, implying a significant income loss. Figure 13-2 depicts the export and import price indexes, terms of trade, and the purchasing power of exports (nominal export values deflated by import prices) for Sub-Saharan Africa from 1965 to 1988. A few countries in

Table 13-3. *Correlation Coefficients for the Nominal Prices of the Top Nine Commodity Exports of Sub-Saharan Africa, 1965–89*

	Cocoa	Coffee	Tea	Cotton	Tobacco	Logs	Copper	Iron ore	Crude oil	Index 33[a]
Cocoa	1.00000	0.92161	0.80796	0.80251	0.73166	0.61288	0.29553	0.71387	0.64582	0.84697
	(0.0000)	(0.0001)	(0.0001)	(0.0001)	(0.0001)	(0.0015)	(0.1609)	(0.0001)	(0.0007)	(0.0001)
Coffee	0.92161	1.00000	0.80967	0.74083	0.78070	0.69343	0.28121	0.77812	0.67415	0.84939
	(0.0001)	(0.0000)	(0.0001)	(0.0001)	(0.0001)	(0.0002)	(0.1831)	(0.0001)	(0.0003)	(0.0001)
Tea	0.80796	0.80967	1.00000	0.73632	0.75323	0.65350	0.20138	0.72773	0.75844	0.78587
	(0.0001)	(0.0001)	(0.0000)	(0.0001)	(0.0001)	(0.0005)	(0.3454)	(0.0001)	(0.0001)	(0.0001)
Cotton	0.80251	0.74083	0.73632	1.00000	0.83881	0.75872	0.50213	0.87814	0.83740	0.92574
	(0.0001)	(0.0001)	(0.0001)	(0.0000)	(0.0001)	(0.0001)	(0.0124)	(0.0001)	(0.0001)	(0.0001)
Tobacco	0.73166	0.78070	0.75323	0.83881	1.00000	0.86809	0.45055	0.93125	0.94600	0.91710
	(0.0001)	(0.0001)	(0.0001)	(0.0001)	(0.0000)	(0.0001)	(0.0271)	(0.0001)	(0.0001)	(0.0001)
Logs	0.61288	0.69343	0.65350	0.75872	0.86809	1.00000	0.67476	0.83752	0.78309	0.87466
	(0.0015)	(0.0002)	(0.0005)	(0.0001)	(0.0001)	(0.0000)	(0.0003)	(0.0001)	(0.0001)	(0.0001)
Copper	0.29553	0.28121	0.20138	0.50213	0.45055	0.67476	1.00000	0.50087	0.37738	0.62104
	(0.1609)	(0.1831)	(0.3454)	(0.0124)	(0.0271)	(0.0003)	(0.0000)	(0.0127)	(0.0691)	(0.0012)
Iron ore	0.71387	0.77812	0.72773	0.87814	0.93125	0.83752	0.50087	1.00000	0.89306	0.93054
	(0.0001)	(0.0001)	(0.0001)	(0.0001)	(0.0001)	(0.0001)	(0.0127)	(0.0000)	(0.0001)	(0.0001)
Crude oil	0.64582	0.67415	0.75844	0.83740	0.94600	0.78309	0.37738	0.89306	1.00000	0.85202
	(0.0007)	(0.0003)	(0.0001)	(0.0001)	(0.0001)	(0.0001)	(0.0691)	(0.0001)	(0.0000)	(0.0001)
Index 33[a]	0.84697	0.84939	0.78587	0.92574	0.91710	0.87466	0.62104	0.93054	0.85202	1.00000
	(0.0001)	(0.0001)	(0.0001)	(0.0001)	(0.0001)	(0.0001)	(0.0012)	(0.0001)	(0.0001)	(0.0000)

Note: Numbers in parentheses are the *p*-values for the correlation coefficients.
a. World Bank nonoil primary commodity price index.
Source: Authors' calculations.

Table 13-4. *Correlation Coefficients for Real Prices of the Top Nine Commodity Exports of Sub-Saharan Africa, 1965–89*

	Cocoa	Coffee	Tea	Cotton	Tobacco	Logs	Copper	Iron ore	Crude oil	Index 33
Cocoa	1.00000	0.74573	0.20972	0.28113	0.13319	-0.16773	0.03494	-0.00951	-0.04050	0.29157
	(0.0000)	(0.0001)	(0.3253)	(0.1833)	(0.5350)	(0.4334)	(0.8712)	(0.9648)	(0.8510)	(0.1669)
Coffee	0.74573	1.00000	0.39410	0.25870	0.17169	-0.19422	0.10733	0.20854	-0.20221	0.33071
	(0.0001)	(0.0000)	(0.0567)	(0.2222)	(0.4224)	(0.3631)	(0.6177)	(0.3281)	(0.3433)	(0.1145)
Tea	0.20972	0.39410	1.00000	0.68141	0.82773	-0.06346	0.82288	0.89363	-0.65161	0.85945
	(0.3253)	(0.0567)	(0.0000)	(0.0002)	(0.0001)	(0.7683)	(0.0001)	(0.0001)	(0.0006)	(0.0001)
Cotton	0.28113	0.25870	0.68141	1.00000	0.68315	-0.13021	0.75813	0.77594	-0.63926	0.88354
	(0.1833)	(0.2222)	(0.0002)	(0.0000)	(0.0001)	(0.5442)	(0.0001)	(0.0001)	(0.0008)	(0.0001)
Tobacco	0.13319	0.17169	0.82773	0.68315	1.00000	-0.03186	0.86460	0.86845	-0.67411	0.83737
	(0.5350)	(0.4224)	(0.0001)	(0.0001)	(0.0000)	(0.8825)	(0.0001)	(0.0001)	(0.0003)	(0.0001)
Logs	-0.16773	-0.19422	-0.06346	-0.13021	-0.03186	1.00000	0.10985	-0.07623	-0.06315	-0.05679
	(0.4334)	(0.3631)	(0.7683)	(0.5442)	(0.8825)	(0.0000)	(0.6094)	(0.7233)	(0.7694)	(0.7921)
Copper	0.03494	0.10733	0.82288	0.75813	0.86460	0.10985	1.00000	0.93219	-0.80026	0.93629
	(0.8712)	(0.6177)	(0.0001)	(0.0001)	(0.0001)	(0.6094)	(0.0000)	(0.0001)	(0.0001)	(0.0001)
Iron ore	-0.00951	0.20854	0.89363	0.77594	0.86845	-0.07623	0.93219	1.00000	-0.77466	0.91708
	(0.9648)	(0.3281)	(0.0001)	(0.0001)	(0.0001)	(0.7233)	(0.0001)	(0.0000)	(0.0001)	(0.0001)
Crude oil	-0.04050	-0.20221	-0.65161	-0.63926	-0.67411	-0.06315	-0.80026	-0.77466	1.00000	-0.75907
	(0.8510)	(0.3433)	(0.0006)	(0.0008)	(0.0003)	(0.7694)	(0.0001)	(0.0001)	(0.0000)	(0.0001)
Index 33[a]	0.29157	0.33071	0.85945	0.88354	0.83737	-0.05679	0.93629	0.91708	-0.75907	1.00000
	(0.1669)	(0.1145)	(0.0001)	(0.0001)	(0.0001)	(0.7921)	(0.0001)	(0.0001)	(0.0001)	(0.0000)

Note: Real prices are prices deflated by the import price index for Sub-Saharan Africa. Numbers in parentheses are the *p*-values for the correlation coefficients.

a. World Bank nonoil primary commodity price index.

Source: Authors' calculations.

Figure 13-2. *Export and Import Price Trends in Sub-Saharan Africa,*
1965–88

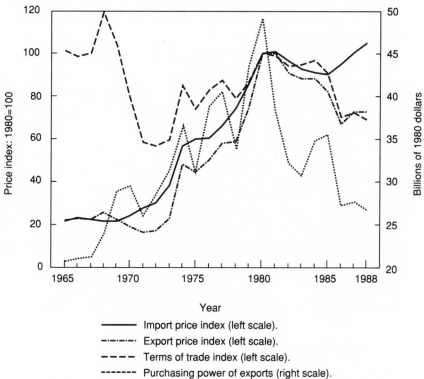

Year

——————— Import price index (left scale).

—·—·—·— Export price index (left scale).

— — — — Terms of trade index (left scale).

------- Purchasing power of exports (right scale).

Source: World Bank data.

Sub-Saharan Africa were able to post a terms-of-trade gain during the
1980s, but most earned in real terms less foreign exchange from exports
in 1989 than in 1980, in spite of increases in the volume of exports.

Thus the heavy dependence of Sub-Saharan African countries on primary commodity exports implies that they have been faced with considerable uncertainty regarding the real value of their exports around a
declining trend. If these countries adopt competitive exchange rates and
reduce the anti-export bias of their current protectionist policies, then, in
the longer term, the development of exports other than primary commodities can be expected, leading to diversification and a reduction in
the volatility of export earnings (see further Culagovski and others
1991). However, it is unlikely that Sub-Saharan Africa will reduce its

reliance on primary commodity exports significantly in the near future. In any case, it is likely that primary commodity prices will remain highly volatile in the 1990s and that many Sub-Saharan African countries will continue to be faced with considerable uncertainty in export revenues, in nominal as well as in real terms.

Currency and Interest Rate Exposures

The external exposure of Sub-Saharan African countries arises not only from their commodity exports but also from their external debt structures (see table 13-5). There are two dimensions here: interest rates and cross-currency exchange rates. About 33 percent of the external debt of Sub-Saharan African countries is variable rate debt (either debt that is indexed to a floating rate or short-term debt that is rolled over). The share that is variable rate debt is substantially below that of all developing countries (and that of the highly indebted, middle-income countries in particular) because of the large share of concessional and official fixed rate debt. Nevertheless, the share that is variable rate debt gives the countries in Sub-Saharan Africa substantial exposure to the volatility of international interest rates.

Currency risk arises because the external debt of Sub-Saharan African countries is denominated in several hard currencies. Approximately 40

Table 13-5. *Debt, Net Flows, and Currency Valuation Effects,*
Sub-Saharan Africa, 1982–89
(billions of dollars)

Year	Debt[a]	Net flows	Currency valuation effect[b]	Currency valuation effect[b] (percent of total debt)
1982	70.3	10.2	−2.3	−3.3
1983	79.3	7.9	−3.1	−3.9
1984	82.7	5.3	−3.6	−4.4
1985	96.0	2.7	6.2	6.5
1986	112.7	5.9	6.7	5.9
1987	137.7	6.8	10.8	7.8
1988	139.5	4.2	−6.0	−4.3
1989	148.5	4.1	—	—

— Not available.

a. Debt outstanding and disbursed.

b. The currency valuation effect is the change in the dollar value of debt resulting from fluctuations of currencies in which debt is denominated against the dollar. It includes the adjustment on loans from the International Bank of Reconstruction and Development and other multicurrency loans.

Source: World Bank data.

Table 13-6. *Currency Composition of Medium- and Long-Term Public External Debt and of New Borrowings, Sub-Saharan Africa, 1988* (percent)

	Dollars	French francs	Yen	Swiss francs	Mixed currencies	Deutsche marks	Other
Debt stock[a]	38.3	13.8	4.2	2.5	11.0	7.1	23.1
Debt stock[a] [b]	40.5	13.8	7.7	4.5	—	8.9	24.6
New borrowings[c]	37.8	15.2	3.8	0.2	10.5	3.8	28.7
New borrowings[b] [c]	39.9	15.2	7.2	2.1	—	5.5	30.1

— Not available.

Note: Except as noted, the currency composition of medium- and long-term debt does not include the currency composition of loans from the International Bank of Reconstruction and Development, which are about one-third U.S. dollar and two-thirds non-U.S. dollar. All figures refer only to public or publicly guaranteed debt.

a. As of the end of 1988.

b. Includes the currency composition of IBRD loans.

c. During 1988.

Source: World Bank data.

percent of Sub-Saharan Africa's medium- and long-term debt is in dollars, 14 percent in French francs, 8 percent in yen, and 43 percent in other currencies (see table 13-6).[5] This composition of debt implies that the debt service for Sub-Saharan Africa, measured in any currency, will be affected by movements in the cross-currency rates between these hard currencies. For instance, the depreciation of the dollar between 1985 and 1988 increased the dollar-measured debt service of Sub-Saharan Africa by approximately 7 percent on an annual basis compared with a situation in which cross-currency rates had remained at their end-1985 level (see further table 13-5).[6] In general, the volatility of nominal (and real) cross-currency exchange rates has been very high during the 1980s (the annual standard deviation of the nominal and real effective U.S. dollar rate has been above 20 percent) and significantly above levels experienced in earlier periods. The fluctuations in the level of debt stocks and debt service (whether measured in dollars or in any other hard currency) are likely to continue, given the fact that the share of non-U.S. dollar currencies in Sub-Saharan Africa's debt, including new borrowings, remains high (see table 13-6) and given the fact that the volatility of cross-currency exchange rates is not likely to decline in the near future. The currency composition of funds borrowed during 1988 (39.9 percent dollars, 60.1 percent other currencies) is similar to the composition of the existing debt stock (40.5 percent dollars, 59.9 percent other currencies), implying that the dollar value of debt will continue to fluctuate as currencies fluctuate.

Interest and currency fluctuations could have affected the countries of

Sub-Saharan Africa adversely if the resulting changes in debt service had not been matched by commensurate changes in the value of net earnings in hard currencies. Whether or not debt service and earnings were matched, and its implications for the measurement and management of exposure, is explored in the next section.

The Impact of Exposures

Sub-Saharan Africa's high dependence on exports of primary commodities for foreign exchange earnings, and the interest and currency composition of its external debt, combined with the high volatilities of these external variables, all imply large external exposures for Sub-Saharan African countries. The likely impact of these external uncertainties and exposures on the economies of Sub-Saharan Africa is threefold. First, it results in a highly variable income and consumption stream, lowering the country's welfare (see Newbery and Stiglitz 1981). Second, it complicates the government's and private sector's planning and investment processes and (as a result) likely leads to lower (private) investment and a lower long-run output level. Third, it makes the economy vulnerable to what is called Dutch (or Nigerian) disease, where, in times of favorable external prices for the major export products, other export activities become less competitive as a result of the real appreciation of the currency and other distortions that take place because of the commodity boom (see Balassa 1989; Cuddington 1989).

The key question this chapter will attempt to answer is whether, from an ex ante point of view, Sub-Saharan Africa's current external liability structure provides the optimal amount of risk sharing between creditors and debtors, or whether a better structure is feasible that allows for gains for both parties. A key concept is ex ante risk sharing. As the experience of the 1980s has shown, ex post, the impact of external shocks on the ability of countries to service their external debts has been shared between creditors and debtors in the form of reschedulings, debt write-offs, and internal and external adjustments by the countries. The end result has been significantly lower growth rates in the countries. This ex post risk sharing has come with considerable lost output–deadweight losses that could have been avoided through a better ex ante structuring of the external debt structure.

Conceptual Issues in the Measurement of Exposure

The previous section clearly established that Sub-Saharan Africa faces large contractual exposures to commodity price and exchange rate uncertainty and, to a lesser extent, to interest rate movements. We now investigate, from a theoretical point of view, whether some of these contractual exposures to price changes may be less in real terms because of some offsetting relationships among these and other external variables. This analysis will become the basis of the calculations used above to measure exposure and determine the optimal liability structure.

Concepts for Measuring Risk Exposure

It has been long recognized in the literature that exposures cannot be measured by contractual (accounting) concepts alone. In the economic literature, this was made clear by Newbery and Stiglitz (1981). One of their insights was that commodity price risks can to a significant extent be offset by quantity risks. In the case of a net commodity exporter, if the price elasticity of demand is different from zero, quantity changes will offset the effect of price changes on total earnings. The net exposure of the country to commodity price risks would then be less than the nominal value exported. In the extreme case, when the price elasticity is −1, revenues would be independent of price movements, because quantity movements would perfectly offset price movements and there would be no need to hedge against price movements. Figure 13-2 illustrates this relationship: the dollar value of exports for Sub-Saharan Africa behaves quite differently from the price index of exports.

In the finance literature, the appropriate measurement of risk has been part of mainstream thinking since the capital asset pricing model was developed in the early 1960s. The main concept of the model is that the risk of holding an individual asset (or, equivalently, an income stream) needs to be defined with respect to a measure of aggregate risk (such as the risk of holding a diversified portfolio of assets). Risks that are diversifiable do not need to be carried and consequently do not receive any higher expected return (risk premium). Only nondiversifiable (systematic) risks require a risk premium.[7] For a country receiving an income stream through its (net) exports, this implies two things. First, risks that arise from movements in commodity prices, interest rates, and exchange rates need to be defined in an integrated fashion and in relation to the country's aggregate economic risks. Second, risks that are in principle diversifiable in the world's capital markets (or can be carried in world capital markets at lower costs) need not be carried by the country and, if they are carried, will not receive a higher rate of return for the country.

The strands of thought coming from both the economics and finance streams have important implications not only for the measurement of commodity price risks, where quantity movements can be important, but also for the measurement of interest and currency price risks. The implications are that changes in debt service which result from movements in interest and exchange rates represent a change in the burden on the country (that is, the country's "risk") only to the extent that the country's capacity to service debt does not move commensurately.

Important for the determination of Sub-Saharan Africa's ability to generate foreign exchange, which will determine the true burden of changes in exchange rates on debt service, will be the relationship between primary commodity prices and the value of the dollar—because Sub-Saharan Africa derives such a large share of its capacity to service its debt from primary commodity exports and because a substantial part of Sub-Saharan Africa's debt is in non-U.S. dollar currencies. It has long been observed that, in general, commodity prices (measured in dollar terms) tend to move inversely with the value of the dollar. That is, when the dollar increases in value, commodity prices tend to decline and vice versa (see, for instance, Dornbusch 1987). This relationship does not appear over shorter periods but manifests itself in general over long cycles.[8] The chapter by Powell applies this concept to Colombia to determine the optimal currency composition of its external debt.

The inverse relationship between the dollar exchange rate and commodity prices is confirmed for the prices of most of the commodities important to Sub-Saharan Africa. For instance, over the period 1974–89, changes in nominal prices of cocoa, coffee, cotton, copper, and sugar had a negative relationship with changes in the index of the nominal effective dollar exchange rate. The negative relationship could imply that a combination of primary commodity exports and nondollar debts has some benefits, because when a depreciation of the dollar makes debt service payments go up, primary commodity export revenues measured in dollars are likely to go up too, and vice versa.

There is an additional aspect important for external risk management: measures such as exports and debt service are nominal and need to be translated into real terms. This can be done through the concept of the purchasing power of exports—the nominal value of exports divided by import prices, which provides a good measuring unit of the real value of exports. Similarly, nominal debt service payments need to be adjusted for price movements.[9]

The outcome of these interactions between commodity prices, exchange rates, and import prices and quantities can be such that the effective exposure of the country to movements in commodity prices, interest rates, and exchange rates is different from what contractual and nominal measures—such as exports and debt service—would indicate. Strategies to manage these risks only on the basis of contractual values could therefore be misleading.

Practical Models for Risk Measurement

Several practical models exist for determining real exposures. Some of these have already been applied to countries with large external exposures.[10] The empirical results indicate that there exist some offsetting effects between commodity price, quantity, import price, and exchange rate movements. For most of these countries, however, the offsetting effects were seen to be small, and, as a result, effective exposures coincided to a considerable extent with nominal measures.

In determining the optimal liability structure of a country, two additional issues need to be recognized. First, external risks should be measured and managed with respect to net liabilities (which are external liabilities minus all external assets such as foreign exchange reserves). Second, (net) external liabilities have to be managed on the basis of a tradeoff between the expected effective cost of a particular financial instrument and the uncertainty of its effective cost (where both cost and uncertainty have to be measured in relation to the economy's ability to pay). This tradeoff implies that the optimal external liability choice can be split up into two components: a speculative component and a hedging component. The speculative component depends, among other things, on the expected costs of the different liabilities. It is reasonable to argue that even though costs of different types of liabilities will differ, these differences will not be significant enough from the point of view of the country to justify taking speculative positions. For instance, the expected costs of borrowing in different currencies, after adjusting for expected changes in exchange rates, will not differ much from one another, because movements in cross-currency exchange rates can be expected to compensate for nominal interest differentials.[11] Similar effects exist for other liabilities. The result of borrowing costs that are expected to be equal is that the speculative portfolio disappears, leaving the hedging portfolio. The hedging portfolio is based on risk minimization. The basic rule for liability choice should therefore be risk minimization, and external exposures should be hedged as much as possible.

The Preferred Liability Structure: A Mixture of Instruments

We will now match up the external exposures of Sub-Saharan Africa with the hedging instruments that are available by calculating the optimal liability structure of Sub-Saharan Africa. We will do this for the Sub-Saharan African countries as a group, realizing that individual countries will have different economic structures and therefore different optimal liability structures. The purpose of this section, therefore, is only to indicate what the benefits could be for the countries of Sub-Saharan Africa as a group to have a liability structure with more ex ante risk sharing.

The derivation of Sub-Saharan Africa's optimal liability structure can be done from two perspectives: for the economy as a whole and for the government's budget alone. The analyses can either be based on historical data or be based on a sensitivity analysis of expected future flows. Thus there are four possible types of analyses, all based on cash flows derived from exports of commodities and other goods and cash flows paid on imports and debt service. Here we perform an empirical analysis only on historical data, but indicate the possibilities of the other approaches.

We use the model developed by Myers and Thompson (1991). The model is also used in the chapter by Coleman and Qian on Papua New Guinea, and we refer the reader to the appendixes of their chapter for further details. The only difference between their application and the application here is that we do not consider currency risk in the determination of the optimal portfolio.[12] Because commodity risk is the most important external risk Sub-Saharan Africa faces, it was decided to include only commodity price–linked bonds and general-obligation dollar loans in the liability portfolio. Coleman and Qian show that the objective function this model uses implies that the optimal liability portfolio will be a hedging portfolio, one that minimizes the impact Sub-Saharan Africa faces from external factors.[13] The model here differs from that used in the chapter by Powell: Powell uses the empirical relationships between commodity prices, interest rates, and exchange rates to determine how conventional borrowings with fixed or variable interest rates can serve as hedges against changes in commodity prices. Thus Powell does not consider commodity price–linked bonds but does include general-obligation nondollar, as well dollar, loans in the liability portfolio, whereas we consider commodity price–linked bonds but include only general-obligation dollar loans.

The model requires as inputs total export earnings, the commodity prices for which financial hedging instruments exist, population numbers, and import prices. Population numbers are used to scale data, and import prices are used to calculate the terms of trade for each commodity. To calculate the optimal liability portfolio (a vector of) conditional covariances between prices and exports and (a matrix of) conditional covariances of prices were estimated from the residuals of a vector autoregressive (VAR) process. The model was run using annual data from

1965 to 1988 for five commodities: coffee, cocoa, copper, cotton, and crude oil. Together, these five commodities accounted for more than 70 percent of Sub-Saharan Africa's total exports over the period 1980–88 (see table 13-1). Estimation of the optimal hedging portfolio starts with a VAR process such as $A(L)y_t = \epsilon_t$, where y_t are the variables of interest in the portfolio selection process and ϵ_t are white noise error terms. The VAR process helps to predict future export revenues and commodity prices. More important, the VAR process generates the conditional covariance matrix from which the theoretical optimal hedging portfolio can be derived.

The stationarity of variables used in the model was investigated before the actual estimation process was carried out. According to results of a set of standard unit root tests, the unit root hypothesis was rejected for all of the model's variables, including export earnings and commodity prices for cocoa, coffee, cotton, copper, and crude oil. Table 13-7 presents statistics from stationarity tests without a time trend. Durbin-Watson (DW) test statistics confirm that export earnings, and prices of cocoa, coffee, and cotton, are stationary at a 95 percent level of significance. The stationarity of the coffee price is also confirmed by the augmented Dickey-Fuller (ADF) test at a 95 percent level of significance. When a time trend is added to the stationarity test, as in table 13-8, all variables are validated as stationary at a 95 percent level according to the DW test, and prices of cocoa, coffee, and cotton are stationary at a 95 percent level according to the Dickey-Fuller (DF) or ADF tests. Before the unrestricted VAR specification was finalized, SAS STEPWISE procedures were applied to search for the best-fitting model, that is, the one with the most significant variables and lag structures. Table 13-9 presents the VAR model in its reduced form.

The seemingly uncorrelated regression (SUR) technique was next applied to estimate the VAR system. It was used because the estimation method for maximum likelihood was not available in SAS. The coefficient matrix $A(L)$ defined by the VAR process, and the conditional covariance matrix derived from the VAR residuals, were then used to determine the optimal portfolio.

Table 13-10 presents two covariance matrixes for variables included in the model. The first matrix is the simple unconditional covariance matrix before the VAR process. The second is the covariance matrix derived from residuals of those variables after the VAR process—which represents the conditional covariance matrix, because any systematic interrelationship among variables has been filtered out. What is left over in the matrix after the VAR process are the truly stochastic errors. The optimal portfolio of commodity-linked bonds is now determined by the conditional

Table 13-7. *Stationarity Tests for Export Earnings and Commodity Prices without Time Trend, Sub-Saharan Africa, 1965–88 (Annual)*

Series	Durbin-Watson (Critical value at 95% = 0.386)	Dickey-Fuller (Critical value at 95% = 3.37)	Augmented Dickey-Fuller (Critical value at 95% = 3.17)	Lags (augmented Dickey-Fuller)	F(3, 20) (Critical value at 95% = 8.66)
Total exports	0.535[a]	1.370	1.231	1	0.845
Cocoa	0.731[a]	2.199	3.057	1	0.072
Coffee	1.138[a]	2.892	3.227[a]	1	0.024
Cotton	0.465[a]	1.453	0.839	1	2.323
Copper	0.199	1.556	2.897	4	1.180
Crude oil	0.233	1.373	1.556	4	0.123

a. Significant at the 95 percent level.
Source: Authors' calculations.

Table 13-8. *Stationarity Tests for Export Earnings and Commodity Prices with Time Trend, Sub-Saharan Africa, 1965–88 (Annual)*

Series	Durbin-Watson (Critical value at 95% = 0.386)	Dickey-Fuller (Critical value at 95% = 3.37)	Augmented Dickey-Fuller (Critical value at 95% = 3.17)	Lags (augmented Dickey-Fuller)	$F_{(3, 20)}$ (Critical Value at 95% = 8.66)
Total exports	0.598[a]	1.757	1.630	1	1.110
Cocoa	0.750[a]	2.314	3.179[a]	1	0.080
Coffee	1.203[a]	2.923	3.287[a]	1	0.052
Cotton	1.853[a]	4.351	4.826[a]	1	0.470
Copper	0.816[a]	1.735	1.770	1	2.834
Crude oil	0.484[a]	0.792	1.077	3	0.100

a. Significant at the 95 percent level.
Source: Authors' calculations.

(*Text continues on the following page.*)

Table 13-9. VAR Estimation Results, Sub-Saharan Africa, 1965–88 (Annual)

$XT =$ $-32.23 + 0.27XTL1 + 0.055CFL3 + 0.21CNL1 +$ $R^2 = 0.93$
       (-3.29) (2.88) (3.84) (5.36) $DW = 2.01$
       $0.25CNL3 - 0.01CPL2$
       (5.96) (-6.02)

$CC =$ $103.36 + 1.18CCL1 - 0.41CFL2 + 0.72CNL1 -$ $R^2 = 0.88$
       (1.84) (7.51) (-3.88) (2.41) $DW = 2.62$
       $0.78CNL2 - 0.06CPL1 + 0.06CPL3$
       (-2.85) (-5.06) (4.78)

$CF =$ $218.32 + 0.43CFL1$ $R^2 = 0.17$
       (2.54) (2.01) $DW = 1.72$

$CN =$ $14.71 + 0.20CNL1 + 0.70XTL3 + 0.03CPL3$ $R^2 = 0.83$
       (0.29) (1.30) (1.73) (4.94) $DW = 2.90$

$CP =$ $1214.10 + 0.77CPL1 + 3.69CCL1 - 6.59CCL3 +$ $R^2 = 0.97$
       (1.41) (5.03) (2.72) (-4.44) $DW = 2.40$
       $5.55CFL3 - 6.16CNL1 - 6.04CNL2 - 4.73CNL3 -$
       (4.41) (-2.13) (-1.87) (-1.62)

$OL =$ $-4.93 + 0.86OLL1 + 0.02CFL3$ $R^2 = 0.80$
       (-1.14) (8.37) (2.15) $DW = 2.39$
       $0.37CPL2 + 0.89CPL3$
       (-2.18) (5.82)

Note: Numbers in parentheses are t-statistics. Variables are as follows: XT is total exports per capita; CC is the price of cocoa; CF is the price of coffee; CP is the price of copper; and OL is the price of crude oil. The notation L is used to denote the nth-order lag of the variable.
Source: Authors' calculations.

348

Table 13-10. *Covariance Matrixes, Sub-Saharan Africa, 1965–88 (Annual)*

Before VAR

	XT	CC	CF	CN	CP	OL
XT	417.4	1172.6	829.3	572.8	3527.5	24.9
CC	1172.6	10069.7	8524.0	1823.1	6413.3	−41.1
CF	829.3	8524.0	12959.8	1910.8	22406.4	−232.3
CN	572.8	1823.1	1910.8	4176.6	3347635.0	−417.7
CP	3527.5	6413.3	22406.4	89643.5	−14805.0	102.2

After VAR

	XTR	CCR	CFR	CNR	CPR	OLR
XTR	33.9	6.7	160.7	8.5	4.2	5.6
CCR	6.7	1323.8	1395.7	−2.1	1693.9	−1.1
CFR	160.7	1395.7	10987.2	−71.3	−2214.1	−96.9
CNR	8.5	−2.1	−71.3	729.3	1655.3	33.1
CPR	4.2	1693.9	−2214.1	1655.3	197.6	19.5

Note: XXR denotes the residual of variable XX after the VAR process.
Source: Authors' calculations.

Table 13-11. *Optimal Liability Portfolios for Sub-Saharan Africa in 1988: Proportions of Commodity-linked Bonds and General Obligation Debt at Various Interest Rates*
(percentage of external debt)

Real interest rate (percent)	Cocoa-linked bonds	Coffee-linked bonds	Cotton-linked bonds	Copper-linked bonds	Oil-linked bonds	All commodity-linked bonds	General obligation debt
1	17.21	6.69	9.16	41.93	8.46	83.45	16.55
3	14.22	5.66	14.87	36.23	6.20	77.18	22.82
5	11.63	4.83	18.93	30.84	4.57	70.81	29.19
7	9.57	3.94	21.65	25.99	3.39	64.54	35.46
9	8.15	2.70	23.45	21.61	2.52	58.42	41.58

Source: Authors' calculations.

covariance matrix of prices and real export earnings multiplied by the inverse of the conditional covariance matrix of commodity prices. The model next calculates the dollar amount to be borrowed in each of five different commodity-linked bonds, under real interest rate assumptions of 1 to 9 percent. The results in table 13-11 are derived by taking the ratio of the dollar amount of each commodity-linked bond in the optimal portfolio to Sub-Saharan Africa's total actual outstanding debt (in dollar terms) in 1988. The amount not borrowed in commodity-linked bonds is categorized as general-obligation dollar debt.

As table 13-11 shows, the optimal portfolios in 1988 should have contained a significant proportion of commodity-linked bonds—about 70 percent. The table indicates also that an optimal liability portfolio for Sub-Saharan Africa would include a large share of copper liabilities—about 30 percent. This share corresponds to an average share of copper exports in total exports over the 1965–88 period of about 11 percent. The shares for the nonmineral commodities (cocoa, coffee, and cotton) may have to be interpreted with caution. Sub-Saharan Africa exports several other agricultural products whose price characteristics are closely related to these commodities. Consequently, the inclusion of these lia-bilities in the portfolio may reflect the fact that instruments whose servic-ing obligations are linked to these commodities also present hedging potential against other commodities whose prices are highly correlated.

The optimal portfolios are sensitive to the assumption made as to the real interest rate. As table 13-12 shows, the total proportion of five commodity bonds in the optimal portfolio decreases as the real interest rate goes up. The decrease can largely be explained by the fact that a higher real interest rate implies a higher servicing cost, thus reducing the

Table 13-12. *Optimal Liability Portfolios for Sub-Saharan Africa in 1988: Values per Capita of Commodity-linked Bonds and General Obligation Debt at Various Interest Rates*
(dollars per capita)

Real interest rate (percent)	Cocoa-linked bonds	Coffee-linked bonds	Cotton-linked bonds	Copper-linked bonds	Oil-linked bonds	All commodity-linked bonds	General obligation debt
1	50.16	19.49	26.69	122.24	24.67	243.25	48.25
3	41.45	16.51	43.35	105.60	18.08	224.99	66.51
5	33.91	14.08	55.19	89.91	13.32	206.41	85.09
7	27.91	11.48	63.10	75.75	9.88	188.12	103.38
9	23.75	7.86	68.36	62.99	7.34	170.30	121.20

Source: Authors' calculations.

demand to borrow and lowering the dollar amount of the bonds. Because the denominator (the total amount of debt) is not changed, the share of commodity-linked bonds declines as the real interest rate goes up.[14] The decline also implies that the hedging effectiveness of commodity bonds is reversely related to the real interest rate assumption.

The composition of the optimal liability structure is shown in dollar amounts per capita in table 13-12. For comparison, the total external debt per capita of Sub-Saharan Africa in 1988 was $291.50.

To estimate the risk reduction benefits of introducing commodity price–linked bonds, we can calculate the variance of the costs of imports with and without the optimal hedging portfolio. The results of doing so are shown in table 13-13. As can be seen, the optimal hedge leads to a very significant risk reduction: a reduction in variance of about 90 percent over the range of real interest rates assumed.

Table 13-13. *Risk Reduction Benefits of Optimal Liability Portfolio*
(dollars per capita)

Real interest rate (percent)	Without hedging	With hedging	Risk reduction	Percentage reduction in risk
1	750.18	52.12	698.07	93.1
2	627.24	57.28	569.95	90.9
5	548.99	60.36	488.63	89.0
7	499.51	61.77	437.74	87.6
9	469.89	62.11	407.78	86.8

Note: Benefits are in terms of variance of import costs.
Source: Authors' calculations.

Table 13-14. *Optimal Liability Portfolios for Sub-Saharan Africa, 1965–82 and 1965–88*

	Cocoa-linked bonds	Coffee-linked bonds	Cotton-linked bonds	Copper-linked bonds	Oil-linked bonds	All commodity-linked bonds	General obligation debt
1965–82							
1980 dollars per capita	9.66	17.95	44.71	11.37	54.69	138.35	55.25
Percentage of external debt	5.00	9.26	23.09	5.87	28.26	71.46	28.54
1965–88							
1980 dollars per capita	33.91	14.08	55.19	89.91	13.32	206.41	85.09
Percentage of external debt	11.63	4.83	18.93	30.84	4.57	70.81	29.19

Source: Authors' calculations.

The effectiveness of the optimal commodity bond portfolio as a hedge against relative price (terms of trade) changes depends on the availability of the different commodity price–linked hedging instruments. To investigate their effectiveness with respect to this assumption, the optimal portfolios were estimated again, this time with a set of four, instead of five, commodity price–linked bonds. These calculations indicate that bonds linked to the prices of cocoa and cotton are the most effective hedging instruments: without these bonds the risk reduction of the optimal portfolio drops to about 65 percent. Surprisingly, the total dollar amount to be borrowed in commodity bonds actually increases when cocoa is dropped, because the dollar amount of the copper bond increases. When cotton is dropped, the total dollar amount borrowed in commodity bonds drops, as expected. The other three commodities appear to be less effective hedges; the risk reduction of the portfolio remains about the same (90 percent) when any one of these three is dropped.

A possible problem with estimating the optimal liability portfolio is stability: estimates of optimal portfolio shares can change from period to period. The possibility of change can reduce the effectiveness of the portfolio strategy because ex post the chosen portfolio may not be the optimal one and because costly (large) portfolio rebalancing can be required in each period when shares (or amounts) change. To check for the stability of our results, we calculated the optimal portfolio shares for a different subperiod, 1965–82. Further sensitivity could be performed by rolling this period forward, changing it, for example, to 1965–84, 1965–85, and so on up to 1965–88. The results are reported in table 13-14 for a real interest rate of 5 percent (similar results were obtained for other interest rates). As can be observed, the dollar amounts to be borrowed in the coffee- and cotton-linked bonds for the period 1965–82 are similar to those for the period 1965–88 (the numbers are all 1980 real dollars). The big changes are for the copper- and oil-linked bonds, and to a lesser extent for the cocoa-linked bonds. These changes are largely the result of differences in the expected future prices of these commodities: for example, the real oil price expected for the next year is almost twice as high in 1982 as in 1988. Changes in expected prices influenced the composition of the optimal portfolio, and because these changes were largest for oil, copper, and cocoa, the borrowings in these bonds were most affected.

The percentage to be borrowed in the form of general-obligation debt was the same for both periods, about 30 percent. The shorter estimation period reduced the fit of the VAR model for the commodity prices and therefore affected the hedging ability of the portfolio. Nevertheless, the relative risk reduction was still high (85 percent), similar to that of the longer estimation period (which was 90 percent). Although a portfolio of commodity-linked bonds can achieve a significant degree of risk reduction, as indicated, rebalancing of the portfolio from year to year may be too costly to aim for the highest degree of risk reduction. There will be a tradeoff between the degree of risk reduction and the degree of rebalancing each period: the costs of rebalancing and the stability of the portfolio will therefore determine an optimal "average" portfolio.

The Exposure of the Economy versus that of the Government

The exposure of the economy to international price changes will be different from the exposure of the government budget to international prices when movements in export earnings are not translated one-to-one into changes in government revenues. For instance, many of the taxes that governments in Sub-Saharan Africa collect (directly and indirectly) do not depend in a linear fashion on commodity prices but go up relatively more than exports when commodity prices increase and, vice versa, fall relatively more than exports when prices decline. Taxes on corporate income from export companies are also usually progressive with respect to commodity prices. Earnings of state enterprises are unlikely to depend in a proportional manner on prices. However, the impact of price fluctuations on government revenues may be somewhat mitigated through the use of stabilization schemes already in place, as long as these schemes involve the use of external liabilities or assets.[15]

No attempt was made here to estimate optimal portfolios for hedging the government budget. However, possible differences in the exposure of governments should be kept in mind when interpreting the results and when designing strategies for individual countries.[16]

Future Exposure

Future exposure to international prices will differ from historic and current exposures as the composition and level of exports and imports change. To analyze the likely future exposure of an individual country to international price movements, sensitivity analysis could be performed on projections of the balance of payments and of government finances. Deviations in the forecasts of the balance of payments and the government budget for varying prices of commodities or goods and varying interest and exchange rates can indicate the sensitivity of the economy and the budget to different external shocks. The differences between the sensitivities of the economy and the budget and those of the existing portfolio indicate the changes that should be made in the portfolios.

Implications and Conclusions

The matching up of the external exposures of Sub-Saharan African countries with the different types of external liability instruments available indicates that Sub-Saharan Africa could improve its liability structure significantly. The use of commodity price–linked instruments would be especially effective in reducing the uncertainty surrounding the resources available for imports after debt service.

Credit risk will impose constraints on the types of instruments and the amount of risk sharing that is feasible between Sub-Saharan Africa and its creditors.[17] However, credit risk does not rule out the use of all financial risk management instruments, and there are ways to make these instruments, such as the use of collateral and marked-to-market mechanisms, available to Sub-Saharan African countries. The fact that firms of all kinds of credit standing in developed countries make extensive use of long-dated tools to manage currency, interest rate, and, more recently, commodity price risk seems to indicate that credit risks can be overcome.

Most important, there are a number of ways in which international institutions and the governments of developed countries can encourage the use of these instruments. They can provide education and training in the use of hedging instruments and technical assistance in the design of strategies. They can directly intermediate and provide guarantees for financial instruments with important risk-sharing characteristics (especially commodity price–linked instruments for Sub-Saharan Africa). They can facilitate ways to overcome technical problems associated with marked-to-market (commodity) swaps, provide the right regulatory and accounting framework for financial risk management instruments in developed countries, and encourage structural changes in the developing countries that will better allow for the use of such instruments. An important opportunity in this last respect can be the restructuring of the external debt of many of the developing countries. This activity provides room for changes in contractual terms and in the ownership of claims to include more risk sharing. However, because of the free-rider problem— introducing more risk sharing by one creditor generates an externality that benefits all creditors—intervention by an international institution may be necessary to achieve this outcome. Other opportunities may present themselves in the privatization of state enterprises involved with commodity production or consumption.

Notes

1. Figures are based on exports for relevant three-digit Standard International Trade Classification codes, except for petroleum, which combines crude (331) with refined petro-

leum products (332), and fish, which combines fresh and simply prepared (031) with tinned (032).

2. Mauritius developed an export processing zone to greatly expand commodity processing and assembly manufacturing operations.

3. Deflating nominal prices by the manufacturers' unit value of the imports of Sub-Saharan African countries.

4. See note 3.

5. Estimated by allocating the World Bank currency pool over these currencies according to the currency pool composition at the end of 1989.

6. Measured in non-U.S. dollar currencies (for example, French francs), the debt stock has decreased since 1985 because of the appreciation of the non-U.S. dollar currencies.

7. Extensions to the capital asset pricing model have stressed that the risk of holding assets has to be defined in relation to movements in individual consumption streams as opposed to movements in the market value of these assets alone. For an exporting country, this implies that the relative riskiness of an income stream derived from exporting a particular good needs to be defined with respect to the country's aggregate income stream.

8. In the period 1985–87 this relationship seemed not to hold when the dollar declined from its peak after 1985 and commodity prices did not increase. The increased need of many developing countries to expand their exports in order to service debt is one argument advanced to explain why commodity prices did not rise (see Gilbert 1989). In the latter part of the 1980s, commodity prices recovered, and the inverse relationship between the value of the dollar and commodity prices seems to be confirmed. More recently, however, both commodity prices and the value of the dollar have declined.

9. One way to do this is to compare nominal debt service payments to other nominal quantities, such as nominal exports. There is another element here, however. High nominal debt service payments do not necessarily imply high debt service burdens. High debt service payments arising as a result of high international interest rates in a high-inflation environment are less of a burden than are low interest payments in a low-inflation environment even if the real interest rate is the same under both scenarios, because in the first scenario interest payments contain a component of principal repayment. Effectively, the interest payments in the high-inflation scenario include repayment of principal and represent less of a real interest burden.

10. See Kroner and Claessens (1991) for Indonesia and Turkey; Myers and Thompson (1991) for Costa Rica; Claessens and Coleman (chapter 10) and Coleman and Qian (chapter 11) for Papua New Guinea; and Claessens (1992) for Mexico and Brazil.

11. Abstracting from transaction costs, a perfect arbitrage can be made between borrowings in different currencies by using the forward exchange (or currency swap) markets. This arbitrage implies covered interest parity: because the forward (or swap) rate represents the interest differential between the alternative currencies, the after forward (or swap) nominal cost of borrowings in alternative currencies will be equal. To the extent that the forward exchange rate represents the equilibrium forecast of the expected future spot rate, the expected effective nominal cost of borrowings in different currencies will be equal, and uncovered interest parity will also hold. Ex ante deviations from uncovered interest parity can be the result of factors such as risk premiums, and to some extent these deviations can therefore be anticipated. Because ex ante risk premiums are largely determined in the capital markets of developed countries, which have a comparative advantage in carrying risks, it can be expected that the risk premiums will be relatively small compared with the risk reduction benefits for the developing country involved. As long as the developing country is more risk-averse than what is implied by the developed countries' capital markets, transferring risks from the developing country to the international capital markets can be an improvement. However, ex post deviations from interest parity cannot be antici-

pated, and active currency management should therefore be employed to reduce risks through proper diversification. A similar comparative advantage for risk bearing can be established in the case of interest rate and commodity price risks.

12. In terms of their notation, we have only U.S. dollar debt (d_t^{us}) for conventional debt and thus do not have the vector d_t of non-U.S. dollar debts in the optimal portfolio.

13. More precisely, the objective function, combined with the market equilibrium condition that the expected percentage changes in the real prices of commodities are equal to the real interest rate, implies that the Myers and Thompson model minimizes the variance of the consumption of tradable goods (imports) in real terms.

14. Notice that the initial level of total external debt is not derived from the model. The model determines only the amounts to be borrowed in each period.

15. Stabilization schemes for domestic purposes (for example, for farmers) that involve the accumulation or depletion of domestic assets (such as government bonds) do not insulate the economy in any way from external risks. Such instruments reallocate risks within the economy, but leave the total risks of the economy unchanged.

16. Important in this respect will be whether most of the external liabilities are public or publicly guaranteed and whether the private sector has access to external risk management techniques.

17. As pointed out by a discussant, Michael Dooley, if commodity prices are nonstationary, creditworthiness may be an especially relevant constraint in the case of long-term commodity price–linked instruments. Leaving aside for the moment whether commodity prices are stationary or nonstationary—which is itself the subject of a continuing debate—if prices are nonstationary, either one of the two parties to a hedging contract is likely to end up with a position that will make defaulting on the contract extremely attractive. Consequently, the credit risk on long-term commodity instruments can be extremely large. Many instruments, however, either involve little if any credit risk for the counterparty or can be structured to minimize credit risk. Credit risk is eliminated altogether through options (on currency, interest, or commodity contracts) bought by the borrowing country, which must pay an up-front premium, or through futures (on currency, interest rates, or commodity prices) bought or sold, which require putting up a margin. In both cases, the legal system in the developed country underwriting the insurance system must ensure that the risk management benefits will be available. Credit risk is minimized without the loss of risk management benefits through currency and interest swaps that are marked to market on a regular basis and which use a margin account. The use of a margin that needs rebalancing does not mean that the instrument is tantamount to self-insurance (see further Folkerts-Landau 1989).

14

The Hungarian Agricultural Commodity Exchange and Liberalization in Hungarian Agriculture

Ronald Anderson and Andrew Powell

Ambitious liberalization programs are under way throughout Eastern Europe. These programs promise great opportunities as economic efficiency is improved and scarce resources within these economies are allocated according to the logic of the market. However, this process is not without dangers. One important potential problem is risk. Prices that are allowed to fluctuate more freely necessarily imply greater price risks.

Adverse consequences of severe price risks include direct welfare loss to consumers and producers, and reduced output in risky sectors. Reduced output is a particular concern in the recently liberalized Eastern European economies because of the general recession brought on by the large changes in relative prices and the abrupt transformation of producer organizations. The major challenge faced by these economies is to stimulate the rapid growth of production and incomes of new or reorganized enterprises. Overcoming the depressing effects of price uncertainty is an important part of that challenge.

One approach to price uncertainty would be for governments to intervene directly to stabilize prices. Indeed, there is considerable evidence that producers would be interested in price stabilization to establish a

The authors wish to thank the World Bank for sponsoring this research and Agromarketing in Budapest for coordinating their visit to Budapest. They especially wish to thank Istvan Mikus and all those who agreed to meet with them. They are also indebted to Andreas Kottering for his excellent background research.

price floor that would allow them to at least recover their costs. Furthermore, the existence of government intervention in agriculture in the European Community and elsewhere encourages the view that price stabilization is not incompatible with a market-based economy.

The main problem with direct price stabilization is that it is difficult to determine the appropriate price targets. This is particularly true in Eastern Europe, where historical cost data give little indication of what average costs are likely to be in the future. Beyond this is the conceptual problem that average costs are of little relevance in a lengthy process of adjustment to a new long-run equilibrium. As a consequence, there is a very serious risk that any efforts to stabilize prices directly will run counter to the aim of allocating resources based on market signals. This makes it worthwhile to consider carefully whether market institutions can make the problem of price risks manageable.

Futures markets provide one method of reducing uncertainty in an environment of fluctuating prices. For this reason there has been a great deal of interest in the role of futures markets in countries pursuing liberalization. In this chapter we consider the case of Hungary. The new Hungarian Agricultural Commodity Exchange, which has been operating since November 1989, is the first futures market to become operational in Eastern Europe. To date, two futures contracts have been traded: in wheat and in maize. Volumes traded have been modest but growing.[1] Interest in the exchange has been high, and its prices are already used regularly as reference prices by producers, bankers, and the government. The target of the exchange is to become a regional exchange and to expand into other (financial) contracts.

The Hungarian exchange, which operates in an environment of great institutional change and economic uncertainty, provides a model for analyzing both the potential of a futures market and the problems in operating one during a liberalization process. We hope that this study will be useful not only to those with an interest in grains in Hungary but also to those with an interest in the potential of futures markets in other countries and for other commodities and financial instruments.

For our study we interviewed representatives of a wide range of bodies having an interest in the exchange. Among those interviewed were representatives from the exchange itself; the ministries of Agriculture, Trade, and Finance; commercial banks; grain-trading companies; and producers. From the interviews we gained an appreciation of how each group perceived the current and potential role of the exchange and what problems they foresaw in its operations.

Futures contracts—and indeed futures markets—are not always successful. Lack of success may stem from sources directly associated with the exchange, for instance, poor contract design (quantity, quality, delivery terms) or poor design of market systems (information and education; membership and membership rules; clearing of contracts; and margins). But futures contracting may fail because of other factors in the operating environment, such as a lack of price variability (possibly because of price controls or government intervention); a lack of competition in the industry (possibly because of government intervention); the availability of an alternative hedging instrument (or the ease of diversification); a poorly functioning credit market; and a poor legal environment. We explore these factors to assess the potential of futures contracting in Hungary and the Hungarian Agricultural Commodity Exchange in particular.

Because the operating environment can determine the success of a futures market, we consider in some detail the changes in the environment for the grain industry in Hungary. In the next section we give a brief introduction to production trends and trade prospects. At present the exchange is devoted to risk shifting within Hungary. However, domestic grain prices are in part a function of the trade policy of the government and of Hungary's major trading partners. We will argue that the uncertainty in the trading environment adds to domestic price uncertainties and hence to the need for futures trading. In the coming years, the exchange may play a more international role, in which case international trends will become increasingly important.

In the third section of the chapter we discuss the changing structure of grain marketing in Hungary. These changes bear directly on the future potential of the exchange. The structure of the marketing system determines which agents carry which risks. In an extreme case of a monopsony purchaser of grain, there may be little role for the exchange. However, different marketing structures will imply different patterns of use of the exchange. In the fourth section we describe the exchange itself and its current status. The fifth section provides an analytical evaluation of futures trading in Hungary, its prospects, and its costs and benefits in relation to various alternatives. The final section presents conclusions and recommendations.

Grain Production Trends and Trade Patterns

In recent years Hungary has produced about 6 million tons of wheat and about 8 million tons of coarse grains annually. The bulk of the latter is maize (about 7 million tons). Although production has varied quite substantially, particularly for wheat, important trends are still discernible. Wheat production increased markedly through the 1960s and 1970s to reach a plateau in the early 1980s. A similar pattern also holds for maize. Recent production figures are detailed in table 14-1.

Table 14-1. *Production and Consumption of Grains in Hungary,*
1981–89
(thousands of tons)

| | Production | | Consumption of wheat | | Wheat exports |
| | Wheat | Coarse grains | | | |
Year	Wheat	grains	Fodder	Other	exports
1981	4,614	8,197	1,732	818	1,438
1982	5,762	9,089	1,995	1,226	950
1983	5,985	7,719	1,905	1,155	1,200
1984	7,392	8,259	2,600	1,315	1,033
1985	6,578	8,178	3,170	626	1,746
1986	5,793	8,461	2,499	248	2,259
1987	5,748	8,327	2,480	910	1,240
1988	6,975	7,604	2,700	1,549	791
1989	6,509	8,460	2,700	224	2,096

Note: "Wheat" includes durum.

Source: International Wheat Council.

Figures for wheat consumption are also given in table 14-1.[2] Total wheat consumption in Hungary has been about 5 million tons, with roughly half of that for animal feed and about 430,000 tons used for seed. Exports have fluctuated widely between a low of 450,000 tons in 1980 to a high of 2.26 million tons in 1986 and were about 2 million tons in 1989. Immediately before the 1990 harvest, stocks stood at about 2 million tons.

The details of Hungarian exports of wheat are given in table 14-2 for the years 1985 to 1989. The former U.S.S.R. has consistently been the most important export target, but even over these four years, quantities have varied between 1.5 million tons and less than 600,000 tons. Tonnages to other economies have also been variable. Exports of coarse grains have been less important. Again, the main trading partners for coarse grains were the former U.S.S.R. and Eastern European countries.

In table 14-3 we show wheat imports for a selection of economies that might be considered potential export markets for Hungarian grain. Clearly, the former U.S.S.R. has been the major grain importer of the region, averaging imports of about 20 million tons of wheat a year. In recent years, Poland has imported about 2 million tons of wheat annually, an amount equivalent to the wheat imports of the whole European Community. The German Democratic Republic managed to reduce wheat imports from over 1 million tons in 1984 to roughly 0.5 million tons in 1987 and 1988. However, it increased imports of coarse grains substantially, from about 1.6 million tons in 1985/86 to 2.6 million tons in 1989/90 (World Bank 1992a). Countries in the Near East provide an

Table 14-2. *Destination of Wheat Exports from Hungary, 1985–89* (thousands of tons)

Economy	1985	1986	1987	1988	1989
Austria	0.0	19.9	0.0	2.6	79.0
Bangladesh	0.0	0.0	0.0	0.0	35.5
Czechoslovakia	133.2	82.9	63.2	31.2	245.4
Ethiopia	1.0	0.0	0.0	0.0	0.0
European Community[a]	0.0	0.8	0.0	0.0	0.5
Finland	0.0	0.0	5.0	5.0	14.4
German Democratic Republic	159.2	159.6	170.4	166.7	177.1
Pakistan	0.0	27.5	0.0	0.0	0.0
Poland	153.7	367.6	3.0		194.5
Romania	0.0	0.1	69.3	0.1	0.1
Sweden	0.0	0.0	0.0	0.0	0.3
Switzerland	0.0	4.6	0.6	0.0	34.8
Syria	19.5	19.8	0.0	0.0	0.0
United Arab Emirates	0.0	0.0	0.0	8.6	0.0
U.S.S.R.	1,268.8	1,490.2	910.0	578.7	1,291.6
Yugoslavia	0.0	91.7	22.3	1.3	25.4
Total	1753.1	2,264.6	1,243.7	794.2	2,098.6

Notes: "Wheat" includes wheat flour, durum, and durum flour. Statistics for wheat flour are in terms of wheat equivalent; usually 0.72 or 0.73 ton of flour equal 1 ton of wheat.

a. Refers to the total exported to all countries in the European Community.

Source: International Wheat Council.

important potential export market for Hungary. Those countries from the region included in the table at present import over 11 million tons of wheat.

Hungarian wheat exports are very small compared with world trade of some 105 million tons in 1988. In 1988, U.S. exports amounted to roughly 44 million tons, followed by Canada (24 million tons), the European Community (14.5 million tons), Australia (12.2 million tons), and Argentina (3.8 million tons).

Hungary's proximity to the former U.S.S.R. should give it a cost advantage over U.S. suppliers. Indeed, the cost advantage is borne out when one compares a selection of free on board (f.o.b.) export prices from the United States and European Community plus appropriate freight rates to the Black Sea or Baltic ports. A selection of such prices is given in table 14-4. Hungarian wheat is slightly softer than North American hard wheat but more like it than the normally cheaper soft wheats of the European Community. Wheat from the European Community, f.o.b. Basle in June 1990, was some $20 a ton more expensive than Hungarian wheat, based on 6,000 forint a ton and 60 forint to the dollar.

Table 14-3. *Wheat Imports in Potential Markets for Hungary, 1984–88* (thousands of tons)

Economy	1984	1985	1986	1987	1988
Austria	—	..	20	49	3
Bulgaria	..	..	412	155	442
Czechoslovakia	14	143	83	74	37
European Community	—	2,207	2,042	2,672	2,179
Finland	7	91	37	33	112
German Democratic Republic	1,253	618	233	535	467
Near East	10,597	10,693	8,465	8,850	11,811
Syria	530	1,309	724	523	1,208
Turkey	518	840	970	407	9
United Arab Emirates	179	207	191	814	114
Yemen	721	848	714	—	947
Norway	330	115	216	259	254
Poland	1,825	1,705	1,662	2,181	2,170
Romania	129	15	..	69	..
Switzerland	534	159	247	302	271
U.S.S.R.	19,749	28,002	16,098	15,561	21,946
Yugoslavia	283	89	137	606	220

— Not available.
.. Less than 1,000 tons.
Note: "Wheat" includes wheat flour, durum, and durum flour.
Source: International Wheat Council.

Transport costs out of Hungary can be substantial, however. Government officials told us that to carry Hungarian wheat by train from the central storage facility south of Budapest to the closest port, Rijeka, in what used to be Yugoslavia, a margin of $30 a ton should be added. Most grain has been transported to the former U.S.S.R. by train via a single border-crossing point. The cost of transporting grain to the Soviet border is as much as $5 to $10 a ton, depending on the origin of the grain within Hungary.

There is considerable uncertainty about the future pattern of trade in Eastern Europe and the former U.S.S.R. in both the short and long run. In 1986, for instance, ruble trade accounted for 44 percent of total Hungarian agricultural trade. Freed from the Council for Mutual Economic Assistance (CMEA) agreements, it is likely that trade in this region will be determined by economic considerations to a much greater extent than previously. However, there is also considerable uncertainty about the grain-marketing structure within the former U.S.S.R.; the purchasing power of both the former U.S.S.R. and Poland during the shock period caused by liberalization in these economies; the status of contracts with the former German Democratic Republic and the likelihood of grain

Table 14-4. *Wheat Prices in International Markets and in Hungary,*
June 1990
(dollars per ton)

	No. 1 CWRS[a] St. Lawrence 13.5%	No. 2 Dark Northern Spring Gulf 14%	EC Standard f.o.b. Basle	Hungarian wheat on Budapest Commodity Exchange
F.o.b. price at port	166.00	156.00	122.00	100.00
C.i.f. price at				
Rotterdam	186.00	156.00	n.a.	n.a.
Freight rates				
To Baltic ports	18.70	20.20	16.11	n.a.
To Black Sea ports	23.70	24.95	27.41	n.a.
F.o.b. price plus freight				
At Baltic ports	184.70	176.20	138.11	n.a.
At Black Sea ports	189.70	180.95	149.41	n.a.

n.a. Not applicable.

a. A category of North American wheat.

Source: International Wheat Council.

purchases from a unified Germany; and the status of the European Community's Common Agricultural Policy. These factors will bear directly on the future pattern of grain trade in the region.

In the longer term it is widely believed that the former U.S.S.R. could be self-sufficient in grains given better incentives for producers and an efficient grain distribution and merchandising system. Poland, too, may not be a large net importer of grains, although for agricultural reasons it is likely to remain an importer of the harder varieties of wheat.

The conclusion from this discussion must be that trading patterns are extremely difficult to predict for this region and that Hungarian exports are likely to remain at least as volatile as in the past. Hungary has historically been an important grain exporter, and recent prices and exchange rates make it appear competitive in the current environment. However, productions costs, exchange rates, and the organizational structure of the sector are potentially subject to large changes, making Hungary's future status as a grain exporter unclear. Still, in view of Hungary's favorable climate and soil conditions, it is reasonable to view the potential for growth of the Hungarian grain trade as good. The main microeconomic issue that will determine whether the potential is fulfilled is whether the merchandising chain can be modernized. Here, the emergence of new agricultural merchandisers, either from new firms or from reorganized cooperatives or privatized state farms, will be key. An important obstacle that any entrant into these activities will face is price uncertainty. For in addition to the usual climatic supply variability, we must expect considerable demand variability as Hungarian incomes vary and the trading regime in Eastern Europe adjusts. All of this indicates that there will be a strong demand for hedging vehicles and that the existence of such vehicles would perform an important economic function.

The Changing Organization of the Grain Sector in Hungary

Hungary, in tandem with other economies in Eastern Europe, has begun an ambitious liberalization program. The government has, for instance, stated its commitment to reform in the following areas: international trade, pricing, taxation, capital markets, banking, enterprise ownership and management, wage differentiation and worker mobility, and direct foreign investment. An important aim of the reforms is to bring about competition by reestablishing markets and reducing the government's role in price formation.

The importance of improving the merchandising system for grains cannot be overemphasized. Agriculture, together with the associated food industry, is vital to the Hungarian economy, accounting for 20 percent of gross domestic product and about 27 percent of convertible currency exports. Approximately 933,000 people are employed full-time on 6.5 million hectares of land, and agriculture and the food industry together account for about 20 percent of total employment. Within agriculture, wheat and maize each account for roughly 11 percent of the gross value of production.

The merchandising system directly affects the likely pattern of use of a commodity exchange. In line with developments in the rest of the economy, there have been important steps away from the central planning system in grain merchandising. In this section we discuss the merchandising process under the state planning system and the changes that have been made.

Under Hungarian central planning there was a complete state system for both the procurement and the processing of grains. A central grain company known as the Grain Trust was established, along with subsidiary trading companies in each of the nineteen provinces. Although these companies had monopoly rights to purchase grain at prices set by the government, the cooperatives and other farms traded grain among themselves. In particular, producers traded grain for fodder and for feed mixing.

Storage facilities in Hungary amount to roughly 10 million tons. About 60 percent of storage facilities are in the hands of producers, and the rest are held by the provincial grain-trading companies. The latter tend to be much more modern. The provincial companies also have the means to conduct quality control tests on the grain purchased, and all mills but one are in the hands of these companies.

Under the central planning system, grain for domestic human consumption was milled, sold as flour to bakeries, and marketed as bread, all at prices set by the government. Grain for domestic consumption as fodder was sold back to the farms and feed producers. Grain for export (almost entirely wheat for human consumption) was sold through the state import-export company for grain, AGRIMPEX. However, even under the state planning system, the arrangement was that AGRIMPEX acted only as an agent for the trading companies and hence did not physically own the grain. As a result, AGRIMPEX does not possess extensive storage or processing facilities.

The Grain Trust had considerable responsibilities. The company was entrusted with the task of coordinating the domestic and export activities of the nineteen provincial companies and of ensuring that the correct quantities and types of grain found their way to the appropriate end uses. Under the trading agreements among the CMEA economies, Hungary was responsible for exporting stipulated quantities of grain of particular qualities. Hence, the coordination role of the Grain Trust was important in ensuring that these quotas were met. Furthermore, in parallel with the CMEA ruble trade, Hungary was selling grain for hard currency to a number of destinations, both in the East and in the West. Once again the Grain Trust was in a position to organize the procurement of the necessary quantities of the appropriate grains. It should be stressed, however, that the export marketing and transportation arrangements were handled by AGRIMPEX, as agent for the exporter.

The Hungarian grain-marketing system is in a state of transition. The institutional structure and government pricing system have changed significantly—although it is too early to observe this system working in practice—and there are great uncertainties about future reforms. Most of the previously fixed prices have been freed. Two fixed producer prices remain: that for wheat for human consumption and that for milk. However, wheat for fodder and maize prices are now free to find their market level. Also, the markets for livestock and flour are free. The prices for breads are also free except for two basic kinds of bread. This mix of free and fixed price systems has already produced a number of contradictions. For instance, in June 1990 the market price for wheat for fodder was above the government-set price for wheat for human consumption. Because producers can choose how to sell their wheat (there is no enforced quota system), there appears to be little point in selling wheat for human consumption. However, the grain traders can reclassify the wheat they have purchased, and because the flour market is free, there may well be incentives for them to do so. In these circumstances there would appear to be little incentive for bakers wishing to buy flour on the free market and bake the basic types of bread to sell at the low government prices and make certain losses on this product. However, bakers may consider it desirable to undertake this activity as a service to long-established customers and to limit the losses by rationing and lowering the quality of the bread.

Up to mid-1980, the organizational structure of crop production and harvesting was still dominated by cooperatives and state farms, private farms being relatively unimportant. At the level of distribution and processing, the Grain Trust has since been split up. The nineteen provincial companies are now independent and free to compete with one another. Furthermore, new firms may enter the grain-merchandising business. However, in view of the historical pattern of regional segmentation and the concentration of each province's modern storage capacity in the hands of the former Grain Trust branch, there is a risk of local monopoly power. Finally, at the national level, the central office of the former state Grain Trust has become the Grain Trading Company. This is a joint-stock company whose shareholders are the nineteen provincial companies. This company has been given permission to trade grain internationally. AGRIMPEX, in turn, has been reorganized as a joint-stock company in which the state is a major shareholder. In light of the general freedom to enter into new economic activities, the Grain Trading Company and AGRIMPEX may evolve into similar competing organizations. Finally, bakers are now also private companies, and, as there are a number of national companies plus many more local bakeries, competition is likely to develop in this sector quite quickly.

Figure 14-1 illustrates the grain-marketing system as it stands at present. The different types of producers are shown at the top of the chart, with the arrows between producers indicating the trade in grain for fodder or for milling. The next level shows the grain-trading companies. A producer is free to sell to any of the provincial grain-trading companies or to one of the private trading companies. The three main uses of grain—for the production of flour, for animal fodder, and for exports—are indicated. Note that many of the provincial grain-trading companies own their own mills and sell flour on the free market.

The form of the contracts between the various entities was of considerable interest to our study. Conflicting reports were given of contracts between producers and the trading companies. Under the central planning system, it appears that producers were given a basic price (published by the government) but that premiums based on quality were paid after results of testing were known. Export bonuses were paid after export

Figure 14-1. *Grain Marketing System in Hungary*

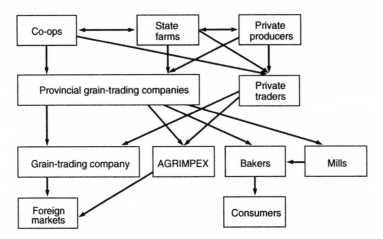

Note: Wheat for fodder and maize are traded at free prices; wheat for human consumption is traded at fixed prices.

prices were known, in practice often with a considerable delay. From time to time there were also ad hoc payments for meeting various yield targets, but the financing of such bonuses was often unconnected to the revenues generated by the improvements. In one system reportedly being used, producers were paid two-thirds of the expected price at the time the grain was purchased and the trading companies would pay the difference between that and the actual "market" price at some later date. It was also reported that some farmers had sold their production forward for the current crop year. In brief, contracts take a variety of forms. The form is important for determining who is taking what risks and thus who might be the main users of risk management tools such as commodity futures contracts.

A second contract of interest is the one between the provincial trading companies and the relevant export agency. AGRIMPEX operates solely as an agent for sales and hence does not legally own the grain. Thus its main source of revenue is from a commission, which at the present time stands at a negotiable 0.3 percent of sales. However, the commission is based on a "limit" price, so if AGRIMPEX obtains a higher price, there is further profit sharing on the additional margin obtained. This share is negotiable but typically is about 20 percent of the profit above the "limit" price. A point to note is that AGRIMPEX never sells grain before finding a supplier. It always ensures that grain is available and then attempts to find a buyer.

The Grain Trading Company may be more flexible in the form of its trading, but as trading is a very new activity for the company there is no standard set of contracts.

An important, but difficult, question is whether the system that is evolving will foster competition and promote efficiency. Under central planning there was total vertical, and considerable horizontal, integration. Because this system existed for more than forty years, very close relationships developed between the various organizations. Although there were serious strains in these relationships at many times, the pattern of responsibilities appeared to be relatively stable.

There is now a danger that the ties that developed will be maintained to promote collusion and local monopoly or monopsony. For instance, if a grain-trading company has a monopoly on storage and processing activities in a region, it may have a considerable monopsony power. Even though many producers have some storage facilities, they have been largely starved of credit, and credit is also extremely expensive. It was reported that perhaps 80 percent of wheat is sold by producers within eight to ten days after harvest. Furthermore, there is at present nothing to stop the former provincial grain-trading companies from making any agreements they may wish between themselves.

Because there is no coherent anti-monopoly regulation in Hungary at present, the authorities are placing great reliance on the threat of entry to ensure competition. However, given present economic conditions in Hungary, in particular the high real interest rates, entry to this activity may not be easy. If entry barriers are high, monopsony power may result in significantly lower prices to producers. Furthermore, it may result in contract forms developing that place price risks with producers who may lack the knowledge of, or access to, means for hedging these risks. This arrangement would imply inefficiencies in risk sharing.

As discussed above, the bakery industry is likely to become truly competitive quite quickly. However, competitiveness has dangers as well as rewards. For instance, a potential embarrassment for the government is that supplies of "basic" breads (provided by bakers at a loss, although their total activities may be profitable) may be reduced. If so, the government may be pressured to introduce a subsidy system for these particular products.

At present the grain-exporting activity is organized as a duopoly. This implies a belief that two firms are enough to ensure a properly competitive environment. However, given the historical relationship between the Grain Trading Company and AGRIMPEX, it is not at all clear how this will function in practice. The Grain Trading Company may have an advantage in procurement because of its close relationship to the nineteen provincial trading companies. For instance, under agreements with the trading companies, the Grain Trading Company gives credit for the purchase of grains. AGRIMPEX, however, has had a monopoly in export marketing and international grain trading and hence clearly has a competitive advantage in these activities. It is also unclear whether the two organizations will cease to cooperate under a more market-oriented system, given that they have been cooperating for forty years under the central planning system.

There is an argument that cooperation between exporting entities may benefit Hungary. At present, in each of Hungary's main grain export markets (including the former U.S.S.R., Poland, and the former Czechoslovakia) there is one monopsonistic purchaser of grain. If Hungarian export marketing of grain is truly competitive, the argument goes, this may place an advantage with the single purchaser and may be welfare-reducing for Hungary as a whole. This argument has not only been submitted by producers but has also been repeated by exporting agencies. It should be recognized, however, that as the process of liberalization proceeds elsewhere in Eastern Europe, the weight of this argument for concentrating grain exports will diminish.

One proposed change is to introduce a quota system for exports. Quotas would be given to producers on the basis of their historical performance and their potential for producing exportable grains. The quotas could be widely traded, however, with other producers or with companies having export licenses. Export licenses could also be applied for by other companies, including the present domestic grain-trading companies, the producers, and perhaps foreign entities. Note that the ethos of central planning is still very much alive in the quota system. The idea behind a system of quotas appears to be twofold. First, there is a concern that Hungary not export such large quantities of grain that it must then import other products for animal feeds or for human consumption. Also, because Hungary has had little previous experience with private storage, there is a fear that Hungary would export grain after the harvest but then be forced to import grain later in the year. Second, domestic producer prices in the past have been low in relation to the world price, and hence exporters (the trading companies, the Grain Trust, and AGRIMPEX) have been felt to be taking too large a share of the value added. The hope is that by giving producers quotas that the eventual exporter must purchase, some of the value added would be transferred back to the producer. The thinking behind the quota system appears to reflect some of the confusion between a mixed, fixed price–flexible price system and a system of central planning. It is not yet clear how the system would operate or whether it would meet the stated objectives.

Perhaps the most serious uncertainty regarding the future of the agricultural sector in Hungary is that of land reform. The present government coalition includes the so-called Smallholders Party, which gained seats largely because of a promise to effect land reform, that is, to reinstate private land ownership and, in particular, to return lands confiscated in the communist revolution. The Smallholders Party has considerable influence and controls the Ministry of Agriculture.

One proposal for land reform is to base redistribution on the Land Roll of 1947. The impact of such a policy may well differ across the various production units. Many of the state farms were formerly large estates that were seized before 1947; these would not be affected by a return to the 1947 rolls. In contrast, cooperatives were mostly formed later and could be affected significantly. If large cooperatives were broken up into small individual plots, there would almost certainly be a loss of economies of scale in some activities. The large cooperatives that produce grain are potentially able to compete with the former state grain-trading companies and with AGRIMPEX. If the cooperatives are broken up or merely preoccupied by a lengthy process of reorganization, this source of competition could be immobilized. Lack of competition would heighten concerns that the former state monopolies would be able to perpetuate themselves.

Development of the Hungarian Agricultural Commodity Exchange

Prior to World War II, a thriving commodity exchange contributed to Budapest's prominence as an agricultural and financial center in Eastern and Central Europe. The Exchange Palace, built in 1904, housed a commodity exchange with 1,340 members. The volume at the exchange was 800,000 tons a year, making it the largest commodity exchange in Europe outside London. With this tradition in mind, there is a feeling that Budapest could once again become a major trading center for grains and for other commodities and is the natural location for a commodity exchange in the region.

In 1989 the Hungarian Agricultural Commodity Exchange (Termenytozsde, Kft.) was formed. The founding organizations were Mezobank and the Commodity Credit Bank (both of which lend to agriculture), AGRIMPEX, and Agromarketing (a recently formed agribusiness consultancy). The purposes of the exchange are to create a marketplace for trading cash contracts and futures contracts for agricultural commodities, to service the needs of exchange members, and to engage in informational and educational activities. The initial scope of the exchange has been limited to grains. There are plans for expansion to include contracts on other commodities and assets and to introduce options contracts. Consequently, the intent is to rename and possibly reconstitute the exchange as the Hungarian Commodity Exchange.

One reason the idea of revitalizing the commodity exchange emerged soon after the liberalization of prices was that AGRIMPEX has been a longtime user of the Chicago Board of Trade (CBOT) soybean complex. In part because of this prior contact, the exchange members have established working relations with the CBOT. The CBOT has sent representatives to the exchange and may assist the exchange in some educational projects.

The exchange started operations in January 1990. Trading has taken place in a trading room shared with the Hungarian Stock Exchange. There are currently two contracts traded: for maize and for semihard winter wheat. The contracts call for the physical delivery of 20 metric tons of grain. These quantities are much smaller than those of the CBOT contracts, which call for delivery of about 127 tons (5,000 bushels of 56 pounds each) for maize and 136 tons (5,000 bushels of 60 pounds each) for wheat.

Trading is organized along the same lines as the grain contracts at the CBOT. Trading is for deferred delivery, with fixed delivery dates. Currently, the longest-dated contracts traded are for about six months. In addition, the exchange serves as a marketplace for spot cash market trades. However, such trades are not official exchange trades.

Trading on the exchange can take place only between members of the exchange. As of mid-1990 there were about twenty-five exchange members. Total membership is limited to fifty, and when that limit is reached, memberships will be bought and sold at negotiated prices. Membership is also limited to individuals; institutions are excluded because it was felt that former components of the state grain procurement process might dominate the exchange and possibly undermine its growth. Individuals are admitted to membership upon passing an examination and posting a financial guarantee. The latter can be in the form of securities and is currently set at 5,000,000 forints (approximately $83,000). Members can trade on their own account or on behalf of customers. All exchange futures trades (long or short) are charged a 0.3 percent exchange fee. Commissions and margins between members and customers are not regulated by the exchange.

Currently, there is a weekly trading session lasting approximately one hour. At this time there is an opening and a settlement (in effect, similar to the two official pricings on the London Metal Exchange). As interest develops, the intent is to move to continuous trading between opening and settlement. Prices are quoted in forints per metric ton with a minimum price move of 10 forints. There is a session price move of 400 forints up or down on all contracts except those of the prompt (spot) month. Initial margins are set to cover an 800–forint move, which is currently about 13 percent of the face value of a contract. Bids and offers are posted on a blackboard in the trading room and, subject to occasional technical problems, on personal computers that are joined on a local area network which is also used to record trades.

All trades are cleared through a clearing association that is formally a separate division of the exchange. All long and short positions must post an initial margin, either as cash or securities. In addition, at the end of each session, a variation margin is charged or paid. Nominally, the clearing time within the Hungarian banking system is three days; in practice, it can be much longer. To deal with this, all exchange members are required to open accounts at the same branch of the Commercial and Credit Bank.

There is one designated delivery location—in Chepal, which is on the Danube, south of Budapest. Delivery can occur anytime within the delivery month. The delivery process is initiated when a short gives notice of an intent to deliver in five days' time. The exchange then matches the short with a long. The paired short and long are free to negotiate for delivery at any mutually convenient location and time other than those specified by the exchange. The exchange assures that the transaction price is the exchange settlement price on the day that notice of the delivery was given. Exchange guidelines allow for transportation savings from not actually delivering to the exchange-designated location to be shared equally between the parties.

In advance of delivery, exchange for physicals is possible along the same lines as occurs on the CBOT. That is, a member with an established long futures position may identify a counterparty with a corresponding amount of deliverable physical grain who would be willing to exchange the physical grain for the futures position. Such an exchange would, in turn, cancel an outstanding short futures contract. At the present time, all physical exchanges are f.o.b. However, there are plans to develop a system of warehouse receipts if the appropriate warehouse facilities can be obtained.

The exchange maintains records of all transactions. Closing bid and asks are reported in a weekly business magazine. In addition, they are displayed on two pages of a Teletex system (similar to Minitel in France), which reaches approximately 100,000 receivers. There is evidence that exchange prices have become a standard reference for grain values. It is widely believed that, in part to avoid the exchange's fixed commission, a number of trades take place off the exchange but that these are based on exchange prices. Furthermore, when discussing recent variations in grain prices, officials of the Ministry of Agriculture made primary reference to the prices on the exchange.

At the present time the responsibility within the government for overseeing the exchange is not fully determined. To some extent the activities of the exchange may be covered by legislation intended to deal with the Budapest Stock Exchange; however, for now this has not been clarified. Exchange officials have requested that the Ministry of Trade and Industry supervise its activities; as yet there has been no decision on this request.

As a consequence, the exchange is a fully self-regulatory body. Among the exchange rules is a reporting limit of 500 contracts. Any member with a position in a single delivery month of more than this will be publicly identified. Another rule concerns dispute resolution. In the case of a disputed trade, the exchange president makes a determination. If the determination is not accepted, the dispute is taken to an expert body.

The level of activity on the exchange has been growing steadily. At a session in June 1990, fifty contracts were exchanged. The face value of these contracts was approximately 6,000,000 forints, a sum that exceeded the value of shares traded simultaneously on the Budapest Stock Exchange. Over the harvest period, volumes rose to about 30 million forints a session, but in November 1990 they settled back to 20 million forints a session, or about 120 lots (2,400 tons). These figures are still some way from showing an active, liquid market, but there are indications that activity could continue to grow. For example, in the June session that was just cited, there were approximately sixty visitors observing the trading and noting the prevailing prices. Most of these visitors were representatives of cooperatives or of newly formed independent grain merchandisers. This strong interest could well be transformed into active participation.

Evaluation of the Hungarian Agricultural Commodity Exchange

The Hungarian Agricultural Commodity Exchange represents one way for the Hungarian economy to adapt the grain sector to the market determination of prices and the sharing of price risks. The model that has guided the exchange is the grain futures market at the CBOT. On the surface using the CBOT as a model looks exceedingly ambitious; in effect, it is an attempt to accomplish in a matter of months what took decades of trial and error to develop in Chicago. In light of the important institutional differences between Hungary and the United States, it is reasonable to look closely at the rationale of building a grain futures exchange in Hungary. Two basic questions need to be answered. First, does the development of the Hungarian grain trade require Chicago-style futures? Second, are Hungary's needs for futures best served by developing its own exchange rather than trading on existing markets?

The generally understood functions of futures or organized forward markets are risk shifting and price discovery. An example of the former is when a farmer or a merchandiser with grain in store sells futures contracts, thus reducing the risks of price fluctuations. The process of price discovery (alternatively, information aggregation) is reflected in the decisions of traders on whether a given futures price is low or high and thus whether to buy or sell futures.

At present, significant amounts of Hungarian grain are not being hedged on the exchange: during the first year of operation, volume on the exchange probably represented less than half of 1 percent of total Hungarian grain production. Furthermore, because little information is available about the customers of the exchange members, it is unclear what percentage of the volume reflects hedging activity. This is not at all surprising for a new futures contract in its early stages. In fact, it is well known that established exchanges actively promote speculative trading among exchange members in new contracts so that the market will be liquid and thus encourage cautious hedgers to participate. In the long run, however, a contract will be successful only if it succeeds in fulfilling a commercial need.

In contrast, the new exchange already appears to have succeeded to a significant extent in its price discovery role. There is recognizable participation by speculators and even more evidence that producers are watching exchange prices to discern supply and demand. Furthermore, off-exchange contracts have been priced using exchange quotes. This is a well-known and economically important aspect of price discovery. Furthermore, the exchange prices are being well publicized. There is even evidence that government officials take the exchange prices to be the best indication of the grain market in Hungary. How can we account for this apparent early success? In part, it is the result of the serious work that has gone into launching the market. In addition, we must recognize that in newly liberalized economies such as Hungary, there is largely a void of valid price information. The first, well-publicized prices of freely negotiated transactions have a very high content of incremental information.

A futures market can facilitate vertical segmentation in a sector. Because price risks can be hedged, a variety of intermediate agents with a minimum of capital can buy the goods and then store, clean, ship, process, or otherwise add value to them before selling them to a later stage. Without an effective hedge, a small middleman would find that even a slightly adverse price change would wipe out his or her small processing or storage margin. Only an integrated producer with a substantial value added would find that price risks were reasonable in relation to the producer's normal returns and normal level of capitalization. Hedging through the futures market thus reduces potential barriers to entry in the market for a variety of services in merchandising and processing. Evidence of this phenomenon can be found in the early history of the CBOT, when a number of relatively small middlemen were active. More recently, independent traders and refiners in the petroleum market have begun to compete with the large international oil firms. This development has gone hand in hand with the strong growth of futures trading for the petroleum complex.

In our view, this role of futures trading is particularly important in Hungary and other recently liberalized economies in Eastern Europe. For, as was described above, liberalization has left intact incumbent firms that have inherited both a highly vertically integrated structure and at least some localized monopoly power. The most aggressive competition for these firms would potentially be from new firms that would target a limited segment of their activities. For example, private companies or local cooperatives with some storage capacity could begin to compete with the regional trading companies in buying grains at harvest time from state farms and elsewhere. Then these firms could merchandise the grains by selling them to the regional trading companies or, more likely, by arranging transport to buyers elsewhere in Hungary or abroad. The major financial obstacle to entering into this business is being able to tolerate fluctuations in the value of stocks purchased and as yet unsold. The grain futures market in Budapest makes this possible for a broader range of operators than otherwise. Indeed, we encountered private traders who were engaging in grain transportation between various locations in Hungary.

If the exchange has made a good start on fulfilling the functions of an effective futures market in Hungary, what then are its prospects for further development? The long-run success of the exchange depends on its ability to satisfy the hedging needs of significant numbers of enterprises engaged in grains or other agricultural products. Hedging demand is most likely to come from enterprises that own grain outright (as opposed to brokering it or processing it for a fee) and which are sensitive to market-based profits or losses. In the current Hungarian context, the small number of private merchandisers most clearly fit into this category. The cooperatives and state farms have the biggest positions in grains; however, their unclear ownership and accounting status means that their degree of market sensitivity is somewhat in doubt. Furthermore, to the extent that their hedging needs occur before the harvest, the uncertainty about yields partially impedes their hedging. For reasons of ambiguous legal status and inertia in mature organizations, the regional trading companies should be expected to follow rather than lead in the transformation of grain marketing and are not likely to be early hedgers. Private exporters would potentially be major users of Hungarian grain futures; however, we have seen that grain exports are currently in the hands of a duopoly composed of the Grain Trading Company and AGRIMPEX. Both of these companies have been observing the exchange closely but have not been trading substantially on it. At some point, it is clear that their decision to participate will become critical to the further growth of the exchange. The practices of the large international grain companies suggest that one of the potential uses of Hungarian grain futures for these agents would be to hedge their forward export contracts prior to the completion of the harvest. However, AGRIMPEX does not have this need as long as it continues the practice of working only as a broker and with a profit participation that leaves it only an upside risk. In sum, the rapidly evolving legal and organizational aspects of enterprises in the Hungarian grain trade make hedging demand for futures particularly changeable.

The second major factor that will strongly affect the development of futures trading in Hungary is inflation and the associated matter of tight credit. In theory, futures trading is not incompatible with high inflation. Interest rates will reflect expected inflation rates and will in turn be built into the carrying costs implicit in the term structure of futures prices. In practice, however, significant problems can emerge for hedgers because, in an inflationary environment, there is typically considerable uncertainty about the rate of inflation. Thus, for example, if a short hedger enters a position when inflation is running at 20 percent and it increases to 40 percent, additional margin will likely be required as the short position loses money. Financing very large margin calls can be problematic in the Hungarian context either because an anti-inflationary monetary policy may make credits unavailable or prohibitively expensive or because margin finance is outside the bankers' established practice. Furthermore, futures prices lock in nominal prices. In a world where there are both relative price risks and a risk that the rate of increase of all prices will change, the demand for futures hedging will decrease. This decrease in futures contracting will be more marked the more that nominal grain prices move closely in tandem with the general price level.

The evolution of the legal environment will have important implications for futures trading and other agricultural merchandising activities. Hungary has a heritage of what might be termed the "socialist contract," in which the terms of economic relationships are often subject to ex post renegotiation. This means that defaults on futures contracts are a particular worry. In this respect, the adoption of a system of initial and variation margin seems a very sensible step. It should be recognized, however, that if hedgers find their cash market contracts difficult to enforce, holding a strictly binding futures position will be very risky. In this sense, the emergence of clear contractual practices and the efficient means of legal recourse would contribute significantly to the growth of futures. A somewhat different legal matter is the problem of fraud. In adopting American-style futures with relatively small contracts and initial margin requirements, the exchange in effect is encouraging the participation of small speculators. Although this has the advantage of promoting liquidity, it raises the problem of investor protection. Experience elsewhere has shown that futures trading can create the problem of asymmetric information between principal (the exchange customer) and agent (the exchange member). This situation can give rise to a variety of trading abuses. In the absence of an effective regulatory apparatus (there is none for the Budapest exchange), the burden then falls on the legal system. Because such problems are largely unprecedented in recent Hungarian experience, the risk for the exchange is that highly publicized disputes might damage the reputation of the exchange and of futures trading generally. To emphasize the seriousness of this concern, we simply note that scandals revolving around commodity options in the 1920s gave rise to a legal ban on commodity options in the United States that was effective for fifty years.

The need for futures markets and other tools to manage price risk is emerging in Eastern Europe as a consequence of the movement away from the fixed price, quantity-based allocation method to a market system. Experience in other countries (for examples, Argentina and Brazil) has made clear that futures exchanges will not be successful in the long term when the cash markets are not efficient and are subject to manipulation or controls. Thus a fundamental determinant of the growth of futures trading is whether the Hungarian liberalization process fully eliminates price fixing by state entities. Currently in the grain sector there are prominent remnants of the old central planning mechanism. Specifically, the purchase price for "wheat for human consumption" is determined through a joint ministerial decision. Given this price, the state determines the price of a basic category of bread and rolls. On the surface this appears to undermine the development of the trading of wheat futures. In reality the importance of the state-set prices of wheat is relatively slight. As stated above, the reason is that there seems to be considerable freedom in reclassifying wheat once it is purchased. At the retail level, the fixed price of common bread is of decreasing significance because bakeries are free to set prices for other breads as they see fit. In recent times the practical implication of this is that bakers have tended to compensate for the low prices of common bread by reducing its quality, which has induced consumers to switch to other categories. Consequently, the fixed price of wheat for human consumption has little operational significance in grain merchandising.

Earlier we indicated that the definition of ownership for cooperatives and other agricultural enterprises would have an important effect in shaping the development of agricultural production and distribution. In the case of grain merchandising and of futures trading in particular, the definition of ownership has importance in determining the objectives and risks for entities involved in handling grain. To the extent that the definition of ownership is unclear or is subject to abrupt changes, the futures contract specifications that will attain commercial success are even more difficult to anticipate than under more settled conditions. This uncertainty creates the need for innovations. It is reasonable to expect that the Hungarian Agricultural Commodity Exchange will need to go through a process of trial and error before reaching the exact combination that fully satisfies commercial needs and attracts correspondingly large volumes.

We now turn to the second question raised at the outset of this section, namely, whether the demand for futures is best met by developing a new exchange in Hungary rather than trading futures on the existing grain futures markets. The advantages of using existing markets are that it is possible to avoid the substantial start-up costs involved in creating a new exchange and that existing markets are likely to be more liquid than a start-up market. There are wheat futures traded on the London Futures and Options Exchange; however, this market is for wheat from the European Community. The internationally traded grain futures are the wheat and maize futures on the Chicago Board of Trade and the wheat futures on the Kansas City Board of Trade. These markets may be useful for hedging risk in Hungarian grain to the extent that their future prices are highly correlated with Hungarian spot prices. The difference between a price on a futures market used for hedging and the spot price relevant to the hedger is the hedger's basis.

The basis between the Hungarian spot price and U.S. grain futures is affected principally by three factors: whether Hungary imports or exports the product, transportation costs, and the exchange rate. Given the unsettled trade situation in Central and Eastern Europe it is not certain that Hungary will routinely export wheat and maize. Consequently, the connection between the Hungarian price and world prices (and thus indirectly Chicago futures) must be considered unstable. Furthermore, even if Hungary is a routine exporter, we have seen that transportation costs are high and are likely to change under increasing competitive pressures. Finally, the forint-dollar exchange rate is subject to significant variation and at present cannot be hedged in a forward or futures market. Thus, it is very likely that the variances associated with the three factors are relatively large. As a consequence it should be expected that the basis for Hungarian-U.S. futures is rather risky.

Even if there were an adequate correlation between Hungarian spot and U.S. futures prices, the usefulness of U.S. hedging would be limited for smaller Hungarian organizations that have little access to international banking relationships and foreign exchange. When Hungary becomes well-integrated into the world grain economy, it may be that some large international traders in Hungary will hedge their net Hungarian positions in U.S. futures. In this situation, a Hungarian futures market could play a role in consolidating domestic grain positions into aggregate Hungarian positions. In this case, the costs associated with international hedging (for example, foreign exchange) would fall on the net position only. For all of these reasons, it is unlikely that U.S. grain futures will be a cost-effective hedging vehicle for most participants in the Hungarian grain market.

Alternatives to developing a traditional futures market in Hungary also include other forms of private risk-sharing contracts. The most obvious alternative is options contracts. Grain producers may find the flexibility of put options rather more attractive than futures. What is less clear is who would be the natural writers of such options. Furthermore, the creation of a liquid options market would pose most of the same difficulties faced in launching a futures exchange. Other alternative contracts would be commodity bonds or commodity-contingent bank loans. The attractions for the potential short hedgers are clear. The problem, however, is that such instruments would tend not to match the risk structure of banks or of most bond purchasers. Indeed, rather than being substitutes for futures trading these types of instruments can be considered as complements. Banks can use futures to offset price risks in innovative lending structures, and options writers can use futures markets to hedge naked positions.

What are the prospects of some form of public intervention in the grain trade or in Hungarian agriculture more generally? The numerous forms of government involvement in grains in other, market-oriented countries suggest that government intervention is a serious alternative. One form of intervention could be a price stabilization scheme implemented through the management of a buffer stock. The experiences of other such schemes have done much to demonstrate the difficulty, particularly for a politically sensitive body, of determining a price band that makes stabilization feasible. Determining a price band is even more problematic in Hungary, where the current configuration of suppliers is far away from what it would be in a steady state where supply matches demand. An alternative to using a price band is to establish a price floor. From the producers' point of view a price floor is similar to giving them a free put option; as such, a price floor is likely to be popular with producer interests. Again the experience elsewhere suggests that setting support prices politically is a poor reflection of economic supply and demand. The risks are particularly high in a recently liberalized economy such as Hungary that such a scheme would be distorted into a routine subsidy for lethargic, uneconomic enterprises.

An alternative view of public involvement in the Hungarian grain sector is as follows. In the absence of a whole series of private market relationships for hedging price risks and granting credits, a governmental agency could temporarily emulate the actions of market institutions. In particular, such an agency could enter into forward purchase contracts with suppliers able to post collateral (perhaps in the form of grain stocks). If the agency maintained a secondary market in such contracts and publicly quoted its prices, it could provide many of the hedging services that would be provided by a liquid futures market. Furthermore, to the extent that it was self-financing and it managed the risks in its forward purchases through forward sales domestically or abroad or, eventually, on foreign futures markets, the agency would be forced to establish contract prices that reflected supply and demand.

Something like this has been proposed for Poland and, to a limited extent, has been implemented in the newly formed Polish Agency for Agricultural Markets. The major advantage of this approach is that with sufficient governmental commitment it is possible to quickly achieve the liquidity provided by a major market maker in the grain sector. Further advantages are that, by confining the participation to professionals with grains as collateral, it is not necessary to establish a system of initial and variation margins, and problems of investor protection are mitigated. The main difficulty with this approach is that of creating within a governmental agency the incentive to respect supply and demand. Such an agency could be vulnerable to political pressures to subsidize uneconomic industries.

Suggested Improvements for the Hungarian Agricultural Commodity Exchange

The Hungarian Agricultural Commodity Exchange is not the only possible avenue to managing price risks, nor is it sure to succeed. But it has had a successful beginning and, more important, creates a valid means of matching supply and demand. We now turn to issues that will affect its success, and we suggest specific actions that could be beneficial.

As currently configured, membership in the exchange is limited to private parties. Companies and nonmember individuals wishing to trade grain futures must engage members to act as their agents on the exchange. According to the rules of the exchange, customers are entitled to "the best possible execution" and have exchange arbitration available as a remedy to any grievances. However, these general rules are not likely to prevent significant problems between principals and agents. In particular, because dual trading (trading for both customers and for oneself) is permitted, the possibility exists for abusive trading practices such as "front running" (buying on one's own account before executing a customer's purchase) and the misallocation of trades (allocating winning trades to one's own account and losers to the client's account). A first step toward combating these practices is to develop more explicit rules on handling customer business. Ultimately, the most effective way for an industrial user to avoid principal-agent problems is to buy a membership and have an employee use this membership to execute company trades exclusively. Under the current rules of the Hungarian Grain Exchange, this arrangement is not possible. It is our view that this particular rule should be reconsidered to see whether memberships, perhaps with limits on their voting rights on exchange decisions, could be extended to companies.

Contract terms are perhaps the most important determinant of a market's eventual success and the most difficult area in which to make specific suggestions. The experience of futures markets in the United States and elsewhere suggests that it is often difficult to find terms that will give the right balance to the conflicting interests of various hedgers. Thus any suggestions to change a contract should be accepted only after careful consideration and widespread screening by potential users. Given this caveat, it is recommended that the exchange pursue directly the possibility of altering contract terms to make warehouse receipts deliverable. Such receipts represent an important step toward standardization and thus fungibility.

In a similar vein, it is important for the exchange to develop new contracts. New contracts involve significant cost in research and development, in education, and in marketing. Thus the exchange must be careful not to dissipate its resources on unpromising proposals. For example, there have been proposals for a high-protein meal contract (perhaps imitating the CBOT's soybean meal contract). In view of the fact that virtually all of Hungary's high-protein meal supplies are imported, it would seem that existing contracts on the CBOT would provide an adequate hedge. Other, perhaps more promising, contracts might be barley, rye, and dry peas. These are important crops in Hungary and elsewhere in Eastern Europe. Effective hedging demand for these contracts could well emerge. A more innovative contract would be for export licenses, which may eventually be introduced in Hungary (see above).

The Hungarian Grain Exchange is aware that education will play an important role in stimulating the growth of futures trading. To date the exchange has engaged in training programs for its members in cooperation with the CBOT. The activities of the exchange were brought to the notice of a broad audience in October 1990 during a successful conference in Budapest that was organized by the exchange. Participants included the heads of both the CBOT and the Chicago Mercantile Exchange. Such training programs and conferences should be encouraged and supported. The exchange should also be encouraged to undertake training of potential hedgers and industry users.

An important function of futures or forward contracting is to facilitate the extension of credit for storing or processing agricultural goods; the usefulness of grain as collateral is compromised if the value of that grain is highly uncertain. Thus the combination of grain plus a short futures position is potentially a more useful form of collateral than is grain alone. However, for this combination to be effective, current lending practices by commercial banks must be adapted. Furthermore, it must be possible, in the event of default on a loan secured by hedged grain, for ownership of the grain and the associated futures position to be assigned to the lending bank. Based on information available to us, it appears that neither commercial bank practices nor legal procedures for assignment have been adopted in Hungary. In our view, failure to make these changes is an important impediment to the eventual integration of the futures market into agricultural merchandising in Hungary.

An efficient credit system that can supply the demands of the members of the exchange is prerequisite to the development of a successful futures market. As argued above, the volatility of grain prices in Hungary is likely to be at least as high as in other parts of the world. Hence margin calls will be significant. Margin finance is a rather specialized business that implies an approach to credit control that is slightly different from that of standard banking practices. If, for instance, a hedger takes a short futures position to cover a percentage of physical stock, margin calls will be made (that is, margin finance will be required) when prices rise. But these calls will be made precisely when profits will be greater on the unhedged part of the physical and, if grain is used as collateral, precisely when the value of the collateral rises. Hence the credit risk may actually be rather small if a sensible hedging strategy is adopted. Thus, attention needs to be given to developing an appropriate system for margin finance.

The absence of a regulating ministry might be viewed as favoring the unfettered development of the marketplace. In fact, the lack of a regulatory framework poses a potential threat to the exchange because, in the event that some political pressure concerning the activities of the exchange should emerge, the result could be an ad hoc intervention into exchange activities, an intervention that might be ill-considered and disruptive. As a result, it would be useful to encourage the government to clarify the legal and regulatory status of the exchange. A priority should be to ensure that senior representatives of the ministries of Trade, Finance, and Agriculture, as well as the Hungarian National Bank, are aware of the economic functions of and regulatory issues concerning the exchange. In our view, education about the exchange should be given to senior civil servants, political appointees, and senior bankers. Because the exchange is relatively young, it is at a disadvantage in pursuing this type of education program.

Conclusions

Historically, Hungary has been a regional force in the European grain economy. Trade statistics indicate that grain exports continue to be important for Hungary, and, that at recent prices and exchange rates, Hungary is competitive in the region. The rapid pace of change in Hungary and elsewhere in Eastern Europe means that extrapolations of the past are not reliable guides to future trading patterns. However, the favorable climate and soil, the large scale of Hungary's producing units, and the stock of relevant technical expertise all suggest that Hungary will maintain or increase its grain exports in coming years.

Making the grain sector more efficient will depend in part on the ability to adapt Hungarian production and merchandising enterprises to operate on free markets. The sector has been reorganized in several important respects: there is, with a few minor exceptions, free trade of grains domestically; the former state Grain Trust has been split up into nineteen provincial grain companies; and the Grain Trading Company has been created out of the former head office of the former state Grain Trust and has been allowed to compete with AGRIMPEX in exporting grains. In other respects, however, the grain sector has changed little. At the local level the former state grain companies have a degree of monopoly power endowed to them by the fact that they control most of the modern storage facilities within their regions. Also, many trade practices reflect the ethos of state planning, which offers little price transparency and is prone to inefficient, ex post renegotiation. In this environment, the most encouraging avenue for improving efficiency is the development of competition in merchandising.

Free-market Hungarian grain prices are likely to be highly volatile in the coming years. Important sources of price uncertainty include crop yields, domestic inflation rates, domestic real income levels, the relative prices of inputs, changing import patterns of the former U.S.S.R. and Eastern European economies, changes in trade restrictions in Hungary, and possible structural changes among Hungarian producers and merchandisers. These factors create a need for price risk management in the Hungarian grain economy. A failure to respond to this need would seriously retard the redirection of the Hungarian grain economy.

The Hungarian Agricultural Commodity Exchange began operations in early 1990. It has been based on the model of a U.S.-style futures market. There is evidence that it has played an important role in Hungary in fulfilling the price discovery function of a futures market. Furthermore, by providing a means of hedging price risks, it has encouraged the entry of new grain merchandisers, which is valuable to Hungary at this stage. However, it is too early for the exchange to have developed into a large, liquid market for hedging significant holdings of Hungarian grain. At this time, price discovery is the most important benefit of the exchange.

The future growth of the exchange could be hampered by a number of factors, including inflation, slowness of the legal system in establishing contract discipline, and fraud or other significant trading abuses involving futures. In the end, however, the success of the exchange will depend on the extent to which potential hedgers perceive the use of exchange contracts to be in their best interest. Currently, hedging by many of the significant participants in the grain sector is hampered by fuzzy internal incentives and organizational inertia. When a critical mass of these participants use exchange contracts, the market could achieve the liquidity that will ensure its subsequent growth. In this regard, it is likely that active participation by the Grain Trading Company and AGRIMPEX will become crucial to the success of the exchange.

The principal alternatives to futures trading as a method for managing price risks in agriculture would likely involve governmental intervention. The practical experiences with price band stabilization and price supports elsewhere point to the propensity of such schemes to degenerate into sources of subsidies for otherwise uneconomic enterprises. Such schemes would be particularly dangerous for Hungary and other recently liberalized economies, where former state enterprises are uneconomic and would probably try to find new ways to tap public revenues. In principle, it would be possible for a new, state-launched enterprise to emulate the actions of the market and to provide a means of hedging. An experiment of this type is under way in Poland. However, the vulnerability of this approach is that it is difficult to prevent political influence from eventually turning the scheme into a routine source of subsidies. One of the major virtues of futures trading in the Eastern European context is that the exchange has all the right incentives to make the market a successful meeting place for the forces of supply and demand.

A number of specific actions would promote the success of the exchange. These include:

- Extending exchange membership to firms
- Developing warehouse receipts as delivery vehicles

- Introducing new contracts
- Educating potential hedgers and public officials
- Modifying banking practices to facilitate margin finance and the collateralization of hedged stocks
- Creating a sensible regulatory environment for futures trading.

If the Hungarian Agricultural Commodity Exchange proves successful, it could have an impact internationally. In particular, it could be important in the development of international grain trading in Eastern Europe and the Middle East. To the extent that trade in this area becomes more integrated, it will become meaningful to talk of the "Eastern European price" of wheat, maize, or other products. In view of the widely noted tendency for both hedging and speculation to flow to the most liquid market, it is likely that one market would emerge as dominant in Eastern Europe. There are other examples of successful regional exchanges, most notably in Asia (for example, the exchanges in Japan, Hong Kong, and Singapore). These have flourished because of a large basis risk and a need for lower transaction costs. If the Hungarian exchange is successful in its domestic market, it will be in a good position to become the dominant market in Eastern Europe. It would then be facilitating more efficient international merchandising, mirroring its role within Hungary. In our view, this is a plausible future scenario. Serious efforts to help the exchange grow out of its current infancy could therefore have significant payoffs.

Notes

1. In 1990 the value of traded commodities was 580 million forints and in 1991 it was 1.92 billion forints. The prediction for 1992 was 5.2 billion forints. The highest daily open interest was 400 contracts in 1989, 3,900 contracts in 1991, and 6,066 contracts in 1992 (January–May only).

2. Data on wheat use are not directly comparable to production data because the latter do not take into account moisture loss and wastage.

15

Tariff-based Stabilization of Commodity Prices in Venezuela

Jonathan R. Coleman and Donald F. Larson

The Venezuelan agricultural sector is highly regulated, with government control over many farm output and input prices as well as over the retail prices of many food items. Domestic prices for many agricultural commodities are set at levels that bear little relation to international prices and that are protected at the border by a strict set of quantitative trade controls, including prohibitions and licensing requirements. An internal World Bank report stated that these restrictions affect more than 70 percent of domestic agricultural production.

Major reforms to Venezuelan agricultural trade policies have been considered as part of an economywide structural adjustment program aimed at redressing macroeconomic imbalances. The overall strategy is to introduce competitive forces into the economy by removing government price controls and liberalizing trade. The agricultural trade reforms are likely to eliminate the quantitative trade restrictions and to replace them with tariffs. Furthermore, the government of Venezuela is committed to a tariff policy that allows price changes and trends in international commodity markets to be reflected in the Venezuelan markets.

If domestic prices become linked to international prices, Venezuelan producers and consumers will be exposed to prices that fluctuate widely. Price fluctuation would represent a dramatic change from the existing price regime, in which agricultural prices are stable and are known at the time production decisions are made. The only source of risk in producer revenues at present is from the uncertainty of crop yields.

Although the government is strongly committed to allowing domestic prices to be closely linked to international prices, it is also concerned that

moving immediately from a fixed price regime without price risk to one
in which prices fluctuate with international prices may be too abrupt a
policy change for the agricultural sector to absorb immediately. The
government feels that it is both economically undesirable and politically
infeasible to bring about such a change without some form of interim
price policy to ease the transition. Fearing both the microeconomic and
macroeconomic consequences associated with extreme price levels, the
government wishes to insulate domestic markets from extremely high or
low international prices by introducing a commodity-price stabilization
scheme.

The government is especially concerned about the microeconomic
effects of commodity price instability on the welfare and economic decisions of individual producers and consumers. Production of many important crops could atrophy if the volatility of prices caused farmers to
reduce investment in farm inputs that provide services over long periods.
Investments in irrigation and soil fertility, for example, are especially
important for the growth of agricultural production, and the government
is concerned that these will be delayed or even postponed if prices cannot
be stabilized within a certain range. This concern is based on the belief
among government officials that Venezuelan producers are highly risk-
averse and that investment incentives for individual farmers are already
poor.

High risk aversion and poor investment incentives are the result of the
institutional structure that has developed from past and current agricultural policies in Venezuela. Because farm prices have been fixed in
Venezuela for more than forty years, Venezuelan farmers have had little
experience in managing price risk. The assurance of price levels removed
the farmers' need to manage price risk on the farm through crop diversification or by modifying use of agricultural inputs. Also because price
uncertainty was removed, third-party, off-farm risk management markets and instruments, such as futures and options contracts and crop
insurance, failed to develop in Venezuela; moreover, no use was made of
international futures and option markets.

The government believes that the effects of price instability on farmers'
willingness to invest will be exacerbated by changes currently taking
place in rural markets. For example, with the relaxation of ceilings on
interest rates, interest on agricultural loans has increased substantially
(although rates on commercial agricultural loans are set 7 percent below
those for general lending). Current nominal rates on agricultural loans
are about 35 percent, compared with only 13 percent in late 1988. Also,
agricultural credit has become tighter because the government relaxed
the requirement that commercial banks keep a certain proportion of their
portfolios as agricultural loans. This proportion was lowered from 22.5

percent to 17.5 percent under the policy changes. Thus, with high real interest rates and the decline in the availability of rural credit, farmers are expected to be less willing to invest in the face of commodity price risk. At the same time, investors are expected to be more reluctant to lend to the agricultural sector, given that the perceived default probability is increased in the face of commodity price risk.

Another important factor that limits farmers' desires and ability to invest in long-run inputs is the system of land tenure in Venezuela. Most farmers do not hold title to the land they cultivate, and tenure is not guaranteed to individual farmers for long periods. Uncertainty about tenure reduces the incentive to invest substantially in fixed inputs. Furthermore, such tenure arrangements reduce the availability of credit because the farmers' landholdings cannot be used as collateral to secure loans.

The government hopes that reforming the rural credit market and land tenure system will bolster agricultural investment, and hence production, but it also sees price stability as important to achieving this end. Price stability will remove some of the risk associated with long-term investment. Furthermore, if Venezuelan farmers are highly risk-averse, the welfare benefits of reducing price and income variability are expected to be substantial (Newbery and Stiglitz 1981).

The government also fears the possibility of extremely high prices for consumers. For a large proportion of the population, food constitutes a major component of the household budget, and higher food prices can reduce purchases considerably. There is much anecdotal evidence that the sharp increase in food prices in 1989 led to malnutrition among the poorer sections of the population, which were previously nourished adequately. The political consequences of sharp increases in food prices were made very clear to the government in February 1989, when the list of products subject to maximum retail prices was sharply reduced and the prices of other regulated commodities were dramatically increased. These actions led to six weeks of food riots in the capital, Caracas.

Although the government is especially concerned about the microeconomic effects of commodity price risk, the macroeconomic consequences are also troublesome. Higher food prices lead to higher wage demands, which fuel inflation. Given that prices and real wages have a downward stickiness, price fluctuations tend to have an upward, ratcheting effect on real wages, creating unemployment (Knudsen and Nash 1990a).

To avoid the problems associated with commodity price fluctuations, the government wishes to introduce stabilization by imposing import tariffs. These tariffs would determine the extent to which price fluctuations in the international market are transmitted to the domestic economy. The government is searching for a tariff structure that neither increases nor decreases the long-run average producer price, yet protects producers against extreme price movements.[1] At the same time it wants to make the tariff structure transparent and to afford protection equitably across manufacturing and agroindustry so as not to distort intersectoral production shares. Furthermore, the government wishes to ensure that levels of protection are uniform, not only across product categories but also within agriculture and the agroindustry processing chain.

This study analyzes price stabilization measures that the Venezuelan government could use in making its new tariff policy for a number of essential agricultural commodities. We first describe various tariff-based price stabilization schemes. Using historical price data, we then determine the levels of protection afforded by each scheme and the effects of the schemes on price stability and government revenues. We then analyze the welfare effects of each scheme, and on the basis of our findings recommend the most appropriate form of tariff structure.

Tariff-based Schemes to Stabilize Commodity Prices

To understand the effects that tariffs have on the economy it is well to first look at the extremes. At one extreme is a variable tariff. A variable tariff adjusts to fluctuations in international prices so that domestic producers and consumers face no price risk. At the opposite extreme is a fixed tariff. A fixed tariff provides no insulation against external shocks from the international market, because changes in world prices are reflected one-for-one in the domestic market. As mentioned above, the government wishes to introduce a tariff structure somewhere between these extremes—that is, a structure that allows changes in the international market to be reflected in the domestic market, yet provides some protection against sharply fluctuating price movements. A variety of tariff structures are discussed below.

Fixed tariffs tax imports at a fixed amount so that domestic prices are set a fixed amount above the world price. Revenue from the tariff is simply the fixed tariff times the quantity of imports. Fixed tariffs are relatively easy to administer and are legal in terms of form under the regulations of the General Agreement on Tariffs and Trade. However, they provide no protection against fluctuating international prices. Also, fixed tariffs are not able to insulate the domestic agricultural sector from unstable domestic prices associated with sharp movements in the exchange rate.

Variable tariffs, which can insulate the domestic market completely from all commodity price risk, can be used as instruments of tariff-based stabilization schemes. Such schemes include reference price schemes, minimum price schemes, and various price band schemes.

A *reference price scheme* has a flexible tariff structure so that a given price, which may be linked to the world price in some way,[2] is guaranteed in each period to producers and consumers. That is,

$$P^d = er(P^r)$$
$$T = P^d - er(P^i) \text{ or } T = er(P^r - P^i)$$
$$GR = T(Q^m)$$

where

P^d is the domestic price,
er is the exchange rate,
P^r is the moving average of the international price,
T is the fixed tariff,
P^i is the international price,
GR is government revenue, and
Q^m is the quantity imported.

If the border price, $er(P^i)$, is below the reference price, P^r, the tariff is positive to ensure that the reference price prevails in the domestic market. However, when the border price exceeds the reference price, a subsidy is required. Given that a moving average of past prices is less variable than the underlying price series itself, this tariff structure lowers the variability of prices facing producers and consumers.

Under this scheme the risk is transferred to the government in the form of unstable tariff revenues. Over the long run, the reference price scheme does not increase the average domestic price, because the mean of the reference price series equals the mean of the underlying world price series. Thus, eventually the tariff revenues and subsidy payments will match. How the reference price is defined has an important effect on government revenues. For example, if a long moving average of prices is chosen as the reference price and real prices have been falling over several years, then the world price will tend to be below the reference price for long periods, requiring persistent government tariffs.

A number of problems are associated with the reference price scheme. For example, as with the fixed tariff scheme, it cannot hedge the risks associated with a sharply fluctuating exchange rate. Most often the reference price will be denominated in dollars. A devaluation of the domestic currency in real terms in relation to the dollar will then cause the reference price in terms of domestic currency to increase while other domestic prices fall. Exchange rates can be highly unstable, as the experience of Venezuela in the late 1980s shows. One solution to this problem is to denominate the reference price in terms of domestic currency. This could be done, for example, by using a five-year moving average of domestic prices as the reference price. However, it can be argued that even though changes in the exchange rate affect the domestic price when the reference price is denominated in foreign dollars, all prices of traded goods are affected in the same way. Therefore, changes in the exchange rate leave the relative prices of traded goods unchanged but affect the relative price of traded to nontraded goods in order to maintain balance of payments equilibrium. Another problem with the reference price scheme is that if it is announced annually, it removes incentives for private storage. However, it can also lead to hoarding immediately prior to the announcement of the new price schedule if it is speculated that new prices will be set at levels above the previous ones.

A *minimum price scheme* is similar to a reference price scheme in that it ensures that prices will not fall below a certain level (or minimum price). When the international price falls below this level, the government levies a tax on imports in order to raise the price to the minimum price. That is,

$$P^d = er\,[\max\,(P^r, P^i)]$$
$$T = P^d - er\,(P^i)$$
$$GR = T\,(Q^m).$$

In contrast to the reference price, when the international price exceeds the reference price, no subsidy payments are made (that is, from the equations above, T can never be negative), so that the international price prevails domestically. In this way, the minimum price scheme offers producers downside price protection and increases the average price to producers at the expense of consumers. The minimum price scheme can therefore be considered a vehicle of producer price support as well as price stabilization.

This scheme has some drawbacks. For example, if the minimum price is set at the moving average of past prices and prices have been falling over long periods, the international price tends to be below the minimum price. The minimum price will become the domestic price for long periods. Furthermore, as in the case of the reference price scheme, the minimum price scheme does not protect domestic producers from fluctuating exchange rates.

A *price band scheme* sets upper and lower limits on the level of domestic prices. The scheme can be represented as follows:

$$P^d = er\,\{\min\,[P^i_{ub}, \max\,(P^i_{lb}, P^i)]\}$$
$$T = P^d - er\,(P^i)$$
$$GR = T\,(Q^m)$$

where P^i_{ub} is the upper limit, or bound, and P^i_{lb} is the lower limit, or bound.

When the international price, P^i, falls below the lower bound, P^i_{lb}, a tariff is levied to raise the price of imports to the lower bound, and if the international price, P^i, exceeds the upper bound, P^i_{ub}, subsidy payments are made to lower the price of imports to the upper bound.

The upper and lower bounds of the price band can be linked to international prices. Different methods are feasible. For example, a reference price could be established and bounds set at a given percentage or number of standard deviations above and below the reference price. Alternatively, a given number (or percentage) of the highest and lowest prices could be removed from a series of past prices (for example, monthly prices over the previous five-year period) and the range of the prices remaining could be used as the upper and lower bounds of the price band. This method is being used to determine price bands for a scheme to stabilize commodity prices in Chile.

The advantage of the price band system is that in the years when the international price is within the band, the international price is also the domestic price, yet in any given year producers and consumers are protected against extremely high or low prices. This scheme does not discourage private storage as much as other schemes do because it allows more price variability (however, the fact that it does reduce price variability discourages some private storage). The disadvantage of this scheme is that if prices remain persistently high or low, the upper or lower price limits prevail for long periods.

An Analysis of the Schemes through Simulations Based on Historical Data

Analysis was undertaken on three tariff regimes. These were (a) a reference price scheme with reference prices set at a five-year moving average of past prices; (b) a guaranteed minimum price scheme with the minimum prices also set at a five-year moving average of past prices; and (c) three variations of a price band scheme. The bands of the first price band scheme (scheme A) were determined by removing a certain number of the top and bottom observations of a series made up of the previous five years of monthly prices and using the minimum and maximum of the remaining prices as the lower and upper bounds, respectively. The bands of the second scheme (scheme B) were set at a reference price (also a five-year moving average of past prices) plus and minus a certain percentage. The bands of the third scheme (scheme C) were set at a reference price (again a five-year moving average of past prices) plus and minus a certain number of standard deviations.

The period being analyzed extended over twenty-five years, between 1965 and 1990. Each of the regimes was analyzed by using both nominal, or current, and real, or constant, prices. The method of denominating prices changed the nature of the results considerably, with important implications for policy design. For example, if the price bounds and reference prices (for example, a five-year moving average of past prices) are denominated in nominal prices, and if prices rise in nominal terms, then in most periods the current price will be above the reference price and frequently will exceed the upper bound. Government tariff rates will need to be lowered to maintain the upper bound, and consequently government revenues will fall. In periods of abnormally high prices, subsidies may be necessary to maintain the upper bound. Alternatively, if prices are denominated in real terms, real prices will fall during periods of stagnant nominal commodity prices. In these periods, the current real price will tend to be below the reference price or even below the lower bound. In this case, it will be necessary to increase the tariff rate in order to maintain the price at the lower bound. Denominating the reference price and price bounds in real prices calls into question the choice of deflator. The most appropriate would appear to be the U.S. producer price index. This index is set at the relevant stage of production (in terms of primary producers), is readily available, and is published regularly.

The various schemes were also analyzed with and without the inclusion of government subsidies on imports. Subsidies are needed to maintain the upper bound when world prices exceed the bound by more than the basic tariff. It is unlikely that the government would subsidize commodity imports, although if subsidies are not given, then the price band scheme becomes, in effect, a minimum price scheme.

The commodities chosen to be analyzed were maize and sugar.[3] Maize is one of the most important commodities produced and consumed in Venezuela and is a good representative of other commodities in the grains and cereals groups. Sugar is also important to the Venezuelan agricultural sector. Sugar prices have been highly volatile throughout the 1970s and 1980s; therefore, the sugar sector would likely benefit greatly from stabilization policies.

Plots of the price series for maize and sugar during 1965–90 are shown in figures 15-1 and 15-2, respectively. To calculate a series of "stabilized" prices that would have prevailed under each stabilization scheme for that period, international monthly commodity price data for the period January 1960 to February 1990 were used to generate initial moving averages. The mean, standard deviation, and coefficient of variation (CV, the ratio of the standard deviation to the mean) for each of the commodities are reported in tables 15-1 to 15-4. Also reported are the same diagnostics for the prices of "unstabilized" historical world prices. Comparison of the means of the stabilized prices with the mean world price provides an indication of the level of price support under each scheme. The differences in the standard deviations and CVs of world prices compared with

Figure 15-1. *Real World Prices for Maize, 1965–90*

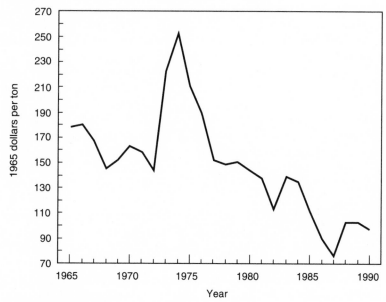

Source: World Bank data.

Figure 15-2. *Real World Prices for Sugar, 1965–90*

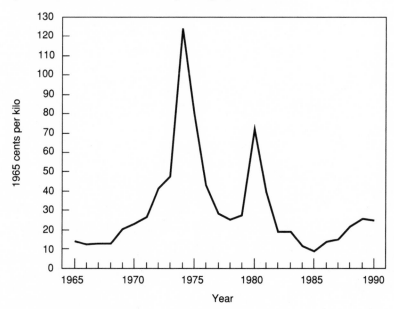

Source: World Bank data.

Figure 15-3. *Reference Price Scheme and Minimum Price Scheme*

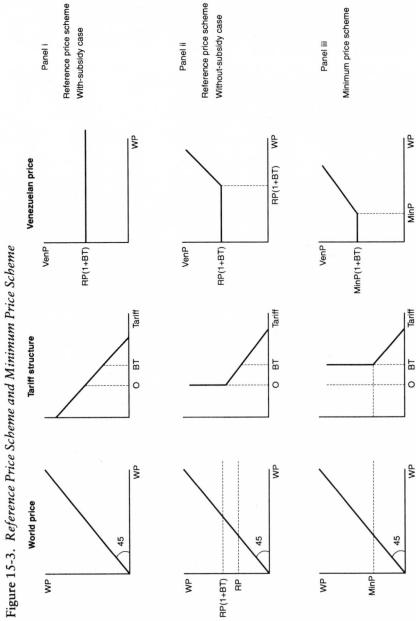

stabilized prices provide a measure of risk reduction. Mean government revenues per ton are also presented in the tables. These include a basic tariff of 20 percent of the world price.

It is important to remember that the prices are denominated in dollars, not local currency. In other words, the analysis has been done in the absence of exchange rate risk and without consideration of shipping, port, and other handling charges. These may be quite unstable and could change the results considerably. Although these components are important, they have an impact on trade in general, not specifically commodity trade. Therefore, the costs and benefits of exchange rate or shipping cost stability should be analyzed separately for the economy as a whole.

Reference Price and Minimum Price Schemes

The reference price and minimum price schemes are illustrated in figure 15-3. Panel 1 of figure 15-3 shows the reference price scheme with government subsidy payments. The internal, or domestic, price is set at the reference price (RP) plus the basic tariff (BT). The domestic price $(VenP)$ in each period is unaffected by the current world price (WP) through adjustable tariffs and subsidies. Panel 2 shows the reference price scheme without government subsidies. The domestic price is set at the reference price plus the basic tariff level. If the world price exceeds this level, then the domestic price is equal to the world price level and the tariff falls to zero. Panel 3 illustrates the minimum price scheme. If the world price is below the minimum price level $(MinP)$ the tariff rate is increased above the basic tariff rate. Otherwise the basic tariff applies to the world price. In the analysis, the reference price and the minimum price in each period were set at a five-year moving average of past prices, and the basic tariff was set at 20 percent. The results for the two commodities in terms of nominal prices are reported in table 15-1.

Looking first at the results under "current dollars," we see that the stabilization policies did not substantially reduce price variability for maize. The largest drop in the CV was for the reference price scheme without subsidies; in that case, the CV was only 4 percent lower than the CV for the world price. The CV for the minimum price scheme was lower than that for the reference price scheme with subsidies. This is a seemingly anomalous result because, by definition, the minimum price series cannot be more stable than the reference price series. Although the standard deviation was lower for the reference price scheme, the mean was lower as well, and together these changes resulted in a CV that was larger than the CV for the minimum price scheme. This result calls into question the appropriateness of the CV as a measure of risk. The refer-

Table 15-1. *Comparison of Alternative Stabilization Policies for Venezuela, 1965–90: Reference Price Scheme and Minimum Price Scheme*

| | Reference price scheme | | | |
	With subsidies	Without subsidies	Minimum price scheme	Unstabilized world price
	Current dollars per ton			
Maize				
Mean price	106.5	110.8	119.4	112.4
Standard deviation	34.1	34.0	37.8	36.0
Coefficient of variation	0.320	0.307	0.317	0.320
Government revenues	12.9	17.1	25.7	n.a.
Sugar				
Mean price	234.0	287.2	312.6	245.3
Standard deviation	128.7	180.3	209.4	218.3
Coefficient of variation	0.550	0.628	0.670	0.885
Government revenues	29.6	82.9	108.2	n.a.
	Constant dollars per ton			
Maize				
Mean price	189.7	192.8	200.2	180.4
Standard deviation	34.3	37.4	44.7	51.1
Coefficient of variation	0.181	0.194	0.223	0.283
Government revenues	39.2	42.3	49.7	n.a.
Sugar				
Mean price	405.0	476.8	515.3	381.3
Standard deviation	200.5	283.2	326.7	343.9
Coefficient of variation	0.495	0.594	0.634	0.902
Government revenues	87.2	159.0	197.6	n.a.

n.a. Not applicable.

Note: Table is based on monthly data from January 1960 to February 1990. Reference prices and minimum prices are set at a sixty-month moving average of past prices.

Source: Authors' calculations, based on World Bank data.

ence price scheme slightly lowered the mean price, whereas the minimum price scheme increased it by about 6 percent. As expected, the tariff revenues were highest under the minimum price scheme—in fact, close to twice the revenues obtained under the reference price scheme with subsidies.

A significant effect on price stability as measured by the CVs was found for sugar. The lowest CV, 0.55, was for the reference price scheme with subsidies. This CV was substantially below the CV for the world price, which was 0.885. The minimum price scheme had a CV of 0.67 and, on average, earned $108.20 a ton in tariff revenue. This amount was more than three times the tariff revenue from the reference price scheme with subsidies. There was a substantial difference between the government revenues for the two reference price schemes. This was because large government subsidies were required to keep prices at the reference price or upper bound when sugar prices rose dramatically in the 1974–75 and 1980–81 periods.

Overall, the results under "constant dollars" were consistent with what was expected in terms of each scheme's effect on the mean price and price variability. For example, the CVs and standard deviations for both commodities were highest for the world price, lower for the minimum price scheme, still lower for the reference price scheme without subsidies, and lowest for the reference price scheme with subsidies. Comparing results for the world price with those of the reference price scheme with subsidies, we see that the CVs fell significantly—36 percent for maize and 45 percent for sugar. The mean real prices were the highest for the minimum price scheme, and were significantly (35 percent) above the world price for sugar. As expected, the mean price under the reference price scheme without subsidies was higher than the world price. This was also true for the reference price scheme with subsidies.

Price Band Schemes

PRICE BAND SCHEME A. The price band schemes analyzed are illustrated in figure 15-4. The bands for scheme A were determined in each period by removing a specified number of the highest and lowest observations of a series of the past five years of monthly prices and using the range of the remaining observations as the lower and upper bounds of the scheme. A number of variations of this scheme were analyzed—eighteen and twenty-four price observations removed, with and without subsidies, and for prices denominated in both current and constant dollars. The results are reported in table 15-2.

The results for maize show that the stabilization effect as measured by the CV and standard deviation was very small. The mean price also changed very little with each scheme although, as expected, the mean price was higher when there were no subsidies than when there were—and for the following reason. When the world price was greater than the upper bound by more than the basic tariff rate, the world price was allowed to become the domestic price (that is, imports entered at zero tariff). Because the means are different, the standard deviations cannot be compared directly. Moreover, the CVs tend to give misleading representations of risk exposure. As a result, in both settings of the scheme (that is, with eighteen and twenty-four observations removed), the CV

Figure 15-4. *Price Band Scheme*

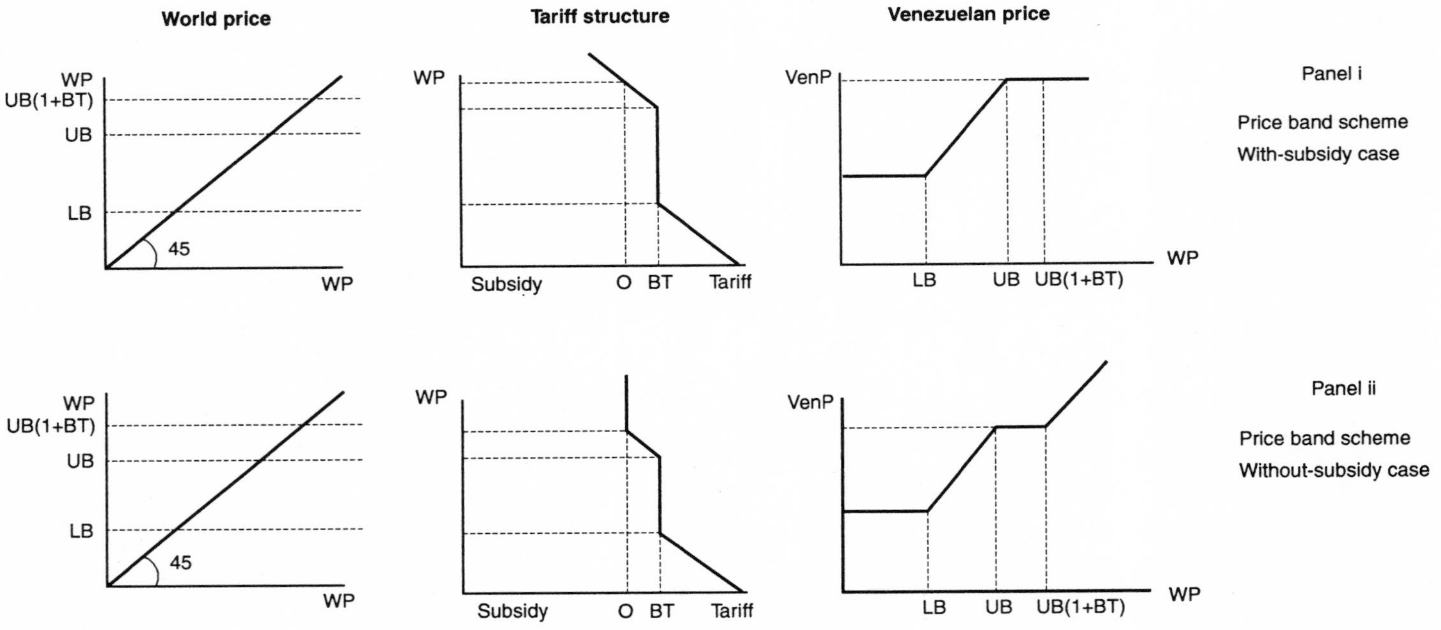

Table 15-2. *Comparison of Alternative Stabilization Policies for Venezuela, 1965–90: Price Band Scheme A*

| | Stabilized prices | | | | |
| | A1: 24 months removed | | A2: 18 months removed | | |
Commodity	With subsidies	Without subsidies	With subsidies	Without subsidies	Unstabilized world price
	Current dollars per ton				
Maize					
Mean price	109.4	111.2	109.9	111.0	112.4
Standard deviation	34.9	34.7	35.3	35.2	36.0
Coefficient of variation	0.319	0.312	0.321	0.317	0.320
Government revenues	15.7	17.5	16.0	17.3	n.a.
Sugar					
Mean price	195.3	231.0	202.5	230.8	245.3
Standard deviation	109.9	179.3	123.1	180.9	218.3
Coefficient of variation	0.563	0.776	0.608	0.784	0.885
Government revenues	−9.2	26.6	−1.9	26.3	n.a.
	Constant dollars per ton				
Maize					
Mean price	183.1	184.2	182.3	183.2	180.7
Standard deviation	39.2	40.5	41.4	42.7	51.1
Coefficient of variation	0.214	0.220	0.227	0.233	0.283
Government revenues	32.6	33.7	31.8	32.6	n.a.
Sugar					
Mean price	327.7	371.2	334.5	368.5	381.5
Standard deviation	177.0	282.1	198.0	284.5	343.9
Coefficient of variation	0.540	0.760	0.592	0.772	0.902
Government revenues	9.9	53.4	16.7	50.7	n.a.

n.a. Not applicable.

Note: Table is based on monthly data from January 1960 to February 1990. Price bands are set by removing 24 or 18 of the highest and lowest monthly price observations made during the sixty months preceding each period and using the range of the remaining observations as the upper and lower limits of the band.

Source: Authors' calculations, based on World Bank data.

fell in the cases without subsidies, although the domestic prices for the cases with subsidies were more variable. The impact of widening the band by removing eighteen observations instead of twenty-four was very small: the CV increased from 0.319 to 0.321 (less than 1 percent) in the case with subsidies and from 0.312 to 0.317 (less than 2 percent) in the case without subsidies. The stabilization schemes did not differ widely in their effect on government revenue; the range in this category was between $15.70 a ton (where twenty-four months were removed and there were subsidies) and $17.50 a ton (where twenty-four months were removed and there were no subsidies).

The effects of the stabilization schemes were more dramatic for sugar than for maize, reflecting the high degree of volatility in the sugar market during the period of study. For the cases with subsidies, the mean domestic price fell by about 20 percent, and the CV fell to 0.563 (compared with a world price CV of 0.885) when twenty-four months were removed, whereas the mean fell about 17.5 percent and the CV fell to 0.608 when eighteen months were removed. Therefore, stability of domestic prices would be increased by 36 percent and 31 percent, respectively. For the cases without subsidies, the mean price fell about 5 percent below the world price. The fluctuations of domestic prices under the schemes were about 12 percent below world price levels when twenty-four price observations were removed and about 11 percent below world price levels when eighteen price observations were removed. The effect on government revenues was quite varied across the various schemes analyzed. In the cases without subsidies, government revenues were between $26 and $27 a ton. However, when the government paid subsidies, average government revenues were negative, despite a basic tariff of 20 percent. Average subsidy payments of $9.20 a ton and $1.90 a ton were required in the cases where, respectively, twenty-four and eighteen months of prices were removed. This finding showed that in the case of sugar, the band setting was an important issue, whereas for maize, the size of the band in terms of risk reduction and government revenues appeared to be of little consequence.

Table 15-2 also reports the results for price band scheme A with prices denominated in constant dollars. With constant prices there was no systematic downward bias in the mean prices. In this respect, a more accurate picture of the level of risk reduction under each of the schemes was obtained from the standard deviation and the CV.

In the case of maize, the mean constant price under the stabilization schemes was slightly higher than the mean constant world price, although the difference was very slight. The reduction in the CV, however, was relatively large, in contrast to the results using current prices. When twenty-four monthly price observations were removed and there were subsidies, the CV was 0.214, a decline of almost 25 percent from 0.283, the CV of the world price. The CV increased from 0.214 to 0.220 when there was no subsidy. As the bands were widened by removing eighteen observations instead of twenty-four, the CV of the domestic price increased, from 0.214 to 0.227 in the with-subsidy case and from 0.220 to 0.233 in the without-subsidy case. Therefore, when constant prices were used, the relative reduction in price variability associated with each of the schemes was captured by differences in the CVs. The impact on government revenues was small, ranging from $31.80 a ton (when eighteen observations were removed and there were subsidies) to $33.70 a ton (when twenty-four observations were removed and there were no subsidies).

For sugar, even with constant prices, the mean domestic prices under the stabilization schemes were substantially different from the world price, especially when subsidies were given. For example, under the most constraining of the schemes (when twenty-four observations were removed and there were subsidies), the mean price of sugar fell 14 percent below the mean world price. The CVs for all of the schemes analyzed were below the CV of the world price by a considerable amount, ranging from 14 percent to 40 percent. The differences in the CV between the cases with subsidies and the cases without were also considerable: the CV increased from 0.54 to 0.76 when twenty-four observations were removed and from 0.592 to 0.772 when eighteen observations were removed. Government revenues were also found to be small under the with-subsidy scenarios, reflecting the high prices of sugar that existed for long periods. In contrast to the analysis based on current prices, the government revenues were positive for all scenarios analyzed.

PRICE BAND SCHEME B. In price band scheme B the bands were set at a given percentage above and below a reference price. The reference price was set at a five-year moving average of past prices, and band widths of 20 percent and 30 percent around this price were analyzed. Schemes with and without subsidy payments were analyzed with both current and constant prices. The results are reported in table 15-3.

The results for maize were similar to those reported for price band scheme A. That is, the measurement of risk reduction given by the CV provided anomalous results: the CV of the unstabilized, world price was lower than the CVs for all the stabilization schemes (except the ±20 percent scheme without subsidies). This was because the mean stabilized prices were much below the mean world price whereas standard deviations were not much below that of the world price, resulting in a higher CV. For both band widths the cases without subsidies had CVs that were lower than the CVs for the cases with subsidies. The lower CVs were the result of higher mean prices. As the band widths were increased from ±20 percent to ±30 percent, the CVs fell between 2 percent and 4 percent. Government revenues amounted to $15.10 a ton and $15.70 a ton for the ±20 percent and ±30 percent band widths, respectively, when subsidy payments were made. Without subsidy payments, government revenues increased about 8 percent, to approximately $16.90 a ton.

Consistent with previous results, the stabilization schemes had a signif-

Table 15-3. *Comparison of Alternative Stabilization Policies for Venezuela, 1965–90: Price Band Scheme B*

| | Stabilized prices | | | | |
| | B1: ± 20 percent | | B2: ±30 percent | | |
	With subsidies	Without subsidies	With subsidies	Without subsidies	Unstabilized world price
	Current dollars per ton				
Maize					
Mean price	108.7	110.7	109.4	110.7	112.4
Standard deviation	34.9	35.1	35.9	36.1	36.0
Coefficient of variation	0.321	0.317	0.328	0.326	0.320
Government revenues	15.1	16.9	15.7	17.0	n.a.
Sugar					
Mean price	220.6	261.9	214.8	250.7	245.3
Standard deviation	111.6	175.2	110.0	175.0	218.3
Coefficient of variation	0.506	0.669	0.512	0.698	0.885
Government revenues	16.3	57.5	10.4	46.2	n.a.
	Constant dollars per ton				
Maize					
Mean price	180.1	180.7	179.3	179.4	180.7
Standard deviation	40.9	41.9	45.4	45.6	51.1
Coefficient of variation	0.227	0.232	0.253	0.254	0.283
Government revenues	29.6	30.1	28.7	28.9	n.a.
Sugar					
Mean price	376.5	427.7	364.6	407.4	381.3
Standard deviation	168.3	271.6	167.0	270.5	343.9
Coefficient of variation	0.447	0.635	0.458	0.664	0.902
Government revenues	58.8	109.9	46.8	89.7	n.a.

n.a. Not applicable.

Note: Table is based on monthly data from January 1960 to February 1990. Bands are set at 20 percent or 30 percent above and below the sixty-month moving average.

Source: Authors' calculations, based on World Bank data.

icant effect on sugar prices: the mean price dropped from an unstabilized $245.30 a ton to $214.80 a ton and $220.60 a ton with subsidy payments. The CVs were likewise reduced significantly. The CV for the world price was 0.885; for the ±20 percent band with subsidy payments it was 0.506—a reduction of more than 40 percent. In contrast to other commodities, the inclusion of subsidies made a big difference in the results. For example, with a ±30 percent band, the CV increased from 0.512 to 0.698 with the removal of subsidy payments. This increase reflected the fact that the upper bound was a constraint on domestic prices for long periods during the time that was studied. Reflecting this constraint, government revenues were considerably lower for the with-subsidy scenarios, increasing from $16.30 a ton to $57.50 a ton when the price band was ±20 percent, and from $10.40 a ton to $46.20 a ton when the price band was ±30 percent.

As was the case for price band scheme A, the CVs showed the stabilization schemes to be much more effective at reducing risk when prices were denominated in constant dollars. For example, for maize, the CV for constant world prices was 0.283, whereas for the ±20 percent band with-subsidy scenario the CV was 0.227. This was a reduction in CV of almost 20 percent, compared with a small increase in the corresponding CVs for almost all schemes denominated in current prices. The inclusion of subsidies increased the CVs, but the increase was slight in both cases. Widening the band had a large impact on the size of the CV (compared with when current prices were used), increasing the CV from 0.227 to 0.253 in the with-subsidy case and from 0.232 to 0.254 in the without-subsidy case.

In the case of sugar, the mean world price in constant dollars a ton was quite different from the mean prices for each of the schemes: for both schemes the mean world price was above the mean price when there were subsidies and below the mean price when there were no subsidies. The CVs for each scheme were substantially lower than the world price CV, and more so when there were subsidies.

Price band scheme C. The third price band scheme analyzed was with bands set at a certain number of standard deviations above and below a reference price. Again, the reference price was based on a five-year moving average of past monthly prices, and these prices were used to calculate the standard deviation for each period. The results are reported in table 15-4 for band widths of 1 and 1.5 standard deviations around the reference price, and for cases with and without subsidies.

The overall results were similar to those of the two price band schemes analyzed above. For example, the results for maize showed the smallest CV, 0.309, for the case using 1 standard deviation without subsidies, compared with 0.320, the CV for the unstabilized, world price. However, there was very little difference between each of the schemes in terms of mean price, standard deviation, and government revenues. The stabilization schemes provided greater constraints on sugar prices than on maize prices. The scheme using 1 standard deviation with subsidies lowered the CV by 30 percent below the CV for the unstabilized, world price. Operating this scheme with a subsidy required average government expenditures of $5.80 a ton (despite the basic tariff of 20 percent).

As was the case for the other stabilization schemes, scheme C was found to be more effective in reducing risk when prices were denominated in constant terms. In the case of maize, the inclusion of subsidies

Table 15-4. *Comparison of Alternative Stabilization Policies for Venezuela, 1965–90: Price Band Scheme C*

| | Stabilized prices | | | | |
| | C1: ±1 standard deviation | | C2: ±1.5 standard deviations | | |
	With subsidies	Without subsidies	With subsidies	Without subsidies	Unstabilized world price
	Current dollars per ton				
Maize					
Mean price	109.3	110.7	110.0	110.7	112.4
Standard deviation	34.2	34.2	35.2	35.2	36.0
Coefficient of variation	0.313	0.309	0.320	0.318	0.320
Government revenues	15.4	17.0	16.2	17.0	n.a.
Sugar					
Mean price	199.2	228.2	207.7	227.5	245.3
Standard deviation	123.7	180.7	140.0	184.0	218.3
Coefficient of variation	0.621	0.792	0.674	0.809	0.885
Government revenues	−5.8	23.2	2.6	22.5	n.a.
	Constant dollars per ton				
Maize					
Mean price	182.7	183.6	180.7	181.1	180.7
Standard deviation	38.6	39.8	42.5	43.1	51.1
Coefficient of variation	0.211	0.217	0.235	0.238	0.283
Government revenues	32.5	33.4	30.5	30.9	n.a.
Sugar					
Mean price	323.4	359.6	330.2	354.8	381.5
Standard deviation	192.7	283.0	220.9	289.5	343.9
Coefficient of variation	0.596	0.787	0.669	0.816	0.902
Government revenues	58.8	42.3	12.9	37.5	n.a.

n.a. Not applicable.

Note: Table is based on monthly data from January 1960 to February 1990. Bands are set at 1 or 1.5 standard deviations above and below the sixty-month moving average.

Source: Authors' calculations, based on World Bank data.

increased the CVs, but the increase was slight in both cases. Widening the band had a significant impact on the size of the CV when the results were in constant dollars instead of current dollars: the CVs for the scenarios in which constant dollars were used increased from 0.211 to 0.235 in the with-subsidy case and from 0.217 to 0.238 in the without-subsidy case.

Consistent with the results reported for other stabilization schemes, significant risk reductions were realized for sugar. The mean world price was significantly above the mean price under each of the schemes. Under the scenario using 1 standard deviation for the band, and subsidies, the

CV fell to 0.596; it fell to 0.669 under the scenario using 1.5 standard deviations for the band, and subsidies.

THE EFFECTIVENESS OF THE PRICE BAND SCHEMES. To gauge the effectiveness of the price band schemes, calculations were made of the percentage of observations showing domestic prices that were constrained to be different from world, or international, prices (see table 15-5). The percentage of observations at the lower and upper bounds are given as well as the percentage of times subsidy payments were required to maintain the upper bound. Consider, for example, price band scheme A1, in which the band was formed by the range of prices remaining after twenty-four of the highest and lowest monthly observations were removed from the preceding sixty months of observations. When price band scheme A1 was applied to current maize prices, 48.7 percent of the domestic prices were inside the price band and therefore equal to international prices. Domestic prices were constrained to be at the lower bound 19.7 percent of the time, and domestic prices were constrained from being higher than the upper bound in 31.6 percent of the observations. The government was required to subsidize imports 10.3 percent of the time in order to maintain the upper bound.

Comparing the different schemes when applied to maize, the most constraining scheme was C1 (bands set at 1 standard deviation around a reference price); under this scheme the domestic price equaled the international price only 44.3 percent of the time. The scheme that put the least constraints on domestic prices was scheme B2 (bands set ± 30 percent around a reference price); under this scheme the domestic price equaled the international price 83 percent of the time (that is, only one in every five periods was the domestic price different from the world price). With prices denominated in current terms, the domestic price was constrained more often by the upper bound, reflecting increasing nominal prices throughout the analysis period. In contrast, with price denominated in real terms, the lower bound provided a constraint on domestic prices more often, reflecting declining real commodity prices over the study period. Widening the price band increased the proportion of observations within the price band, increasing the proportion by 10 to 15 percent when current prices were used and 7 to 20 percent when constant prices were used.

The volatility of sugar prices is clearly reflected in table 15-5. For example, for price band scheme B1 (bands set ± 20 percent around a reference price), measured in both current and constant terms, only 13 to 14 percent of domestic prices were equal to the international price, 38 to 41 percent of domestic prices being constrained at the upper bound and between 45 and 50 percent at the lower bound. For all schemes analyzed

Table 15-5. *Percentages of Price Observations at the Upper and Lower Bounds of Various Price Band Schemes, and Percentages for which Subsidies Were Paid*

Commodity and scheme	At lower bound	Inside band	At upper bound (including subsidies)	Subsidies paid
Maize				
A1-Current	19.7	48.7	31.6	10.3
A1-Constant	38.0	47.7	24.3	3.3
A2-Current	16.0	58.3	25.7	8.0
A2-Constant	32.7	54.7	12.7	3.3
B1-Current	8.3	71.3	20.3	9.0
B1-Constant	20.3	71.7	8.0	4.3
B2-Current	4.3	83.0	12.7	6.7
B2-Constant	6.7	87.0	6.3	1.0
C1-Current	21.9	44.3	33.8	9.3
C1-Constant	42.7	41.1	16.2	4.3
C2-Current	13.9	59.9	26.2	6.6
C2-Constant	26.8	61.6	11.6	2.0
Sugar				
A1-Current	26.7	34.0	39.3	8.3
A1-Constant	35.0	28.0	37.0	23.3
A2-Current	24.0	40.3	35.7	21.1
A2-Constant	32.3	35.3	32.3	16.0
B1-Current	45.7	13.7	40.7	33.0
B1-Constant	49.3	13.0	37.7	29.0
B2-Current	42.7	18.7	38.7	26.7
B2-Constant	45.0	20.0	35.0	22.0
C1-Current	16.9	45.0	38.1	29.1
C1-Constant	25.8	38.1	36.1	24.2
C2-Current	0.0	67.9	32.1	18.5
C2-Constant	0.0	72.2	27.8	12.6

Note: Table is based on monthly data from January 1960 to February 1990. "Current" and "Constant" refer to the prices used.

A1: Twenty-four of the largest and smallest observations removed from a series of the past five years of monthly prices and the range of the remaining observations providing the upper and lower bounds of the band.

A2: Eighteen of the largest and smallest observations removed from a series of the past five years of monthly prices and the range of the remaining observations providing the upper and lower bounds of the band.

B1: Bands set at ±20 percent above and below the five-year moving average of past monthly prices.

B2: Bands set at ±30 percent above and below the five-year moving average of past monthly prices.

C1: Bands set at ±1 standard deviation above and below the five-year moving average of past monthly prices.

C2: Bands set at ±1.5 standard deviations above and below the five-year moving average of past monthly prices.

Source: Authors' calculations.

in current terms, government subsidy payments were often required, ranging from about 18 percent to 33 percent of the time. As with maize, the upper bound constrained prices more frequently and subsidies were paid more often when the schemes were denominated in current terms.

A Comparison of the Schemes

It is useful to conclude this section of the analysis by briefly comparing the different schemes. This comparison is based on the analysis of maize and sugar presented above as well as an analysis of seven other commodities by Coleman and Larson (1990).

In terms of current dollars, the impact of the schemes on risk reduction as measured by standard deviations and CVs was surprisingly small; in most cases the CV was reduced very little below the CV of world prices. This result was consistent across all commodities analyzed, with the exception of sugar (and to a lesser extent rice), for which prices were the most unstable. One could conclude therefore that using tariffs to stabilize domestic prices (which are linked to world prices) would be an ineffective way to manage commodity price risk. However, although this conclusion may be valid in terms of monthly prices averaged over a twenty-five-year period, the benefits of commodity price stabilization in periods of extremely high or low prices may be large.[4] The low level of risk reduction as measured by the CVs calls into question the appropriateness of the CV as a measure of riskiness. Perhaps a different measure of instability should be applied that weights the outlying observations more heavily (than does, for example, the standard deviation). When the analysis was based on real prices instead of nominal prices, there was a much greater difference in the CVs of domestic prices under the tariff regimes compared with the CVs of the world price.

The reference price scheme reduces the price risk more than the other schemes, and there seems to be very little to choose from between the three price band configurations, except in the case of sugar. When nominal prices were used for the price band schemes, the mean prices fell, indicating that deviations in prices on the upside tended to exceed deviations on the downside. Price bands set at certain percentage levels below and above the reference price afforded more reduction in price risk.

In terms of mean prices and government revenues, and again with the exception of sugar, there was little difference between the price band schemes. Government revenues were largest for the minimum price scheme because no subsidy payments were made in periods of high prices. The minimum price scheme increased the average price across all commodities, because the downside of price fluctuations was supported whereas no subsidy payments were made on the upside. Therefore the minimum price scheme was an instrument of price support as well as risk management. Because no subsidy payments were made when domestic prices were above the guaranteed minimum price level, government revenues for the minimum price scheme were approximately double those for the others. In this respect, price band schemes where no subsidy payments were paid should be considered price support mechanisms as well. Whereas the minimum price scheme and price band schemes without subsidies were both instruments of risk management and price supports, the other schemes did not systematically support prices and were mechanisms only for reducing price variability.

A Welfare Analysis of the Schemes

An analysis of the welfare benefits of each of the tariff-based price stabilization schemes described above was undertaken. The purpose of this exercise was to provide estimates of the dollar value of the benefits derived from the risk reduction associated with each of the schemes. The framework employed was developed by Newbery and Stiglitz (1981) and has been applied in recent studies (Akiyama and Varangis 1990; Jolly, Beck, and Bodman 1990; Hinchy and Fisher 1988).

Newbery and Stiglitz begin by assuming that a country can be modeled as if it were an individual with a von Neumann–Morgenstern utility function of income given by $U(Y)$. The Arrow-Pratt approximation of the coefficient of relative risk aversion is given by

$$R = Y \left[\frac{U''(Y)}{U'(Y)} \right].$$

The effect of price stabilization on income is to transform the distribution of income (Y) from the random variable Y_0 to Y_1. The money value benefits of stabilization are such that $EU(Y_0) = EU(Y_1 - B)$. This formula can be manipulated by using a Taylor series expansion to give the welfare equation

$$B/Y = \Delta Y/Y_0 + 0.5R(Y_0)[\sigma_{Y1}^2 (\overline{Y}_1/\overline{Y}_0)^2 - \sigma_{Y0}^2]$$

where

B is the money value of stabilized benefits,
Y_i is income ($i = 0$ unstabilized income; $i = 1$ stabilized income),
$\overline{Y}_i$ is the mean of Y_i ($i = 0, 1$),
$\sigma_{Y_i}^2$ is the square of the CV of Y_i, and
ΔY is $Y_1 - Y_0$.

The interpretation of B/Y_0 is the dollar value of benefits to producers of stabilized income, expressed as a proportion of average income before stabilization. The first term in the welfare equation (that is, $\Delta Y / Y_0$) is an expression for the transfer benefit because it shows the percentage change in mean producer income before and after the introduction of the stabilization scheme and represents a transfer to producers from consumers or the government, or both, depending on how the stabilization scheme is designed. It is possible for the transfer benefits to be negative, indicating that transfers are made to consumers or the government, or both, by producers. The second term in the equation—that is, $0.5R$ $(Y_0) [\sigma_{Y1}^2 \ (\overline{Y}_1 / \overline{Y}_0)^2 - \sigma_{Y0}^2]$—is the risk benefit to producers, which is positive when the price stabilization scheme lowers the CV of income.

The welfare benefits to the producer of stabilizing prices of maize, sorghum, rice, and sugar are presented in table 15-6. The analysis was based on annual data for 1980–89. Estimates of producer income for these years under the stabilized and unstabilized price scenarios were derived for each of the four commodities as follows. First, the percentage changes in prices between years were combined with an estimate of the elasticity of supply to obtain percentage changes in production. This was done for each of the ten years. This procedure was repeated for the stabilized and unstabilized price series, giving stabilized and unstabilized production series. Then the stabilized price series were multiplied by the stabilized production series to obtain a stabilized income series, and the unstabilized price series and production series were multiplied to give an unstabilized income series. The means and CVs of the income series were used in the welfare equation. This procedure was repeated for each of the four tariff-based price stabilization schemes under consideration. Given that estimates of the elasticity of supply are not available, the welfare benefits are reported for assumed elasticities of 0.1 and 0.3. The coefficient of relative risk aversion was assumed to be equal to one.

From table 15-6 we see that the total benefits were quite small for maize and sorghum and fairly large in the cases of rice and sugar. Most of the benefits were transfer benefits, reflecting an increase in mean income values over the period taken. The risk benefits were small, with the exception of sugar. The low risk benefits reflected the fact that the CVs of the stabilized income series were not much different from the CVs of the unstabilized income series in most cases. Overall, the benefits were larger when the elasticity was assumed to be 0.3 than when it was assumed to be 0.1.

For maize the total benefits were all less than 10 percent of the average unstabilized income level. The risk benefits were below 3 percent and did not differ significantly across the schemes. The transfer benefits for the price bands were negative when the elasticity was assumed to be 0.1, indicating that the mean of stabilized income was less than the mean of

Table 15-6. Simulated Welfare Benefits of Various Commodity Price Stabilization Schemes for Maize, Sorghum, Rice, and Sugar in Venezuela, 1980–89 (percentage of total revenue)

	Reference price scheme		Minimum price scheme		Price band scheme A[a]		Price band scheme B[b]		Price band scheme C[c]	
	0.1[d]	0.3[d]	0.1	0.3	0.1	0.3	0.1	0.3	0.1	0.3
Maize										
Transfer benefit	4.6	7.4	6.2	7.3	-2.5	-0.9	-1.9	-1.1	0.9	1.1
Risk benefit	1.5	1.9	1.3	1.8	0.9	2.2	0.9	2.2	1.6	2.8
Total benefit	6.1	9.3	5.5	9.1	-1.6	1.3	-1.0	1.1	2.5	3.9
Sorghum										
Transfer benefit	6.0	9.6	9.7	10.9	-0.3	1.6	6.7	8.1	3.3	4.6
Risk benefit	1.2	1.5	1.1	1.4	0.9	1.2	1.2	1.6	0.8	1.0
Total benefit	7.2	11.1	10.8	12.3	0.6	2.8	7.9	9.7	4.1	5.6
Rice										
Transfer benefit	11.7	18.6	16.7	18.7	-3.6	-2.2	-2.1	-0.3	-1.7	-0.5
Risk benefit	2.0	2.6	0.6	0.8	2.3	3.2	2.5	3.4	1.9	2.6
Total benefit	13.7	21.2	17.3	19.5	-1.3	1.0	0.4	3.1	0.2	2.1
Sugar										
Transfer benefit	21.8	26.1	38.2	40.9	-8.8	-10.4	35.3	37.8	20.1	33.4
Risk benefit	1.4	1.4	3.3	4.5	6.0	8.0	2.9	4.0	7.7	9.1
Total benefit	23.2	27.5	41.5	45.4	-2.8	-2.4	38.2	41.0	27.8	42.5

Note: All schemes shown have subsidies.

a. Band set by removing twenty-four of the highest and lowest monthly price observations made during the sixty months preceding the period, and incorporating the rest in the band.

b. Band set at ±20 percent of the sixty-month moving average of past prices.

c. Band set at ±1 standard deviation from the sixty-month moving average of past prices.

d. Supply elasticity.

Source: Authors' calculations.

unstabilized income. Similar results were obtained for sorghum. In all schemes the risk benefits were less than 2 percent of the average unstabilized income. Large differences were found for the transfer benefits associated with the three price band schemes. This was because during the 1980s sorghum prices were at the upper bounds of these schemes, and the upper bound for scheme B is significantly higher than for schemes A and C.

The transfer benefits of stabilizing the income from rice production were positive for the reference price and minimum price schemes and negative for the price band schemes. The negative numbers reflected a fall in average income that resulted from prices being held at the upper bound. The risk benefits were small, the maximum being 3.4 percent.

The largest risk benefits were realized for sugar. This result reflected the large fall in the CV for sugar in every scheme considered. In the case of price band scheme C, the risk benefit was more than 9 percent, the highest reported in table 15-6. Wide differences were found between the price band schemes in terms of transfer benefits. The reason for this was the same as in the case of sorghum: the price was constrained by the upper bound, which was much higher for price band scheme B than for the other schemes.

This analysis showed that the risk benefits of price stabilization were quite small when based on the Newbery and Stiglitz framework. This finding is consistent with the other applications of the framework cited above. However, the analysis ignores important factors such as the distribution of income of individual producers and differences in their risk attitudes. Also, the results are sensitive to the choice of the instability measure and to the assumptions made about the value of the coefficient of relative risk aversion.

Another important omission from the analysis and discussion so far is the efficiency losses associated with each of the schemes. When tariffs and subsidies are used to make domestic prices different from international prices, efficiency losses are incurred. This is because the international price represents the opportunity cost of resources used in producing domestically. These costs should be traded off against the welfare benefits associated with risk reduction. However, a considerably more complicated model would be required to measure the welfare losses associated with such stabilization schemes.

Recommendations

In deciding which tariff-based stabilization program to recommend for Venezuela, we first put forward the characteristics we thought a stabilization scheme should have. These characteristics became criteria against which the schemes were judged.

The first criterion was that the scheme should allow changes in the world price to be reflected in the domestic market. This criterion is based on economic efficiency arguments, which state that when domestic prices differ from border prices, welfare and efficiency losses are incurred. Of the schemes analyzed, the ±30 percent band without subsidies was found to meet the criterion best.[5] It placed the fewest constraints on domestic prices and allowed the greatest range of international prices to prevail directly in the domestic market. In contrast, the reference price scheme did not allow changes in international prices to be reflected in the domestic market other than to move the reference price marginally in the direction of the price change. Therefore, price band schemes with wide bands and without subsidies are preferred.[6]

The second criterion was that the mean stabilized producer price should not be above or below the long-run international price. In other words, because the goal of the policy is to stabilize the domestic price, the tariff structure should not increase or decrease the price over the long term. Otherwise there will be a transfer between producers and consumers. As shown in tables 15-1 to 15-4, whenever the schemes had a reference price based on a five-year moving average of past prices (denominated in current terms), the mean prices of the stabilized series tended to be below the mean of the unstabilized, international price. Thus a transfer from producers to consumers occurred. However, the results showed that this transfer was small (less than 5 percent of the world price in most cases). The transfer was lower for a reference price based on fewer years of past prices and if subsidy payments were not made.

An alternative approach would be to denominate the reference price and price bands in terms of real prices. As shown in tables 15-1 to 15-4, the mean price of schemes denominated in constant dollars was not consistently above or below the mean of the world price. Even with prices denominated in constant terms, the minimum price scheme (which only supported the domestic price when international prices were low) systematically increased the mean domestic price. Also, price band scheme A may not preserve the mean price even when constant prices are used, because the upper and lower bounds are not set symmetrically around the reference price.

The third criterion was that the scheme should not impose an excessive financial burden on the government. For importing countries such as Venezuela, a tariff-based stabilization scheme can become a burden, because when international prices are high, the reference price (in a reference price scheme) or upper bound (in a price band scheme) can be maintained only by reducing the basic tariff and, if the basic tariff then falls to zero, by paying subsidies. For exporting countries, such schemes can become a burden because the government must pay subsidies to exporters to maintain the reference price or lower bound when international prices are very low.

For the scenarios analyzed above, if subsidies are not made, there will clearly be no budgetary difficulties for the government. For an importing country, when international prices are very high, the basic tariff on imports will fall to zero but never go negative. In this regard, all schemes without subsidy payments are equally desirable. However, in terms of the stability of government revenues from import tariffs, the price band schemes with the widest bands are the most desirable because under these schemes the basic tariff applies most often. In contrast, the reference price scheme requires that the tariff rate change every period.

In times of very high international prices the government may decide to subsidize imports to maintain the reference price or upper bound. Providing the subsidies could become a heavy fiscal burden, especially if the high international prices persist for long periods.[7] Subsidies are more likely to be given under the following conditions: if the basic tariff is set at a relatively low level; if the stabilization scheme is very constraining (for example, if a price band is narrow); if the scheme is denominated in current prices; and if the world price is above the reference price.[8] On the basis of these conditions, of the stabilization schemes employing subsidies, the price band scheme with the most relaxed band and denominated in constant prices is least likely to impose a fiscal burden. Therefore, the most desirable scheme analyzed is the price band scheme with bounds set at 30 percent around the reference price. This scheme provides even greater flexibility than the scheme with band widths 1.5 standard deviations around the reference price.

In the long run, there should not be a heavy fiscal burden if the stabilization scheme in any period is centered on the current long-run price and if border prices are normally distributed. Defending a price above the long-run average will eventually lead to a financial deficit. Commodity price series may exhibit distributional characteristics leading to large single-year or multiple-year expenditures that may still strain fiscal budgets in the medium term.

The fourth criterion was that the scheme should be transparent and predictable. Transparent rules allow economic agents to act more efficiently, remove advantages to "insiders," and are easier to administer. All of the schemes discussed above are transparent, with the exception, perhaps, of price band scheme A, where the rules of the scheme can be changed slightly to give large changes in the band widths.[9] However, it can be argued that if a government wishes to manipulate or change the stabilization policy it will do so whatever the mechanism employed.

The stabilization schemes denominated in real terms are generally more difficult to interpret and tend to be much less transparent. Also, such schemes require that a suitable index be chosen. These concerns can be accommodated if a common and well-known deflator is used, such as the U.S. producer price index.

From the single standard of economic efficiency, it is clear that a policy of no intervention is preferred, with risks hedged by using standard market mechanisms such as futures, options, swaps, and multiperiod contracts. Based on the multiple criteria cited earlier, however, and in conjunction with the further criterion that it must be workable and acceptable to the government operating the scheme, the most appropriate, "second best" scheme for Venezuela appears to be the price band scheme, in particular, price band scheme B. It would provide producers and consumers protection against extremely high and low prices and would be very transparent. It would be even more transparent if it were operated in terms of nominal prices.

It is recommended that the price bands be set at a given percentage above and below a reference price that is the five-year moving average of monthly prices. To ease the transition in Venezuela's agricultural sector from a system of fixed market prices to one in which prices are allowed to fluctuate freely, the bands could be widened over time. For example, bands could be set at ± 10 percent for an initial period (say, six months) and then widened to ± 20 percent after one year. Later the bands could be widened even further to, say, ± 30 percent, by which time the bands would rarely constrain domestic prices (see table 15-5).

In order to maintain an effect on average prices, the scheme would require subsidies when prices are at the upper bound and additional taxes when they reach the lower bound. This combination of subsidies and taxes may not be practicable. If trade across borders is profitable, then targeting only domestic consumers is impossible. Furthermore, such subsidies encourage circular trade. Given the limited resources of the government, such a program would soon fail. As a result, the band might have to operate without subsidies, despite the subsequent distortions.

Conclusions

The research presented in this chapter was prompted by agricultural trade reforms being discussed by the Venezuelan government. The purpose of this study was to analyze a number of tariff-based commodity price stabilization schemes in terms of their effect on the average level and stability of domestic prices, on government revenues, and on producer welfare.

Three tariff-based stabilization schemes were analyzed: a reference price scheme, a guaranteed minimum price scheme, and three varieties of a price band scheme. Each of the schemes was analyzed using both nominal and real prices and with and without the government paying import subsidies.

In terms of risk reduction, when measured in current dollars and as measured by the standard deviations and CVs, the impact of employing any of these schemes was surprisingly small. With the exception of sugar, whose prices were very unstable, the CVs of the commodities analyzed fell very little below the CVs of world prices. The difference in CVs was greater when real prices instead of nominal prices were used.

Overall, the reference price scheme reduced the price risk more than the other schemes, and there seemed to be very little difference in results between the three price band configurations, except in the case of sugar. Government revenues were largest for the minimum price scheme because no subsidy payments were made in periods of high prices. Across all commodities, the minimum price scheme increased the average price the most, because only downward price fluctuations were supported and no subsidy payments were made when prices moved up.

In addition to these analyses, the welfare effects of the schemes were calculated using a framework developed by Newbery and Stiglitz. Overall, the results showed that the welfare benefits were small. This result followed mainly from the fact that the measure of risk reduction used in the approach (that is, the change in the CVs of stabilized, compared with unstabilized, income) was found to be small.

Based on a number of criteria, the most appropriate tariff-based stabilization scheme for Venezuela appears to be the price band scheme. It is recommended that bands be set at a certain percentage above and below a reference price, which could be set at the five-year moving average of monthly prices. To ease the transition to a free market, the band widths could be set quite narrowly initially (for example, at ± 10 percent) and then be widened over time (for example, to ± 20 percent after six months and to ± 30 percent after one year). Such a scheme should be operated in nominal prices.

Notes

1. The problem with a tariff scheme that seeks to maintain a price around its long-run average is the pressure, both from budgetary demands and from producers, to avoid domestic price reductions. One would anticipate that the stabilized price would be above the long-run average.

2. For example, in the case of Venezuela a reference price equal to a five-year moving average of past world prices was used.

3. In an extended version of this paper, Coleman and Larson (1990) report the results for

nine commodities—maize, wheat, sorghum, rice, sugar, soybeans, soybean meal, soybean oil, and palm oil.

4. Empirical evidence, for example, Binswanger (1978), indicates that risk aversion increases in the face of larger potential loses. Thus, extreme prices are likely to place extraordinary pressures on producers, consumers, and government officials.

5. The exception to this is for sugar, for which bands set at ±1.5 standard deviations from the reference price provide the greatest flexibility.

6. Such schemes may not be the most efficient, however. For the same reduction in price variability achieved without subsidies, efficiency losses are lower if the scheme operates with subsidies. Operating on two margins to reduce risk extracts the smallest marginal efficiency losses.

7. Targeting the effects of import subsidies in a country with otherwise liberal trade policies may prove untenable as well, because subsidized imports may be reexported or smuggled.

8. These features are borne out by the results for sugar. Using current prices, and with a tight price band, even with a basic tariff of 20 percent a subsidy payment averaging $9.20 a ton would be required to maintain the scheme.

9. When this scheme was used in Chile, the rules over the number of observations removed from the scheme were adjusted continuously, with the result that the price band widths changed unpredictably.

16

Integration of the International Rice Market: Implications for Risk Management

Jeannette Herrmann

For more than half the population of the world, rice is the predominant food staple. Many people eat rice at every meal, and their health depends on the ability to purchase sufficient quantities of this basic foodstuff. In Thailand, where the word for eating is synonymous with the term "eating rice," per capita consumption of rice is almost half a kilogram a day—about a pound of uncooked rice.

Rice is pervasive in many cultures—in households where it is produced and consumed; in religious, marketing, and fiscal institutions; and in national political and economic structures, whose fortunes rise and fall with rice. One factor that may have precipitated the recent unrest in Myanmar (formerly Burma) may well have been the 530 percent increase in the price of rice during early 1988 (Mydans 1988). The upheaval is hardly surprising when one calculates the daily cost of food: the half kilogram of rice eaten by the average Myanmar costs half the minimum daily wage.[1]

The importance of rice as a staple food and as a source of income for

The author wishes to express her appreciation for the thoughtful comments of Robert Dohner, Walter Falcon, Peter Timmer, Christopher Owens, Anne Peck, and the late Robert West on earlier versions of this chapter. Most of the work on this chapter was completed prior to the author's employment as an advisory economist at the Chicago Board of Trade. The author is currently a consulting economist with offices in Boston and Chicago. The opinions expressed are her own and do not represent those of the Chicago Board of Trade.

small farmers creates strong incentives for governments to protect both groups from price variation by maintaining barriers between domestic and international markets. International trade becomes a function of excess domestic supply and demand—a trade of residual supply, not responsive to current world prices. As a result, the international market is thin in relation to world production: less than 5 percent of annual production is traded internationally. The small international market is thus very sensitive to variations in supply and demand. The resulting price volatility creates added incentives for self-sufficiency in rice, further thinning the market. The evidence summarized in table 16-1 indicates that world prices are much more variable than either world production or world trade.

This price instability combined with uncertainty regarding annual trade volumes translates into substantial risk exposure for many countries for which rice is an important source and use of foreign exchange. Bangladesh spends about 10 percent of its annual export earnings on rice imports. Between 1981 and 1983, Myanmar received, on average, 43.2 percent of its export earnings from rice. During the same period, Thailand received 15.1 percent of its foreign exchange from rice exports (a decline from 35.6 percent in 1964). Nepal, contributing only 0.6 percent of the world rice trade, received 26 percent of its export earnings from rice sales (World Bank, various years).

The insulation of domestic markets from international variability creates conditions under which neither producers nor consumers observe signals that accurately reflect supply conditions. Economic efficiency

Table 16-1. *Variability of World Rice Production, Trade, and Prices, Selected Years 1950–89*

	Coefficient of variation[a]				
	1950–59	*1960–69*	*1970–79*	*1980–89*	*Average*
World production	0.12	0.07	0.10	0.08	0.09
World trade	0.18	0.09	0.12	0.08	0.12
U.S. price in constant U.S. dollars	n.a.	0.07	0.37	0.33	0.26
Thai price in constant U.S. dollars	0.11	0.15	0.40	0.35	0.25

n.a. Not applicable.

a. The ratio of the standard deviation to the mean.

Source: Production and trade figures for 1950–79 from International Rice Research Institute (1986); for 1980–89, U.S. Department of Agriculture, Foreign Agricultural Service, *World Grain Situation and Outlook* (various issues). Prices from World Bank (various years).

losses result from this divergence from the assumptions underlying competition. Information usually found in prices permits efficient decision-making regarding the allocation of resources, including those resources allocated to risk management. Failure of the market to establish a price under competitive conditions decreases the efficiency of rice trading and thus increases the magnitude of the risk to which trading nations are exposed.

This chapter explores the potential of a rice futures market for hedging price risks. It also evaluates the performance of the rice futures market and discusses its contribution to reducing inefficiencies in the rice cash market.

The Rice Market

World Production and Consumption

The rice crop, annually about 345 million metric tons (milled) worldwide (see table 16-2), represents the second highest volume of production of any crop, next to wheat. Together, production of these two grains uses one-fourth of the world's arable land.

In contrast to wheat, roughly 20 percent of which is used as livestock feed, rice is used almost exclusively for food. The U.S. Department of Agriculture (USDA) estimates that average per capita consumption of rice is about 64 kilograms a year—four-tenths of a pound per day. In many populations, nutritional status can be estimated by rice consumption.

Supply Elasticities

Determinants of supply are primarily technical, such as area planted and yields (themselves a function of irrigation, fertilizer, and so forth). Other determinants are climatological and political.

Rice supply elasticities in the range of zero to one-third are reported in Thailand, West Malaysia (where it is more than one in the long run), Japan, and the Philippines and between one-third and two-thirds in Java and Iraq (again where it is more than one in the long run; see Askari and Cummings 1976). Rice supply is not highly price-responsive, although some evidence indicates that higher prices reduce on-farm consumption and thus increase the marketed surplus (Barker, Herdt, and Rose 1985). Countries contribute little price-responsive supply to the world market. Siamwalla and Haykin (1983) found only seventeen of fifty-five countries to be at all price-responsive. China is the most responsive, followed by the United States, where the response comes primarily though changes in planted area.

Table 16-2. *Rice Production and Consumption*

	1989–90 (millions of tons)		Per capita consumption, in 1986[a] (kilograms)
	Production	Consumption	
Exporters			
China	126.1	123.3	113.9
India	74.1	71.7	76.6
Myanmar	13.5	7.0	—
Pakistan	3.2	2.4	20.6
Thailand	13.7	8.6	163.8
United States	5.1	2.7	8.9
Vietnam	12.0	10.3	—
Importers			
Bangladesh	18.0	17.9	—
Brazil	5.0	7.4	50.7
Indonesia	29.1	28.2	145.8
Japan	9.4	9.7	80.7
Korea, Rep. of	5.9	5.7	—
World	344.5	337.6	63.7

— Not available.

a. Excludes feed.

Source: Production and consumption data from U.S. Department of Agriculture, World Agricultural Outlook Board. Per capita consumption data from U.S. Department of Agriculture, Economic Research Service (1987).

Demand Elasticities

Determinants of demand can be viewed at a national level, where population growth is clearly the dominant influence, or at an individual level, where income and price are critical. As household income rises, the proportion of the household budget spent on food decreases. At low income levels, very high (close to one) income elasticities for food are observed; these fall off as incomes rise.

Estimates of Asian income elasticities of demand for rice have varied and are largely dependent on income levels. Estimates by the Food and Agriculture Organization (FAO) range from −0.1 for Japan to 0.7 for Indonesia. The USDA finds an elasticity of 0.3 for rice in South Asia, 0.0 in Southeast Asia, and 0.2 in East Asia. The International Food Policy Research Institute estimates income elasticities of below 0.1 for Thailand, Malaysia, Korea, and Nepal, and of approximately 0.5 for Indonesia, Myanmar, India, and Sri Lanka. Estimates of Asian price elasticity range from −0.6 to −0.3.[2]

Substitutions

Households with very low incomes substitute maize and cassava for rice. In global trade, however, wheat is the most common substitute for rice. The ratio of rice prices to wheat prices has more than doubled over the last sixty years. Siamwalla and Haykin (1983) offer three possible explanations: the supply of wheat has grown faster than the supply of rice; the population in predominantly rice-consuming areas has grown faster than that in wheat-eating areas; and income elasticities are higher among rice eaters than among wheat eaters. Barker, Herdt, and Rose (1985) also argue that the growth of wheat production in Asia may be a major factor in the decline in wheat prices in relation to rice prices. One-third of the world's wheat is now produced and consumed in China and the former Soviet Union. Nevertheless, the change in relative prices appears to drive the growth of wheat imports at an annual rate of about 4 percent in monsoon Asia. Specifically, the average annual change in wheat imports between 1960 and 1980 was negative in South Asia (the Indo-Gangetic plain produces 10 percent of world wheat) but nearly 9 percent in Southeast Asia (notably Indonesia, Vietnam, and the Philippines) and 5 percent in East Asia (Barker, Herdt, and Rose 1985).

Managing Instability in the Rice Market

Siamwalla and Haykin (1983) describe the international rice market as thin, based on the high search costs associated with rice transactions: a market with few participants would be expected to develop established trading patterns and thereby decreased search costs. The distinguishing thinness found in the rice market derives from the instability of participants on both the purchasing and sales sides, they argue. The thinness is exacerbated by increasing desires for self-sufficiency expected to be realized through modern technology. With no central market for rice, each decision to enter the market may require a new search for trading partners.

The thinness of the international market leads to increased price volatility. If, for example, Indonesia has a poor harvest and needs to buy in the world market, the impact of such a large purchase shocks the market. Based on the 1984 rice market, each additional million tons that Indonesia might import would raise the world price about $50 a ton, starting from $200 a ton (including cost, insurance, and freight [c.i.f.]) under conditions of Indonesian self-sufficiency. If on the other hand, Indonesia were to export a million tons of rice, from the same starting position, rice prices would drop to $120 a ton (free on board [f.o.b.]), the level at which it becomes economic to use rice as livestock feed and therefore the level at which the price stabilizes (Timmer 1986).

Food prices play a dual role: they determine both food consumption levels, especially among the poor, and food production levels, through incentives to farmers (Timmer, Falcon, and Pearson 1983). In response to this food price dilemma, governments generally intervene. The less developed countries tend to have pricing policies that favor consumers; more developed countries generally have producer-biased policies, as found in the United States and the European Community. Both approaches result in large government subsidies.

The impact of price volatility is generally absorbed by the government subsidy needed to protect the domestic market. China spends 30 percent of its national budget to maintain its food price structure—more than is spent on health, education, and defense combined (Timmer 1988). Chinese grain and edible oil price subsidies alone, as a percentage of government revenues, increased an average of 50 percent annually between 1978 and 1985, reaching 15 percent of government revenues in 1984 (Liu 1989).

Domestic price stabilization policies may insulate domestic consumers and producers from the changes experienced in the world market, although they shift the risk to the government. The most popular of these stabilization schemes are buffer stock mechanisms. These can be effective seasonal price stabilizers but are generally considered unlikely to be cost-efficient protection against the kind of serious drops in production that occur in Asia about once every decade (World Bank 1986). Grain insurance plans have been proposed but are difficult to implement for rice (Johnson 1981). Participation in international trade is considered the most efficient strategy for providing food security, because global production is generally less variable than domestic production. It is highly unlikely that all countries would need large stocks in the same year; stockpiling purchasing power is preferable to stockpiling grain.

Futures and options markets can improve decisionmaking among grain-trading nations. These markets integrate information about expectations surrounding future prices, aid in price discovery, and provide a mechanism for risk transfer. Information from futures markets can be used to guide domestic price policy or to hedge projected trade. Below, a description and evaluation of the rice futures market follows a review of domestic stabilization policies and international trade in rice.

Domestic Stabilization Policies

Governments absorb price risk: domestic price variation is rarely as great as world price variation. This relative stability is not the result of stable domestic production. Although a few major rice-consuming nations have less variable production than the world as a whole has, almost all major importing nations have much greater production variability than the world does, as demonstrated by the data in table 16-3.

Stocks moderate seasonal price fluctuations and provide security against the possibility of a poor harvest. Storage, the temporal integration of markets, represents large costs in rice marketing. Storing rice is very risky: estimates of loss range from below 1 percent to as high as 10 percent (Barker, Herdt, and Rose 1985).[3] Furthermore, risk in storing products is amplified where politics may change a commodity's value. Nevertheless, stocks are one of the most important tools in domestic short-run price stabilization plans.

Siamwalla and Haykin (1983) found that the major rice-producing and -consuming nations do not transmit all of their domestic variability to the international market. Overstocking, rather than export, appears to be the main response to excess production. Levels of ending stocks (carryover stocks from one crop year to the next) have varied from 10 percent to 21 percent of consumption levels during the past twenty-five years. However, government stocks are not immediately available to the world market. Private speculative stockholding in countries where rice could be traded across borders unimpeded by national taxes and quotas should, in theory, stabilize prices. In practice, speculative private stockholding is minimal—probably for lack of legal devices and physical storage space (Siamwalla and Haykin 1983).

Trade

Although international trade is considered the most efficient strategy for providing food security, international trade in rice is very risky because the market is so thin and imperfectly competitive. In contrast, the international wheat market trades about 20 percent of annual production (of about 500 million metric tons) and has active cash and futures markets that provide vehicles for speculative storage. Rice prices are more volatile than prices for other grains, including wheat, the production of which is slightly more variable than that of rice. The reason for the comparative volatility of rice prices is that the demand for rice as food is relatively inelastic, whereas the demand for other grains, because they are also used as livestock feed, is more elastic.

Another characteristic of rice trade is that much rice stays within the region where it is grown, not entering even the domestic market. Siamwalla and Haykin (1983) found that between 1953 and 1968 only 12.2 to 14.2 percent of total production was marketed in Bangladesh; even in Thailand, the largest exporter, the marketed surplus was only 56.9 per-

Table 16-3. *Variability of Domestic Rice Production of High-consuming Producers and Major Importing Producers, 1950–89*

	Coefficient of variation[a]				
	1950–59	1960–69	1970–79	1980–89	Average
World production	0.12	0.07	0.10	0.08	0.09
Producers with annual per capita consumption of over 100 kg					
Cambodia	0.12	0.13	0.53	0.15	0.23
Korea, Dem. People's Rep. of	0.13	0.17	0.29	0.06	0.16
Korea, Rep. of	0.17	0.16	0.17	0.09	0.15
Vietnam	0.28	0.04	0.06	0.13	0.13
Laos	0.09	0.21	0.05	0.12	0.12
Malaysia	0.12	0.16	0.10	0.08	0.12
Indonesia	0.10	0.09	0.13	0.14	0.12
Thailand	0.13	0.14	0.10	0.08	0.11
Nepal	0.06	0.14	0.09	0.14	0.11
Myanmar	0.09	0.08	0.11	0.09	0.09
Bangladesh	0.09	0.10	0.10	0.08	0.09
Taiwan	0.10	0.09	0.05	0.12	0.09
Producers with large annual import volumes					
Iraq	0.37	0.49	0.45	0.23	0.39
Iran	0.16	0.19	0.14	0.06	0.14
Brazil	0.12	0.13	0.13	0.15	0.13
India	0.15	0.10	0.12	0.13	0.12
Philippines	0.10	0.11	0.15	0.07	0.11
Bangladesh	0.09	0.10	0.10	0.08	0.09

Note: Countries are ranked by average coefficient of variation.

a. The ratio of the standard deviation to the mean.

Source: Production figures for 1950–79 from International Rice Research Institute (1986); for 1980–89, U.S. Department of Agriculture, World Agricultural Outlook Board.

cent in 1971. Thus, fluctuations in production are magnified in their impact on the domestic markets. Worldwide, the rice marketing system shares characteristics common to many food crops. A small number of middlemen buy from a large number of producers and, in turn, sell to a large number of consumers. Such a bottleneck in the marketing sector offers opportunities for oligopolistic behavior and high price volatility.

Rice dealers are quick to point out that rice is not a homogeneous commodity. Different varieties and grades are preferred by different consumers. Within a grade, many factors influence the value of a given lot, and large price differentials exist. These price differentials between grades are much greater than between grades of wheat (Barker, Herdt, and Rose 1985).

Of the rice traded internationally, much moves as food aid. In the early 1970s, one quarter of the rice traded was to meet aid needs, compared with about 15 percent of the wheat traded. By 1984, about 10 percent of each of these grains traded was shipped as aid. The major providers of rice aid are the United States and Japan, followed by the European Community and Australia. On the whole, developing countries in Asia receive less rice aid now than in the early to mid-1970s; African and Latin American countries receive more—about 15 percent of their rice imports are aid (Smith 1987).

The Mechanics of a Futures Market

A futures market is designed to allocate risk efficiently. Buyers and sellers trade a standardized contract to deliver a specific quantity and quality of a commodity at a specified time and place. Participants in a futures market are generally divided into hedgers and speculators. Hedgers protect themselves against a price change between now and a future purchase or sale of the actual commodity by locking in a price on a futures contract. Speculators, or risk takers, seek to profit from price movements. The key third party to each transaction is the clearinghouse that makes contracts impersonal, protecting both parties from default by guaranteeing each trade.

The market's basic role is to provide rational forward prices. All new information that might affect the commodity market is embodied in both the spot (cash) and futures prices. Evidence shows that both these prices are equally variable for continuously stocked commodities (Peck 1985). Although most contracts are settled in cash, the option of delivery is fundamental to the working of the futures market. In an efficient market the basis, the difference between the futures price and the spot price, moves to zero over the life of the contract, with the result that the cash and futures prices of the deliverable quality are equal at the time of delivery in the delivery locations. In this fashion, the futures market increases the predictability of returns from storing the commodity and thus contributes to seasonal stability. The evidence shows that insofar as production, storage, and consumption decisions are based on rational forward prices rather than on retrospective expectations, ex ante social costs are reduced (Peck 1985). Hedgers, who have traded price risk for basis risk (the fraction of price volatility that remains unhedged), depend on such rational forward prices.

Rationality can be considered from two aspects: bias and predictability. Bias (chronic under- or overestimation of the future price) is not a characteristic problem in futures markets, although some thin markets do demonstrate lopsidedness over extended periods—probably the result of inadequate speculative participation (Gray 1987a).

Evidence on predictability (the value of the futures price as a forecast) is mixed. Futures prices for nonstorable commodities often demonstrate poor predictive capacity across crop years. Evidence from the potato market shows that potato futures prices are not useful predictors, because they create a self-defeating supply response from one season to the next (Gray 1987b). Similar observations have been made in other markets for nonstorable commodities (see Martin and Garcia's work on hog and cattle markets and Leuthold and Hartmann's work on hog markets, both cited by Peck 1985).

For storable commodities, where inventories link crop years, prices in the cash and futures markets are equally variable and reflective of available information; here futures prices are better predictors of cash prices (see Peck 1985 on Tomek and Gray's work on maize and soybeans). Inventories add a "self-fulfilling" aspect to these forecasts that improve their predictive value.

Futures trading serves as a centralized market. One value of a centralized market is that potential buyers and sellers of the commodity, as well as of risk, can find trading partners efficiently at all times, minimizing search costs. Another value is the broadcasting of prices. Forward prices for the commodity guide sales negotiations as well as decisions about resource allocation. It is often the case that the contract traded may not be for the exact quality or terms being negotiated elsewhere but may provide a benchmark, or reference price, to which a premium or discount can be applied. Studying the relationship between prices for related qualities, terms, and commodities allows efficient pricing decisions that reflect the integration of the markets.[4]

The revelation of expectations about future supply and demand increases the efficiency of production, marketing, and consumption. Peck (1985, p. 73) states that futures markets are the "primary price discovery markets for most of the storable agricultural products . . . [and are] widely used to complement the fundamental purchase and sales decisions. Futures prices are the referent prices in all transactions . . . because they provide a standardized, competitively determined reflection of underlying current and future value."

Futures markets increase the number of speculators in a commodity market because transaction costs in a commodity market are lower than in a cash market. Returns to these speculators depend on the accurate prediction of price movements; thus greater incentives exist to search out information. This information should be reflected in both the futures and cash prices and, as responses to information are considered, prices should become increasingly rational. Tests of such informational efficiency in futures prices show mixed results. Nevertheless, overall these studies demonstrate that "speculation in futures clearly improves both market liquidity and the information content of prices" (Peck 1985, pp. 72–73).

A Futures Market for Rice

The history of rice contracts is sparse. A futures market for rice existed in Japan in the 1930s and 1940s until it was closed by the occupation forces. Thirty contracts were traded on the New York Mercantile Exchange in 1964. In April 1981 the New Orleans Cotton Exchange (NOCE) opened, trading both rough and milled rice futures. The milled rice contract was never very popular, but more than a thousand rough rice contracts were outstanding when the market closed in June 1983 following Merrill Lynch's decision to quadruple the margin requirement in response to increased futures market volatility. In September of that year, the Chicago Rice and Cotton Exchange (CRCE) got permission to trade the NOCE contracts on the MidAmerica floor. In August of 1986, MidAmerica became affiliated with the Chicago Board of Trade.

The CRCE rice contract now specifies 2,000 hundredweight, the equivalent of 90.7 metric tons, of U.S. Number 2 or better long grain rough rice for delivery in one of twelve counties in eastern Arkansas. The rice must have at least 48 percent head rice (whole grains) and a milling yield of at least 65 percent. The par milling yield is 55/70 (55 percent head rice and 15 percent broken rice, for a total milling yield of 70 percent). Six contract months in each year (January, March, May, July, September, and November) are traded by the CRCE on the floor of the Chicago Board of Trade.[5] Trades are cleared through (and guaranteed by) the Board of Trade Clearing Corporation.

Since the NOCE contracts moved to the floor of the Chicago Board of Trade, the volume of trade on the rough rice contract has grown to the extent that the rough rice contract no longer meets the Commodity

Table 16-4. Prices for Rough Rice Futures Contracts on the Chicago Rice and Cotton Exchange, Selected Months, 1986–89

Futures contract	Trading period	Low price (dollars)	High price (dollars)	Last price (dollars)	Average volume (number of contracts)	Average open interest (number of contracts)
Nov 86	08/20/86–10/31/86	3.97	4.21	4.20	21	158
Jan 87	11/05/86–12/31/86	3.95	4.35	3.95	12	117
Mar 87	01/02/87–02/27/87	4.03	4.26	4.10	11	123
May 87	02/27/87–04/30/87	4.05	4.27	4.17	7	129
Sep 87	04/30/87–08/31/87	4.40	5.93	5.60	13	211
Nov 87	08/31/87–10/30/87	5.73	10.89	9.10	126	915
Jan 88	10/30/87–12/31/87	8.47	10.57	10.46	102	1,171
Mar 88	01/04/88–02/29/88	10.82	13.11	12.04	175	1,531
May 88	02/29/88–04/29/88	7.51	12.40	7.51	141	1,423
Sep 88	05/01/88–08/31/88	6.53	9.30	7.05	47	751
Nov 88	09/01/88–10/31/88	6.91	7.45	6.96	60	904
Jan 89	11/01/88–12/30/88	6.54	7.15	6.67	50	677

Source: Chicago Board of Trade.

Futures Trading Commission's criterion of a "thin" market (fewer than a thousand contracts traded in four of six consecutive months). Activity in the rice futures market for each contract nearing its delivery period is summarized in table 16-4.

The danger of a thin market is that single actors can manipulate it. Position limits (250 contracts net in one month and 500 net in all contracts) are designed to minimize the potential for manipulation, but bona fide hedgers can apply for exemptions to these limits. Even so, hedgers are limited in the amount of risk that they can lay off in a thin market (general wisdom dictates that no one party should hold more than 10 percent of the open interest). The limited price variability reduces speculative interest, further reducing market liquidity.

In the future the most beneficial aspect of the rice futures market may be its price discovery function. The rice trade has traditionally been marked by a high degree of secrecy, although rice market information has become more available since 1986.

There is no central cash rice market comparable to the market for wheat, which equilibrates global supply and demand and broadcasts a world cash price. Nevertheless, benchmarks exist. Common international prices are for milled rice; rough rice is less frequently traded, because hulls have very low value. Within an area having common milling technologies and markets for by-products, rough rice offers a more fundamental price.

Rice prices do not arise in a purely competitive or open market and are not all equally available. Because an examination of the international rice market must be based on these cash prices, a description and assessment of some of the more commonly cited price series is in the Appendix.

Evaluating the Performance of the Rice Futures Market

What is the relationship between rice prices in futures and cash markets? To what extent are rice markets integrated, so that price movements are synchronized? It is very difficult to evaluate these relationships, given the complete lack of daily cash prices, the scarcity of a weekly cash price series, and the even greater paucity of U.S. cash price information in the spring and summer. Nevertheless, the potential contribution of a rice futures market makes analysis using the best available data valuable.

Market Integration

Markets can be integrated across space and across time. If prices differ by more than transportation costs between two geographically distinct markets, arbitraging traders profit by shipping goods. Similarly, when prices for immediate delivery differ from prices for forward delivery by more than the cost of storage, arbitragers integrate markets across time by storing goods. A full set of competitive markets ensures efficient consumption and production across space and time.

TESTING THE INTEGRATION OF CASH MARKETS. Exports of U.S. long grain rice are the product flows necessary to consider the hypothesis that the U.S. rice market is integrated with the international market. U.S. commercial exporters compete with Thai traders in the European Community and the Middle East. Within the United States, some millers and cooperatives specialize regionally but nevertheless face a nationwide market for their products.

Petzel and Monke (1979) found that U.S. milled rice prices lagged Thai prices by a month in their study of market integration between 1967 and 1978. Did the development of futures trading in Chicago have an integrating effect on cash markets? Do prices in these markets move together? Did they appear to move more closely in 1988 than in 1986?

To examine these questions, this analysis compares price movements across markets and across time. Price trends during the marketing year obscure the relationships among actual prices. Therefore, first differences (weekly price changes) are used to study the tracking of prices in geographically disparate markets. One would expect well-integrated markets to have tightly related price changes, and thus regression coefficients close to one.

The USDA-announced world price is taken as the proxy for world prices. Louisiana prices are the average of public bid sales. Arkansas prices are privately obtained farm and elevator price quotes. Brinkley, Arkansas, prices are derived from logs of confirmed public bid sales. Details of these price series are provided in the Appendix. The greatest marketing activity in the delivery area is during the first five months of the marketing year. In the delivery area, most rice is harvested in August and September and is out of the hands of most farmers by January. The time from harvest through delivery is thus presumably the period of greatest liquidity in the cash market and the most competitively discovered prices. For each price series, the change in price is the difference over one week, assembled as a series of changes from August through January of the 1986, 1987, and 1988 crop years.

The analysis regresses Louisiana and Arkansas cash price changes against changes in the announced world price and regresses the Louisiana and Brinkley cash price changes against changes in the Arkansas cash price. The general model expresses the price change in one cash market as a linear function of the price change in another cash market:

$$(CP_{a,t} - CP_{a,t-1}) = \beta_0 + \beta_1 (CP_{b,t} - CP_{b,t-1})$$

where $CP_{a,t}$ is the price in cash market a at time t, $CP_{a,t-1}$ is the price in cash market a one week before time t, and $CP_{b,t}$ and $CP_{b,t-1}$ are the comparable prices in cash market b, β_0 is the constant, and β_1 is the slope coefficient. The results of estimating this model on 1986, 1987, and 1988 crop year price series are summarized in table 16-5.

Although an argument might have been made in 1987 that these three markets, or at least these three price series, were becoming increasingly well integrated, this does not appear to be the case with the addition of data from the 1988 marketing year. The Arkansas market seems more closely related to the world market (as interpreted by the USDA) than is the Louisiana market in 1986 and 1987, but the world market price does not appear to guide the Arkansas market in 1988. One would expect that price movements in the Arkansas cash series collected from farms and elevators and in the series describing the Brinkley sales would be tightly related, because they describe sales at the same time and in the same area. They are not.

The relatively high degree of integration in 1987 across the three markets suggests the somewhat speculative hypothesis that increased integration in the United States is a by-product of an unusually active period in the market. The 1987 crop year was marked by U.S. prices that rose dramatically as the year progressed, far above the announced world market price. U.S. prices diverged far from Thai prices before the speculative bubble burst. The model used above to examine geographic integration of markets was also applied to U.S. and Thai milled rice prices from the 1987 and 1988 periods under study. Cash price movements were unrelated in both years.

TESTING THE INTEGRATION OF FUTURES WITH CASH MARKETS. Do price movements in the futures markets reflect price movements in the underlying cash markets? Is there any sign that these markets were better integrated in 1988 than in 1986?

Using the same series of cash prices described above, this analysis regresses the changes in the price of the nearby future against changes in the announced world price and in the Louisiana, Arkansas, and Brinkley cash prices. The nearby future is the currently traded contract that is closest to expiring; it is usually more heavily traded than more distant contracts and should reflect cash prices most closely. Liquidity in the nearby contract usually diminishes as the delivery (or expiration) month progresses. Although a contract may be traded more than a year before it expires, it becomes the spot contract on the seventh business day before the end of the month when the previous contract was delivered. For

Table 16-5. Geographic Integration of Cash Rice Markets, 1986–88

Markets and year	Regression equation	Standard error of slope	F-statistic df	F-statistic Value	p	R^2
Louisiana vs. world						
1986	$\Delta LA = -0.01 + 0.593\Delta WP$	1.137	1,10	0.272	0.6135	0.026
1987	$\Delta LA = 0.04 + 1.918\Delta WP$	0.985	1,15	3.789	0.0706	0.202
1988	$\Delta LA = 0.023 + 1.975\Delta WP$	1.659	1,13	1.418	0.255	0.098
Arkansas vs. world						
1986	$\Delta AR = -0.004 + 0.879\Delta WP$	0.167	1,23	27.770	0.0001	0.547
1987	$\Delta AR = 0.114 + 1.61\Delta WP$	0.284	1,23	32.237	0.0004	0.584
1988	$\Delta AR = -0.024 + 0.293\Delta WP$	0.336	1,23	0.761	0.3922	0.032
Louisiana vs. Arkansas						
1986	$\Delta LA = -0.002 + 0.505\Delta AR$	1.059	1,10	0.228	0.6434	0.022
1987	$\Delta LA = -0.162 + 1.324\Delta AR$	0.361	1,15	13.491	0.0023	0.474
1988	$\Delta LA = -0.019 + 0.819\Delta AR$	1.508	1,13	0.295	0.5963	0.022
Brinkley vs. Arkansas						
1988	$\Delta BAR = 0.081 + .53\Delta AR$	0.970	1,12	0.299	0.5946	0.024

Source: Author's calculations.

example, the January 1989 contract is defined as the nearby contract between November 21, 1988, and January 20, 1989.[6]

The general model regresses the change in the price of the nearby future against the change in the cash price:

$$(FP_t - FP_{t-1}) = \beta_0 + \beta_1 (CP_t - CP_{t-1})$$

where FP_t is the futures price at time t, FP_{t-1} is the futures price the week before time t, and CP_t and CP_{t-1} are the comparable cash prices.

The results of tests of this model are summarized in table 16-6.

Changes in the futures price appear to be increasingly closely related to changes in the announced world price, reaching statistical significance with the 1988 crop year, when prices hovered near the announced price. Insofar as the world price acts as a domestic floor price through the loan rate mechanism (see the Appendix), it is consistent that when market prices are near the floor, movements in the floor price are reflected in the futures price.

The futures price movements do not show a relationship to movements in the Louisiana price, except as the regression approaches statistical significance in 1987. The positive relationship and significance at the 10 percent level is consistent with the findings of Traylor, Zapata, and McCann (1989) for that crop year.[7]

The Arkansas results hold hope for hedgers. For all three crop years, the model shows a statistically significant relationship between changes in the futures price and changes in the Arkansas cash price. In all cases, the regression coefficient is positive, as might be expected, and it appears to increase over the three years. A statistically significant coefficient close to one would support the argument that the futures market offers a good hedge for rice in the delivery area.[8]

The Brinkley data do not replicate the favorable hedging scenario observed in the Arkansas prices. Some participants have suggested that the Brinkley market follows the futures market. Tests of such a lagged relationship (which are not reported here) do not support their hypothesis.

Efficiency

Another way to examine the efficiency of a futures contract is to observe the behavior of the basis, the difference between the cash and the futures prices, as a contract matures. Ideally, the basis should narrow over time and the prices should converge in the delivery area during the delivery month.

Table 16-6. *Temporal Integration of Rice Markets, 1986–88*

Markets and year	Regression equation	Standard error of slope	F-statistic df	F-statistic Value	p	R^2
Futures vs. world spot						
1986	$\Delta FP = 0.009 + 0.463\Delta WP$	0.337	1,20	1.89	0.1844	0.086
1987	$\Delta FP = 0.201 + 1.029\Delta WP$	0.527	1,23	3.818	0.063	0.142
1988	$\Delta FP = 0.011 + 1.029\Delta WP$	0.493	1,23	4.366	0.0479	0.16
Futures vs. Louisiana spot						
1986	$\Delta FP = 0.008 - 0.023\Delta LA$	0.115	1,70	0.041	0.8452	0.006
1987	$\Delta FP = 0.184 + 0.342\Delta LA$	0.162	1,15	4.477	0.0515	0.23
1988	$\Delta FP = 0.005 + 0.045\Delta LA$	0.140	1,13	0.104	0.7521	0.008
Futures vs. Arkansas spot						
1986	$\Delta FP = 0.01 + 0.64\Delta AR$	0.251	1,20	6.475	0.0193	0.245
1987	$\Delta FP = 0.056 + 0.865\Delta AR$	0.201	1,23	18.629	0.0003	0.448
1988	$\Delta FP = 0.008 + 0.955\Delta AR$	0.261	1,23	13.438	0.0013	0.369
Futures vs. Brinkley spot						
1988	$\Delta FP = -0.021 + 0.08\Delta BAR$	0.093	1,12	0.738	0.4072	0.058

Source: Author's calculations.

Because the delivery area for the rice futures contract is in eastern Arkansas, one would expect basis behavior closest to the ideal in that market. To test the basis, this analysis compares world, Louisiana, Arkansas, and Brinkley cash prices with the futures price.

To measure the integration of January futures contracts with cash markets and to determine whether the basis behaves in an orderly fashion during the early (more active) part of the marketing year, this model regresses the basis over time. The basis is defined as the price of the January future less the cash price each week; the time variable is simply a counter of weeks (one in August to twenty-six in January). The general case can be represented as BASIS $= (JF_t - CP_t) = \beta_0 + \beta_1 \text{WEEK}_t$, where JF_t is the price of the January contract at time t, CP_t is the cash price at time t, and WEEK_t is the time counter.

One would expect the basis with regard to each cash price to fall over time as the contract nears maturity, representing positive but decreasing returns to storing rice. Such ideal behavior would be reflected in the equations below with statistically significant negative regression coefficients (regression lines with negative slopes). Table 16-7 provides the results of this model when applied to price series from 1986, 1987, and 1988.

With regard to announced world prices, statistical significance is only obtained in 1987, but a positive relationship between the basis and time is observed, implying a negative return to storage.[9] Although Louisiana prices show some improvement in statistical significance, the regression coefficients are not significantly different from zero. These findings suggest that there is no relationship between the Louisiana basis and the maturing of the January contract. These results are not surprising, given the weak geographic integration found among U.S. markets.

The Arkansas market demonstrates behavior more typical of an efficient futures market, in which the basis should be predictable. Regression coefficients are consistently negative, with p values that suggest an increasing degree of confidence, achieving statistical significance in the 1987 and 1988 basis equations. This finding means that cash prices that fell below futures prices in August 1988 converged with futures prices through January 1989, suggesting orderly returns to storage.

The Brinkley basis behaves as expected: the equation is statistically significant and the regression coefficient is negative. In absolute terms, the slope is steeper than was observed in the 1988 Arkansas cash market. Both cases describe orderly behavior with decreasing returns to storage over time, as indicated in figure 16-1 below.[10]

Hedgers seek a predictable basis. However, the similarity of regression coefficients is difficult to assess with only three estimates in each market. More years of experience will make such judgments possible.

Table 16-7. Basis of Rough Rice Futures Contracts on the Chicago Rice and Cotton Exchange, 1986–88

Price basis and year	Regression equation	Standard error of slope	F-statistic df	F-statistic Value	p	R^2
World price basis						
1986	$\text{BASIS}_W = 0.48 + 0.006 \text{ WEEK}$	0.003	1,20	3.93	0.0613	0.164
1987	$\text{BASIS}_W = 1.31 + 0.15 \text{ WEEK}$	0.017	1,23	78.168	0.0001	0.773
1988	$\text{BASIS}_W = 0.748 + 0.0001 \text{ WEEK}$	0.004	1,23	0.0004	0.9839	0.00002
Louisiana price basis						
1986	$\text{BASIS}_L = 0.332 - 0.007 \text{ WEEK}$	0.011	1,12	0.458	0.5115	0.037
1987	$\text{BASIS}_L = 0.99 + 0.021 \text{ WEEK}$	0.028	1,19	0.533	0.4743	0.027
1988	$\text{BASIS}_L = 0.876 - 0.031 \text{ WEEK}$	0.017	1,16	3.307	0.0878	0.171
Arkansas price basis						
1986	$\text{BASIS}_A = 0.169 - 0.003 \text{ WEEK}$	0.002	1,20	2.476	0.1313	0.110
1987	$\text{BASIS}_A = 1.51 - 0.028 \text{ WEEK}$	0.012	1,23	5.093	0.0338	0.181
1988	$\text{BASIS}_A = 0.39 - 0.014 \text{ WEEK}$	0.003	1,23	17.772	0.0003	0.436
Brinkley price basis						
1988	$\text{BASIS}_{BAR} = 0.815 - 0.038 \text{ WEEK}$	0.015	1,17	6.808	0.0183	0.286

Source: Author's calculations.

Figure 16-1. *Rough Rice Basis, Arkansas and Brinkley, 1988 Crop*

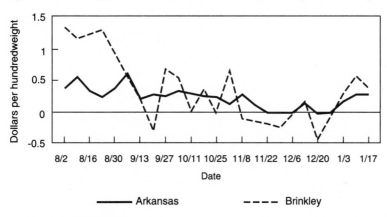

Source: See the Appendix.

Implications for the International Rice Market

In summary, this analysis demonstrates connections between futures prices and cash prices in Arkansas but poorer integration of prices among other markets examined. The analysis of the geographic integration of rice markets shows inconsistent relationships in cash prices between markets. Although the Arkansas price changes track USDA world price changes in 1986 and 1987, the integration is not sustained in 1988 or in Brinkley, Arkansas. Looking at the integration of rice markets over time, Arkansas price changes track futures price changes in all three years tested. However, the relationships of Louisiana, Brinkley, and world price changes to futures price changes were inconsistent. The basis, or difference between cash and futures prices, behaves in a manner consistent with orderly returns to storage in Arkansas in 1987 and 1988 and in Brinkley for the one year examined, 1988.

Efficient markets that integrate prices geographically and temporally provide a risk management tool for commodity trading. Given a preference for trade over other domestic stabilization schemes, a liquid futures market offers protection against unanticipated price changes. The ability to lock in prices for traded rice would permit countries to set more appropriate domestic prices and thus better manage domestic subsidies.

Rumors of successes and failures in trading rough rice futures abound. There is much talk of players who are profiting from arbitrage opportunities between the cash and futures markets and also talk of informed participants who lost their shirts. It seems extremely unlikely that the futures market will fail again as it did in 1983, and committed traders claim that they will maintain open interest in the CRCE contract at a level sufficient to prevent the withering away of the futures market. But will it prosper? Will the futures market ever offer an efficient hedge to U.S. farmers and millers? Will the contract display sufficient predictive capacity to support foreign forward pricing decisions? Will increased revelation of information lead to better integrated rice markets worldwide?

The amount of market information available has increased since futures trading began, and the amount of reliable information has increased as well, although not proportionately. Improved communications worldwide have contributed to the efficiency of information flows. Increased interest in risk management tools, notably futures markets, has encouraged curiosity about futures prices. Monitoring futures prices leads to efforts to assess their validity and thus to a search for reliable cash prices. Having found, or believing to have found, a related cash market leads some traders to arbitrage between those markets, producing increased pricing efficiency.

One result of increased market orientation in U.S. policy would be to make U.S. cash markets more active and U.S. cash prices more reflective of domestic conditions. As cash prices become more reliable and the cash market more competitive and more liquid, trading in futures should be more attractive to speculators. The resulting increase in volume should lead to a more efficient futures market and thus more opportunities for hedging.

Because the United States is the second largest exporter of rice, market-determined forward prices could lead to a more competitive international rice market as traders from abroad arbitrage internationally as well as temporally in the U.S. market. The key to a more efficient global rice market, therefore, may well lie in a more efficient cash market in the United States.

Appendix. Description and Assessment of Cited Rice Prices

Thai Rice Prices

Substantial confusion arises from the source of Thai price quotes. The Thai Board of Trade posts a price, but discounts of 10 to 15 percent are usual and can range to 20 to 30 percent, depending on market conditions. Since mid-1984, nominal price quotes have been solicited from exporters by the U.S. agricultural attaché in Bangkok. These nominal prices are felt to be more representative of actual prices, although further discounts are generally negotiated.

Thai "5 percent brokens" were cited for years as the standard for the world price. The grade represents milled indica rice with a minimum of 90 percent long grain rice and 3 to 7 percent broken grains, f.o.b. Bangkok. Now, the more commonly tracked milled rice is Thai 100 percent B rice, milled long grain indica rice that may have up to 5 percent short grain rice and up to 5 percent brokens (Barker, Herdt, and Rose 1985).

More frequent price estimates based on information about actual sales are tightly guarded. Nevertheless, two series of milled rice prices were used for comparison in this analysis: weekly estimates of Thai 100 percent B, f.o.b. Bangkok prices and estimated U.S. Number 2, 4 percent, f.o.b. Gulf prices.[11]

USDA-announced World Market Prices

Exports of Thai rice represent 30 to 40 percent of rice traded in recent years. Its price is therefore important, but other prices are also important. The USDA attempts to collect and digest information about prices in order to offer a benchmark price—its estimate of the price U.S. exporters must meet in order to be competitive in the world market. These prices are announced every Tuesday afternoon by the Secretary of Agriculture. Price analysts review actual sales rather than nominal quotes or posted prices for different classes of rice traded in all markets, then weight the prices to reflect quality differences and adjust them to reflect equivalent values for U.S. Number 2, 4 percent brokens, f.o.b. Houston.

Using this estimated price for milled rice, the analysts work backward to estimate the price at which U.S. rough rice would have to sell in order to be processed and sold at the world market price. The processing costs reflect milling costs (relatively high in the United States), costs of bagging and transportation, and the market for by-products. Calculations are based on industry estimates of milling yields, which are updated as the season progresses. The loan-rate basis price for any yield of rough rice is a weighted average of whole and broken (milled) grain prices. For this analysis, the world market price for rough rice with the milling yield specified on the futures contract is derived from the world market price for milled rice after using such averaging, as announced by the USDA.

This effort was mandated by the Food Security Act of 1985 for use in determining marketing loan repayment rates. Crop loans made in 1988 may be repaid at either the loan rate for the specified class of rice, or at the higher of the world market price (at time of repayment) or 60 percent of the loan rate. Producers who put their rice under loan have essentially a one-way option on the price: if local prices fall below the announced world price, they need not redeem their rice from the government. This floor price forces millers to compete with the government when the world price falls below the loan rate or, alternatively, allows the government to undercut farmers when selling the rice that they accumulate from the loan program.

Louisiana Prices

The Louisiana Department of Agriculture and Forestry assembles a weekly summary of public bid sales of rough rice in Crowley, Louisiana. It reports the volume, weighted average milling yield, and price for both long and medium grain sales during the prior week and lists some representative lots. Reports are fairly regular during the early part of the marketing year, from late August through January (with interruptions at Thanksgiving and Christmas) but rare from March through July. This information appears weekly in *Rice Market News,* a publication of the USDA in Arkansas. *Rice Market News* provided a series of prices for use in this analysis. Weekly average public bid sales prices were adjusted to reflect the par milling yield for delivery on the futures contract using the premium and discount schedule of the futures exchange. Nevertheless, the price used here is biased upward because nondeliverable grades (those below Number 2 or with poor milling yields, or both) are included in the average price. Without proof that the markets for different grades of rice are integrated, such bias diminishes its use for comparability to futures prices.

Arkansas Prices

Most rice in Arkansas is marketed through rice cooperatives that receive the rice directly from member farmers, then dry, mill, store, and market it. Increasingly, the cooperatives are integrating higher value-added products, such as rice cakes, into their operations. No cash prices apply in this seasonal pool-marketing system; members receive a share of the annual income of the cooperative in proportion to their quality-adjusted rice deliveries.[12]

The most widely disseminated cash price information is from the public bid sales in Brinkley, Arkansas. Similar sales are held in England, Arkansas. As in Louisiana, the market is most active in fall and early winter; later in the year, cash prices are less available. Two Arkansas price series are used in this analysis. One is a series collected on Tuesdays (prior to the USDA announcement) from three to five farms and elevators by Scott Minton, of Stotler and Co. (now of Rodman and Renshaw), in Chicago. The second is a series of weekly average Brinkley cash prices derived from confirmed sales data provided by Southern Rice Marketing, of Brinkley.

Southern Rice Marketing made available its bid sheets from public bid sales and its confirmed sales log from the period under study. Because no charges were levied on the information and no restrictions placed on its use, such data have characteristics of information in the public domain.

The data thereon are not readily accessible to the casual observer but can be transformed to yield prices that are comparable to other series. Bid sheets show the range of prices under consideration but should not be used for analyses such as these, because the seller is under no obligation to accept any of the bids and the offers are valid for only twenty-four hours. An examination of confirmed sales data demonstrates the divergences; only actual sales should be included in price summaries.

Each lot sold between August 1988 and January 1989 was considered. Only lots that would be deliverable under the rules of the exchange were included (Number 2 or better long grain rough rice, with a head milling yield of at least 48 percent and a total yield of at least 65 percent); lots beyond $0.10 a bushel freight of the delivery area were excluded. In the 155 lots that were included, 777,785 hundredweight of rice were sold. Sales prices, given in a variety of forms, straight or as a premium over the world market price, were standardized to a price per hundredweight, with a 55/70 milling yield using the CRCE milling yield adjustment schedule. Where terms were not f.o.b. the seller's bins, an average freight adjustment was made to the price.

Futures Prices at the CRCE

The rough rice futures contract traded on the CRCE, which has been affiliated with the Chicago Board of Trade since August 1986, provides futures prices daily for U.S. Number 2 long grain rough rice in lots of 2,000 hundredweight, with a par milling yield of 55/70, delivered in eastern Arkansas. A price adjustment is made for milling yield variations above the specified minimums of at least 48 percent head rice and 65 percent total yield.[13] Location differentials apply to warehouses within the delivery area. Because the USDA price announcement is made on Tuesday afternoons, the Tuesday settlement price of the futures contract, determined prior to the announcement, is used as the futures price in this analysis.

Notes

1. Even making this expenditure, one would consume only 1,725 calories, 22 percent below the FAO estimated daily requirements for Asia of 2,200 calories per capita.

2. These elasticities are summarized in Barker, Herdt, and Rose (1985).

3. Barker, Herdt, and Rose (1985) do not specify the period. Storage costs appear to be in a range of 1 to 10 percent a year.

4. Two mechanisms bear mentioning in this context. A basis contract specifies the price as an agreed discount or premium applied to a fluctuating referent price to be fixed on an agreed date. A cross-hedge is a hedge arranged in a commodity whose price fluctuations are closely related to the price movements in the actual commodity being traded.

5. Five contracts a year were traded in the period under study. The year 1989 brought the first July contract; it is traded with reduced position limits.

6. Two exceptions arise in this analysis in the start-up year of futures trading. No September 1986 futures were traded. Thus the first contract traded was November 1986, making it the nearby contract from the start of trading on August 20, 1986. The second exception is the January 1987 contract, which had no trades and no open interest after January 2nd; the March contract is thus the nearby contract as of that date.

7. Traylor, Zapata, and McCann (1989), in their work evaluating the efficiency of the futures contract, limit their assessment to the postharvest marketing periods of 1986 and 1987. They use cash prices from sales in Crowley, Louisiana, but do not demonstrate any integration between cash rice markets in Arkansas and Louisiana. They find very low correlation coefficients between Louisiana cash and nearby futures prices, little impact of cash prices on futures, and very erratic basis behavior in both the 1986 and 1987 rice markets. A two-period autoregressive model demonstrates that rice futures prices were significantly related to prior period prices, suggesting nonrandom price movement and therefore market inefficiencies.

8. I am indebted to Walter Falcon and Anne Peck for pointing out to me that cash prices and futures prices cannot track each other perfectly if the two prices will converge at delivery. I suggest that hedgers planning to liquidate their futures positions prior to expiration will want to examine the integration of futures and cash price movements. Hedgers planning to maintain their positions until expiration will analyze the convergence of prices (basis behavior), as discussed below.

9. The January 1988 contract price rose dramatically from October through January, reflecting speculation in the U.S. market based on projections of poor crops in Asia. The announced world price, reflecting the current international market, never reacted to these expectations. As a result, the basis grew over time as cash prices diverged from futures prices.

10. Because the basis for the deliverable quality in the delivery area should equal the costs of carrying the commodity, volatility in the basis as the contract nears expiration may represent changes in deliverable supply in relation to immediate demand.

11. Thai 100 percent B and U.S. Number 2, 4 percent price series were provided by Scott Minton, of Stotler and Co. (now of Rodman and Renshaw), Chicago.

12. The cooperatives are extremely important in the U.S. marketing system, but members reported few standards by which they could judge the performance of co-op management. Improved cash and futures price reporting may make evaluation easier, but the overhead of drying and marketing rice deters many farmers from leaving the co-ops. Although a more open rice market offers competition for supplies, the leverage that the co-ops offer farmers for their rice as they move into value-added production in what remains an oligopolistic industry strengthens their position.

13. The milling yield adjustment for the period under study is 1.75 percent premium or discount for each percentage of head rice above or below 55 percent, respectively, and 0.5 percent premium or discount for each percentage of broken rice above or below 15 percent, respectively. This discount schedule is applied consistently throughout this analysis to adjust prices to the CRCE par milling yield, making prices directly comparable.

Bibliography

The word "processed" describes informally reproduced works that may not be commonly available through library systems.

Aitchison, John, and James Alan Calvert Brown. 1957. *The Lognormal Distribution.* Cambridge, U.K.: Cambridge University Press.

Akiyama, Takamasa, and Panos Varangis. 1989. "Impact of the International Coffee Agreement's Export Quota System on the World Coffee Market." PRE Working Paper 148. World Bank, International Economics Department, International Trade Division, Washington, D.C. Processed.

————. 1990. "The Impact of the International Coffee Agreement's Export Quota System on Producing Countries." *World Bank Economic Review* 4 (2, May):157–74.

Anderson, Ronald W., and Christopher L. Gilbert. 1988. "Commodity Agreements and Commodity Markets: Lessons from Tin." *Economic Journal* 98 (March):1–5.

Askari, Hossein, and John T. Cummings. 1976. *Agricultural Supply Response: A Survey of the Econometric Evidence.* New York: Praeger.

Baillie, Richard, and Robert J. Myers. 1989. "Modeling Commodity Price Distributions and Estimating the Optimal Futures Hedge." Working Paper CSFM 201 (December). Columbia Business School, Center for the Study of Futures Markets, New York. Processed.

Balassa, Bela. 1986. "Policy Responses to Exogenous Shocks in Developing Countries." *American Economic Proceedings* 76 (2, May):75–8.

————. 1988. "Temporary Windfalls and Compensation Arrangements." World Bank, Vice Presidency Development Economics, Washington, D.C. Processed.

Bank for International Settlements. 1991. "Commodity Swaps and Other Commodity-related Derivative Instruments." *Annual Report* Vol. 62. Basle, Switzerland.

Banque Paribas. 1989. *News from Paribas* (July). New York.

Barker, Randolph, Robert W. Herdt, and Beth Rose. 1985. *The Rice Economy of Asia.* Washington, D.C.: Resources for the Future.

Bauer, T. 1967. *West African Trade,* 2d ed. New York: Kelley.

Besley, Timothy, and Andrew Powell. 1989. "Commodity Indexed Debt in International Lending." PRE Working Paper 161. World Bank, International Economics Department, International Trade Division, Washington, D.C. Processed.

Bevan, D. L., Paul Collier, and J. W. Gunning. 1987. "Consequences of a Commodity Boom in a Controlled Economy: Accumulation and Redistribution in Kenya 1975–83." *World Bank Economic Review* 1 (May):489–514.

Binswanger, Hans. 1980. "Attitudes towards Risk: Experimentation Measurement Evidence in Rural India." *American Journal of Agricultural Economics* 62 (3, August):395–407.

Brogan, Brian, and Joseph Remenyi, eds. 1987. "Commodity Price Stabilization in PNG: A Work-in-Progress Seminar." Australian Centre for International Agricultural Research, Sydney. Processed.

Caballero, Ricardo, and Vittorio Corbo. 1989. "The Effect of Real Exchange Rate Uncertainty on Exports: Empirical Evidence." *World Bank Economic Review* 3(2):263–78.

Cartiglia, Filippo. 1989. "A Note on the Optimal Currency Composition of the External Debt of Colombia." World Bank, Country Operations, Latin America, Washington, D.C. Processed.

Claessens, Stijn. 1988. "The Optimal Currency Composition of External Debt." PRE Working Paper 14. World Bank, International Economics Department, Debt and International Finance Division, Washington, D.C. Processed.

———. 1992. "The Optimal Currency Composition of External Debt: Theory and Applications to Mexico and Brazil." *World Bank Economic Review* 6(1):503–28.

Coleman, Jonathan R., and Donald F. Larson. 1990. "Tariff-based Commodity Price Stabilization Schemes: The Case of Venezuela." PRE Working Paper No. 611. World Bank, International Economics Department, International Trade Division, Washington, D.C. Processed.

Commodity Futures Trading Commission. 1989. *Annual Report 1989.* Washington, D.C.

Coopers and Lybrand. 1989. *Mining and Petroleum Taxation: A Guide for Operators and Contractors.* New York.

Cox, John C., and Mark Rubinstein. 1985. *Options Markets.* Englewood Cliffs, N.J.: Prentice-Hall.

Cuddington, John. 1989. "Commodity Booms in Developing Countries." *World Bank Research Observer* 4 (2, July):143–65.

Culagovski, Jorge, Victor Gabor, Maria Christina Germany, and Charles Humphreys. 1990. "African Financing Needs in the 1990s." In Ishrat Husain and John Underwoods, eds., *African External Finance in the 1990s.* Washington, D.C.: World Bank.

Danthine, Jean-Pièrre. 1978. "Information, Futures Prices, and Stabilizing Speculation." *Journal of Economic Theory* 17 (1, February):79–98.

Deaton, Angus S., and Guy Laroque. 1992. "On the Behavior of Commodity Prices." *Review of Economics* 59 (January):1–23.

De Graaff, J. 1986. *The Economics of Coffee.* Wageningen, Netherlands: Pudoc.

Dornbusch, Rudiger. 1987. "Exchange Rates and Prices." *American Economic Review* 77(1):93–102.

Euromoney. Various issues. London.

FEDESARROLLO. Various issues. *Coyuntura Economica.* Bogota.

Figlewski, Stephen. 1986. *Hedging with Financial Futures for Institutional Investors.* Cambridge, Mass.: Ballinger.

Fischer, Stanley. 1989. "Resolving the International Debt Crisis." In Jeffrey D. Sachs, ed., *Developing Country Debt and Economic Performance.* Boston: National Bureau of Economic Research.

Folkerts-Landau, David. 1989. "Marked-to-Market Interest Rate Swaps: A Solution to the Interest Rate Risk Management Problem of Indebted Developing Countries." In Jacob Frenkel, Michael Dooley, and Peter Wickham, eds., *Analytical Issues in Debt.* Washington, D.C.: International Monetary Fund.

Gemmill, Gorden. 1985. "Optimal Hedging on Futures Markets for Commodity-Exporting Nations." *European Economic Review* 27(2):243–61.

Ghosh, Shyamal K., Christopher L. Gilbert, and Andrew J. Hughes-Hallett. 1987. *Stabilizing Speculative Commodity Markets.* New York: Oxford University Press.

Gilbert, Christopher L. 1986. "Commodity Price Stabilization: The Massell Model and Multiplicative Disturbances." *Quarterly Journal of Economics* 100 (August):635–40.

――――. 1987. "International Commodity Agreements: Design and Performance." *World Development* 15 (May):591–616.

――――. 1988. "Optimal and Competitive Storage Rules: The Gustafson Problem Revisited." In O. Guvenon, ed., *International Commodity Market Models and Policy Analysis.* Dordrecht, Netherlands: Kluwer.

――――. 1989. "The Impact of Exchange Rates and Developing Country Debt on Commodity Prices." *Economic Journal* 99 (September):773–84.

――――. 1990. "Primary Commodity Prices and Inflation." *Oxford Review of Economic Policy* 6(4):77–99.

――――. 1991. "The Response of Primary Commodity Prices to Exchange Rate Changes." In L. Philips, ed., *Commodity, Futures, and Financial Markets.* Dordrecht, Netherlands: Kluwer.

Grabbe, J. Orlin. 1986. *International Financial Markets.* New York: Elsevier.

Gray, Roger W. 1987a. "The Characteristic Bias in Some Thin Futures Markets." In Ann E. Peck, ed., *Selected Writings on Futures Markets: Basic Research in Commodity Markets.* Chicago: Chicago Board of Trade.

――――. 1987b. "The Futures Market for Maine Potatoes: An Appraisal." In Ann E. Peck, ed., *Selected Writings on Futures Markets: Basic Research in Commodity Markets.* Chicago: Chicago Board of Trade.

Guest, James. 1987. "Problems in Managing the MRSF." *Quarterly Economic Bulletin* 15 (2, June):17–24. Bank of Papua New Guinea.

Gustafson, R. L. 1958a. "Carryover Levels for Grains: A Method for Determining Amounts That Are Optimal under Specified Conditions." *Technical Bulletin.* Vol. 1178. U.S. Department of Agriculture, Washington, D.C.

———. 1958b. "Implications of Recent Research on Optimal Storage Rules." *Journal of Farm Economics* 40:290–300.

Hansen, Lars, and Thomas Sargent. 1980. "Formulating and Estimating Dynamic Linear Rational Expectations Models." *Journal of Economic Dynamics and Control* 2(1):7–46.

Helleiner, G. K. 1964. "The Fiscal Role of the Marketing Boards in Nigerian Economic Development, 1947–61." *Economic Journal* 74(296):582–610.

Hesp, Paul, and H. L. van der Laan. 1985. "Marketing Boards in Tropical Africa: A Survey." In Kwame Arhin, Paul Hesp, and H. L. van der Laan, eds., *Marketing Boards in Tropical Africa.* London: Kegan Paul International.

Hinchy, M., and B. Fisher. 1988. "Benefits from Price Stabilization to Producers and Processors: The Australian Buffer-Stock Scheme for Wool." *American Journal of Agricultural Economics* 70 (August):604–15.

Hughes-Hallett, Andrew J., and Prathap Ramanujam. 1990. "Marketing Solutions to the Problem of Stabilizing Commodity Earnings." CEPR Working Paper 48. Center for Economic Policy Research, London.

Husain, Ishrat, and John Underwood, eds. 1991. *African External Finance in the 1990s.* Washington, D.C.: World Bank.

International Financing Review. Various issues. London.

International Monetary Fund. Various issues. *International Financial Statistics.* Washington, D.C.

———. 1989. *Managing Financial Risks in Indebted Developing Countries.* Occasional Paper 65. Washington, D.C.

———. 1990. "Request for Stand-By Arrangement and Compensatory Financing of Export Fluctuations under the Compensatory and Contingency Financing Facility." *IMF Survey* (March). Washington, D.C.

International Rice Research Institute. 1986. *World Rice Statistics 1985.* Manila.

Jaramillo, Felipe. 1989. "A Study of Costa Rica's Coffee Marketing System." World Bank, Country Operations, Latin America, Washington, D.C. Processed.

Jennings, Richard W., Harold Marsh, Jr., and John C. Coffee, Jr. 1992. *Federal Securities Laws: Selected Statutes, Rules, and Forms.* Westbury, N.Y.: Foundation Press.

Johnson, D. Gale. 1981. "Grain Insurance, Reserves, and Trade: Contributions to Food Security for LDC's." In Alberto Valdés, ed., *Food Security for Developing Countries.* Boulder, Colo.: Westview Press.

Jolly, L. O., A. C. Beck, and P. M. Bodman. 1990. "Commodity Price Stabilization in Papua New Guinea." Discussion Paper 90.2. Australian Bureau of Agricultural and Resource Economics, Sydney.

Jordan, James, Robert Mackay, and Eugene Moriarity. 1990. "The Regulation of Commodity-Linked and Depository Instruments." In Clifford Smith, Jr., and Charles Smithson, eds., *The Handbook of Financial Engineering*. New York: Harper and Row.

Just, Richard E., Darrell L. Hueth, and Andrew Schmitz. 1982. *Applied Welfare Economics and Public Policy*. Englewood Cliffs, N.J.: Prentice-Hall.

Kamas, L. 1986. "Dutch Disease Economics and the Colombian Export Boom." *World Development* 14(9):1177–98.

Kolb, Robert. 1985. *Understanding Futures Markets*. London: Scott, Foresman.

Knudsen, Odin, and John Nash. 1990a. "Agricultural Price Stabilization and Risk Reduction in Developing Countries." In R. Bautista and Alberto Valdéz, eds., *Macroeconomic Policies' Impact on Agriculture*. Washington, D.C.: International Food Policy Research Institute.

————. 1990b. "Domestic Price Stabilization Schemes in Developing Countries." *Economic Development and Cultural Change* 38 (April):539–58.

Kroner, Kenneth, and Stijn Claessens. 1991. "Optimal Dynamic Hedging Portfolios and the Currency Composition of External Debt." *Journal of International Money and Finance* 10 (March):131–48.

Labuszewski, John W., and John E. Nyhoff. 1988a. *Trading Options on Futures*. New York: John Wiley & Sons.

————. 1988b. *Trading Financial Futures*. New York: John Wiley & Sons.

Lapan, Harvey, Giancarlo Moschini, and Steven D. Hanson. 1991. "Production, Hedging, and Speculative Decisions with Options and Futures Markets." *American Journal of Agricultural Economics* 73(1):66–74.

Larson, Donald, and Jonathan Coleman. 1991. "The Effects of Option-Hedging on the Costs of Domestic Price Stabilization Schemes." PRE Working Paper 653. World Bank, International Economics Department, International Trade Division. Washington, D.C. Processed.

Laughlin, Terrence J., and William D. Falloon. 1990. "Catch-22 Solutions for Less Developed Countries." *Corporate Risk Management* 2 (5, September):26–29.

Lessard, Donald. 1986. "The Management of International Trade Risks." *Geneva Papers on Risk and Insurance* 11:255–64.

Liu, Zhichen. 1989. *Study on Grains in China*. Beijing: Chinese Agricultural Science Academy.

Massell, B. F. 1969. "Price Stabilization and Welfare." *Quarterly Journal of Economics* 83:284–98.

McNicol, D. 1978. "Political Economy of an Integrated Commodity Program."

In F. Gerard Adams and Sonia Klein, eds., *Stabilizing World Commodity Markets*. Lexington: Heath-Lexington.

Middle East Business Weekly. Various issues.

Miranda, M. J., and P. G. Helmberger. 1988. "The Effects of Commodity Price Stabilization Programs." *American Economic Review* 78:46–58.

Mirrlees, J. A. 1988. "Optimal Commodity Price Intervention." World Bank, International Economics Department, International Trade Division, Washington, D.C. Processed.

Moffett, Matt, and Peter Truell. 1991. "Mexico's Move to Lock in Oil Prices in Gulf Crisis Means It Can Stay Calm Now as the Market Softens." *Wall Street Journal,* March 11, p. C14.

Mundlak, Yair, and Donald Larson. 1990. "On the Relevance of World Agricultural Prices." PPR Working Paper 383. World Bank, International Economics Department, International Trade Division, Washington, D.C. Processed.

Mydans, Seth. 1988. "Uprising in Burma: The Old Regime under Siege." *New York Times,* August 12, p. 1.

Myers, Robert J. 1991. "Estimating Time-Varying Optimal Hedge Ratios on Futures Markets." *Journal of Futures Markets* 2(1):39–53.

———. 1992. "Incomplete Markets and Commodity-Linked Finance in Developing Countries." *World Bank Research Observer* 7 (1, January):79–97.

Myers, Robert J., and J. Oehmke. 1988. "Instability and Risk as Rationales for Farm Programs." In D. Sumner, ed., *Agricultural Stability and Farm Programs: Concepts, Evidence, and Implications*. Boulder, Colo.: Westview Press.

Myers, Robert J., and Stanley R. Thompson. 1989a. "Generalized Optimal Hedge Ratio Estimation." *American Journal of Agricultural Economics* 71(2):858–68.

———. 1989b. "Optimal Portfolios of External Debt in Developing Countries: The Potential Role of Commodity-linked Bonds." *American Journal of Agricultural Economics* 71(2):517–22.

———. 1991. "Optimal External Debt Management with Commodity-linked Bonds." In Theophilos Priovolos and Ronald C. Duncan, eds., *Commodity Risk Management and Finance*. New York: Oxford University Press.

Nash, John. 1984. "Pricing for Rice in Peru." World Bank, Country Operations Department, Washington, D.C. Processed.

———. 1985. "The Organization and Management of the Coffee Economy." In Vinod Thomas, ed., *Linking Macroeconomic and Agricultural Policies for Adjustment with Growth: The Colombian Experience*. Baltimore, Md.: Johns Hopkins University Press.

Newbery, David. 1987. "Agricultural Taxation: The Main Issues." In David

Newbery and Nicholas Stern, eds., *The Theory of Taxation for Developing Countries*. New York: Oxford University Press.

————. 1988. "The Analysis of Agricultural Price Reform." *Journal of Public Economics* 35 (February):1–24.

————. 1989. "The Theory of Food Price Stabilization." *Economic Journal* 99 (December):1065–82.

————. 1990. "Optimal Trade Taxes on Agriculture in Developing Countries." *Economic Journal* 100:180–92.

Newbery, David, and Joseph E. Stiglitz. 1981. *The Theory of Commodity Price Stabilization: A Study in the Economics of Risk*. Oxford: Clarendon University Press.

————. 1982. "Optimal Commodity Stock-Piling Rules." *Oxford Economic Papers* 34 (3, November):403–27.

Ocampo, José A. 1989. "Ciclo Cafetero y Comportamiento Macroeconómico en Colombia." *Coyuntura Economica* 19 (3, October):125–58.

Overdahl, J. 1986. "The Use of Crude Oil Futures by the Governments of Oil Producing States." Working Paper CSFM 136. Columbia University, Center for the Study of Futures Markets, New York. Processed.

Patrikis, Ernest, and D. Cook. 1989. "Bank Supervisory Aspects of Swaps." Federal Reserve Bank of New York. Processed.

Peck, Ann E. 1985. "The Economic Role of Traditional Commodity Futures Markets." In Ann E. Peck, ed., *Futures Markets: Their Economic Role*. Washington, D.C.: American Enterprise Institute for Public Policy Research.

Perry Rubio, Guillermo. 1987. "El Petroleo en la Economia Colombiana. *Coyuntura Economica* 17 (March):95–121.

Petzel, Todd E., and Eric A. Monke. 1979. "The Integration of the International Rice Market." *Food Research Institute Studies* 17(3):307–26.

Powell, Andrew. 1989. "Management of Risk in Developing Country Finance." *Oxford Review of Economic Policy* 5(4):69–87.

Priovolos, Theophilos. 1987. "Commodity Bonds: A Risk Management Instrument for Developing Countries." International Trade Division Working Paper 1987, No. 12. World Bank, International Economics Department, Washington, D.C. Processed.

————. 1991. "Experience with Commodity-linked Issues." In Theophilos Priovolos and Ronald Duncan, eds. *Commodity Risk Management and Finance*. New York: Oxford University Press.

Priovolos, Theophilos, and Ronald Duncan, eds. 1991. *Commodity Risk Management and Finance*. New York: Oxford University Press.

Sah, Rah, and Joseph E. Stiglitz. 1987. "The Taxation and Pricing of Agricultural and Industrial Goods in Developing Countries." In David Newbery and Nicholas Stern, eds., *The Theory of Taxation for Developing Countries.* New York: Oxford University Press.

Salant, Stephen W. 1983. "The Vulnerability of Price Stabilization Schemes to Speculative Attack." *Journal of Political Economy* 91 (February):1–38.

Siamwalla, Ammar, and Stephen Haykin. 1983. *The World Rice Market: Structure, Conduct, and Performance.* Research Report 39. Washington, D.C.: International Food Policy Research Institute.

Smith, Mark E. 1987. "Government Programs in World Rice Trade." *Rice: Situation and Outlook Report* (September). U.S. Department of Agriculture, Economic Research Service, Washington, D.C.

Stewart, Roberto. 1990. "A Study of Costa Rica's Coffee Marketing System." World Bank, Agricultural Research Department, Agricultural Policies Division, Washington, D.C. Processed.

Stiglitz, Joseph E. 1987. "Some Theoretical Aspects of Agricultural Policies." *World Bank Research Observer* 2(1):43–60.

Thomas, Vinod, ed. 1985. *Linking Macroeconomic and Agricultural Policies for Adjustment with Growth: The Colombian Experience.* Baltimore, Md.: John Hopkins University Press.

Thompson, Stanley, and G. Bond. 1987. "Offshore Commodity Hedging under Floating Exchange Rates." *American Journal of Agricultural Economics* 69(1):46–55.

Timmer, C. Peter. 1986. *Getting Prices Right.* Ithaca, N.Y.: Cornell University Press.

———. 1988. Lecture, March 8, Harvard University. Processed.

Timmer, C. Peter, Walter P. Falcon, and Scott R. Pearson. 1983. "Food Policy Analysis." World Bank, International Economics Department, International Trade Division, Washington, D.C. Processed.

Toevs, Alden, and W. Haney. 1986. "Measuring and Managing Interest Rate Risk: A Guide to Asset/Liability Models Used in Banks and Thrifts." Morgan Stanley, New York. Processed.

Traylor, Harlon D., John F. Denison, Hector O. Zapata, and Kyle M. McCann. 1989. "An Analysis of the Efficiency of Rough Rice Futures Contracts." Paper presented at the 1989 Southern Agricultural Economics Association Meeting, Nashville, Tenn.

Turnovsky, Stephen. 1976. "The Distribution of Welfare Gains from Price Stabilization: The Case of Multiplicative Disturbances." *International Economic Review* 17:133–48.

Turnovsky, Stephen, Haim Shalit, and Andrew Schmitz. 1980. "Consumer's Surplus, Price Instability and Consumer Welfare." *Econometrica* 48(1):135–52.

U.S. Department of Agriculture, Economic Research Service. 1987. *Rice: Situation and Outlook Report* (April). Washington, D.C.

U.S. Department of Agriculture, Foreign Agricultural Service. Various issues. *Circular: Coffee* (now *The World Coffee Situation*). Washington, D.C.

————. Various issues. *World Grain Situation and Outlook Report.* Washington, D.C.

Walters, Alan. 1987. "The Mischief of Moving Average Pricing." World Bank, Vice Presidency Development Economics, Washington, D.C. Processed.

Waugh, Frederick V. 1944. "Does the Consumer Benefit from Price Instability?" *Quarterly Journal of Economics* 58:602–14.

World Bank. 1986. *Poverty and Hunger: Issues and Options for Food Security in Developing Countries.* Washington, D.C.

————. 1989. *World Debt Tables 1989–90.* Vol. 2. Washington, D.C.

————. 1990. "Quarterly Review of Financial Flows to Developing Countries." (September). International Economics Department, Debt and International Finance Division, Washington, D.C. Processed.

————. 1992a. "Market Outlook for Primary Commodities." Vol. 2. International Economics Department, Washington, D.C. Processed.

————. 1992b. *World Debt Tables 1992–93.* Washington, D.C.

————. Various years. "Commodity Trade and Price Trends." World Bank, International Commodity Division, Washington, D.C. Processed.

Wright, Brian D., and Jeffrey C. Williams. 1982. "The Economic Role of Commodity Storage." *Economic Journal* 92 (September):596–614.

————. 1990. "The Behavior of Markets for Storable Commodities." Presented to the Thirty-Fourth Annual Conference of the Australian Agricultural Economics Society. University of Queensland, Brisbane, Australia.

————. 1991. *Storage and Commodity Markets.* Cambridge: Cambridge University Press.

Yeats, Alexander. 1990. "Do African Countries Pay More for Imports? Yes." *World Bank Economic Review* 4 (1, January):1–20.

Index